PC/MS DOS **FUNDAMENTALS**

This belongs to
Marie Dunseath

PC/MS DOS **FUNDAMENTALS**

C A R O L Y N   Z .   G I L L A Y

Franklin, Beedle & Associates
Publishers
4521 Campus Dr., #327
Irvine, CA 92715-9877
Telephone (714) 552-4155

Publisher: James F. Leisy, Jr.
Manuscript Editor: Sheryl Rose
Interior Design: Neo Nova
Composition: Highpoint Type & Graphics, Inc. (Pomona, CA)
Cover Design: Neo Nova
Book Manufacturing: Malloy Lithographing (Ann Arbor, MI)

Franklin, Beedle & Associates
4521 Campus Drive, #327
Irvine, CA 92715-9877

Printed in the United States of America

Library of Congress Cataloging-in-Publication Data

Gillay, Carolyn Z., 1943-
PC/MS DOS fundamentals.

Includes index.
1. PC DOS (Computer operating system) 2. MS-DOS (Computer operating system) I. Title.
QA76.76.063G55 1988 005.4'469 88-3638
ISBN 0-938661-09-4

Y X W 0 1

Special thanks to Michael and G Heilpern, Jim Yarrow, Pam Nash, Lisa Biddle and the whole crew at Highpoint Graphics for all the attention and care.

Thank you Malloy Lithographing for another fine book and great schedule!

DEDICATION

To My Father, Walter Gillay, for all he gave me.

PREFACE

PC/MS DOS FUNDAMENTALS is for Beginners

This book assumes no prior experience with computers, software, or PC/MS DOS. It is intended to be used as the core textbook for a course which focuses exclusively on PC/MS DOS. (Note: For those requiring a short course book, please consider my book, *The PC/MS DOS Companion* published by Franklin, Beedle and Associates.)

Parallel Coverage of Floppy Disk Drive and Hard Disk Drive Systems

To use this book effectively, students must have access to an IBM PC work alike computer system. The commands covered in this book are compatible with PC/MS DOS versions 2.X and 3.X. The unique design of this book allows parallel treatment, throughout the book, of both floppy disk drive and hard disk drive based computer systems. This eliminates translation problems which can occur because of the differences between the two system environments.

Step Through Approach (with the Rationale)

Each PC/MS DOS command covered in this book is presented in a careful step-by-step activity. A floppy disk containing the data files for each activity accompanies the book. Interspersed with the steps are the reasons for and results of each action. I have class tested this material during the past four years and found this to be the most effective way for students to master PC/MS DOS.

Intermediate DOS Concepts

The DOS line editor, EDLIN is covered in the latter third of the book. Creating, modifying, and printing EDLIN text files is presented in the same thorough step-by-step approach used throughout the book. Batch files are discussed and, to aid in mastering them, many activities are provided. Many DOS users require the ability to use AUTOEXEC.BAT and CONFIG.SYS in customizing their software; so, special attention has been paid to their use and implementation.

Software and file management is difficult without a working knowledge of subdirectories. The concept of organizing directories through the use of roots and trees is presented in a capstone chapter. Included in this chapter are the routine commands for creating and deleting directories, and switching from one directory to another.

Please note that BACKUP and RESTORE commands have been treated outside the main body of the text, in Appendix A. These are powerful file commands. Thus, their presentation is left to the discretion of the instructor.

Self Mastery and Reference Tools Provided

Each chapter includes a Chapter Summary and Chapter Exercises. These features help to reinforce the material covered in the chapter. At the back of the book there are Chapter Tests which I use, throughout my course, to gage mastery of the concepts and commands. The Chapter Tests have been designed to be torn out and turned in for grading.

This book is useful as a reference to PC/MS DOS commands. The Appendices provide a tutorial using the BACKUP and RESTORE commands, an explanation of bits and bytes, a DOS Commands Quick Reference Chart, a list of Special Keys, a list of Batch File commands, and a list of EDLIN commands.

ACKNOWLEDGEMENTS

A Project of this scope is difficult to successfully complete without the contributions of many individuals. Thank you:

Theresa Flores-Gibbs, for your effort on the book's glossary;
Fred Papay, for reading and commenting on the manuscript;
Steven Tuttle, my son, for working through each activity and exercise in the book;
Nancy Wilson, for keeping my head above water in the final days of writing the book and teaching a full load;
Nick Markiw, my brother, for creating some of the book's software and for networking my DEC with my IBM;
Emily Markiw, my mother, for encouraging me in this undertaking and everything else;
Karin Ellison, Walter Babchuk, Nick Babchuk, Sophie Nyles, Nick Markiw, Sr. and *Kathryn Maurdeff,* for your encouragement and belief in me;
to the students, at Saddleback College, who took the DOS course and provided me with many insights into the learning process;
Marly Bergerud and *Don Busche,* for providing a supportive academic environment in which to conceive and write this book;
California Business Education Association and *National Business Education Association,* for providing a forum in which to present ideas on the development and teaching of PC/MS DOS courses;
Jim Leisy, my publisher, for your contributions to this book and your friendship;
and most of all I thank you, *Frank Panezich,* my husband, for your patience, encouragement, suggestions, and dedication to helping me see this project through.

Lastly, a BIG thank you to the following individuals for critiqueing various drafts of the manuscript and sharing experiences in teaching the DOS course:
Lindsey Graves (Pima Community College)
Jim Gross (Cochise College)
Susan Flanogan and *Trudy DiSelettes* (and their students at the Fremont-Newark ROP Center)
Peter Walther (Salish Kootenai College)
Steve Murtha (Tulsa Junior College)
Carl Penziul (Corning Community College)

—*C. Z. G.*
Orange, CA

IMPORTANT NOTE TO MS DOS USERS

PC/MS DOS files with the file extension ".COM" are used in the activities and exercises contained in this book. However, some versions of MS DOS use ".EXE" as a file extension, instead of ".COM". If, while working with a file that has a ".COM" extension, you get the message, "File not found", key in the file name with the ".EXE" file extension. For example, in Chapter 3, Page 56, Step 4, the instruction is to key in DIR DISKCOPY.COM. If you get the message, "File not found", key in DIR DISKCOPY.EXE. You may need to modify file extensions, from ".COM" to ".EXE", for CHKDSK.COM to make it work, as well.

See Chapter 8, Sections 8.9 through 8.12, on comparing files. The command used in the text is COMP.COM. Some versions of MS DOS use FC.EXE (File Compare command). To see what version of the compare command you have, key in DIR COMP.COM and press <ENTER>. Then key in DIR FC.EXE and press <ENTER>. Depending upon the version of DOS you are working with, the computer will either retrieve the file or report with the message, "File not found".

If you have FC.EXE instead of COMP.COM, substitute FC every place the text uses COMP.

CONVENTIONS USED IN THIS TEXT

Certain conventions have been followed in the text to allow the user to follow the instructions easily. These include:

1. If a key is surrounded by angle brackets, it indicates that this is a key to be pressed. It is not something that the user types in. These include:

   <Shift> The key labeled 'Shift' or that has an up arrow on it. ↑

   <Enter> The key labeled 'Enter' or that has the following symbol on it: ↵

   <Backspace> The key labeled 'Backspace' or that has the following symbol on it: ←

<Alt>	The key labeled 'Alt'.	<ESC>	The key labeled 'Esc'.
<Ctrl>	The key labeled 'Ctrl'.	<Num Lock>	The key labeled 'Num Lock'.
<Del>	The key labeled 'Del'.	<Break>	The key labeled 'Break'.
<Ins>	The key labeled 'Ins'.	<PrtSc>	The key labeled 'PrtSc'.

2. All DOS commands will be in uppercase letters, such as DIR.
3. Files or commmands treated as files will be in lowercase letters, such as `format.com.`
4. Because DOS is not case sensitive, you can key in text using either uppercase or lowercase letters. However, DOS will display files in uppercase letters on the screen.
5. When the phrase, key in is used, it means that the user will type in whatever follows the key in statement. In addition, what is to be keyed in will appear in a special typeface as follows:

   STEP 1: Key in the following:

   ```
   A>DIR jan.txt   <Enter>
   ```

6. The A>, B> or C> represents the drive letter displayed on the screen and should never be keyed in.
7. <ENTER> means to press the <Enter> key. Do not key in the word 'Enter'.
8. When the phrase "displayed on the screen" is stated, it means that it should appear on the video monitor. In addition, it will appear in a special typeface and look like this:

   ```
   A>TYPE jan.txt
   This is my january file.
   It is file one.
   ```

9. The microcomputer will be referred to as the computer.
10. The original disk that is included with the DOS manual will be referred to as the master DOS System Disk.
11. The working copy of DOS that the user copies, will be referred to as the DOS System Disk.
12. If a user has a hard disk and DOS is installed on the hard disk, that portion of the hard disk will also be referred to as the DOS System Disk.
13. If a user has a hard disk and DOS is installed in a subdirectory, the user will have to refer to the documentation to find out the name of the subdirectory. Common names for that area on the hard disk include \DOS, \BIN, and \UTILITIES. In addition to knowing the subdirectory name, the user will have to log into the subdirectory where the DOS programs are located. He would do this by keying in CD followed by the name of the subdirectory. Thus, if the subdirectory name was \DOS, the user would key in the following:

   ```
   C>CD \DOS   <Enter>
   ```

14. The disk that comes with this text will be referred to as the ACTIVITIES disk.
15. The two disks that the user provides for the exercises and the back up will be referred to respectively as the DATA disk and the Backup Data disk.

CONTENTS

1 MICROCOMPUTER SYSTEMS: Hardware, Software, and the Operating System — 1

2 GETTING STARTED WITH DOS: Booting the System, Using the Keyboard, and Making a System Disk — 25

3 COMMAND SYNTAX: Using the DIR Command with Parameters and Wildcards — 51

4 DISKS AND FORMATTING 76

5 USING INTERNAL COMMANDS: COPY and TYPE 94

6 EXPANDING THE USE OF THE COPY COMMAND 118

7 FILE MAINTENANCE: Using ERASE, DEL and RENAME 145

8 INFORMATIONAL COMMANDS: CHKDSK, COMP, VER and LABEL 173

9 EDLIN, THE TEXT EDITOR 204

10 MANAGING THE PRINTER WITH THE MODE AND PRINT COMMANDS 243

11 INTRODUCTION TO BATCH FILES 266

12 CUSTOMIZED BATCH FILES 288

13 SUBDIRECTORIES 307

APPENDIX A: BACKUP AND RESTORE A1

APPENDIX B: DATA REPRESENTATION: Bits and Bytes A18

APPENDIX C: DOS COMMANDS QUICK REFERENCE CHART A21

APPENDIX D: SPECIAL KEYS A30

APPENDIX E: BATCH FILE COMMANDS A31

APPENDIX F: EDLIN COMMANDS A32

MICROCOMPUTER SYSTEMS: Hardware, Software, and the Operating System

CHAPTER

1

CHAPTER OBJECTIVES

This chapter discusses the elements that make up a microcomputer system and the role and use of the operating system, specifically DOS. After reading this chapter, you will:

Understand the parts of a microcomputer system.

Understand the CPU, RAM, and ROM.

Understand what input devices are and how they are used.

Understand what output devices are and how they are used.

Understand what external storage devices are, both floppy disks and hard disks.

Understand the differences between system software and application software.

Understand the functions of an operating system.

1.0 AN INTRODUCTION TO COMPUTERS

The desire to automate repetitive calculations, as well as complex ones, is a very old one. For hundreds of years the Chinese have automated their business transactions with a wooden calculator called an abacus. English mathematician Charles Babbage invented a mechanical calculator in the middle of the last century. A little over forty years ago, a professor at Iowa State University, John Atanasoff, designed the first known workable electronic computer to store student grades and calculate final grades.

Today's personal computers, at the most basic level, are calculators. But this is a very narrow definition. Now we use these machines to handle accounting chores (spreadsheets), to write books (word processing), to organize and retrieve information (data bases), and to design automobiles (computer-aided design).

1.1 CATEGORIES OF COMPUTERS

Computers are divided into categories based on a variety of factors such as size, processing speed, information storage capacity, and cost. However, in the ever-changing technical world, these classifications are not absolute. Technical lines blur the categories. For instance, some microcomputers today exceed the capability of mainframes manufactured five years ago. Table 1.1 shows the major categories of computers.

Table 1.1 Computer Types

COMPUTER	APPLICATIONS
Supercomputer: Very large computer	Used most often in sophisticated scientific applications such as nuclear physics, atomic physics, and seismology.
Mainframe: Large computer	General purpose business machines. Typical applications include accounting, payroll, airline reservations, and banking functions.
Minicomputer: Smaller version of mainframe	Specialized applications such as engineering and industrial research.
Microcomputer: Small, general-purpose, single-user computers	Applications include word processing, accounting for a small business, time and record keeping for attorneys and medical accounting.

1.2 COMPUTER COMPONENTS

All computers operate in the same way, regardless of their category. Information is input, processed, and stored, and the results are output. Figure 1.1 is a graphic representation of this.

Figure 1.1 Components of a Computer System

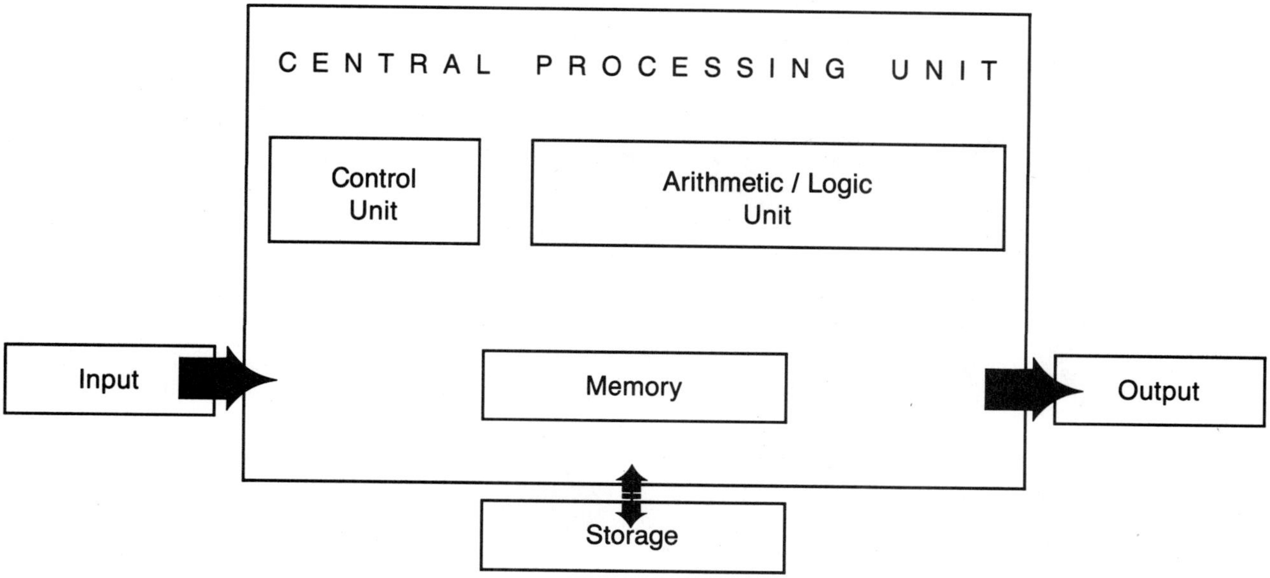

The figure shows the physical components of a computer system, referred to as **hardware**. All computer systems, large or small, have these basic components. However, hardware by itself can do nothing. A computer system needs a **program** (software). **Software** is a set of detailed instructions that tell the hardware what operations to perform on the data.

Data, in its simplest form, is related or unrelated numbers, words, or facts that, when arranged in a particular way, provide information. For example, if you wanted to add 2 plus 3 using a computer, you would need the hardware to do the work. Next, you would need the software instructions to tell the computer how to add. Last, you would have to input the data, the numbers 2 and 3, so the program would know what was to be processed.

1.3 MICROCOMPUTER HARDWARE COMPONENTS

This text is devoted to microcomputers. Microcomputers, which may be called micros, personal computers, home computers, PCs, or desktop computers, are comprised of hardware components. In other words, a complete microcomputer system has several parts, much like a stereo system. The basic components of a complete system, also called the **system configuration**, include an input device (typically a keyboard) for inputting data and programs; a system unit that houses the electronic circuitry for storing and processing data and programs (CPU, adapter cards, ROM, and RAM); a display unit (commonly a monitor); an external storage unit that allows you to store data and programs on disks (disk drives) and a printer for producing hard copy or a printed version of the results. Figure 1.2 represents a typical microcomputer system.

Figure 1.2 A Typical Microcomputer System

1.4 THE SYSTEM UNIT

The system unit, as shown in Figure 1.3, is the "black box" that houses the electronic and mechanical parts of the computer. If the outer case were removed and the unit were opened up, it would look like the diagram in Figure 1.4.

Figure 1.3 The System Unit

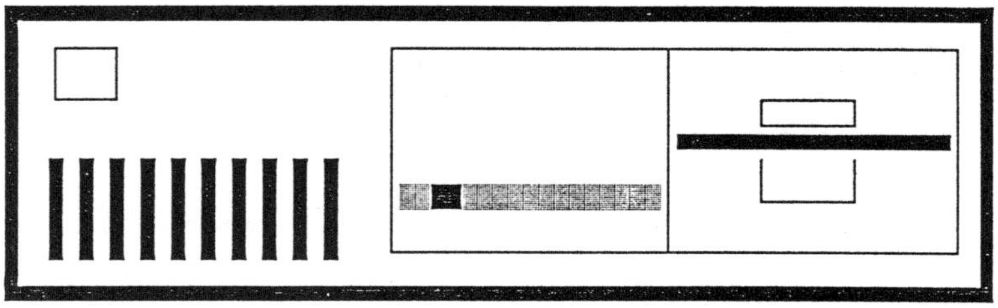

Figure 1.4 Inside the System Unit

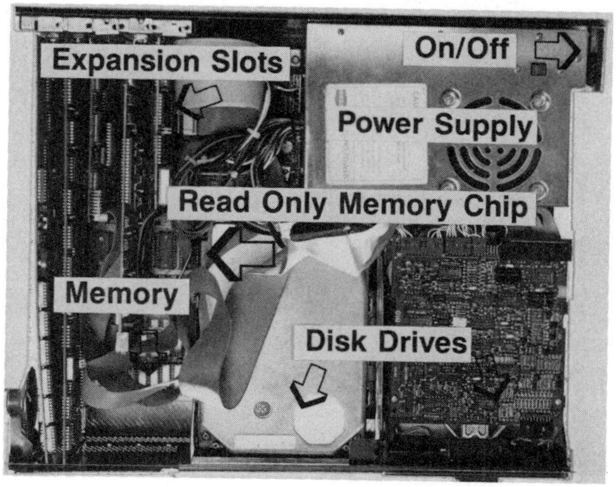

The system unit has some mechanical parts, such as the power supply (to get power to the computer) and the disk drives. In addition, it contains many electronic printed circuit boards, also called cards. One of these boards is a special printed circuit board, the system board, sometimes called the "mother board." The **system board** is shown in Figure 1.5.

Figure 1.5 The System Board

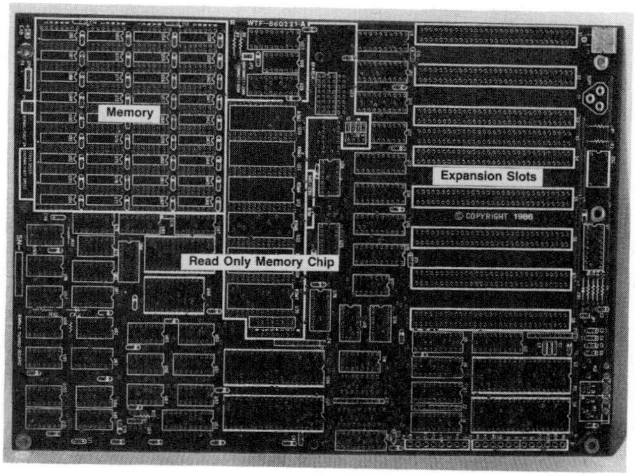

Attached to the system board is the microprocessor chip that is the central processing unit or CPU, Random Access Memory and Read-Only Memory.

1.5 CENTRAL PROCESSING UNIT

The **central processing unit**, most commonly referred to as the CPU, is the brain of the computer, composed of transistors on a silicon chip. It comprehends and carries out instructions sent to it by a program and directs the activity of the computer. It is comprised of two parts, the **control unit** and the **arithmetic/ logic unit (A/LU)**. The control unit is responsible for directing and coordinating program (software) instructions. It does not actually execute the instructions but directs the other parts of the system to carry them out. The A/LU performs the arithmetic functions: addition, subtraction, multiplication and division and the logical functions, which in most cases are comparisons. Programs are designed to take action based on these comparisons.

1.6 RANDOM ACCESS MEMORY

Random Access Memory (RAM) is the work space of the computer, often referred to as main memory. Physically, RAM is contained in many electrical circuits. However, a computer's memory is not like a person's memory; RAM is not a permanent record of anything. RAM is where the programs and data are placed while the computer is working. It is like a desk. When you are working on a project, you spread it out on the desk. When you finish the project, you clear off the desk and ready it for the next project. The programs (set of instructions that tell the computer what to do) and the data (the user's information) are stored in RAM. The computer can read and write information to and from RAM. Its memory size is measured in bytes. The programs and data must fit into RAM in order for the user to be able to work with the microcomputer.

Computer memory is temporary, useful only while the computer is on. This is why RAM is considered volatile. Think of RAM as read/write memory. You can write data into it, change it, or write data out.

1.7 READ-ONLY MEMORY

Read-Only Memory (ROM) holds permanently stored programs, usually installed by the manufacturer of the specific computer. ROM is also made of electronic circuits. "Read only" means exactly what it says. The CPU can only read the instructions from ROM; it cannot write, erase, or alter the contents of ROM in any way. ROM is nonvolatile which means that when you turn off the computer, none of the information stored on ROM is lost. In reality, ROM has programs etched on it; it is a program-on-a-chip. Here, however, is where the terms hardware and software get somewhat blurred. ROM is hardware because it is a chip. However, it is also software because it contains instructions. Hence, ROM is sometimes called **firmware**, halfway between hardware and software. Nearly all computers use ROM to hold start-up programs, which are routines that include instructions for loading the operating system into memory.

1.8 ADAPTER CARDS

Adapter cards, other printed circuit boards, are installed in the system unit when purchased or as a later addition. Adapter cards allow the user to add more memory, use a printer or a video display, or utilize a modem or a mouse. These items are considered peripheral devices.

1.9 DISKS AND DISK DRIVES

If RAM is volatile and disappears when the power is turned off and if ROM is "read only," how does the computer user retain data and programs on a permanent basis? As mentioned previously, one reason for using a computer is to handle repetitive tasks that deal with large volumes of information (data). For example, if you have keyed in the names of 200 employees and their hourly rates, a repeated task, for doing payroll, the next time you want to "run" the payroll, you do not wish to key in all the employee names and rates again. You just want to key in the current hours so that the payroll program can do the new calculations and print paychecks. This problem is handled with secondary or external storage media, which are actually magnetic media that store data and programs in the form of magnetic impulses. Such media can include floppy disks, hard disks, tape, magnetic cards, and tape cartridges. In the microcomputer world, the most common secondary storage media are **floppy disks** and **hard disks**.

Disks serve a dual purpose. First, disks provide a permanent way of holding data. When power is turned off, the disk retains what has been recorded on it. Second, disks are transportable. Programs or data developed on one computer can be used by another merely by inserting the disk. If it were not for this capability, programs such as the operating system or other application packages could not be used. Each time you wanted to do some work, you would have to write your own instructions.

Storing information on a disk is the equivalent to storing information in a file cabinet. Like a file cabinet, disks store information in disk files. When the computer needs the information, it goes to the disk, opens a file, "reads" the information from the disk file into memory (RAM), and works on it. When the computer is finished working on that file, it closes the file and returns ("writes") it back to the disk. In the payroll example, once the employees' names and hourly rates are stored on a disk, the user just tells the computer to "read" the program that does the work and to "read" the employee file into memory. Now, all the user has to do is key in the weekly hours. The program does the calculations necessary to generate the paychecks.

1.10 MINIFLOPPY DISKS: THE 5 1/4-INCH DISK

Floppy disks come in several sizes: 8 inch, 5 1/4 inch, and 3 1/2 inch. The 8-inch disk is rarely used today. The standard size is the 5 1/4-inch floppy, but the 3 1/2-inch floppy is becoming very popular.

The 5 1/4-inch floppy disk, technically known as a **minifloppy diskette**, is a circular piece of plastic, polyurethane, or Mylar covered with magnetic oxide (see Figure 1.6). It is always enclosed inside a relatively rigid nonremovable protective jacket with a lined inner surface. Like a phonograph record, the disk has a hole (called a hub) in the center so that it can fit on the disk drive's spindle. The disk drive can spin the disk to find information on it or to write information to it. Once the disk is locked into the disk drive, it spins at about 300 revolutions per minute. The disk has an exposed opening called the **head slot** where data is written to and read from by the computer's disk drive. This is where the disk drive's magnetic heads actually touch the surface of the disk. There is also a cutout on the side of the disk known as a **write-protect notch**, which can be covered with a **write-protect tab**. If a disk is write-protected, with the notch covered, the programs and data on the disk cannot be written over, so the original data and programs can never be lost. If the write-protect notch is not covered, data can be read from the disk as well as written to it. Some disks, like the original DOS System Disk, have no notch and, therefore, can never be written on. This is known as write-protection. This disk can only be read, never written over.

There is a small hole in the jacket near the center of the disk called the index or timing hole. If you rotated the plastic disk, you could find a small hole in the actual disk itself. The disk drive uses this hole to indicate where a circle has begun and ended, to help determine where information is stored on the disk. If a disk has only one hole, it is considered soft-sectored; if it has many holes, it is considered hard-sectored. Most personal computers use a soft-sectored disk that indicates the first sector and track. This disk can store approximately 360K worth of information. You can also get a high-capacity disk which holds 1.2 megabytes of information. The high-capacity disk can only be read or written to with a high-density disk drive

Figure 1.6 A Minifloppy 5 1/4-Inch Disk

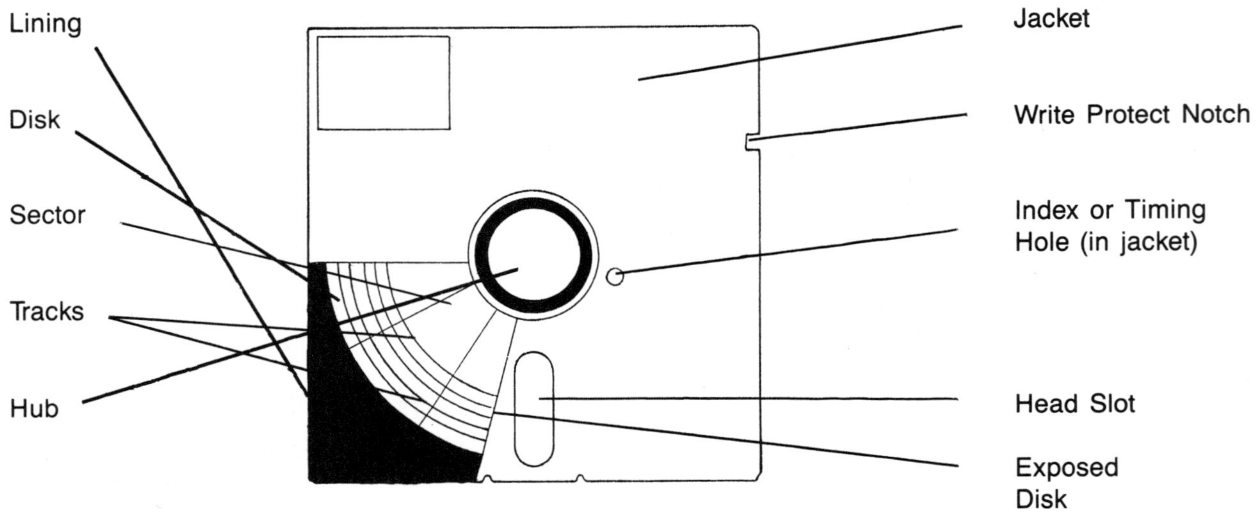

1.11 MICROFLOPPY DISKS: THE 3 1/2-INCH DISK

The new IBM PS/2 family, portable, and lap-top computers are using this new disk, technically called a **microfloppy disk**. In principle, these 3 1/2-inch disks work the same way that the 5 1/4-inch disks do, except that they are smaller and are enclosed in a rigid plastic shell. In addition, these disks have a shutter that covers the read/write head. The computer's disk drive opens the shutter only when it needs access. When the disk is not in the drive, the shutter should be closed. This disk does not use an index or timing hole; this function is performed by the disk drive's spindle. The write-protect notch can be either a built-in slider or a breakaway tab. Figure 1.7 shows the 3 1/2-inch disk.

Figure 1.7 A Microfloppy: 3 1/2-inch Disk

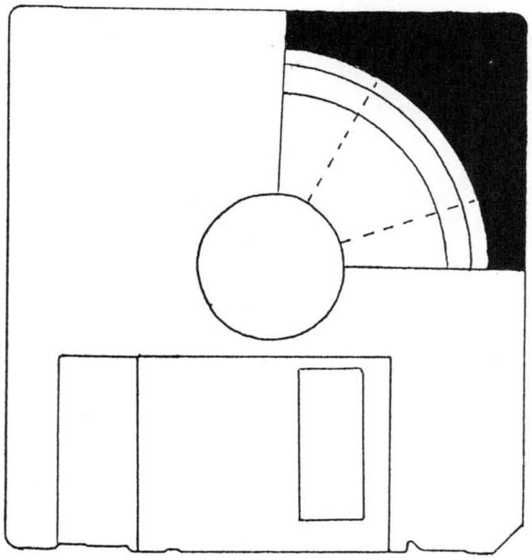

1.12 HARD DISKS

A hard disk, also called a fixed disk, a Winchester disk, or a hard drive, is a non-removable disk that is usually permanently installed in the system unit (See Figure 1.8). A hard disk holds much more information than a removable floppy disk. It is composed of two or more rigid platters, usually made of aluminum and coated with oxide, which allow data to be encoded magnetically. Both the platters and the read/write heads are permanently sealed inside a box; the user cannot touch or see the drive or disks. These platters are affixed to a spindle that spins at about 3600 RPM, although this speed can vary, depending on the type of hard disk. This speed makes it much faster than a standard floppy disk drive. The rapidly spinning disks in the sealed box create air pressure that lifts the recording heads above the surface of the platters. As the platters spin, the read/write heads float on a cushion of air.

A floppy disk drive has only one read/write head while a hard drive has more than one. Because the hard disk rotates faster than a floppy disk and because the head floats above the surface, the hard disk can store much more data and access it much more quickly than a floppy disk. Today a common hard disk storage capacity is 20 megabytes, much more than a floppy disk capacity of 360K.

Figure 1.8 A Hard Disk

1.13 DIVIDING THE DISK

A disk's structure is essentially the same whether it is a hard disk or a floppy disk. Disks are organized or divided into numbered tracks and sectors so that the computer can locate information. The disk itself is much like a file cabinet with numbered file dividers.

Data is recorded on the surface of a disk in a series of concentric circles known as **tracks**, similar to a record's grooves. However, each track on the disk is a separate circle divided into **sectors**. The amount of data that can be stored on a disk depends on the density of the disk—the number of tracks and the size of the sectors.

Sectors are the basic unit of disk storage. Whenever a computer reads or writes to a disk, it always reads and writes a full sector, regardless of the space the data needs. The location, size, and number of sectors are determined by the software in a process known as **formatting**.

A disk is a random-access medium, which does not mean that the data and/or programs are randomly arranged on the disk. It means that the head of the disk drive, which reads the disk, does not have to read all the information on the disk to get a specific item. The CPU can have the head of the disk drive go directly to the track and sector that holds the specific item of information.

1.14 DISK DRIVES

A disk drive is used to write information to and from a disk. If a disk contains the information you wish to use, it is the disk drive that "plays" it back. All disk drives have read/write heads much like the ones on tape or video recorders, which read and write information back and forth between RAM and the disk. While floppy disks have one head, most hard disks have more than one head. In addition, all disk drives have a means of spinning the disk. Since a hard disk is sealed, all the mechanics of the spinning are internal. The user never interacts directly with the hard disk; or in other words, the user never has to "change the record." The mechanics are different with a floppy disk drive because the user does have to interact with the disk drive to "change records" (disks) in order to "play" different information.

A floppy disk drive is the device that holds the floppy disk. The user inserts the floppy disk into the disk drive (See Figure 1.9). The hub of the disk fits onto the hub mechanism that grabs the disk. When the disk drive door is shut, the disk

Figure 1.9 A Floppy Disk Drive

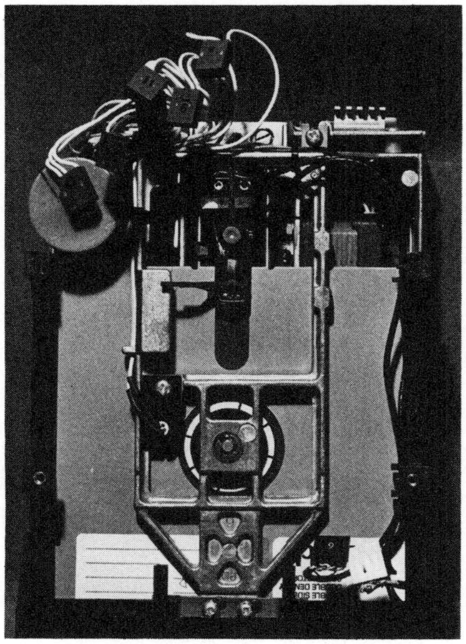

is secured to the hub mechanism. The jacket remains stationary, and the floppy disk rotates at about 300 revolutions per minute. The disk drive's head reads and writes information back and forth between RAM and the disks through the exposed head slot. Some floppy disk drives are single-sided, which means that they can only read and write to one side of a floppy disk. Others are double-sided, which means that they can read and write to both sides of a floppy disk. Another type of floppy disk drive is known as a high-capacity floppy disk drive, which means that it can not only read and write to both sides of a disk but the disk can accept more information than a standard disk because more data can be packed on the high-capacity disk, nearly four times more than the storage capacity of a standard floppy disk.

1.15 DISK DRIVE DEVICE NAMES

Disk drives come in a variety of sizes and door configurations. A disk drive is an example of a device name. A **device** is a place for the computer to send information (write) or a place from which to receive information (read). Disk drives are not the only devices that the system uses. However, in order for the operating system to know which device it is supposed to be communicating with at any given time, every device is given a specific and unique name by the system. Disk drives are given one-letter names followed by a colon. You must determine the configuration of disk drives you have in your microcomputer. Some common configurations are illustrated in Figure 1.10.

Figure 1.10 Disk Drive Configurations

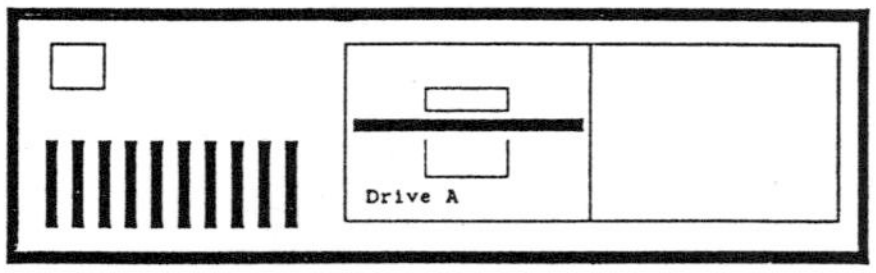

Single Floppy Disk Drive

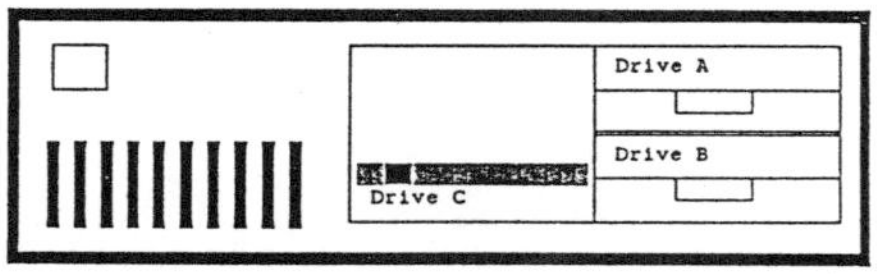

Hard Disk Drive and Dual Floppy Disk Drives

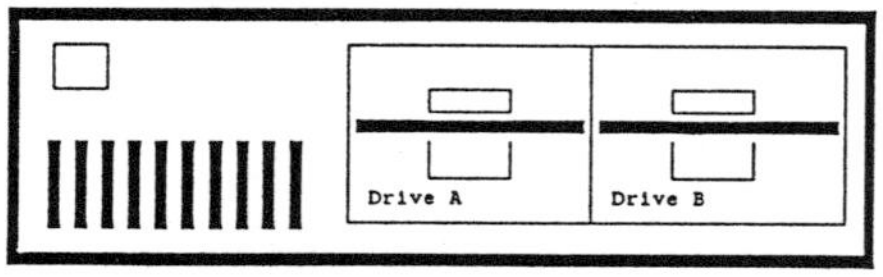

Dual Floppy Disk Drives

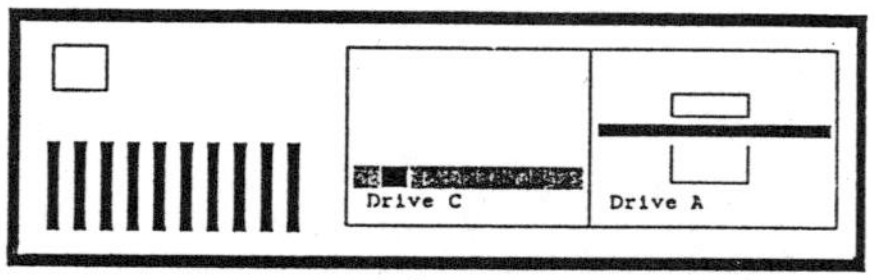

Hard Disk Drive and Floppy Disk Drive

Floppy disk drives have doors so that the user can insert a floppy disk. The doors are either shut or latched. The first floppy disk drive (either the one on top in a half-height configuration or the one on the left in a two-floppy configuration) is always known as **A:** or Drive A. The second floppy disk drive (either the one on the bottom or the one on the right) is always known as **B:** or Drive B. The sealed hard disk is always known as **C:** or Drive C. Any other drives are lettered alphabetically through the letter Z, or use the letters **D:** through **Z:**. Device names are also known as reserved names and cannot be used for any other purpose.

1.16 CAPACITY MEASUREMENT: BITS AND BYTES

How do you measure the capacity of RAM or a disk? A computer does not understand actual words, letters, or numbers. A computer is primarily made of switches. All it can do is turn a switch on or off. The CPU controls RAM; 0 represents an off state and 1 represents an on state. A **bit** (from binary digit) is the smallest unit a computer can recognize; it is an on or off state. However, while a bit may be meaningful to a computer, it is not meaningful to human beings. What we want represented are letters, numbers, and symbols such as ? or &. So bits are combined in meaningful groups, much as letters of the alphabet are combined to make words. The most common grouping is eight bits, called a **byte**. Thus a byte can be thought of as one character.

RAM, ROM, and disk capacities are measured in bytes, typically in thousands of bytes or kilobytes. **K** is the symbol for 1024 bytes. If your computer has 64K of memory, its actual memory size is 64 times 1024 or 65,536 bytes. For simplification, K is rounded off to 1000, so that 64K of memory means 64,000 bytes. You should know the capacity of your computer's memory because it determines how big a program and/or data the computer will hold. For instance, if you had a 64K computer and a program that required 256K, your computer could not hold that program.

Disk capacity is also measured in bytes. A single-sided disk holds 180K of data (180,000 bytes); a double-sided disk holds 360K (360,000 bytes). Because a hard disk holds so much more than a floppy disk, hard disks are measured in millions of bytes, or **megabytes (MB)**. Typical hard disks have a capacity of 20 million bytes and more. However, most computer users, when referring to megabytes, use the word **meg**. A hard disk with 20 million bytes would be referred to as a 20 meg hard disk.

1.17 PERIPHERALS: INPUT DEVICES

The most common input device is the typewriterlike keyboard attached to the system unit by means of a cable. By keying in instructions and data, you transmit to the computer, which places the information into RAM. Another input device is a **light pen**, which has a light-sensitive cell. When the tip of the pen comes in contact with the monitor, it identifies a point on the screen. Through this, you can draw or enter data. There are also touch-sensitive display screens, which allow the user to the screen with a finger to input data. A **mouse** is a hand-held device that is moved around on a flat surface, allowing the user to move information on the screen. A disk drive can also be considered an input or an output device because programs and data can be read off or read to the disk by the disk drive.

1.18 PERIPHERALS: OUTPUT DEVICES, MONITORS

A monitor, also called a terminal, a display screen, the screen, Cathode Ray Tube (CRT), or Video Display Tube (VDT) looks like a television. The CPU writes information to the screen where it is displayed. Information that appears on the screen is sometimes referred to as **soft copy** because it can be changed. The three most common screens are:

1. Monochrome displays. These screens display in one color. The user can choose the color: green characters on a black screen, amber characters on a black screen, etc. The clarity or resolution of the text displayed on the screen is very good. If there is a graphics adapter card it is possible to produce "shaded" graphics on a monochrome monitor.
2. Color displays. These screens display in a variety of colors. The resolution of text is usually not as good as on a monochrome display; however, a color display does provide graphic capabilities in a variety of colors.
3. Extended graphics displays. These screens display not only colors but also high-resolution or high-quality text.

1.19 PERIPHERALS: OUTPUT DEVICES, PRINTERS

The most common output device is the printer. A printer is attached to the system unit with an adapter card. The printer allows the user to have a **hard copy** (unchangeable because it is on paper) of information. The two major types of printers are impact and nonimpact.

An impact printer works like a typewriter. The element strikes some kind of ribbon, which strikes the paper and leaves a mark. A dot-matrix printer, the most common type, forms characters by selecting dots from a grid pattern on a movable print head, which permits printing in any style of letters and graphics (pictures). A dot-matrix printer operates from 80 cps (characters per second) to over 200 cps. There are also impact printers that have elements which have formed letters. A type of element printer is a daisy-wheel printer. It is considered a letter-quality impact printer. It operates from 12 cps to 55 cps. A dot-matrix impact printer tends to be faster, less expensive, and more versatile than a daisy-wheel printer, but its output does not have the "finished" quality of that produced by the daisy-wheel printer.

Nonimpact printers include thermal printers that burn images into paper using a dot-matrix grid. Some thermal printers heat the ribbon and melt ink onto the paper.

Ink-jet printers spray drops of ink to shape characters. However, the most exciting recent news in printers is the laser printer. Also a nonimpact device, this printer uses a laser beam instructed by the computer to form characters with powdered toner fused to the page by heat, as a photocopying machine does. This printer produces high-quality character and graphic images. Laser printers operate at speeds up to 300 cps (eight pages per minute) and are noiseless.

1.20 SOFTWARE

Up to this point, we have been discussing primarily hardware. However, software is what makes a computer useful. In fact, without software, hardware has no use. You can think of hardware as a box to run software. Software is the step-by-step instructions that tell the computer what to do. These instructions are called **programs**. Programs need to be installed or "loaded" into RAM, where the CPU executes them. The total execution of a program is called running the program. Programs usually come stored on disks. You insert the disk into a drive, and the program is read into memory and stored there until it is done executing. Software can also be divided into categories. The most common divisions are system software and application software.

Application software as its name suggests, is a set of instructions, a complete program, that directs the computer to solve a particular problem. Application software solves problems, handles information, and is user-oriented. It may also be called packages, off-the-shelf software, or canned software. For example, it would be useful to purchase a payroll package to run on the computer. All you would have to do would be to key in the information needed by the program, such as hours worked, and the package would have the instructions needed to complete the calculations and print the paychecks. There are thousands of commercially available application packages. Most people purchase a computer because of the application programs available.

System software is also a set of instructions or programs. However, these programs coordinate the operations of all the various hardware components. System software is usually supplied by the computer manufacturer because it is necessary to run application software. It is computer-oriented rather than user-oriented. It takes care of what the computer needs so it can run application software.

Table 1.2 summarizes the characteristics of both kinds of software.

Table 1.2 Application and System Software

APPLICATION SOFTWARE	SYSTEM SOFTWARE
Solves problems	Coordinates operation of hardware
Handles information	Necessary to run application software
User-oriented	Computer-oriented

System software can also be divided into three categories: operating systems, system utilities, and programming language processors (See Table 1.3).

The **operating system** supervises the processing of application programs and all the input/output of the computer. Running a computer is somewhat analogous to producing a concert. The hardware is like the musicians and their instruments. They do not change. The application software is like the score the musicians play, anything from Ludwig von Beethoven to Paul McCartney. The computer hardware can "play" any application software from accounting to a game. Like the conductor who tells the violins or trumpets when to play and how loudly, the operating system makes the computer work. It is the first and most important program on the computer and must be loaded into memory before any other program. Working with the operating system is known as being at the system level.

Typically, operating systems are comprised of several important programs. These include **disk handlers**, which transfer data to and from the disk and into and out of memory, and perform other such disk-related tasks. **Nondisk peripheral programs** handle the input/output (I/O), such as input from the keyboard and output to the printer or screen. These programs check such things as whether a key has been pressed. If it has, they encode it so the computer can read it and then decode it so it can be written to the screen. The operating system also includes a **command processor**. The command processor has some built-in commands known as internal or resident commands that are always available as long as the power is on. These internal commands allow the user to manage disk files at a system level and to perform such activities as looking into the directory of a specific disk. In addition, the command processor allows the user to instruct the computer to load a system utility or an application package into RAM.

System utilities are special programs stored on an operating system disk. However, system utilities are not necessary to run the computer. They are only loaded and executed when the user needs them. Also known as external command or transient programs, system utilities do useful tasks such as formatting a disk. A system utility program formats a disk with the proper tracks and sectors to make it a readable single-sided or double-sided disk.

Programming language processors are programs that support the use of a programming language on a computer system. They are tools for the development of application packages. Programmers who wish to write step-by-step instructions that tell the computer what to do use these programs.

Table 1.3 System Software

OPERATING SYSTEM	SYSTEM UTILITIES	PROGRAMMING LANGUAGE
Handles input/output of computer	Enhances usefulness of computer	Supports use of programming languages
Manages computer resources	Adds capabilities	
Enables the running of application software		

The term operating system is generic. There are "brand names" for mainframe, minicomputer, and microcomputer operating systems. Brand names for microcomputer systems include CP/M, Unix, Xenix, Apple-DOS, TRS-DOS, UCSD-P. However, the standard operating system for microcomputers today is **DOS**, pronounced dahs. DOS, which stands for disk operating system, was developed and is owned by Microsoft Corporation. Their version is known as **MS-DOS**. MS-DOS can run on the majority of personal computers on the market today. In addition, Microsoft also supports the IBM Personal Computer with a version of DOS known as **PC-DOS**. If you are going to use a computer and run application packages, you are going to need to know how to use the operating system first. Since DOS is the major microcomputer operating system in use today, this text is devoted to teaching the concepts of the operating system in general and DOS operations in particular.

Most people who use a computer are really interested in application software. They want programs that are easy to use. However, in order to get the applications, the user must know the operating system since it is the primary program that is loaded into the computer. Operating systems typically have programs stored as system files that take care of the mandatory functions for computer operations. When you purchase a computer, you also purchase a disk labeled DOS. On this disk are the programs that comprise the system software and the system utilities.

1.21 OPERATING SYSTEM FUNDAMENTALS

PC-DOS is a program that is always working. No computer can work unless it has an operating system in memory or RAM. When you boot the system, you are loading the system software or operating system programs into memory. This is what DOS is all about. DOS is comprised of three parts: the programs that handle input and output to peripherals and files, the command processor, and the utility programs. The utility programs are not a mandatory part of the operating system.

Some of the software is built into the hardware. When you turn on the power to the computer it would not know what to do if it were not for programs or sets of instructions. The first thing that is necessary is to communicate with the computer using peripheral devices. When you key in a character on the keyboard, that character moves to the CPU and RAM (memory); this is input. When a character is displayed (written) to the monitor or the printer, it moves from the CPU and RAM; this is output. Input and output take place within the CPU, memory, and the different peripherals. **BIOS** (basic input/output system) routines or programs provide some of the control for the I/O devices.

Where is BIOS? It is actually found in two places. First, it is built into the hardware of the microcomputer on the system board in a read-only memory chip called ROM-BIOS (read-only memory—basic input/output system). (This ROM-BIOS chip is abbreviated to RIOS, pronounced RYE-ose). Here, terminology can get confusing. Is ROM hardware or software? It is some of both. It is hardware because it is permanently installed in the computer. On the other hand, it is software because nonerasable, read-only programs are written on it. Sometimes it is called firmware. Since ROM-BIOS is a built-in part of the computer, it is technically not part of DOS. However, it is a part of any operating system that runs on the computer.

Thus, when you turn on power to the computer, it goes to the RIOS. One of the things this programmed chip does is to execute the power on self-diagnostic test (POST) routine programs. This simply means that this is the first set of instructions to be followed, including checking the memory and equipment that is attached to the computer. Thus, before getting started, the user knows whether or not there is a hardware failure. Once this self-test is completed successfully, the next job or program to execute is to load the operating system.

Loading the operating system entails ROM-BIOS checking to see if a disk drive is installed. The program then checks to see if there is a disk in Drive A. If there is no disk in Drive A and if there is a hard disk, the program will check Drive C. It is looking for the **DOS system disk**. A DOS system disk has a special program on it called the **boot record**. If ROM-BIOS does not find this boot record or if there is something wrong with the boot record, control is turned over to the BASIC interpreter (on an IBM Personal Computer). If the program does find the proper boot record, it reads the record from the DOS disk into memory and turns control over to this program. The boot record is also a program that executes; its job is to read into memory the rest of the operating system, in essence, pulling the system up by its bootstraps. Thus, one "boots" the computer instead of merely turning it on.

The purpose of the operating system files that are loaded into RAM is to manage the resources and primary functions of the computer so that each application run does not have to reinvent the wheel. The application program can concentrate on doing its job, such as word processing, without having to worry about how the document gets from the keyboard to RAM and from RAM to the screen. The operating system takes care of those mundane but critical functions. This can be considered analogous to the automobile. Most of us use our cars to get from point A to point B. Put your key in the ignition and go. Most of us would not like it if every time we wanted to drive, we first had to open the hood and attach the proper cables to the battery and to all the other parts that are necessary to start the engine. The operating system is the engine of the computer that lets the user run the application.

Nondisk peripheral handlers is a complicated name for the software that extends the capability of ROM-BIOS or the input/output handling, also known as device handling. Here is the second location for the BIOS routines. The main job of the boot record for DOS is to load the hidden system file called IBMBIO.COM (on IBM PC-DOS) which is stored at a predefined location on the system disk. (Another version of DOS, MS-DOS, would have the same file but it has the file name of IO.SYS. It serves the same function.) The term **hidden system file** means that it is hidden from the user but resident in RAM. This means that when the user asks to have the files on the disk displayed on the screen, any file that is marked hidden will not be shown. The boot record reads this file into memory, and it remains there until the computer is turned off.

These programs take care of the operating details of the I/O (input/output) devices. In addition, any errors in ROM-BIOS can be corrected by making changes in the programs in IBMBIO.COM, rather than having to install a new ROM chip. IBMBIO.COM can also handle the addition of new peripheral devices, such as a hard disk, a new printer, or a display screen. It tells the computer that these devices exist and how to handle the I/O, without making major hardware changes. These programs extend the capability of RIOS and handle the input and output between the CPU and the peripherals.

Disk handlers are the next group of programs to be loaded into RAM. They are stored on the DOS System disk in a file called IBMDOS.COM on the IBM PC-DOS. (MS-DOS would have the same file but it has the name MSDOS.SYS. It serves the same function.) IBMDOS.COM is another hidden system file of programs that handle most of the disk routines. It is a high-level interface. These programs deal with intermediate level input-output routines such as reading what is input from the keyboard or writing on the screen. In addition, these programs also handle disk operations and take care of reading and writing onto a disk, including opening and closing files on a disk, searching the table of contents or directory of a disk, deleting files, reading and writing data, or placing and retrieving information on the disks. This file is the other hidden system file. This, then, is the first part of the operating system, DOS—the two hidden files, IBMBIO.COM and IBMDOS.COM.

The last group of programs to be loaded into RAM is stored on the DOS System disk as a file called COMMAND.COM. This program is not a hidden file like IBMDOS.COM and IBMBIO.COM, but it is a very important part of the operating system. Also known as the command processor, it is the second major part of DOS. It is what you actually communicate and interact with. When you key something in on the keyboard, this program reads what you key in and decides what to do with it; this is why it is called the command processor or command interpreter. It processes or interprets what you have keyed in. However, you cannot just key in anything. COMMAND.COM is looking for programs, specific predefined instructions, to execute.

Inside COMMAND.COM are built-in commands or subroutines, also called **internal** or **resident** commands. Once you have loaded DOS, these internal commands remain in memory until you turn off the power. You do not need to have the DOS System disk in any drive to "call" or run these programs; that is why they are called internal commands. These internal commands are programs that are routines for functions regularly used in file management such as finding out what is on a disk using the DIR command; deleting a file from a disk the ERASE command; or changing the name of a file with the RENAME command. These commands or programs are listed in a table. When you key in a command name, COMMAND.COM looks it up in the table or does a match. When it finds a match, it can run the program. Because these programs are resident in RAM, you can take out the disk and still use the programs because they are always in RAM.

Utility programs, also called **external** or **transient** commands because they are not resident in RAM make up the third part of DOS. These programs reside in program files located on the DOS System disk. When you wish to use one of these utilities, you key in the command name at the keyboard. COMMAND.COM looks for it in the table. If it cannot find a match, it must go to the disk and look for a match. When it finds a match on the appropriate disk, it loads that program into RAM and executes it. The utility programs must be on the disk that DOS reads in order for DOS to be able to locate them. Thus, the program is only loaded when you need it; it is transient because it is not retained in RAM unless you have called it. COMMAND.COM can recognize a program because it will have a file name with the file extension .COM, .EXE, or .BAT.

Remember that although external commands or utilities are handy programs, they are not mandatory to running the operating system. Any program, including an application program, is external and stored as a file on a disk.

Thus the IBM PC-DOS operating system is comprised of two hidden files, IBMBIO.COM and IBMDOS.COM, and the file COMMAND.COM. These files are loaded into memory when you place the disk in the drive and boot up the system. The programs remain in memory until you turn off the computer.

To recap, the operating system is comprised of the following:

RIOS	ROM-BIOS (Read Only Memory—Basic Input/Output System) a preprogrammed chip that handles the start-up routines and loads the operating system.
BOOT	The bootstrap routine that loads the remainder of DOS into memory.
IBMBIO.COM	A hidden system file that is loaded into RAM and manages the basic input and output devices or peripherals.
IBMDOS.COM	A hidden system file that is loaded into RAM and manages the disks.
COMMAND.COM	The command processor that interprets what is keyed in and contains the subroutines or internal commands.

In general, using the operating system, particularly the two hidden files, is **transparent** to the user, which means that the work is being done but the user does not see the operating activities, just the results. In other words, the first two system files take care of the tedious but vital routines such as moving information to and from disks. However, the user actually interfaces with COMMAND.COM, the third system file.

Figure 1.11 illustrates the operation of the command processor. When the prompt is displayed on the screen, the command processor is done running one program or command and is waiting for the next. When the user keys in something on the keyboard, the command processor tries to follow the instructions. It is looking for a program to execute. Some built-in internal or resident commands are listed in a table. These are routines for commonly used functions such as displaying the table of contents. These internal commands are always available after you've loaded DOS because they are in memory. The command processor does not have to go the disk to find these programs. The major internal commands include `DIR`, `ERASE`, `TYPE`, `RENAME`, and `COPY`. Even though these are programs, the internal commands are not listed when you do a directory display.

If the command processor does not find the command internally, it goes to the default disk to locate and load the program. Hence, these commands are called external or transient because they are outside of memory, reside on a disk, and are only loaded and executed when the user requests them. External programs are stored on a disk with a file extension of `.EXE`, `.COM`, or `.BAT`. All application programs are external. There is a special group of external programs or external commands on the DOS System Disk called utility programs. These are not a mandatory part of the operating system but are very useful.

Figure 1.11 Operation of the Command Processor

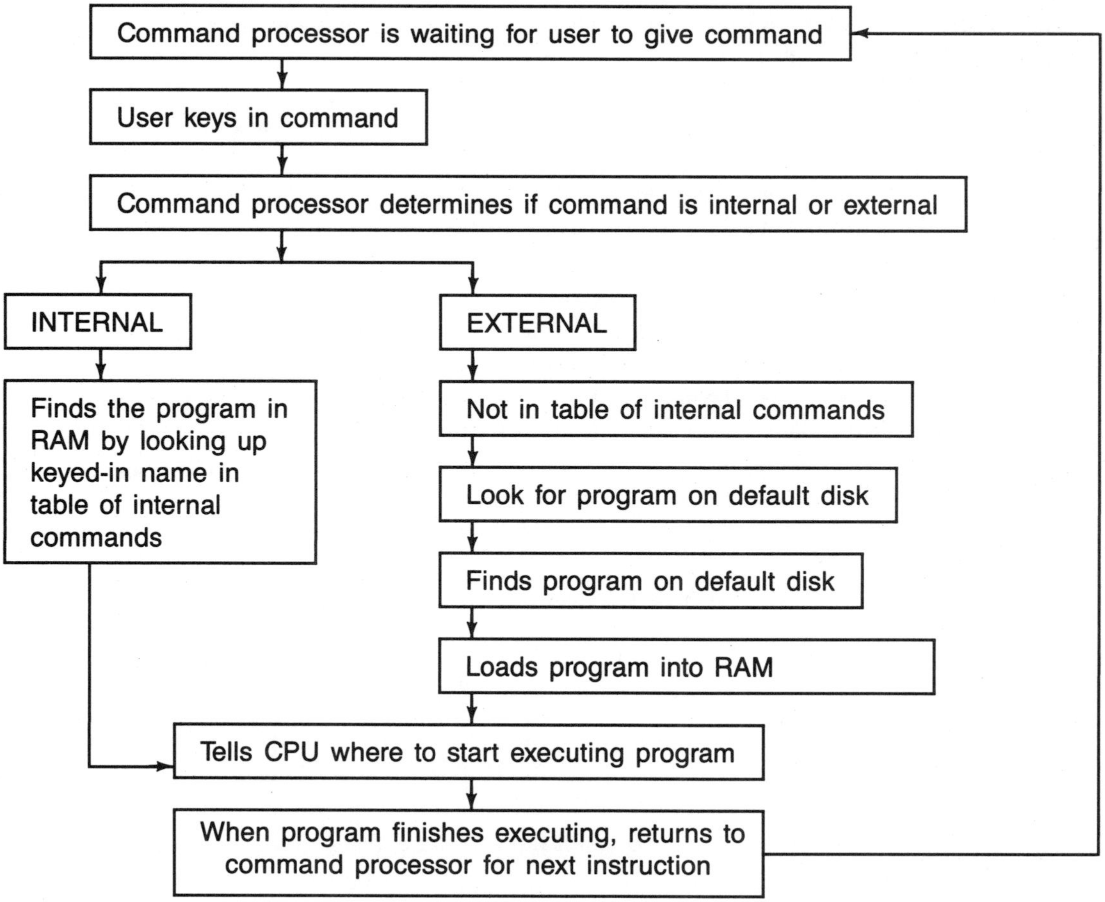

If what was keyed in does not match the above scenario, the system returns an **error message**, "`Bad command or file not found.`" It means that the system could not find a matching program in its vocabulary. It did not comprehend the command. Remember, a computer has a limited vocabulary. You have to speak its language; it does not speak yours.

CHAPTER SUMMARY

1. All computers function in the same way. Data is input, processed, and stored and the results are output.
2. Hardware components include the system unit, the monitor, the keyboard, and the printer.
3. The central processing unit is the brain of the computer and can comprehend and carry out instructions sent to it by a program.
4. Random Access Memory is the work space of the computer. RAM is volatile and is only there when the computer has power.
5. Read-Only Memory are chips with programs written on them. They are not volatile. They often contain start-up routines of the computer.
6. Adapter cards are other printed circuit boards that allow the user to add various peripheral devices.
7. Disks are a means of permanent storage for data and programs. A floppy disk is a piece of plastic inside a jacket. Floppy disks come in two popular sizes, 5 1/4-inch (minifloppy disk) and 3 1/2-inch (microfloppy). A hard disk is made of rigid platters that are permanently sealed inside a box.
8. All disks are divided into numbered tracks and sectors so that the computer can locate the needed information.
9. A floppy disk drive is the device where a floppy disk is inserted so that the computer can read or write to the inserted disk.
10. Disk drives have reserved names made of a letter of the alphabet followed by a colon. The lefthand disk drive is known as `A:` or Drive A; the righthand disk drive is known as `B:` or Drive B; and the hard disk is known as `C:` or Drive C.
11. A byte represents a single character. The capacity of RAM, ROM, and disks is measured in bytes, usually thousands of bytes or kilobytes (K). The capacity of hard disks is measured in millions of bytes or megabytes (MB) usually referred to as meg.
12. Peripherals are different devices that are attached to the system unit. The most common input device is a keyboard. The most common output device is the printer.
13. Software is the step-by-step instructions that tell the computer what to do. These instructions are called programs which are loaded into RAM where the CPU executes each instruction. Programs are referred to as "running" or "executing."
14. Programs are stored on disks and loaded into memory or RAM.
15. Software is divided into application software and system software.
16. Application software solves problems, handles information, and is user-oriented.

17. System software coordinates the operation of the hardware, is mandatory to be able to run applications software, and is computer-oriented.
18. An operating system is comprised of programs called system software that perform the functions necessary to control the operations of the computer. The operating system tells the computer what to do and interfaces with the user.
19. ROM-BIOS (Read Only Memory—Basic Input/Output System) is a chip that is built into the hardware of the system unit. Its job is to run self-diagnostics and load the boot record, which loads the rest of the operating system.
20. On an IBM PC-DOS System disk, the system files have specific names. The nondisk peripheral handler is stored as a hidden file called `IBMBIO.COM`. The disk handler is stored as a hidden file called `IBMDOS.COM`. The command interpreter is stored as a file called `COMMAND.COM`.
21. Internal commands are programs loaded with the operating system in `COMMAND.COM`. They remain in memory until the power is turned off.
22. External commands are stored on a disk and must be loaded into memory each time used. External commands are transient and do not remain in memory after they are executed.
23. The external commands that come with the DOS System disk are also known as system utilities.
24. Booting the system is more than powering up the system; it means loading the operating system.
25. Application packages are external to the computer and must be loaded in order to be executed.

REVIEW QUESTIONS

1. Define hardware.
2. Define RIOS.
3. What is meant by the system configuration?
4. Describe a typical microcomputer configuration.
5. Define DOS.
6. Why is an operating system important?
7. What files comprise DOS? What is the purpose of each file?
8. Where is DOS stored for use by the computer?
9. Can application packages run without an operating system?
10. What is an internal command?
11. What is an external command?
12. What purpose do disks serve?
13. How many types of disks are there? Describe them.
14. What is the difference between a hard disk and a floppy disk?
15. What are tracks and sectors? Where are they found?

TRUE/FALSE

1. A program is a set of instructions that tells the computer what to do.
2. External commands are stored on a disk.
3. An operating system is not needed if you want to run an application package.
4. The file IBMBIO.COM is used by the computer for communication with input/output peripherals.
5. Floppy disks are no longer used with microcomputers.
6. If a write-protect notch is covered with special tape, the computer cannot write on it.
7. The two hidden system files are IBMDOS.COM and IBMBIO.COM.
8. Data and programs are written to ROM.
9. The terms memory and RAM can be used interchangeably.
10. A monochrome screen displays in color.
11. The computer's memory is where data is stored permanently.
12. The central processing unit (CPU) is the brains of the computer and carries out instructions sent to it by programs.
13. A floppy disk drive allows the user to "play" data from the disk the user inserts.
14. A byte represents one character.
15. Each disk drive has a specific letter of the alphabet to represent it and is followed by a colon.

GETTING STARTED WITH DOS: Booting the System, Using the Keyboard, and Making a System Disk

CHAPTER

2

CHAPTER OBJECTIVES

This chapter discusses loading the operating system, using the keyboard, and using some DOS commands. After completing this chapter, you will:

Be able to boot the system.

Be able to reboot the system.

Understand and be able to use the computer keyboard.

Be able to make a copy of the DOS system disk.

Be able to compare the copy of DOS that you made with the original system disk.

Be able to end a work session with the computer.

2.0 USING DOS

The "brand name" of a microcomputer's operating system is usually DOS, either PC-DOS or MS-DOS. You must know how to get programs from the DOS System Disk to memory or RAM so that you can use the computer. This process is known as booting the system. The following activity allows you to have your first hands-on experience with the microcomputer using the DOS System Disk. You are going to load DOS, or boot the system. Be sure to follow the instructions exactly for your system configuration. The instructions for users who have two floppy disk drives will always be in the lefthand column. The instructions for users who have a hard disk and one floppy disk drive will always be in the righthand column. If the righthand column says "Same," read and follow the lefthand column instructions.

MATERIALS NEEDED:

1. A microcomputer
2. Master DOS System Disk, Version 2.0 or higher.

ACTIVITY 2.1 BOOTING THE SYSTEM: COLD START

STEP 1: Check to see if the monitor has a separate on/off switch. If it does, turn on the monitor	STEP 1: Same.
STEP 2: Get the disk labeled DOS. If the master DOS System Disk is in a paper envelope, remove it from this envelope.	STEP 2: Same.
STEP 3: The master DOS System Disk should have a label. It also has an exposed opening where you can see the actual plastic disk. This is called the head slot, where the magnetic head reads and writes information to the disk. **Never** put your fingers on this area. To insert a disk properly into the disk drive, hold it label side up, with the head slot facing away from you and toward the floppy disk drive. The write-protect notch should be facing left.	STEP 3: Same.
STEP 4: Gently lift the latch or open the door of Drive A on the system unit. Insert the master DOS System Disk, label up, into Drive A. Shut or latch the drive door.	STEP 4: Same.
STEP 5: Power on the computer by locating the on/off switch and lifting it. Often it is a red switch. On an IBM PC the switch is located on the righthand side of the system unit.	STEP 5: Same.

WHAT'S HAPPENING? The system will check itself in the diagnostic routine. You will see displayed on the screen a blinking horizontal bar called the **cursor**. (**Cursor** is a Latin word for runner). After the system checkout is complete, the computer reads DOS into RAM from the master DOS System Disk, that is two hidden files, `IBMBIO.COM` and `IBMDOS.COM`, and the other system file, `COMMAND.COM`. The computer boots DOS from the master DOS System Disk. When this happens, the disk drive makes a brief buzzing noise and the red light on the drive flashes on, letting you know the system is reading the disk. The computer beeps. If the boot is successful, the screen will display the following prompt:

```
Current date is Tue 1-01-1980
Enter new date (mm-dd-yy):_
```

STEP 6: Enter the current date and press `<Enter>`. You must enter the date in the format displayed, mm-dd-yy (month-day-year). You can also use the slash to separate the numbers as in mm/dd/yy. You must use only numbers, not alphabetic characters.

```
Current date is Tue 1-01-1980
Enter new date (mm-dd-yy):_
```

STEP 6: Same.

```
Current time is 0:00:16:25
Enter new time:_
```

STEP 7: Do not be concerned if the time displayed is different than what is shown above. The computer is on a 24-hour clock, i.e., 1:00 p.m. is 13:00. Entering the hours and minutes is sufficient. Enter the current time and press `<Enter>`.

```
Current time is 0:00:16:25
Enter new time:_
```

STEP 7: Same.

NOTE: The following display will appear on both floppy and hard disk systems.

```
The IBM Personal Computer DOS
Version 3.10 (C)Copyright International Business Machines Corp 1981,1985
             (C)Copyright Microsoft  Corp 1981, 1985

A>_
```

WHAT'S HAPPENING? You have successfully booted the system when you get the date and time prompt and then see the A> on the screen. The A>, known as the A prompt, is the drive that the system read to get the operating system into memory.

2.2 REBOOTING THE SYSTEM

Rebooting the system means reloading the operating system from the disk. When you reboot, everything that is in memory disappears and DOS is read into memory from the master DOS System Disk. The only difference between rebooting and booting is that when you reboot you do not have to turn on the power to the computer by pressing the red switch. Also, during a reboot the self-diagnostic routine is not run.

ACTIVITY 2.3 REBOOTING THE SYSTEM: WARM START

STEP 1: On the keyboard, locate the keys labeled <Ctrl>, <Alt> and <Del>.

STEP 1: Same.

STEP 2: To reboot the computer, hold down the <Ctrl> key, then simultaneously press the <Alt> key and the <Del> key.

STEP 2: Same.

```
Current date is Tue 1-01-1980
Enter new date (mm-dd-yy):_
```

```
Current date is Tue 1-01-1980
Enter new date (mm-dd-yy):_
```

WHAT'S HAPPENING? This activity is intentionally made awkward so you do not reboot accidentally, since rebooting erases everything in RAM. When you pressed the three keys, the system went to the master DOS System Disk in Drive A and read the operating system into RAM. Remember that a reboot does not go through the process of the self-diagnostic routine.

STEP 3: At the date prompt, key in the invalid formatted date shown below:

STEP 3: Same.

```
Current date is Tue 1-01-1980
Enter new date (mm-dd-yy):May 5, 1986
```

```
Invalid date
Enter new date (mm-dd-yy):_
```

```
Invalid date
Enter new date (mm-dd-yy):_
```

WHAT'S HAPPENING? The operating system must have information entered in the proper format. Like all programs, the operating system has rules that must be followed. If you do not follow the format, the computer cannot recognize the information and will reject it. That is why you got the error message "`Invalid date`" with an opportunity to correct the error.

STEP 4: Key in the current date in the proper format. Press <Enter>.

```
Current time is 0:00:16:25
Enter new time:_
```

STEP 4: Same.

```
Current time is 0:00:16:25
Enter new time:_
```

STEP 5: At the time prompt, key in the invalid formatted time shown below:

STEP 5: Same.

NOTE: The following display is for both floppy and hard disk systems:

```
Current time is 0:00:14:25
Enter new time: 75:00 am
```

```
Invalid time
Enter new time:_
```

WHAT'S HAPPENING? Not only must information be entered in the proper format, but it must also be correct information. The system knows that there is no such time as 75:00 and, thus, will not process the information.

STEP 6: Key in the correct time and press <Enter>.

STEP 6: Same.

NOTE: The following display will appear on both floppy and hard disk systems:

```
The IBM Personal Computer DOS
Version 3.10 (C)Copyright International Business Machines Corp 1981,1985
             (C)Copyright Microsoft  Corp 1981, 1985

A>_
```

WHAT'S HAPPENING? Now that you have entered a valid date and time, you see the `A>` prompt displayed on the screen. You have rebooted the system and again loaded the operating system, which is stored on the master DOS System Disk in

Drive A. DOS was read into RAM or memory from the disk that you inserted into Drive A. It is much like using a turntable (the disk drive) to play a record (the master DOS System Disk).

2.4 OVERVIEW OF FILES AND DISKS

Each time you turn off the computer, whatever was in memory, programs, or data is gone. The memory is temporary. You need a way to store this information permanently. In the microcomputer world, the only way to save data and programs permanently is to store them on a disk. After you have booted up your computer, DOS reads the programs or data it needs from the disk back into its memory. However, in order for DOS to find this information, it has to have a way of organizing it, which it does by keeping programs and data in files on the disk. Just as you organize your written work in files, DOS organizes computer information in disk files.

A disk file is much like a file folder stored in a file cabinet. The file cabinet is the floppy disk. A file consists of related information stored on the disk in a "file folder" with a unique name. All information with which a computer works is contained and stored in files on the disk. Thus an analogy might be:

A file cabinet is equivalent to a box of disks or a hard disk.

A file drawer is equivalent to one disk.

A file folder is equivalent to one file on the disk.

The name on the file folder is equivalent to the file name of the disk file.

A command or program, the set of instructions that tells the computer what to do, is stored in files on a disk. When you wish to use a program or a command, you call the file by keying in the file name or the command. DOS responds by opening the file on the disk, reading the contents of the file from the disk into RAM, and executing or running the program. If the computer did not have the ability to store information permanently on disk, all the work you did would be lost every time you turned off the computer.

2.5 FILE NAMES

Because computers must follow very specific rules, there is a specific format for file names. Technically, a file name is called the **file specification**. The first rule is that the file specification must be unique. Second, the file specification is broken down into two parts, a **file name** and a **file extension**. The file name typically describes or identifies the file and the file extension typically identifies the kind of data in the file. Since the term file specification is rather awkward, most people simply refer to the file name, meaning both the file name and the extension.

2.6 THE DIR COMMAND

When you booted the system by placing the master DOS System Disk in Drive A and powering on the computer, you loaded the operating system into RAM or memory. The system programs that reside or are stored on the master DOS System Disk are read into RAM. You are going to be using the operating system commands, those programs that you call by keying in the command name and pressing `<Enter>`. The command then executes or runs.

Certain commands, known as internal commands or resident commands, always remain in memory for you to use until you turn off the computer. The other commands, known as external or transient commands, reside only on the master DOS System Disk and must be read into RAM each time you key in the command name. When using external commands, you will find that if the DOS System Disk is not in the drive where the computer looks, the command or program will not be found and hence cannot be run.

The master DOS System Disk is in Drive A. How do you know what files are on the disk? There is an internal command called `DIR` for directory. This command was loaded into memory when you booted the system as part of the file called `COMMAND.COM`. When you key in `DIR`, you are asking the system to run this program. The purpose of this command is to display on the screen the names of all the files that are located on the disk in Drive A, in other words, the table of contents for the disk. The `DIR` command is the first DOS command you will use.

ACTIVITY 2.7 USING DIR

STEP 1: The master DOS System Disk should be in Drive A. The `A>` prompt should be displayed on the screen.	STEP 1: Same.

STEP 2: Key in the following:

```
A>DIR  <Enter>
```

```
FORMAT   COM     9398   3-07-85    1:43p
GRAFTABL COM     1169   3-07-85    1:43p
GRAPHICS COM     3111   3-07-85    1:43p
JOIN     EXE    15971   3-07-85    1:43p
KEYBFR   COM     2473   4-12-85    4:22p
KEYBGR   COM     2418   4-12-85    4:23p
KEYBIT   COM     2361   4-12-85    4:25p
KEYBSP   COM     2451   4-12-85    4:24p
KEYBUK   COM     2348   4-12-85    4:26p
LABEL    COM     1826   3-07-85    1:43p
MODE     COM     5295   3-07-85    1:43p
MORE     COM      282   3-07-85    1:43p
PRINT    COM     8291   3-07-85    1:43p
RECOVER  COM     4050   3-07-85    1:43p
RESTORE  COM     5410   3-07-85    1:43p
SELECT   COM     2084   3-07-85    1:43p
SHARE    EXE     8304   3-07-85    1:43p
SORT     EXE     1664   3-07-85    1:43p
SUBST    EXE    16611   3-07-85    1:43p
SYS      COM     3727   3-07-85    1:43p
TREE     COM     2831   3-07-85    1:43p
VDISK    SYS     3307   3-07-85    1:43p
    36 File(s)     61440 bytes free

A>
```

STEP 2: Same.

```
FORMAT   COM     9398   3-07-85    1:43p
GRAFTABL COM     1169   3-07-85    1:43p
GRAPHICS COM     3111   3-07-85    1:43p
JOIN     EXE    15971   3-07-85    1:43p
KEYBFR   COM     2473   4-12-85    4:22p
KEYBGR   COM     2418   4-12-85    4:23p
KEYBIT   COM     2361   4-12-85    4:25p
KEYBSP   COM     2451   4-12-85    4:24p
KEYBUK   COM     2348   4-12-85    4:26p
LABEL    COM     1826   3-07-85    1:43p
MODE     COM     5295   3-07-85    1:43p
MORE     COM      282   3-07-85    1:43p
PRINT    COM     8291   3-07-85    1:43p
RECOVER  COM     4050   3-07-85    1:43p
RESTORE  COM     5410   3-07-85    1:43p
SELECT   COM     2084   3-07-85    1:43p
SHARE    EXE     8304   3-07-85    1:43p
SORT     EXE     1664   3-07-85    1:43p
SUBST    EXE    16611   3-07-85    1:43p
SYS      COM     3727   3-07-85    1:43p
TREE     COM     2831   3-07-85    1:43p
VDISK    SYS     3307   3-07-85    1:43p
    36 File(s)     61440 bytes free

A>
```

NOTE: The screen shown above is a display of PC-DOS, Version 3.1. Your screen display could be different if you are using another version of DOS. It is all right if some different files are displayed. Just be sure you have the master DOS System Disk in Drive A. The number of bytes may vary, but this too is not significant.

WHAT'S HAPPENING? You will see text moving past you on the screen. This is known as **scrolling**, the result of executing the `DIR` command. DOS is displaying, or listing, all the files on the disk in Drive A. This list of files stops scrolling when the list ends. The `DIR` command has displayed the files on the disk in Drive A, and it also gave information about the files. Look at the top line of the screen. You will see `FORMAT`, the name of the file. Going from left to right is `COM`, the file extension. (`FORMAT.COM` is the file specification.) The number `9398` is the size of the file in bytes. Next is `3-07-85` followed by `1:43p`, which represents the date and time this file was created or last modified. Now look at the bottom line of the display: `36 File(s) 61440 bytes free`. This line indicates the total number of files on the disk—36. It also tells you how much room is left in bytes (`61440 bytes free`), so you will know if you have room on this disk for more files. All the files listed on this disk are programs or commands that you will learn to use. If you can see the file name on the master DOS System Disk, it is an external command.

2.8 THE KEYBOARD

The keyboard on a microcomputer is similar to a typewriter keyboard with more than 40 additional special keys. Many of these keys have symbols rather than alphabetic characters. The keyboard can be broken down into three categories:

1. Alphanumeric keys. These keys, located in the center of the keyboard, are the standard typewriter keys and therefore consist of the letters of the alphabet and Arabic numbers.
2. Function keys. Keys labeled Fl, F2, etc., often located on the left side of the keyboard or across the top, are known as function keys. These keys are program-dependent or programmable keys. Their function is dependent on the software used.
3. Numeric keys. These keys, located to the right of the alphabetic keys, are known as a number pad. Numeric keys can be used two ways: like a calculator keypad, or with the directional arrows and other commands. The directional arrows and other commands are program dependent. The user must activate the mode desired (numeric keypad or directional arrows) with the <Num Lock> toggle switch. A toggle switch acts like an on/off switch. Press the <Num Lock> key once, and the numbers are turned on. Press the <Num Lock> key again, and the numbers are turned off. There are other toggle keys, but they will be discussed later. Some keyboards separate the directional keys and the numeric keypad.

The following activity will familiarize you with some of the special keys and features of a computer keyboard. Figure 2.1 shows some of the major keyboards used today. Identify the keyboard used with your system so that you can locate the keys on the keyboard.

Figure 2.1 Various Keyboard Layouts

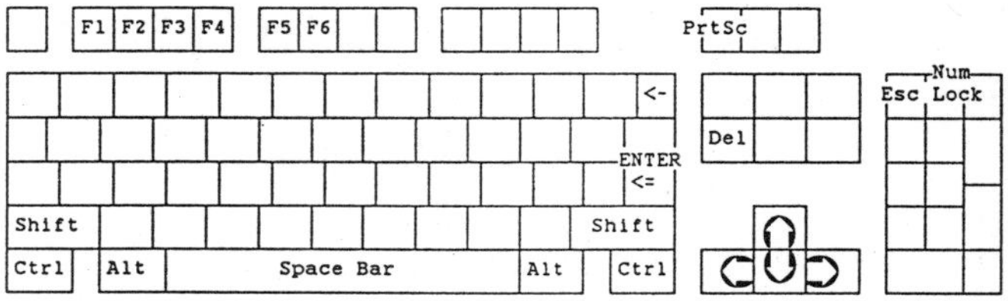

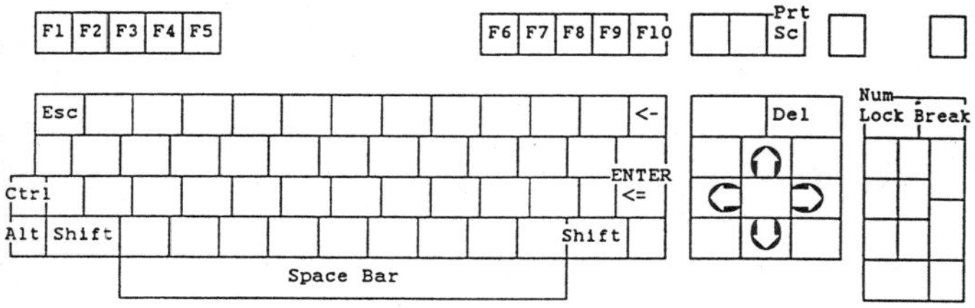

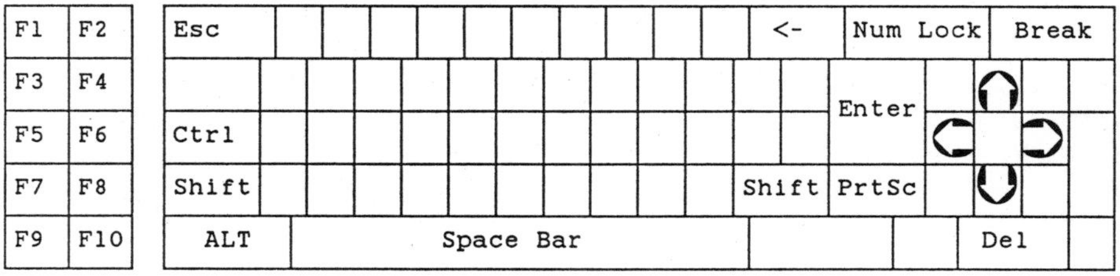

2.9 THE BACKSPACE KEY

The <Backspace>, the key with the symbol ⇦ on it, allows you to erase or delete characters you have keyed in, prior to hitting <Enter>.

ACTIVITY 2.10 CORRECTING TYPOGRAPHICAL ERRORS USING THE BACKSPACE KEY

STEP 1: Key in the following:

```
A>The quick brown fox
```

STEP 1: Same.

STEP 2: Press the <Backspace> key until you reach the A prompt (A>). As you see, each time you press this key, you delete a character.

STEP 2: Same.

2.11 THE ESCAPE KEY

<Esc> is an abbreviation for Escape. Look for the key labeled <Esc>. When you press this key, it cancels a line you have keyed in, provided you have not yet hit <Enter>. When you hit the <Esc> Key, DOS ignores what you have keyed in and waits for you to key in something else.

ACTIVITY 2.12 USING THE ESC KEY

STEP 1: Key in the following:

```
A>The quick brown fox
```

STEP 1: Same.

STEP 2: To erase this line, you could repeatedly press the <Backspace> key. However, you can use the <Esc> key to cancel the line instead. Press the <Esc> key.

```
A>The quick brown fox\
 _
```

STEP 2: Same.

```
A>The quick brown fox\
 _
```

WHAT'S HAPPENING? DOS displayed a backslash (\) to show you that the line you keyed in was canceled. DOS then moved the cursor to the beginning of the next line. Note that the A> is not shown where the cursor is blinking. This cursor indicates that DOS is ready for you to key in a command. DOS will ignore the line you had keyed in.

STEP 3: Press <Enter>. DOS will again display the A> on the next line.

```
A>The quick brown fox\
A>_
```

STEP 3: Same.

```
A>The quick brown fox\
A>_
```

2.13 THE SHIFT KEY

The <Shift> key will be labeled Shift or will have an up arrow symbol, ⇧ . This key allows you to shift to uppercase letters and the special characters such as the * above the number 8. There are usually two <Shift> keys, one on either side of the alphabet keys.

ACTIVITY 2.14 USING THE SHIFT KEY

STEP 1: Press the letter m.

```
A>m_
```

STEP 1: Same.

```
A>m_
```

STEP 2: Hold down the <Shift> key and press the letter m.

```
A>mM_
```

STEP 2: Same.

```
A>mM_
```

STEP 3: Press either the <Backspace> or the <Esc> key to delete the letters.

STEP 3: Same.

2.15 THE SHIFT KEY AND THE PRINT SCREEN KEY

Look for the key labeled <PrtSc> which means print the screen. If you want to print what is displayed on the screen, hold down <Shift> and press the <PrtSc> key. This gives you a hard copy or printed version of what the screen displays, like a "snapshot" of the screen at a specific moment in time. **Be sure the printer is turned on** prior to doing this exercise.

ACTIVITY 2.16 USING THE SHIFT KEY AND THE PRINT SCREEN KEY

STEP 1: Key in the following:

STEP 1: Same.

```
A>DIR  <Enter>
```

STEP 2: Wait until the table of contents has stopped scrolling. Hold the <Shift> key down and then press the <PrtSc> key.

STEP 2: Same.

WHAT'S HAPPENING? You should see the cursor moving along the screen and at the same time, you should see that the printer is printing what is displayed on the screen.

2.17 THE CONTROL KEY AND THE PRINT SCREEN KEY

Look for the key labeled <Ctrl>. This is known as the Control key. It has many functions, depending on what other key it is used with. Pressing the Control key has no meaning by itself. However, when used with another key, it "triggers" another meaning for that key. When you see the notation <Ctrl> or ^ or Control key, it means to hold down the Control key with the other specified key. <Ctrl>-C or ^C is computer notation for pressing the control key and another key, which in this instance is the letter C. Whenever you see the notation Control, <Ctrl>, or ^, this means to press the <Ctrl> key and the key name following the <Ctrl>. Do not type or key in the word Control, <Ctrl>, or ^. In the last example, when you printed the screen, you could only get what was displayed on the screen. The files that scrolled by were not printed. If, however, you hold down the <Ctrl> key and the <PrtSc> key, DOS will print everything as it is displayed. **Be sure the printer is turned on.**

ACTIVITY 2.18 USING THE CONTROL KEY AND THE PRINT SCREEN KEY

STEP 1: Press the <Ctrl> key. While pressing the <Ctrl> key, press the <PrtSc> key.

STEP 1: Same.

STEP 2: Key in the following:

STEP 2: Same.

```
A>DIR  <Enter>
```

WHAT'S HAPPENING? Note that as the directory is displayed, it is also being printed. The table of contents or the directory is displayed much more slowly than when you use the DIR command by itself because DOS waits until a line is printed before going on to the next line. Pressing <Ctrl>-<PrtSc> creates what is known as a toggle switch, much like a light switch. In one position, the light is turned on; in the other position, the light is turned off. This is also true with <Ctrl>-<PrtSc>. You have turned on this printing function and it will stay turned on, printing everything you key in and display on the screen, until you turn it off. To turn off a toggle switch, simply press the same keys again.

STEP 3: Press the <Ctrl> key. While pressing the <Ctrl> key, press the <PrtSc> key.

STEP 3: Same.

2.19 FREEZING THE DISPLAY

You have already seen that when you use the DIR command, the display scrolls by very quickly on the screen, making it very difficult to read. There is a way to stop displays from scrolling by on the screen. DOS allows you to read a long display by temporarily halting it. Once again you use the <Ctrl> key, but now you use it in conjunction with the key labeled <Num Lock>. Locate the key with <Num Lock> on it.

ACTIVITY 2.20 USING THE CONTROL KEY AND THE NUM LOCK KEY

STEP 1: Key in the following:

STEP 1: Same.

```
A>DIR  <Enter>
```

STEP 2: Press the <Ctrl> key. While pressing the <Ctrl> key, press the <Num Lock> key.

STEP 2: Same.

WHAT'S HAPPENING? Pressing these keys will halt or "freeze" the display on the screen. The display stops with a blinking cursor set when you pressed these two keys. To continue scrolling, press any key.

STEP 3: Press any key.

STEP 3: Same.

2.21 CANCELLING A COMMAND

If you keyed in a command and pressed <Enter>, but you either made an error or changed your mind about executing the command, you can cancel the command or cause it to stop executing. This command is not the same as <Esc>, which is used prior to pressing <Enter>. To cancel a command after you have pressed <Enter>, press the <Ctrl> key in conjunction with the <Break> key or the letter C. Look for the key labeled Break. It is often paired with the <Scroll Lock> key.

ACTIVITY 2.22 USING DIR AND CANCELLING THIS COMMAND

STEP 1: Key in the following:

STEP 1: Same.

```
A>DIR  <Enter>
```

STEP 2: As soon as the directory starts displaying on the screen, hold the <Ctrl> key down. While holding down the <Ctrl> key, press the <Break> key.

STEP 2: Same.

WHAT'S HAPPENING? DOS will stop running or executing the DIR command. You will be returned to the A prompt. You interrupted or stopped the program or the command from running and therefore you see only a partial directory display. At the point where you hit the <Ctrl> key and the <Break> key, you will see ^C displayed on your screen. Note that it is a Control and the letter C. <Ctrl>-C has the same function and meaning as <Ctrl>-<Break>.

STEP 3: Key in the following:

STEP 3: Same.

```
A>DIR <Enter>
```

STEP 4: As soon as the directory starts displaying on the screen, hold the <Ctrl> key down. While holding down the <Ctrl> key, press the letter C.

STEP 4: Same.

WHAT'S HAPPENING? Note that this worked exactly like `<Ctrl>-<Break>`. DOS ceased executing the program or the `DIR` command and returned you to the A prompt, ready for another command.

2.23 THE CLS, DATE AND TIME COMMANDS

So far, the only internal command you have been working with is the `DIR` command. There are many other internal commands. The next three commands that will be demonstrated are minor but useful.

NOTE: Both two disk drive users and hard disk users will have the master DOS System Disk in Drive A for Activities 2.25 and 2.27.

2.24 THE CLS COMMAND

As you will note, your screen is filled with the display of the directory and other commands that you have keyed in. If you would like to have a "fresh" screen, with nothing displayed on it except the `A>` prompt and the cursor in its "home" position (the upper lefthand corner of the screen), there is an internal command, `CLS`, which clears or "refreshes" the screen. This means that whatever is displayed on the screen will go away, as if you erased a blackboard. This command has no effect on files.

ACTIVITY 2.25 USING THE CLS COMMAND

STEP 1: Key in the following:

```
A>CLS  <Enter>
```

```
A>_
```

STEP 1: Key in the following:

```
A>CLS  <Enter>
```

```
A>_
```

WHAT'S HAPPENING? The screen is now cleared and the `A>` is back in the upper lefthand corner of the screen.

2.26 THE DATE AND TIME COMMANDS

You have used the DATE and TIME commands every time you booted up the system and entered the date and time in response to the DATE/TIME prompts. This is known as the **system date** and the **system time**. The system date and time are the date and time the computer uses when it opens and closes files (last date/time accessed) or when another program asks for the date and time. Some computer systems have a built-in clock, which usually is an "add-on." You add it after you purchase the computer system. This built-in clock is simply a 24-hour battery operated clock that sets the date and time automatically when you boot up the system so that you never see the DATE/TIME prompts when you start. However, regardless of whether you entered the date and time when you booted up the system or whether you have an automatic clock, you can change or check the system date and system time whenever you wish by using the internal DATE and TIME commands.

ACTIVITY 2.27 USING THE DATE AND TIME COMMANDS

STEP 1: Key in the following:

A>DATE <Enter>

```
Current date is Fri 1-16-1987
Enter new date (mm-dd-yy):_
```

STEP 1: Key in the following:

A>DATE <Enter>

```
Current date is Fri 1-16-1987
Enter new date (mm-dd-yy):_
```

WHAT'S HAPPENING? The date displayed on your screen will be the one you entered when you booted the system, not the above example. Note that this prompt is exactly like the one you saw when booting up. This displays the system date. If you did not wish to change the date, you would just hit <Enter>. This would retain the date displayed and return you to the A>. However, if you do want to change the date, you respond to the prompt.

STEP 2: Key in the following for both systems:

12-31-99 <Enter>

```
A>_
```

```
A>_
```

WHAT'S HAPPENING? You did change the date, and we will examine this in a moment. You can also change the time in the same fashion with the TIME command.

STEP 3: Key in the following:

A>TIME <Enter>

```
Current time is 10:44:14.42
Enter new time:_
```

STEP 3: Key in the following:

A>TIME <Enter>

Current time is 10:44:14.42
Enter new time:_

WHAT'S HAPPENING? The time displayed on your screen will be the current time not the above example. Note that this prompt is exactly like the one you saw when booting up. This displays the system time. If you did not wish to change the time, you would just hit <Enter>. This would retain the time displayed and return you to the A>. However, if you do want to change the time, you respond to the prompt.

STEP 4: Key in the following:

23:59:59 <Enter>

STEP 4: Key in the following:

23:59:59 <Enter>

WHAT'S HAPPENING? You have just reset the computer clock with the DATE and TIME commands. These are internal commands. How do you know the system date and time have been changed? You can check by keying in the commands.

STEP 5: Key in the following:

A>DATE <Enter>

```
Current date is Sat 01-01-2000
Enter new date (mm-dd-yy):_
```

STEP 5: Key in the following:

A>DATE <Enter>

Current date is Sat 01-01-2000
Enter new date (mm-dd-yy):_

STEP 6: Press <Enter>.

STEP 6: Press <Enter>.

STEP 7: Key in the following:

A>TIME <Enter>

```
Current time is 0:01:16.40
Enter new time:_
```

STEP 7: Key in the following:

A>TIME <Enter>

Current time is 0:01:16.40
Enter new time:_

STEP 8: Press <Enter>

STEP 8: Press <Enter>

WHAT'S HAPPENING? Your time display numbers may be slightly different. What have you done? You have changed the system date and time. You entered the date of December 31, 1999 (12-31-99), prior to changing the time. The date now displayed is January 1, 2000. How did that happen? Why is the displayed date different than the date that you keyed in? After you entered the date of 12-31-99, you entered the time of 23:59 p.m. (23:59:59). When you set the time or clock, it will run until you turn off the power. Seconds went by; the time rolled over to past midnight, and when you are past midnight, you are into a new day. Hence the day "rolled over" from December 31, 1999 to January 1, 2000. In other words, DOS is keeping the date and time current based on the information you originally gave it. Note that the day of the week is displayed in the date. You can play around with the system to find out on what day of the week any date will fall. For instance, you can find the day of the week of your birthday in any future year by using the DATE command.

STEP 9: Key in the following:

A>DATE <Enter>

```
Current date is Sat 1-01-2000
Enter new date (mm-dd-yy)_
```

STEP 9: Key in the following:

A>DATE <Enter>

Current date is Sat 1-01-2000
Enter new date (mm-dd-yy)_

STEP 10: At the prompt, date (mm-dd-yy)_ on the screen, key in your birthdate for 1995. In the example below, I will use my birthday, 5-7-95. Key in the following for both systems:

```
Current date is Sat 01-01-2000
Enter new date (mm-dd-yy):05-07-95   <Enter>
```

STEP 11: Key in the following:

A>DATE <Enter>

```
Current date is Sun 5-07-1995
Enter new date (mm-dd-yy):_
```

STEP 11: Key in the following:

A>DATE <Enter>

Current date is Sun 5-07-1995
Enter new date (mm-dd-yy):_

WHAT'S HAPPENING? The screen display will show you the exact day of the week of your birthday in 1995. In this case, my birthday will fall on a Sunday in 1995. If you wish to see or change the system date or time, use the DATE command and the TIME command.

STEP 12: Use the **DATE** and **TIME** commands to enter the current date and time.

STEP 12: Use the **DATE** and **TIME** commands to enter the current date and time.

2.28 MAKING A SYSTEM DISK

MATERIALS NEEDED

1. Master DOS System Disk
2. Blank floppy disk

You are now going to make a working copy of the master DOS System Disk. You will work from a copy of the master DOS System Disk so that if anything happens to it, you can go back to the original master DOS System Disk and make another copy. Whenever possible, always work from a copy, never the original. This copy of the master DOS System Disk will be used for all future exercises.

You are going to use your first external program, called **DISKCOPY**. It is stored as a file on the master DOS System Disk called **DISKCOPY.COM**. It does exactly what it says; it copies all the information on one disk to another disk.

NOTE 1: The master DOS System Disk should be in Drive A. The A> should be displayed on the screen. If you do not have the A>, boot or reboot the system.

NOTE 2: Hard disk users please be especially careful to follow the instructions exactly. Be sure your screen looks like the sample, especially the prompt. **You do not want C> displayed, only A>.**

ACTIVITY 2.29 MAKING A SYSTEM DISK

STEP 1: Get a blank disk and a blank label and write on it: DOS System Disk. Put the label on the blank disk, label side up. If the disk has no label, you can determine which is "label side up" by laying the disk down on a flat surface with the read/write area facing away from you and the write-protect notch facing left. Here is the side on which to place the label. If you ever need to write on a label that is already affixed to the disk, be sure to use only a felt-tip pen, and write very gently.

STEP 1: Same.

STEP 2: Insert the blank disk, label side up, into Drive B. Close the drive door.

STEP 3: Key in the following:

```
A>DISKCOPY A: B:  <Enter>
```

```
Insert SOURCE diskette in drive A:
Insert TARGET diskette in drive B:

Press any key when ready.....
```

STEP 2: The master DOS System Disk is in Drive A.

STEP 3: Key in the following:

```
A>DISKCOPY  <Enter>
```

```
Insert SOURCE diskette in drive A:

Press any key when ready.....
```

WHAT'S HAPPENING? By keying in `DISKCOPY`, you are asking the command processor to find a program called `DISKCOPY`. It first looked in the table of commands and when it could not find a match, it went to the disk in Drive A and found the program, loaded it into memory, and started executing the program. This program has some prompts, which are simply instructions to follow. The program asks you to put the SOURCE disk that you wish to copy in Drive A. In this case, you have the master DOS System Disk which you want to copy, already in Drive A. Because two disk drive users have two disk drives, A and B, DOS is telling you to put the TARGET disk in Drive B. The TARGET disk will be the recipient of the information. Two disk drive users have already placed a blank disk, the TARGET disk, in Drive B ready to receive the information. Hard disk users only have one floppy drive and are going to have to swap disks when prompted. To make the copy or begin executing the command `DISKCOPY`, both users just need to press any key. (There is no key labeled "any." This instruction literally means any key on the keyboard.) Typically, you use `<Enter>`.

STEP 4: Press `<Enter>`.

```
Copying 40 tracks
9 Sectors/Tracks, 2 side(s)
```

STEP 4: Press `<Enter>`.

```
Copying 40 tracks
9 Sectors/Tracks, 2 side(s)
```

WHAT'S HAPPENING? This command tells DOS to copy everything on the disk in Drive A (the SOURCE) to RAM. Since two disk drive users have two disk drives with a second disk in Drive B (the TARGET), the `DISKCOPY` command can immediately begin copying to the disk in Drive B. But since hard disk users have only one floppy disk drive, the program will instruct you to insert the destination disk. While this program is doing the copying, the screen will show a flashing cursor. When the command is completed or the program is finished executing (copying), two disk drive users will be done, but hard disk users need to take another step. Hard disk users will get the following prompt:

```
Insert TARGET DISK in drive A:
Press any key when ready...
```

WHAT'S HAPPENING? This prompt is telling you to remove the SOURCE disk from Drive A and insert the blank or target disk in Drive A so DOS has a place to copy the information.

STEP 5: Do nothing. You will see the screen display shown below.

STEP 5: Remove the master DOS System Disk from Drive A. Insert the blank disk into Drive A. Close the drive door. Press `<Enter>`.

WHAT'S HAPPENING? Again, you see the flashing cursor. Now, whatever was copied into RAM is being copied or written to the blank disk in Drive A.

```
Copy another diskette (Y/N)_
```

```
Copy another diskette (Y/N)_
```

WHAT'S HAPPENING? Note the prompt, which will tell you that the program has finished executing. This command is asking you a question. Do you want to execute this program again to make another copy of a disk? In this case, you do not wish to make another copy.

STEP 6: Key in the letter n.

STEP 6: Key in the letter n.

```
A>_
```

```
A>_
```

WHAT'S HAPPENING? You are returned to the `A>`. DOS is ready for a new command.

2.30 VERIFYING THE COPY

MATERIALS NEEDED

1. Master DOS System Disk
2. Working copy of DOS that you just made.

How do you know that the disks were copied correctly? One way to confirm this is to use another command, **DISKCOMP**. **DISKCOMP** is stored as a file on the master DOS System Disk called **DISKCOMP.COM**. This command does exactly what it sounds like. It compares two disks track by track, sector by sector, making sure that the two disks are exact or identical copies. It is also an external command.

ACTIVITY 2.31 VERIFYING THE COPY

STEP 1: Verify that the master DOS System Disk is in Drive A and that the working copy of DOS that you DISKCOPIED is in Drive B.

STEP 2: Key in the following:

```
A>DISKCOMP A: B:  <Enter>
```

```
Insert FIRST diskette in drive A:
Insert SECOND diskette in drive B:

Press any key when ready...
```

STEP 3: The disks you want to compare are already in Drive A and Drive B. Press **<Enter>**.

```
Comparing 40 tracks
9 sectors per track, 2 side(s)
```

STEP 1: Place the master DOS System Disk is in Drive A.

STEP 2: Key in the following:

```
A>DISKCOMP  <Enter>
```

```
Insert FIRST diskette in drive A:

Press any key when ready...
```

STEP 3: Press **<Enter>**.

```
Comparing 40 tracks
9 sectors per track, 2 side(s)
```

WHAT'S HAPPENING? By keying in DISKCOMP, you are asking the command processor to find a program called DISKCOMP. It first looked in the table of commands and when it could not find a match (since DISKCOMP is external), it went to the disk in Drive A, found and loaded the program into memory, and began executing it. Its job is to verify that the two disks are alike. This command is only used with floppy disks, since you cannot compare a hard disk and a floppy disk. Hard disk user are working with one floppy disk drive. DISKCOMP read the disk in Drive A into RAM. Now it needs a disk to compare with. Do not do anything until you see the following prompt displayed on the screen:

```
Insert SECOND diskette in drive A:
Press any key when ready....
```

STEP 4: Do nothing.

STEP 4: Remove the master DOS System Disk from Drive A. Insert the working copy of the DOS System Disk you made. This is the second disk that you wish to compare to the original. Press <Enter>.

WHAT'S HAPPENING? Again, you see the flashing cursor while the program is working. It read into memory whatever was on the second diskette and is checking this against the original information.

```
Compare OK
Compare another diskette (Y/N)_
```


```
Compare OK
Compare another diskette (Y/N)_
```


WHAT'S HAPPENING? The DISKCOMP command told you that it checked the disks and they are exactly the same (Compare OK). It also asks you a question. Do you want to compare any more disks? Since you do not, you select n for no.

STEP 5: Press n.

STEP 5: Press n.

WHAT TO DO WHEN IT DOESN'T WORK: If you get beeps from the computer and the following screen display ("n" represents any numerical value):

"Compare error on side n, track n"

Press the <Ctrl> key and the <Break> key simultaneously. Return to Step 1 and repeat the steps.

2.32 ENDING THE WORK SESSION

You can stop working with the computer any time you wish. Since your programs are stored on the disks, you will not lose them. Whatever is in RAM or memory will go into the "byte bucket," i.e., disappear, but that does not affect what is on your disk any more than when you turn off your tape deck; you do not lose what is on the tape. The only thing you need to be cautious about is the red light. When the red light is on, that indicates that the head is reading or writing to the disk. Removing the disk at this time is the equivalent of taking a record off the turntable without first removing the needle.

ACTIVITY 2.33 ENDING THE WORK SESSION

STEP 1: Be sure no red lights are on.

STEP 2: Remove any disks that are in the disk drives. Place the floppy disks in their envelopes.

STEP 3: Turn off the printer, the monitor, and the system unit.

STEP 1: Be sure no red lights are on.

STEP 2: Remove any disk that is in the disk drive. Place the floppy disk in its envelope.

STEP 3: Turn off the printer, the monitor, and the system unit.

CHAPTER SUMMARY

1. Booting the system, also know as a cold start, means inserting the DOS System Disk in Drive A and powering on the system. This loads the operating system into memory and includes the execution of the self-diagnostic test routine.
2. Rebooting, also known as a warm start, involves pressing the `<Ctrl>`, `<Alt>`, and `<Del>` keys. This erases everything from memory and reloads the operating system from the disk. Rebooting does not execute the self-diagnostic test routine.
3. Internal commands are programs loaded with the operating system in `COMMAND.COM`. They remain in memory until the power is turned off.
4. External commands are stored on a disk and must be loaded into memory each time they are used. They are transient and do not remain in memory after being executed.
5. Programs and data are stored on disks as files. The formal name is file specification, which includes the file name and file extension.
6. The `DIR` command is an internal command that displays the table of contents or directory of a disk.
7. The `<Backspace>` key deletes characters to the left.

8. The <Esc> key ignores what was previously keyed in.
9. The <Shift> key shifts letters to uppercase.
10. The <PrtSc> key and <Shift> key, when held down together, print the screen.
11. The <Ctrl> key and the <PrtSc> key, when held down together, toggles the printer on or off.
12. A toggle switch is like a light switch. In one position, the function is on. By pressing the same toggle switch the function is turned off.
13. The <Num Lock> key and the <Ctrl> key, when held down together, freeze the screen display.
14. The <Ctrl> key and the <Break> key or the <Ctrl> key and the letter C, when held down together, cancel a command.
15. Minor internal commands include CLS, DATE, and TIME.
16. CLS clears the screen.
17. DATE and TIME allow you to look at and/or change the system date and system time.
18. DISKCOPY is an external command that makes an identical copy of any disk, track for track, and sector for sector. It was used to make a working copy of the master DOS System Disk but can be used to make exact copies of any two floppy disks.
19. DISKCOMP is an external command that compares two disks, track for track, sector for sector. It was used to verify that the copy of DOS that was made was correct but can be used to verify any two floppy disks.
20. To end a work session with the computer, remove any disks and turn off the monitor, printer, and system unit.

REVIEW QUESTIONS

1. How do you boot the system?
2. How do you reboot the system?
3. What happens when you boot the system?
4. What happens when you reboot the system?
5. Is there any difference between rebooting and booting a system?
6. Define disk file.
7. Define file specification.
8. Name two ways the display screen can be printed.
9. What is DIR? What is it used for?
10. What is CLS? What is it used for?
11. How is the Ctrl key used?
12. Define a toggle switch.
13. How can you freeze the display?
14. Describe how to cancel a command.
15. Define the system date and system time.
16. How can you change the system date and system time?

17. What are function keys?
18. What is DISKCOPY used for?
19. What is DISKCOMP used for?
20. How do you end a work session with the computer?

TRUE/FALSE

1. A program is a set of instructions that tells the computer what to do.
2. When you key in the time, you must specify a.m. or p.m. by keying in AM or PM.
3. DISKCOPY is an external command that makes an identical copy of a disk.
4. When you key in the date, you must key it in the format mm/dd/yy or mm-dd-yy.
5. The DOS System Disk must be inserted in Drive A prior to turning on the power.
6. DISKCOMP is an internal command that compares two files.
7. The two hidden system files are IBMDOS.COM and IBMBIO.COM.
8. External commands are stored permanently on a disk.
9. DISKCOPY.COM is a program that is stored as a file on a disk.
10. When you see <Ctrl>-C, this means to key in Control and then the letter C.
11. You cannot print what is displayed on the screen.
12. CLS erases everything in memory.
13. When the printer is toggled on, everything that is displayed is printed.
14. Freezing the display allows the user to halt what is scrolling past on the screen.
15. If you press the <Backspace> key, you get many spaces.

COMMAND SYNTAX: Using the DIR Command with Parameters and Wildcards

CHAPTER

3

CHAPTER OBJECTIVES

This chapter discusses command syntax, file names, defaults, parameters, using the `DIR` command with parameters, and wildcards.

After completing this chapter, you will:

Be familiar with the DOS command structure.

Understand the purpose and use of the `DIR` command.

Understand prompts.

Understand defaults.

Be able to change the default drive.

Understand wildcards and be able to use them with the `DIR` command.

3.0 COMMAND SYNTAX

All languages have rules or conventions to be followed when speaking or writing. The syntax or order of the language is important. For example, in English the noun (person, place or thing) is followed by the verb (the action). In another language, however, the syntax or order might be different: first comes the verb, followed by the noun. When you learn a language, you learn its syntax.

Computers also communicate with language, but you must speak the computer's language and follow its syntax exactly because the computer has a very limited understanding of language. This is why you cannot just key in any word and expect the computer to understand. Anything you key in must be a recognized word, actually a program that you are asking the system to execute. And not only must you use the computer's vocabulary, you must also use the proper syntax. The computer cannot guess what you mean. If, for example, I said, "Going I store," people would still understand what I meant. A computer is different. First of all a computer must have a vocabulary or know the meaning of words. In addition, the words must be expressed in the proper order or syntax. If I key in an incorrect word or put correct words in the wrong order, the computer will respond with a message that it does not understand: "`Bad command or file name.`" This is the computer equivalent of saying, "I do not understand you."

In computer language, the command can be compared to a verb, the action you wish to take. In other words, when you key in `DIR`, you are asking DOS to take an action: run the program called `DIR` that lets you see the table of contents or the directory of a disk. However, you are also allowed to add one or more qualifiers or modifiers to the command to make it more specific. These qualifiers are called **parameters**. This process is the same in English. If I give my son my Visa card and tell him "Go buy," I have given him an open-ended statement—he can buy anything (and I also have made him one happy guy). However, if I add a qualifier, "Go buy shoes," I have limited what he can do. This is precisely what parameters do to a command. Some commands require parameters, while other commands let you add them if needed.

3.1 USING PARAMETERS

`DIR` is one of the commands that has optional parameters. As you have noted, there is a problem with the `DIR` command. There are so many files on the disk that when you key in `DIR` and the files scroll by, they move so quickly that you cannot read them. In the previous chapter, you learned that you could halt the display by pressing the `<Ctrl>` and `<Num Lock>` keys. However, there is a more efficient way to solve this problem. `DIR` has two modifiers or parameters that allow you to control the way the operating system displays the table of contents on the disk. These are the two switches, `/P` for "pause display" and `/W` for "wide display."

NOTE: From now on, unless otherwise specified, the DOS System Disk refers to the working copy of the DOS disk you made with the `DISKCOPY` command from the DOS Master System Disk in the previous chapter.

ACTIVITY 3.2 USING PARAMETERS WITH THE DIR COMMAND

STEP 1: The DOS System Disk should be in Drive A with the `A>` displayed.

STEP 1: The DOS System Disk should be in Drive A with the `A>` displayed.

STEP 2: Key in the following:

```
A>DIR /P  <Enter>
```

```
ANSI     SYS     1651  3-07-85   1:43p
ASSIGN   COM     1509  3-07-85   1:43p
ATTRIB   EXE    15091  3-07-85   1:43p
BACKUP   COM     5577  3-07-85   1:43p
BASIC    COM    17792  3-07-85   1:43p
BASICA   COM    27520  3-07-85   1:43p
CHKDSK   COM     9435  3-07-85   1:43p
COMMAND  COM    23210  3-07-85   1:43p
COMP     COM     3664  3-07-85   1:43p
DISKCOMP COM     4073  3-07-85   1:43p
DISKCOPY COM     4329  3-07-85   1:43p
EDLIN    COM     7261  3-07-85   1:43p
FDISK    COM     8173  3-07-85   1:43p
FIND     EXE     6403  3-07-85   1:43p
FORMAT   COM     9398  3-07-85   1:43p
GRAFTABL COM     1169  3-07-85   1:43p
GRAPHICS COM     3111  3-07-85   1:43p
JOIN     EXE    15971  3-07-85   1:43p
KEYBFR   COM     2473  4-12-85   4:22p
KEYBGR   COM     2418  4-12-85   4:23p
KEYBIT   COM     2361  4-12-85   4:25p
KEYBSP   COM     2451  4-12-85   4:24p
KEYBUK   COM     2348  4-12-85   4:26p
Strike a key when ready..._
```

STEP 2: Key in the following:

```
A>DIR /P  <Enter>
```

```
ANSI     SYS     1651  3-07-85   1:43p
ASSIGN   COM     1509  3-07-85   1:43p
ATTRIB   EXE    15091  3-07-85   1:43p
BACKUP   COM     5577  3-07-85   1:43p
BASIC    COM    17792  3-07-85   1:43p
BASICA   COM    27520  3-07-85   1:43p
CHKDSK   COM     9435  3-07-85   1:43p
COMMAND  COM    23210  3-07-85   1:43p
COMP     COM     3664  3-07-85   1:43p
DISKCOMP COM     4073  3-07-85   1:43p
DISKCOPY COM     4329  3-07-85   1:43p
EDLIN    COM     7261  3-07-85   1:43p
FDISK    COM     8173  3-07-85   1:43p
FIND     EXE     6403  3-07-85   1:43p
FORMAT   COM     9398  3-07-85   1:43p
GRAFTABL COM     1169  3-07-85   1:43p
GRAPHICS COM     3111  3-07-85   1:43p
JOIN     EXE    15971  3-07-85   1:43p
KEYBFR   COM     2473  4-12-85   4:22p
KEYBGR   COM     2418  4-12-85   4:23p
KEYBIT   COM     2361  4-12-85   4:25p
KEYBSP   COM     2451  4-12-85   4:24p
KEYBUK   COM     2348  4-12-85   4:26p
Strike a key when ready..._
```


WHAT'S HAPPENING? Note that you keyed in the command DIR followed by a slash / and the parameter P. The slash, which must be included, is known as a **delimiter** or a switch. This character is used to separate other characters. The slash is the signal to the command DIR that there are more instructions than just to display the directory or table of contents. P, the parameter that tells the program what to do, is the additional information. The slash and P stop the directory from scrolling. Thus, /P told the DIR command to fill the 24 lines on the screen and then pause until the user takes some action. You should see displayed on your screen the directory that halted, with a bottom line prompt that says, "Strike a key when ready..._."

STEP 3: To continue the display of the directory, press any key.

```
GRAFTABL COM     1169   3-07-85    1:43p
GRAPHICS COM     3111   3-07-85    1:43p
JOIN     EXE    15971   3-07-85    1:43p
KEYBFR   COM     2473   4-12-85    4:22p
KEYBGR   COM     2418   4-12-85    4:23p
KEYBIT   COM     2361   4-12-85    4:25p
KEYBSP   COM     2451   4-12-85    4:24p
KEYBUK   COM     2348   4-12-85    4:26p
Strike a key when ready...
LABEL    COM     1826   3-07-85    1:43p
MODE     COM     5295   3-07-85    1:43p
MORE     COM      282   3-07-85    1:43p
PRINT    COM     8291   3-07-85    1:43p
RECOVER  COM     4050   3-07-85    1:43p
RESTORE  COM     5410   3-07-85    1:43p
SELECT   COM     2084   3-07-85    1:43p
SHARE    EXE     8304   3-07-85    1:43p
SORT     EXE     1664   3-07-85    1:43p
SUBST    EXE    16611   3-07-85    1:43p
SYS      COM     3727   3-07-85    1:43p
TREE     COM     2831   3-07-85    1:43p
VDISK    SYS     3307   3-07-85    1:43P
       36 File(s)    61440 bytes free
A>_
```

STEP 4: Key in the following:

`A> DIR /W <Enter>`

STEP 3: To continue the display of the directory, press any key.

```
GRAFTABL COM     1169   3-07-85    1:43p
GRAPHICS COM     3111   3-07-85    1:43p
JOIN     EXE    15971   3-07-85    1:43p
KEYBFR   COM     2473   4-12-85    4:22p
KEYBGR   COM     2418   4-12-85    4:23p
KEYBIT   COM     2361   4-12-85    4:25p
KEYBSP   COM     2451   4-12-85    4:24p
KEYBUK   COM     2348   4-12-85    4:26p
Strike a key when ready...
LABEL    COM     1826   3-07-85    1:43p
MODE     COM     5295   3-07-85    1:43p
MORE     COM      282   3-07-85    1:43p
PRINT    COM     8291   3-07-85    1:43p
RECOVER  COM     4050   3-07-85    1:43p
RESTORE  COM     5410   3-07-85    1:43p
SELECT   COM     2084   3-07-85    1:43p
SHARE    EXE     8304   3-07-85    1:43p
SORT     EXE     1664   3-07-85    1:43p
SUBST    EXE    16611   3-07-85    1:43p
SYS      COM     3727   3-07-85    1:43p
TREE     COM     2831   3-07-85    1:43p
VDISK    SYS     3307   3-07-85    1:43P
       36 File(s)    61440 bytes free
A>_
```

STEP 4: Key in the following:

`A> DIR /W <Enter>`

NOTE: The following display will appear on both floppy and hard disk systems:

```
ANSI     SYS   ASSIGN   COM   ATTRIB   EXE   BACKUP   COM   BASIC    COM
BASICA   COM   CHKDSK   COM   COMMAND  COM   COMP     COM   DISKCOMP COM
DISKCOPY COM   EDLIN    COM   FDISK    COM   FIND     EXE   FORMAT   COM
GRAFTABL COM   GRAPHICS COM   JOIN     EXE   KEYBFR   COM   KEYBGR   COM
KEYBIT   COM   KEYBSP   COM   KEYBUK   COM   LABEL    COM   MODE     COM
MORE     COM   PRINT    COM   RECOVER  COM   RESTORE  COM   SELECT   COM
SHARE    EXE   SORT     EXE   SUBST    EXE   SYS      COM   TREE     COM
VDISK    SYS
         36 File(s)    61440 bytes free
```

WHAT'S HAPPENING? The directory display is different. It is displayed across the screen, five files wide. In addition, all you see is the file specification, the file name and extension. You do not see the file size, date, or time. You still see the total number of files and the number of bytes free. Thus, the **/W** parameter allows you to see all the files at one time.

3.3 USING FILE NAMES AS PARAMETERS

In the previous activities, you used the **DIR** command with two different parameters, **/P** and **/W**. There is another parameter you can use with the **DIR** command: the name of the file.

Files are formally called file specifications. A file specification is broken into two parts, the file name and the file extension. The words file or file name really mean the file specification, which is the file name and file extension. In this case, the files are already named. But all files follow the DOS rules or naming conventions.
These are:

1. All files on one disk or one subdirectory must have a unique name.
2. File names are mandatory. All files must have a file name that may be less than but no longer than eight characters. Typically, file names refer to the subject of the file, for example, employee, taxes.
3. File extensions are optional. An extension may be less than but not longer than three characters. Typically, file extensions refer to the type of data in the file, for example, `.txt` (text), `.dat` (data), `.dbf` (data base), `.wks` (spreadsheet).
4. Any alphanumeric character can be used in a file name or file extension, except the following illegal or forbidden characters:
   `<space> . " / \ [ ] : ; ¦ < > + = , * ?`

When you key in the command, **DIR** you get the entire table of contents or directory. Usually you do not care about all the files. Most often you are only interested in whether or not one specific file is located or stored on the disk. If you use one of the parameters, **/P** or **/W**, you still have to look through all the files. You can locate a specific file by using only the file name, giving the **DIR** command specific information about what you are looking for.

ACTIVITY 3.4 USING FILE NAMES AS PARAMETERS WITH THE DIR COMMAND

NOTE: Both two disk drive and hard drive users should have the DOS System disk in Drive A with the **A>** displayed.

STEP 1: Key in the following:

```
A>CLS  <Enter>
```

STEP 2: Key in the following:

```
A>DIR  <Enter>
```

STEP 1: Key in the following:

```
A>CLS  <Enter>
```

STEP 2: Key in the following:

```
A>DIR  <Enter>
```

WHAT'S HAPPENING? The first thing you did was to clear the screen by using the internal command `CLS`. Then you keyed in `DIR` and the entire table of contents of the disk in Drive A scrolled by on the screen. When it stopped scrolling, it looked as follows:

```
FORMAT   COM     9398   3-07-85   1:43p
GRAFTABL COM     1169   3-07-85   1:43p
GRAPHICS COM     3111   3-07-85   1:43p
JOIN     EXE    15971   3-07-85   1:43p
KEYBFR   COM     2473   4-12-85   4:22p
KEYBGR   COM     2418   4-12-85   4:23p
KEYBIT   COM     2361   4-12-85   4:25p
KEYBSP   COM     2451   4-12-85   4:24p
KEYBUK   COM     2348   4-12-85   4:26p
LABEL    COM     1826   3-07-85   1:43p
MODE     COM     5295   3-07-85   1:43p
MORE     COM      282   3-07-85   1:43p
PRINT    COM     8291   3-07-85   1:43p
RECOVER  COM     4050   3-07-85   1:43p
RESTORE  COM     5410   3-07-85   1:43p
SELECT   COM     2084   3-07-85   1:43p
SHARE    EXE     8304   3-07-85   1:43p
SORT     EXE     1664   3-07-85   1:43p
SUBST    EXE    16611   3-07-85   1:43p
SYS      COM     3727   3-07-85   1:43p
TREE     COM     2831   3-07-85   1:43p
VDISK    SYS     3307   3-07-85   1:43p
      36 File(s)    61440 bytes free

A>_
```


```
FORMAT   COM     9398   3-07-85   1:43p
GRAFTABL COM     1169   3-07-85   1:43p
GRAPHICS COM     3111   3-07-85   1:43p
JOIN     EXE    15971   3-07-85   1:43p
KEYBFR   COM     2473   4-12-85   4:22p
KEYBGR   COM     2418   4-12-85   4:23p
KEYBIT   COM     2361   4-12-85   4:25p
KEYBSP   COM     2451   4-12-85   4:24p
KEYBUK   COM     2348   4-12-85   4:26p
LABEL    COM     1826   3-07-85   1:43p
MODE     COM     5295   3-07-85   1:43p
MORE     COM      282   3-07-85   1:43p
PRINT    COM     8291   3-07-85   1:43p
RECOVER  COM     4050   3-07-85   1:43p
RESTORE  COM     5410   3-07-85   1:43p
SELECT   COM     2084   3-07-85   1:43p
SHARE    EXE     8304   3-07-85   1:43p
SORT     EXE     1664   3-07-85   1:43p
SUBST    EXE    16611   3-07-85   1:43p
SYS      COM     3727   3-07-85   1:43p
TREE     COM     2831   3-07-85   1:43p
VDISK    SYS     3307   3-07-85   1:43p
      36 File(s)    61440 bytes free

A>_
```


WHAT'S HAPPENING? You are looking at all the file specifications on the disk in Drive A. You see the file names and, separated by some space, the file extensions. The other information is the size in bytes and the date and time the files were last updated.

STEP 3: Key in the following:

```
A>CLS <Enter>
```

STEP 3: Key in the following:

```
A>CLS <Enter>
```


STEP 4: Key in the following:

```
A>DIR diskcopy.com   <Enter>
```

STEP 4: Key in the following:

```
A>DIR diskcopy.com   <Enter>
```

```
A>DIR diskcopy.com

  Volume in Drive A has no label
  Directory of A:\

DISKCOPY     COM      4329    3-07-85     1:43p
      1 File(s)      61440 bytes free

A>_
```

```
A>DIR diskcopy.com

  Volume in Drive A has no label
  Directory of A:\

DISKCOPY     COM      4329    3-07-85     1:43p
      1 File(s)      61440 bytes free

A>_
```

WHAT'S HAPPENING? You asked the operating system a question. Does the table of contents on the disk in Drive A (DIR) have a specific file (diskcopy.com) located on it? DIR is the command; diskcopy.com is the parameter. Note that when you entered diskcopy and com, you separated the file name from the file extension with a period, called a **dot**. The dot must be entered between diskcopy and com because it separates the file name from the file extension. The dot, a delimiter, tells DOS that the file name is over and the file extension is about to begin. The DIR program will search the entire list of files on the disk in Drive A and look for an exact match to diskcopy.com. DOS answered your question with the above screen display. DOS is telling you that, yes, it found a file called diskcopy.com on the disk in Drive A. The file name is diskcopy. The file extension is com. The file size is 4329. The date and time are 3-7-85 and 1:43p. It also tells you that it only found one file with that name.

DOS is not case sensitive. This means that you can key in information in either uppercase or lowercase letters. However, this book uses the convention that if a file is being treated as a file it is in lowercase letters. If a file is being treated as a command, it is in uppercase letters. diskcopy.com is a file and a program. In chapter 2, you used it as a program by keying in the command name, DISKCOPY. In that instance, DOS not only found the program, it also loaded it into memory and executed the program. The "work" of DISKCOPY was to make an exact copy of a disk. In this example, you are using diskcopy.com as a file. The command or program you are running is DIR. You are not asking to execute the program DISKCOPY.COM; you are asking DIR if it has a file called diskcopy.com on the disk. This is like going to your file cabinet and looking for a file folder called diskcopy.com. When you locate the folder, you know where the folder is; you don't yet know what is in the folder.

STEP 5: Key in the following:

```
A>DIR format.com   <Enter>
```

```
Volume in Drive A has no label
Directory of A:\

FORMAT    COM     9398     3-07-85      1:43p
       1 File(s)       61440 bytes free

A>_
```

STEP 5: Key in the following:

```
A>DIR format.com   <Enter>
```

```
Volume in Drive A has no label
Directory of A:\

FORMAT    COM     9398     3-07-85      1:43p
       1 File(s)       61440 bytes free

A>_
```


WHAT'S HAPPENING? This command tells you that DOS did find the file `format.com` located on the disk in Drive A. What happens if there is no file by that name? You get the answer "`File not found.`"

STEP 6: Key in the following:

```
A>DIR nofile.ext   <Enter>
```

```
Volume in Drive A has no label
Directory of A:\

File not found

A>_
```

STEP 6: Key in the following:

```
A>DIR nofile.ext   <Enter>
```

```
Volume in Drive A has no label
Directory of A:\

File not found

A>_
```


WHAT'S HAPPENING? "`File not found`" is a **system message** or an **error message**. DOS is telling you that it looked through the entire list of files on the disk in Drive A and could not find a "match" or the file called `nofile.ext`. This message is the equivalent of going to your file cabinet and not locating the folder called `nofile.ext`. You can't "open" this folder because it is not in this file cabinet.

3.5 DRIVES AS DEVICE NAMES AND DEFAULTS

You have gotten used to seeing the **A>** or A prompt. What is the A prompt? **A>** indicates the disk drive, or the device, where the floppy disk is "playing." A disk drive is an example of a **device name**. A device is a place to send information (write) or a place from which to receive information (read). Disk drives are not the only places where the system sends or receives information. Other common devices are the keyboard, the printer, and the monitor.

In addition to device names, it is also important to understand the concept of **defaults**. Computers must have very specific instructions for anything they do. However, to save keystrokes, there are implied instructions that the system "falls back to" or defaults to in the absence of other instructions. If you do not specify what you want, the system will make the assumptions for you. For example, not only is `A>` called the A prompt, but it is also the default drive. When you want any activity to occur, if you don't specify where you want it to happen, the system will assume that you must mean the `A>` or what is displayed on the screen. Thus, when you key in `DIR` at the `A>`, how does DOS know that you are asking for the system to give you a table of contents of the disk that is in Drive A? It knows for two reasons. First, devices have very specific names and DOS must have a specific place to look. Second, the `A>`, or default drive, is displayed on the screen. Since you did not specify which disk you wanted DOS to see, it made the assumption (programmed in by the programmer) that since you did not give any instructions to the contrary, you must mean that you want the table of contents or directory listing for the default drive or the disk in drive A.

The prompt displayed on the screen can also be known as the **designated drive** or the **logged drive**. All commands, if given no other specific instructions to the contrary, will assume that all activities must take place or default to the prompt shown on the screen.

ACTIVITY 3.6 USING DEFAULTS AND CHANGING DEFAULTS

NOTE: Both two disk drive and hard drive users have the DOS System Disk in Drive A and the `A>` displayed.

STEP 1: Key in the following:

A>DIR <Enter>

```
FORMAT   COM     9398   3-07-85   1:43p
GRAFTABL COM     1169   3-07-85   1:43p
GRAPHICS COM     3111   3-07-85   1:43p
JOIN     EXE    15971   3-07-85   1:43p
KEYBFR   COM     2473   4-12-85   4:22p
KEYBGR   COM     2418   4-12-85   4:23p
KEYBIT   COM     2361   4-12-85   4:25p
KEYBSP   COM     2451   4-12-85   4:24p
KEYBUK   COM     2348   4-12-85   4:26p
LABEL    COM     1826   3-07-85   1:43p
MODE     COM     5295   3-07-85   1:43p
MORE     COM      282   3-07-85   1:43p
PRINT    COM     8291   3-07-85   1:43p
RECOVER  COM     4050   3-07-85   1:43p
RESTORE  COM     5410   3-07-85   1:43p
SELECT   COM     2084   3-07-85   1:43p
SHARE    EXE     8304   3-07-85   1:43p
SORT     EXE     1664   3-07-85   1:43p
SUBST    EXE    16611   3-07-85   1:43p
SYS      COM     3727   3-07-85   1:43p
TREE     COM     2831   3-07-85   1:43p
VDISK    SYS     3307   3-07-85   1:43p
       36 File(s)     61440 bytes free

A>_
```

STEP 1: Key in the following:

A>DIR <Enter>

FORMAT   COM   9398   3-07-85   1:43p
GRAFTABL COM   1169   3-07-85   1:43p
GRAPHICS COM   3111   3-07-85   1:43p
JOIN   EXE   15971   3-07-85   1:43p
KEYBFR   COM   2473   4-12-85   4:22p
KEYBGR   COM   2418   4-12-85   4:23p
KEYBIT   COM   2361   4-12-85   4:25p
KEYBSP   COM   2451   4-12-85   4:24p
KEYBUK   COM   2348   4-12-85   4:26p
LABEL   COM   1826   3-07-85   1:43p
MODE   COM   5295   3-07-85   1:43p
MORE   COM   282   3-07-85   1:43p
PRINT   COM   8291   3-07-85   1:43p
RECOVER COM   4050   3-07-85   1:43p
RESTORE COM   5410   3-07-85   1:43p
SELECT   COM   2084   3-07-85   1:43p
SHARE   EXE   8304   3-07-85   1:43p
SORT   EXE   1664   3-07-85   1:43p
SUBST   EXE   16611   3-07-85   1:43p
SYS   COM   3727   3-07-85   1:43p
TREE   COM   2831   3-07-85   1:43p
VDISK   SYS   3307   3-07-85   1:43p
       36 File(s)   61440 bytes free

A>_

WHAT'S HAPPENING? This is the display after it has finished scrolling. You asked to execute the command **DIR**. Since you did not specify which disk DOS should look into, it assumed or defaulted to the disk in Drive A.

STEP 2: Key in the following:

A>DIR A: <Enter>

STEP 2: Key in the following:

A>DIR A: <Enter>

```
FORMAT   COM     9398   3-07-85   1:43p
GRAFTABL COM     1169   3-07-85   1:43p
GRAPHICS COM     3111   3-07-85   1:43p
JOIN     EXE    15971   3-07-85   1:43p
KEYBFR   COM     2473   4-12-85   4:22p
KEYBGR   COM     2418   4-12-85   4:23p
KEYBIT   COM     2361   4-12-85   4:25p
KEYBSP   COM     2451   4-12-85   4:24p
KEYBUK   COM     2348   4-12-85   4:26p
LABEL    COM     1826   3-07-85   1:43p
MODE     COM     5295   3-07-85   1:43p
MORE     COM      282   3-07-85   1:43p
PRINT    COM     8291   3-07-85   1:43p
RECOVER  COM     4050   3-07-85   1:43p
RESTORE  COM     5410   3-07-85   1:43p
SELECT   COM     2084   3-07-85   1:43p
SHARE    EXE     8304   3-07-85   1:43p
SORT     EXE     1664   3-07-85   1:43p
SUBST    EXE    16611   3-07-85   1:43p
SYS      COM     3727   3-07-85   1:43p
TREE     COM     2831   3-07-85   1:43p
VDISK    SYS     3307   3-07-85   1:43p
       36 File(s)     61440 bytes free

A>_
```


```
FORMAT   COM     9398   3-07-85   1:43p
GRAFTABL COM     1169   3-07-85   1:43p
GRAPHICS COM     3111   3-07-85   1:43p
JOIN     EXE    15971   3-07-85   1:43p
KEYBFR   COM     2473   4-12-85   4:22p
KEYBGR   COM     2418   4-12-85   4:23p
KEYBIT   COM     2361   4-12-85   4:25p
KEYBSP   COM     2451   4-12-85   4:24p
KEYBUK   COM     2348   4-12-85   4:26p
LABEL    COM     1826   3-07-85   1:43p
MODE     COM     5295   3-07-85   1:43p
MORE     COM      282   3-07-85   1:43p
PRINT    COM     8291   3-07-85   1:43p
RECOVER  COM     4050   3-07-85   1:43p
RESTORE  COM     5410   3-07-85   1:43p
SELECT   COM     2084   3-07-85   1:43p
SHARE    EXE     8304   3-07-85   1:43p
SORT     EXE     1664   3-07-85   1:43p
SUBST    EXE    16611   3-07-85   1:43p
SYS      COM     3727   3-07-85   1:43p
TREE     COM     2831   3-07-85   1:43p
VDISK    SYS     3307   3-07-85   1:43p
       36 File(s)     61440 bytes free

A>_
```


WHAT'S HAPPENING? You did specify `A:`. Note that the display is the same as `DIR` without the `A:`. Since `A>` is the default, it is unnecessary to key in `A:` but not wrong to do so. However, what if two disk drive users want to see what files are on the disk in Drive B? Or what if hard disk users want to see what files are on the disk in Drive C? You must tell DOS to look on the drive you are interested in, the disk in Drive B or the disk in Drive C. In other words, you must be specific.

NOTE 1: A brief word on subdirectories: `Subdirectories` are used primarily with hard disks. This is because hard disks, which range in capacity from 10 million bytes to over 40 million bytes, are very difficult to manage because of the number of files that can be stored on them. Subdirectories allow a hard disk to be divided up into smaller, more manageable portions. Just as disk drives have a name, like A: or B: or C:, subdirectories have names. Since subdirectories are part of the C: drive, their names are referred to as **paths**. A name for a subdirectory is not just a letter; it is also a text name, as in Utility. The way you tell DOS to look on the subdirectory is to tell it the path name, as in `C:\Utility`.

NOTE 2: Hard disk assumptions for hard disk system users: If you have a hard disk system (one hard disk drive and one floppy disk drive), the hard disk is designated as C: and the floppy disk drive is A:. Typically, DOS is already copied onto your hard drive. This process is usually done at the time of purchase. Thus, when you boot up the system, you do not need to insert the DOS System disk into Drive A.

The system boots from the disk in Drive C because that is where the operating system files have been copied. For the remainder of this text, it will be assumed that Drive C is where the operating system and utility files are located. (If the hard disk has been set up with subdirectories, refer to your installation documentation to see where the DOS utility programs are located. If you have this configuration, you will need to log into the proper subdirectory where the DOS utility programs are located to follow the rest of this text.)

STEP 3: Do nothing.

STEP 3: Key in the following:

```
A>C: <Enter>
```

```
C>_
```

WHAT'S HAPPENING?

NOTE: You may have to issue another command at this point depending on where the DOS utility programs are located. The command could be `C>CD \BIN` or `C>CD \DOS`. The actual name or subdirectory where the DOS utility programs are located is machine-specific. Your screen display or prompt can vary - it could look like `C:\DOS>` or `C:\BIN>` or other displays depending on the setup of the hard disk. In this text, `C>` will indicate that you are logged into the hard disk and subdirectory with the DOS utility programs. In addition, the DOS System Disk will refer to this area (subdirectory) of the hard disk. You are changing the logged or default drive so that you will be using the hard disk as the DOS System Disk. This should be where the DOS utility programs are located.

STEP 4: Get the disk labeled ACTIVITIES. Insert it into Drive B. Be sure to close the drive door.

STEP 4: Remove the DOS System disk from Drive A. Get the disk labeled ACTIVITIES. Insert it into Drive A. Be sure to close the drive door.

STEP 5: Key in the following:

```
A>DIR B: <Enter>
```

STEP 5: Key in the following:

```
C>DIR A: <Enter>
```

```
FEB         87      74     11-23-87   1:19p
MAR         87      70     11-23-87   1:19p
APR         87      71     11-23-87   1:19p
FILE2       CZG     18     11-23-87   2:51p
FILE3       CZG     18     11-23-87   2:51p
FILE2       FP      18     11-23-87   2:53p
FILE3       FP      18     11-23-87   2:53p
FILE4       FP      18     11-23-87   2:53p
FILE2       SWT     18     11-23-87   2:54p
FILE3       SWT     18     11-23-87   2:54p
RIGHT       RED     25     11-23-87   2:57p
DRESS       UP      25     11-23-87   2:57p
LEFT        RED     24     11-23-87   3:03p
MIDDLE      RED     28     11-23-87   3:04p
RIGHT       UP      25     11-23-87   2:57p
MIDDLE      UP      28     11-23-87   3:04p
BLUE        JAZ     17     11-23-87   3:07p
GREEN       JAZ     17     11-23-87   3:08p
ADDRESS     DAT    601     11-23-87   3:13p
BYE         TXT     44     11-23-87   3:14p
GOODBYE     TXT     33     11-23-87   3:15p
TEST        TXT     67     11-23-87   4:46p
        70 Files(s)   173056 bytes free

A>_
```


```
FEB         87      74     11-23-87   1:19p
MAR         87      70     11-23-87   1:19p
APR         87      71     11-23-87   1:19p
FILE2       CZG     18     11-23-87   2:51p
FILE3       CZG     18     11-23-87   2:51p
FILE2       FP      18     11-23-87   2:53p
FILE3       FP      18     11-23-87   2:53p
FILE4       FP      18     11-23-87   2:53p
FILE2       SWT     18     11-23-87   2:54p
FILE3       SWT     18     11-23-87   2:54p
RIGHT       RED     25     11-23-87   2:57p
DRESS       UP      25     11-23-87   2:57p
LEFT        RED     24     11-23-87   3:03p
MIDDLE      RED     28     11-23-87   3:04p
RIGHT       UP      25     11-23-87   2:57p
MIDDLE      UP      28     11-23-87   3:04p
BLUE        JAZ     17     11-23-87   3:07p
GREEN       JAZ     17     11-23-87   3:08p
ADDRESS     DAT    601     11-23-87   3:13p
BYE         TXT     44     11-23-87   3:14p
GOODBYE     TXT     33     11-23-87   3:15p
TEST        TXT     67     11-23-87   4:46p
        70 Files(s)   173056 bytes free
```


```
C>_
```

WHAT'S HAPPENING? The display of files is completely different from the one you have been observing. Because you keyed in **DIR** and a drive letter (**B:** for two disk drive users and **A:** for hard disk users), you were saying to DOS, "I want a display of the directory (**DIR**), but this time I don't want you to default or look at the DOS System disk, I want you to look only on the ACTIVITIES disk." The ACTIVITIES disk is in Drive B for two disk drive users and in Drive A for hard disk users. As long as you tell DOS on which disk drive to look, you can work with any drive you wish. If you are not specific, DOS will always default to the disk drive shown on the screen (**A>** or **B>** or **C>**). DOS (or any computer system) will follow your instructions. It is not smart enough to take alternate action.

STEP 6: Key in the following:

A>DIR hello.txt <Enter>

```
Volume in drive A has no label
Directory of A:\

File not found

A>_
```

STEP 6: Key in the following:

C>DIR hello.txt <Enter>

```
Volume in drive C is HARD DRIVE
Directory of C:\

File not found

C>_
```

STEP 7: Key in the following:

```
A>DIR B:hello.txt   <Enter>
```

```
Volume in drive B is ACTIVITIES
Directory of B:\

HELLO    TXT   51   11-23-87   1:12p
    1 File(s)   173056 bytes free

A>_
```

STEP 7: Key in the following:

```
C>DIR A:hello.txt   <Enter>
```

```
Volume in drive A is ACTIVITIES
Directory of A:\

HELLO    TXT   51    11-23-87   1:12p
    1 File(s)   173056 bytes free

C>_
```

WHAT'S HAPPENING? In Step 6, you asked DOS to look for a file on the DOS System Disk called `hello.txt`. The DOS System Disk is in Drive A for two disk drive users and in Drive C for hard disk users. The prompt displayed on the screen (`A>` or `C>`) is the default drive. Since you did not specify which drive to look on for the file called `hello.txt`, the default drive was assumed. DOS could not find the file on the default drive and gave you that information, "`File not found.`" Note that DOS is not smart enough to say, "Oh, this file is not on the disk in the default drive. Let me go check the ACTIVITIES disk in a different disk drive." DOS followed your instructions exactly. In Step 7, you were specific. You made the same request: "Look for a file called `hello.txt`." However, first of all, you told DOS what disk drive to look on (`B:hello.txt` for two disk drive users or `A:hello.txt` for hard disk users). The drive designator (`B:` or `A:`) preceded the file name (`hello.txt`) because you always tell DOS which "file cabinet" to look in (the disk drive) before you tell it which "folder" you want (`hello.txt`). Not only can you tell DOS which drive to look on, you can also change the default.

STEP 8: Key in the following:

```
A>B:   <Enter>
```

```
B>_
```

STEP 8: Key in the following:

```
C>A:   <Enter>
```

```
A>_
```

WHAT'S HAPPENING? Devices have specific reserved names. The name of the hard disk drive is `C:`. The name of the first floppy disk drive (the one on the left) is `A:`. The name of the second floppy disk drive (the one on the right) is `B:`. If you have more disk drives, each would have a lettered name. By keying in a letter followed by a colon, you are telling DOS that you want to change your work area to the designated drive that you keyed in. Thus, two disk drive users, when you keyed in `B:`, you changed the work area from the disk in Drive A to the disk in Drive B. You have made `B:` the default drive. The assumption DOS will now make is that all files and work will come from the disk in Drive B. It will not look at the disk in Drive A unless you specifically tell it to do so. Hard disk users, when you keyed in **A:**, you changed the work area from the hard disk, Drive C, to the floppy disk in Drive A. You have now made A: the default drive. The assumption DOS will make is that all files and work will come from the disk in Drive A. It will not look at the hard disk, Drive C, unless you specifically tell it so.

STEP 9: Key in the following:

B>DIR <Enter>

```
FEB          87     74    11-23-87   1:19p
MAR          87     70    11-23-87   1:19p
APR          87     71    11-23-87   1:19p
FILE2        CZG    18    11-23-87   2:51p
FILE3        CZG    18    11-23-87   2:51p
FILE2        FP     18    11-23-87   2:53p
FILE3        FP     18    11-23-87   2:53p
FILE4        FP     18    11-23-87   2:53p
FILE2        SWT    18    11-23-87   2:54p
FILE3        SWT    18    11-23-87   2:54p
RIGHT        RED    25    11-23-87   2:57p
DRESS        UP     25    11-23-87   2:57p
LEFT         RED    24    11-23-87   3:03p
MIDDLE       RED    28    11-23-87   3:04p
RIGHT        UP     25    11-23-87   2:57p
MIDDLE       UP     28    11-23-87   3:04p
BLUE         JAZ    17    11-23-87   3:07p
GREEN        JAZ    17    11-23-87   3:08p
ADDRESS      DAT   601    11-23-87   3:13p
BYE          TXT    44    11-23-87   3:14p
GOODBYE      TXT    33    11-23-87   3:15p
TEST         TXT    67    11-23-87   4:46p
        70 Files(s)    173056 bytes free

B>_
```

STEP 9: Key in the following:

A>DIR <Enter>

```
FEB          87     74    11-23-87   1:19p
MAR          87     70    11-23-87   1:19p
APR          87     71    11-23-87   1:19p
FILE2        CZG    18    11-23-87   2:51p
FILE3        CZG    18    11-23-87   2:51p
FILE2        FP     18    11-23-87   2:53p
FILE3        FP     18    11-23-87   2:53p
FILE4        FP     18    11-23-87   2:53p
FILE2        SWT    18    11-23-87   2:54p
FILE3        SWT    18    11-23-87   2:54p
RIGHT        RED    25    11-23-87   2:57p
DRESS        UP     25    11-23-87   2:57p
LEFT         RED    24    11-23-87   3:03p
MIDDLE       RED    28    11-23-87   3:04p
RIGHT        UP     25    11-23-87   2:57p
MIDDLE       UP     28    11-23-87   3:04p
BLUE         JAZ    17    11-23-87   3:07p
GREEN        JAZ    17    11-23-87   3:08p
ADDRESS      DAT   601    11-23-87   3:13p
BYE          TXT    44    11-23-87   3:14p
GOODBYE      TXT    33    11-23-87   3:15p
TEST         TXT    67    11-23-87   4:46p
        70 Files(s)    173056 bytes free

A>
```

WHAT'S HAPPENING? DOS does not display the directory of the DOS System Disk. It displays the directory of the ACTIVITIES disk (in Drive B for two disk drive users and in Drive A for hard disk users). You have changed the assumption or default, and since you did not specify which drive you wanted to look at, DOS "defaulted" to the displayed prompt (**A:** or **B:**) and showed the directory of the ACTIVITIES disk. Since the default is now **B>** for two disk drive users and **A>** for hard disk users, if you wish to locate any information on any other disk, you must specify the parameters and include the letter of the drive where you are looking for a file. For instance, in a prior activity, you asked to find a file called **diskcopy.com** (**DIR diskcopy.com**). You did not include a drive designator in front of the file name because the file was on the default disk drive where the DOS System Disk was (**A>** for two disk drive users and **C>** for hard disk users). If you now want to locate that same file, you need to specify where it is located.

STEP 10: Key in the following:

```
B>DIR diskcopy.com  <Enter>
```

```
Volume in drive B is ACTIVITIES
Directory of B:\

   File not found
B>_
```

STEP 10: Key in the following:

```
A>DIR diskcopy.com  <Enter>
```

```
Volume in drive A is ACTIVITIES
Directory of A:\

   File not found
A>_
```

WHAT'S HAPPENING? Because the default is the drive with the ACTIVITIES disk, DOS looked for this file only on the ACTIVITIES disk (in Drive B for two disk drive users and in Drive A for hard disk users). You must be aware of where you are (what the default is) and where your files are located.

STEP 11: Key in the following:

```
B>DIR A:diskcopy.com  <Enter>
```

```
Volume in drive A has no label
Directory of A:\

DISKCOPY  COM  4329 3-07-85 1:43p
   1 File(s)  61440 bytes free

B>_
```

STEP 11: Key in the following:

```
A>DIR C:diskcopy.com  <Enter>
```

NOTE: If the DOS System Disk is in a subdirectory, you must include the path name with the drive letter. If the DOS System Disk area was called `\DOS`, the above command would be keyed in as: `A>DIR C:\DOS\diskcopy.com`. You are asking DOS not only to look on Drive C but more specifically to look on Drive C in the subdirectory called `\DOS` for the file called `diskcopy.com`.

```
Volume in drive C is HARD DRIVE
Directory of C:\

DISKCOPY  COM  4329 3-07-85 1:43p
   1 File(s)   15441920 bytes free

A>_
```

3.7 GLOBAL FILE SPECIFICATIONS: WILDCARDS, THE ? AND THE *

Using the `DIR` command and a file specification, you can find one specific file that matches what you keyed in. Every time you wish to locate a file, you can key in the entire file specification. Often, however, you wish to work with a group of files, or to find a group of files that have similar names, or to find a file or group of files whose names you do not know. DOS has a "shorthand" system that allows you to operate on a group of files rather than a single file. This system is formally called **global file specifications**; informally, it is called using **wildcards**. In concept, this is similar to playing cards, where the joker can stand for another card of your choice. In DOS, the question mark (?) and the asterisk (*) are the wildcards. These symbols can stand for unknowns. The * represents or substitutes for a group of characters; the ? represents or substitutes for a single character. Many commands allow you to use global file specifications. You will use the `DIR` command to demonstrate the use of wildcards.

ACTIVITY 3.8 DIR AND WILDCARDS

NOTE: Two disk drive users will have the DOS System disk in Drive A and the ACTIVITIES disk in Drive B. Hard disk users will have the ACTIVITIES disk in Drive A. Remember that for hard disk users, if the DOS System disk is in a subdirectory, you will have to take two steps. First key in `C:` and then, log into the correct subdirectory by keying in `CD` and the subdirectory name. For example, if the subdirectory was named `\DOS`, you would key in: `C>CD \DOS`.

STEP 1: Change the default drive back to A where the DOS System disk is by keying in:

```
B>A: <Enter>
```

STEP 1: Change the default drive back to C where the DOS System disk is by keying in:

```
A>C: <Enter>
```

WHAT'S HAPPENING? You have changed the default drive to where the DOS utility programs are located. If you wanted to locate a file and all you remembered about the file name was that it began with the letter m and it was located on the default drive, you could not find that file. You have insufficient information.

STEP 2: Key in the following:

```
A>DIR m  <Enter>
```

```
Volume in drive A has no label
Directory of A:\

    File not found

A>_
```

STEP 2: Key in the following:

```
C>DIR m  <Enter>
```

```
Volume in drive C is HARD DRIVE
Directory of C:\

    File not found

C>_
```

WHAT'S HAPPENING? You were correct, to a point. You first entered the work you wanted done, then the command `DIR`. You did not need to enter the drive letter. Since you did not specify otherwise, DOS assumed the default. However, DOS specifically looked for a file called `m`. There was no file just called `m`; that was simply the first letter of the file. You could find out what files you had by using the wildcard symbol `*` to represent all other characters.

STEP 3: Key in the following:

```
A>DIR m*.* <Enter>
```

```
Volume in drive A has no label
Directory of A:\

MODE COM    5295  3-07-85   1:43p
MORE COM     282  3-07-85   1:43p
    2 File(s)  61440 bytes free

A>_
```

STEP 3: Key in the following:

```
C>DIR m*.* <Enter>
```

```
Volume in drive C is HARD DRIVE
Directory of C:\

MODE COM    5295  3-07-85   1:43p
MORE COM     282  3-07-85   1:43p
    2 File(s)  61440 bytes free

C>_
```

WHAT'S HAPPENING? In this example, you asked DOS what files began with the letter `m` were located on the disk in the default drive. You did not know anything else about the file names or even how many files you might have that began with the letter `m`. You represented any and all characters following the letter `m` with the asterisk, separated the file name from the file extension with a period, and represented all the characters in the file extension with the second asterisk. Thus, `m*.*` (called m, star dot star) means all the files that start with the letter `m`, can have any or no characters following the letter `m`, and can have any or no file extension. Now DOS could look for a match. Although you keyed in a lowercase `m`, DOS returns uppercase `M` since all file names are stored in uppercase letters. The first file DOS found that had an `m` that matched the first `m` that you specified was `MODE.COM`. DOS could display this file because the `*` following the `M` matched `ODE`. Remember, the `*` represents any group of characters. The second `*`, representing the file extension, matched `.COM` because, again, the `*` represents any group of characters. For another example, if all you knew about a group of files on the disk in the default drive was that the group had a file extension of `.sys` in common, you could display these files on the screen using wildcards.

STEP 4: Key in the following:

```
A>DIR *.sys  <Enter>
```

```
Volume in drive A has no label
Directory of A:\

ANSI  SYS  1651  3-07-85  1:43p
VDISK SYS  3307  3-07-85  1:43p
    2 File(s)   61440 bytes free

A>_
```

STEP 4: Key in the following:

```
C>DIR *.sys  <Enter>
```

```
Volume in Drive C is HARD DRIVE
Directory of C:\

ANSI  SYS  1651  3-07-85  1:43p
VDISK SYS  3307  3-07-85  1:43p
    2 File(s) 15441920 bytes free

C>_
```

WHAT'S HAPPENING? In response to your query, `DIR *.sys`, the above screen display answered the question. The * represented any file name, but all the files must have `.sys` as a file extension. The next activities will demonstrate the differences between the * and the ?.

STEP 5: Key in the following:

`A>DIR s*.* <Enter>`

```
Volume in drive A has no label
Directory of A:\

SELECT   COM  2084  3-07-85 1:43p
SHARE    EXE  8304  3-07-85 1:43p
SORT     EXE  1664  3-07-85 1:43p
SUBST    EXE 16611  3-07-85 1:43p
SYS      COM  3727  3-07-85 1:43p
    5 File(s)    61440 bytes free

A>_
```

STEP 5: Key in the following:

`C>DIR s*.* <Enter>`

```
Volume in drive C is HARD DRIVE
Directory of C:\

SELECT   COM  2084  3-07-85 1:43p
SHARE    EXE  8304  3-07-85 1:43p
SORT     EXE  1664  3-07-85 1:43p
SUBST    EXE 16611  3-07-85 1:43p
SYS      COM  3727  3-07-85 1:43p
    5 File(s) 15441920 bytes free

C>_
```

WHAT'S HAPPENING? You asked DOS what files that began with the letter `s` were located on the default drive. You did not know anything else about the file names or file extensions. DOS searched the table of contents in the default drive and found five files that matched `s*.*`. Now, how does the question mark work?

STEP 6: Key in the following:

`A>DIR s????.*  <Enter>`

```
Volume in drive A has no label
Directory of A:\

SHARE   EXE  8304  3-07-85 1:43p
SORT    EXE  1664  3-07-85 1:43p
SUBST   EXE 16611  3-07-85 1:43p
SYS     COM  3727  3-07-85 1:43p
    4 File(s)  61440 bytes free

A>_
```

STEP 6: Key in the following:

`C>DIR s????.*  <Enter>`

```
Volume in drive C is HARD DRIVE
Directory of C:\

SHARE   EXE  8304  3-07-85 1:43p
SORT    EXE  1664  3-07-85 1:43p
SUBST   EXE 16611  3-07-85 1:43p
SYS     COM  3727  3-07-85 1:43p
    4 File(s) 15441920 bytes free

C>_
```

WHAT'S HAPPENING? This time you asked your question a little differently. You still asked for any file that started with the letter `s`. However, instead of "any number of characters," you used the ? four times. To DOS, this means look for any file name that starts with the letter `s` and has a file name that is no longer than five characters in length. It can be less than five characters but no longer. Thus, the `s` is one character and the `????` represented the next four characters. You then separated the file name from the file extension with a period and the * to indicate any file extension is fine. This time only four files matched your request. Note the above screen display and how it differs from the screen display for Step 5. This time you do not see the file called SELECT.COM displayed on the screen. SELECT has six characters in its name. Note also that SYS.COM was displayed even though it is not five characters in length, but three. This is because s???? means five characters or less. SYS is only three characters long. That is less than five characters. Let's try this again.

STEP 7: Key in the following:

```
A>DIR s???.* <Enter>
```

```
Volume in drive A has no label
Directory of A:\

SORT EXE 1664  3-07-85 1:43p
SYS  COM 3727  3-07-85 1:43p
2 File(s)    61440 bytes free

A>_
```

STEP 7: Key in the following:

```
C>DIR s???.* <Enter>
```

```
Volume in drive C is HARD DRIVE
Directory of C:\

SORT EXE  1664  3-07-85 1:43p
SYS  COM  3727  3-07-85 1:43p
2 File(s)  15441920 bytes free

C>_
```

WHAT'S HAPPENING? This time you asked DOS for any file name that started with the letter s that was four characters or less in length (s counts as one character and ??? makes a total of four), and had any file extension (*). You separated the file name and file extension with a period. Note the differences in the screen displays. The * is used most often. In fact ????????.??? is the same as *.*. However, there are occasions when the ? is extremely useful.

STEP 8: Key in the following:

```
A>DIR B:exp*.*  <Enter>
```

```
Volume in drive B is ACTIVITIES
Directory of B:\

EXP87JAN  DAT 293  11-23-87 1:00p
EXP87FEB  DAT 295  11-23-87 1:00p
EXP87MAR  DAT 291  11-23-87 1:00p
EXP86JAN  DAT 293  11-23-87 1:01p
EXP86FEB  DAT 294  11-23-87 1:01p
EXP86MAR  DAT 293  11-23-87 1:01p
EXP85JAN  DAT 293  11-23-87 1:01p
EXP85FEB  DAT 294  11-23-87 1:01p
EXP85MAR  DAT 291  11-23-87 1:01p
    9 File(s) 210944 bytes free

A>_
```

STEP 8: Key in the following:

```
C>DIR A:exp*.*  <Enter>
```

```
Volume in drive A is ACTIVITIES
Directory of A:\

EXP87JAN  DAT 293  11-23-87 1:00p
EXP87FEB  DAT 295  11-23-87 1:00p
EXP87MAR  DAT 291  11-23-87 1:00p
EXP86JAN  DAT 293  11-23-87 1:01p
EXP86FEB  DAT 294  11-23-87 1:01p
EXP86MAR  DAT 293  11-23-87 1:01p
EXP85JAN  DAT 293  11-23-87 1:01p
EXP85FEB  DAT 294  11-23-87 1:01p
EXP85MAR  DAT 291  11-23-87 1:01p
    9 File(s) 210944 bytes free

C>_
```

WHAT'S HAPPENING? This time your request to DOS was to show you all the files (DIR) located on the ACTIVITIES disk (Drive B for two disk drive users or Drive A for hard disk users) that start with the letters exp, and that's all you know (exp*.*). The *.* following the exp represented the rest of the file name and the file extension. These files are some budget files that I created. EXP means expenses, followed by the year (87, 86, or 85), followed by the month (January, February, or March). The file extension I choose was .DAT, meaning that there is data in these files; they are not programs. However, often I am not interested in all the files. I only want some of them. A typical example would be that I want to know what expense files I have on the ACTIVITIES disk for the year 1987.

STEP 9: Key in the following:

```
A>DIR B:exp87*.*   <Enter>
```

```
Volume in drive B is ACTIVITIES
Directory of B:\

EXP87JAN  DAT 293  11-23-87 1:00p
EXP87FEB  DAT 295  11-23-87 1:00p
EXP87MAR  DAT 291  11-23-87 1:00p
    3 File(s) 210944 bytes free

A>_
```

STEP 9: Key in the following:

```
C>DIR A:exp87*.*   <Enter>
```

```
Volume in drive A is ACTIVITIES
Directory of A:\

EXP87JAN  DAT 293  11-23-87 1:00p
EXP87FEB  DAT 295  11-23-87 1:00p
EXP87MAR  DAT 291  11-23-87 1:00p
    3 File(s) 210944 bytes free

C>_
```

WHAT'S HAPPENING? Here you asked for all the files (DIR) on the ACTIVITIES disk (B: for two disk drive users and A: for hard disk users) that were expense files for 1987 (exp87). The rest of the file names were represented by *.*. Note that on your screen display you get only the 1987 files. However, what if your interest was in all the files for all the months of January? You no longer cared which year but only which month.

STEP 10: Key in the following:

```
A>DIR B:exp*JAN.*  <Enter>
```

```
Volume in drive B is ACTIVITIES
Directory of B:\

EXP87JAN  DAT 293  11-23-87 1:00p
EXP87FEB  DAT 295  11-23-87 1:00p
EXP87MAR  DAT 291  11-23-87 1:00p
EXP86JAN  DAT 293  11-23-87 1:01p
EXP86FEB  DAT 294  11-23-87 1:01p
EXP86MAR  DAT 293  11-23-87 1:01p
EXP85JAN  DAT 293  11-23-87 1:01p
EXP85FEB  DAT 294  11-23-87 1:01p
EXP85MAR  DAT 291  11-23-87 1:01p
    9 File(s) 210944 bytes free

A>_
```

STEP 10: Key in the following:

```
C>DIR A:exp*JAN.*  <Enter>
```

```
Volume in drive A is ACTIVITIES
Directory of A:\

EXP87JAN  DAT 293  11-23-87 1:00p
EXP87FEB  DAT 295  11-23-87 1:00p
EXP87MAR  DAT 291  11-23-87 1:00p
EXP86JAN  DAT 293  11-23-87 1:01p
EXP86FEB  DAT 294  11-23-87 1:01p
EXP86MAR  DAT 293  11-23-87 1:01p
EXP85JAN  DAT 293  11-23-87 1:01p
EXP85FEB  DAT 294  11-23-87 1:01p
EXP85MAR  DAT 291  11-23-87 1:01p
    9 File(s) 210944 bytes free

C>_
```

WHAT'S HAPPENING? This is not quite the display you wanted. Note that this display looks just like the display following Step 8 when you asked for `DIR B:exp*.*` or `DIR A:exp*.*`. Why weren't only the `JAN` files displayed? Because when you state your request as `DIR B:exp*JAN.*` or `DIR A:exp*JAN.*`, everything in the file name segment after the first `*` is ignored. Hence, the `DIR` command picked up all the files with exp and ignored your specific `JAN`. Here is where the question mark is useful.

STEP 11: Key in the following:

```
A>DIR B:exp??JAN.*  <Enter>
```

```
Volume in drive B is ACTIVITIES
Directory of B:\

EXP87JAN  DAT 293  11-23-87 1:00p
EXP86JAN  DAT 293  11-23-87 1:01p
EXP85JAN  DAT 293  11-23-87 1:01p
    3 File(s) 210944 bytes free

A>_
```

STEP 11: Key in the following:

```
C>DIR A:exp??JAN.*  <Enter>
```

```
Volume in drive A is ACTIVITIES
Directory of A:\

EXP87JAN  DAT 293  11-23-87 1:00p
EXP86JAN  DAT 293  11-23-87 1:01p
EXP85JAN  DAT 293  11-23-87 1:01p
    3 File(s) 210944 bytes free

C>_
```

WHAT'S HAPPENING? This time the ? was critical. It acted as a place holder. You asked for a file name that specifically started with `exp` and ended with `JAN`. The middle two characters, represented by `??`, could be any characters but had to be alphanumeric. Either `87`, `86`, or `85` matched `??` because any character could have been there as long as there was something in that place in the file name.

ACTIVITY 3.9 PRINTING THE SCREEN

You can print whatever is displayed on the screen at any time by using the `<Shift>` key or the `<up arrow>` key in conjunction with the `<PrtSc>` key.

STEP 1: To print the screen display, first be sure the printer is turned on.

STEP 2: Press the `<Shift>` key. While pressing the `<Shift>` key, press the `<PrtSc>` key.

STEP 1: To print the screen display, first be sure the printer is turned on.

STEP 2: Press the `<Shift>` key. While pressing the `<Shift>` key, press the `<PrtSc>` key.

WHAT'S HAPPENING? You will see what is displayed on the screen printed by the printer.

CHAPTER SUMMARY

1. Command syntax means the proper order or sequence in which to key in commands.
2. Parameters allow a command to be made more specific.
3. The `DIR` command is an internal command that displays the table of contents or directory of a disk.
4. `DIR` has three parameters: `/P` to stop the display from scrolling, `/W` to have a wide display of only file names, and the third parameter is to search the directory with a file name of your choice.
5. A file specification has two parts, the file name and the file extension. The file name may be no longer than eight characters. The file extension may be no longer than three characters. A file name is mandatory, but a file extension is optional. If you use a file extension, separate it from the file name by a period, called a dot.
6. A valid file name contains legal characters, most often alphanumeric characters. It cannot contain illegal characters.
7. Every device attached to the computer has a reserved, specific and unique name so that the operating system knows what it is communicating with. Disk drives are designated by a letter followed by a colon, as in `A:`.
8. Defaults are implied instructions to which the operating system falls back when no specific instructions are given.
9. The system prompt displayed on the screen is the default drive.
10. A user can change the default drive.
11. A user can look for files on other drives than the default, if he or she tells DOS where to look by prefacing the file names with a drive designator.
12. If the file is in a subdirectory, the file name must be prefaced by the drive designator, then the subdirectory name. A user may have to include the subdirectory in the command, as in `C:\DOS\filename`.
13. Global file specifications (*, ?) or wildcards allow the user to substitute a wildcard for an unknown.
14. ? represents one character in a file name. * matches a group of characters.
15. The screen display may be printed by pressing the `<Shift>` key and the `<PrtSc>` key.

REVIEW QUESTIONS

1. Define command syntax. Why is syntax important when using a computer?
2. Define parameters.
3. Name two parameters that can be used with the `DIR` command. Explain why you would use the parameters.
4. Define default or designated drive.
5. What is the default drive? How can you tell which drive is the default drive?
6. How can you change the default drive?
7. What does `A>` mean?
8. Define a file specification.
9. What is the difference between a file name and a file extension?
10. What are the rules for naming files?
11. How do you separate a file name from a file extension?
12. Define global file specifications.
13. How are wildcards used?
14. Define delimiters. Give an example of a delimiter.
15. You key in `DIR B:my*.*`. Where would DOS look for these files?
16. You key in `DIR B:my*.*`. Which of the following files would DOS find?
    `B:myfile.old`
    `B:nofile.new`
    `B:mynext.one`
    `B:diskcopy.com`
17. You key in `DIR A:book??.*`. Which of the following files would DOS find?
    `A:booktest.txt`
    `A:bktst.txt`
    `A:bookrt.sys`
    `A:book.txt`
18. You are looking for a file on the disk in Drive B. The default drive is A:. You key in `A>DIR myfile.txt B:`. Is there anything wrong with this command? If so, correct the command.
19. The system prompt is `B>`. You want a display of the default directory that shows only the file names and their extensions across the screen. What command would you key in?
20. I have fifty files on my disk in drive A. The system prompt is `B>`. When I want to see all the file names, I used `DIR A:`, but the names scroll by too fast for me to read them. Is there anything I can do?

TRUE/FALSE

1. `DIR /P` is an example of using a parameter.
2. A file specification cannot be used as a parameter.
3. When you see `B>` displayed on the screen, you know that B: is the default drive.
4. You cannot change the default drive.
5. `DIR f*.*` would find all the files that started with the letter `f`.
6. You cannot print what is on the screen.
7. `A>` is referred to as the A prompt and is also know as the system prompt.
8. Command syntax refers to the order in which to key in commands.

9. `A>` is displayed on the screen. To locate the file called `myfile.txt` on the disk in Drive B, I would key in `A>DIR B:myfile.txt`.
10. I keyed in `A>DIR B:myfile.txt` and got a message on the screen, "`File not found.`" This tells me that the file called `myfile.txt` is not on the disk in Drive B.

SUGGESTED ACTIVITIES

Note 1: The following activities will use the `<Shift>` and `<PrtSc>` keys to get the output to the printer. Be sure the printer is turned on.

Note 2: Two disk drive users will have the DOS System Disk in Drive A with the `A>` displayed and the ACTIVITIES disk in Drive B. Hard drive users will be logged into the DOS System Disk on Drive C and have the `C>` displayed. The ACTIVITIES disk will be in Drive A.

1. Clear the screen. Find all the files on the ACTIVITIES disk that have the file extension `.txt`. Display the file names on the screen. Print this screen.
2. Clear the screen. Find the file on the DOS System Disk called `diskcomp.com`. Display this file name on the screen. Print this screen.
3. Clear the screen. Do a wide display of the directory on the DOS System Disk. Print this screen.
4. Clear the screen. Find all the files on the DOS System Disk that begin with the letter C. Display these file names on the screen. Print this screen.
5. Clear the screen. Find all the files on the DOS System Disk that begin with the letter C, whose file names are four characters or less and have any file extension. Display the file names on the screen. Print this screen.
6. Clear the screen. Do a wide display of the ACTIVITIES disk. Print this screen.
7. Clear the screen. Do a directory display of the ACTIVITIES disk. The screen will scroll. Wait until it has stopped scrolling. Print only the last screen displayed.
8. Change the default drive to where the ACTIVITIES disk is located. The prompt of the default directory will be on the screen. Print this screen.
9. Find all the files on the DOS System Disk that have a file extension of `.exe`. Display these file names. Print this screen.
10. Display the system date. Print this screen.

DISKS AND FORMATTING

CHAPTER

4

CHAPTER OBJECTIVES

This chapter discusses how DOS uses disks and discusses how disks are prepared for use. After completing this chapter, you will:

Understand the nature of disks.

Understand internal and external commands.

Understand the use of the `FORMAT` command.

Be able to format a floppy disk.

Be able to format a floppy disk with a system and a volume label.

Understand the difference between bootable and nonbootable disks.

Understand and use the `VOL` command.

4.0 STRUCTURE OF A DISK: FORMATTING A DISK

A new disk is a blank disk that must be prepared before it is used. DOS is what prepares it for use. This is done by a DOS utility program called `FORMAT`. **Formatting** determines the size of the sectors and establishes a framework in which DOS works. Part of the formatting process is to assign a number to each disk side, track, and sector so that every space on the disk is accounted for. Formatting a disk means that the physical layout of the information on the disk is defined to determine how the information is stored on the disk. Each disk is divided into tracks (concentric circles on the disk, similar to the grooves on a record), and each track is divided into sectors, a block of 512 bytes. A **cluster** is the smallest unit of disk space that DOS will work with. On a single-sided disk, one sector is a cluster; on a double-sided disk, two sectors equal one cluster. The number of sectors that make up a cluster can vary on a hard disk. Formatting also determines how many sides of the disk will be used. The formatting process determines the amount of information that can be stored on the disk. In addition, through the use of the `FORMAT` command, DOS sets up the boot record, the file allocation table (FAT), the root directory, and the data sectors on each disk. Although the size of each portion can vary, the order of the sections is always the same. The boot record, the FAT, and the directory, always located in the first sectors, control how the files are stored on a disk. The data sectors are where the data or files are actually stored.

BOOT RECORD

The **boot record**, located on Side 0, Track 0, Sector 0, includes the bootstrap routine that DOS uses to load itself, if it is a system disk. All disks have a boot record that indicates which version of DOS was used to format the disk.

FILE ALLOCATION TABLE (FAT)

Following the boot record are several sectors reserved for the **file allocation table** (FAT). The FAT is a map of the disk associated with the file names in the directory and is made up of entries that correspond to every cluster on the disk. The FAT entries include information about which clusters contain data (in use), which clusters are marked as "bad" or unusable, and which clusters have no data (available for use). If a data file is longer than one cluster, which it usually is, the FAT entry has the number of the next cluster that file occupies. The FAT keeps linking these clusters until it finds an end-of-file marker, indicating that there is no more data in the file. The FAT tells DOS which sectors on the disk actually have the data and points to those locations. It is the record of the disk's format and since it is used to control the entire disk, two copies of the FAT are kept on the disk in case one is damaged. The FAT can occupy as many sectors as it needs to map out the disk.

DIRECTORY

Next on the disk are the **directory sectors**. When you ask for the `DIR`, the information that is displayed on the screen comes right from these directory sectors. The directory stores information about every file, including the file name, the file extension, and the file attributes. A file can be marked by the following attributes: (1) read-only, which means the file cannot be normally erased; (2) hidden status, which means that a file will not be displayed when you issue the `DIR` command; (3) system status, which typically marks the file as the system files, `IBMBIO.COM` and `IBMDOS.COM`; (4) volume label; (5) subdirectory status, if needed; (6) archive status, which is set when the file is opened and closed and is used by some backup and restore utilities. Further information about the files in the directory sectors include the time and date of creation/update, the file's starting cluster entry in the FAT, and the file size in bytes. The DOS directory does not say where a specific file is located on a disk; instead, it points to an entry in the FAT. Thus, the directory sectors keep track of what the files are, and the FAT keeps track of where the files are located.

DATA SECTORS

The rest of the disk, and its the largest part, is used for storing the files or data. As far as DOS is concerned, all files, programs, data, and so forth are just chains of bytes laid out in sequence. Space is allocated to files on an as-needed basis, one cluster at a time. When a file is written to a disk, DOS begins writing at the first available cluster. It writes in adjacent or contiguous clusters, if possible, but if any adjacent sectors are already in use (allocated by FAT), DOS skips to the next available space (unallocated). Thus, a file can be noncontiguous, or physically scattered over the disk.

4.1 FORMATTING A FLOPPY DISK

A new disk must be formatted so that the operating system can read from the disk and write on it. In addition, the **FORMAT** command can be used to erase a disk completely, if it contains information you no longer want. However, you must be very careful when using the **FORMAT** command. Formatting deletes or eliminates everything on a disk, and the data cannot be recovered. Although the format routine can be used on a hard disk, you must be very careful as **FORMAT** does not distinguish between a floppy disk and a hard disk. It will format any disk, including the hard disk. This means that everything stored on a hard disk would be gone, both programs and data. Thus, in the next activity, you will only be formatting floppy disks.

4.2 MATERIALS NEEDED

1. DOS System Disk. Throughout the rest of this text, two disk drive users will use the DOS System Disk, the working copy of DOS that you made in Chapter 2. You should know how to boot the system and have the **A>** displayed on the screen. Hard disk users will boot off Drive C. You will not place the DOS System Disk in Drive A but simply power on the computer. You should then get the **C>**. You may have to log into the subdirectory that has the DOS System Utility Programs, like **C>CD \DOS**, and your prompt may then read **C:\DOS>**. Whenever the DOS System Disk is referred to, it means the C drive or whatever subdirectory holds the DOS System Utility Programs.
2. A blank or new disk. Whenever a new or blank disk is referred to, you may use a brand-new disk or an old disk with information on it. However, it will be assumed that if there is information on the disk, you no longer want it, because it will be written over in the **FORMAT** process.

ACTIVITY 4.3 FORMATTING A DISK

WARNING: Never format an application disk you have purchased or a disk that has data you wish to keep. Also, if you have a hard disk/fixed disk, you must be exceedingly careful. Never, never key in C>FORMAT or C>FORMAT C:. If you do, you will completely erase, forever, all the information on the hard disk.

STEP 1: Be sure the DOS System Disk, copied in Chapter 2, is in Drive A and the A> is displayed.

STEP 1: Be sure you are in the DOS System Utility program areas. The C> should be displayed.

WHAT'S HAPPENING? To format a disk, you use the FORMAT command. FORMAT is an external command located on the DOS System disk. This DOS System Disk should be in Drive A. You know that your default drive is A because A> should be displayed on the screen. If you are using a hard disk, the C> should be displayed on the screen. This is the default drive for hard disk users. Hard disk users do not have a disk in Drive A yet. The default drive is a very important concept. Whenever you key in a command and/or file name, the operating system only looks for that command and/or file on the default drive unless you tell it otherwise. In this case, the default is the prompt displayed on the screen, which means when the operating system looks for an external command and/or file, it will only look on the default drive (A or C) for that command or file that you keyed in. You can tell the system to look or do something on a different disk drive by specifying that disk drive. In this case, you are looking for the command FORMAT. You can see whether or not this command, which is stored as a file called format.com, is located on the disk in the default drive.

STEP 2: Key in the following:

A>DIR format.com <Enter>

```
Volume in Drive A has no label
Directory of A:\

FORMAT COM  9398  3-07-85  1:43p
    1 File(s)   61440 bytes free

A>_
```

STEP 2: Key in the following:

C>DIR format.com <Enter>

```
Volume in Drive C is HARD DRIVE
Directory of C:\

FORMAT COM  9398  3-07-85  1:43p
    1 File(s) 15441920 bytes free

C>_
```

WHAT'S HAPPENING? This screen display tells you that the FORMAT command, stored as the file named format.com, is located on the default drive (Drive A for two disk drive users and Drive C for hard disk users). The command used in Step 2 was DIR. To use, execute, or run the program FORMAT, you key in the name of the command.

STEP 3: Key in the following:

```
A>FORMAT B:  <Enter>
```

STEP 3: Key in the following (Be sure to use A):

```
C>FORMAT A:  <Enter>
```

WHAT'S HAPPENING? Note how this differs from Step 2. In this example, you called the program by keying in the name of the command. FORMAT is the command that tells the system what work you want it to do. For two disk drive users, B: tells the system where the disk that you want formatted is located (in the disk drive labeled B). For hard disk users, A: tells the system where the disk that you want formatted is located (in the disk drive labeled A). If you did not specify a lettered drive, B: or A:, the operating system would format the default drive. For two disk drive users the default is A, which has the net effect of erasing the operating system disk. For hard disk users, the default is C, which has the net effect of erasing the hard disk. You do not want to do this.

```
Insert new diskette for drive B:
and strike ENTER when ready_
```

```
Insert new diskette for drive A:
and strike ENTER when ready_
```

WHAT'S HAPPENING? You are getting a message or prompt that tells you what to do. Get the blank disk out and prepare a label for the disk. Write your name and DATA disk on the label. Place the label on the disk. Two disk drive users, open the door to Drive B. (the righthand drive door or the lower drive door), insert this new disk into Drive B, label side up, and shut the drive door. Hard disk users, open the door to Drive A (the lefthand drive door), insert this new disk into Drive A, label side up, and shut the drive door. Be sure that this disk is blank. Anything on it will be eliminated.

STEP 4: Press <Enter>.

STEP 4: Press <Enter>.

```
Formatting......
```

```
Formatting......
```

WHAT'S HAPPENING? The red light on the floppy disk drive will glow, indicating that some activity is taking place on the disk you are formatting. "Formatting..." is a message telling you that DOS is working, carrying out the command that you keyed in. Do not do anything until you see the following displayed on the screen:

```
Formatting...Format complete

   362496 bytes total disk space
   362496 bytes available on disk

Format another (Y/N)?_
```

```
Formatting...Format complete

   362496 bytes total disk space
   362496 bytes available on disk

Format another (Y/N)?_
```

STEP 5: Press n. Press `<Enter>`.

STEP 5: Press n. Press `<Enter>`.

WHAT'S HAPPENING? The command called `FORMAT` was executed. Two disk drive users formatted the disk in Drive B and hard disk users formatted the disk in Drive A. DOS can now can read and write to this disk because it has set up the tracks and sectors, FAT, and directory as needed.

ACTIVITY 4.4 UNDERSTANDING INTERNAL/EXTERNAL COMMANDS

NOTE: Two disk drive users will have the DOS System Disk in Drive A with the `A>` displayed and the disk just formatted in Drive B. Hard disk users will be logged into the DOS System Disk on Drive C and have the `C>` displayed. The disk just formatted will be in Drive A.

STEP 1: Key in the following:

```
A>DIR B:  <Enter>
```

```
Volume in drive B has no label
Directory of B:\

File not found

A>_
```

STEP 1: Key in the following:

```
C>DIR A:  <Enter>
```

```
Volume in drive A has no label
Directory of A:\

File not found

C>_
```

WHAT'S HAPPENING? You asked DOS to display a table of contents for the DATA disk located in Drive B for two disk drive users and in Drive A for hard disk users. You just completed formatting this disk. You get a message, "`File not found.`" There are no files on this disk because formatting only prepares the disk for files; it does not place any files on the disk.

STEP 2: Key in the following:

```
A>B:  <Enter>
```

```
B>_
```

STEP 2: Key in the following:

```
C>A:  <Enter>
```

```
A>_
```

STEP 3: Key in the following:

```
B>DIR  <Enter>
```

```
Volume in drive B has no label
Directory of B:\

File not found

B>_
```

STEP 3: Key in the following:

```
A>DIR  <Enter>
```

```
Volume in drive A has no label
Directory of A:\

File not found

A>_
```

WHAT'S HAPPENING? You have changed the default to the drive that has the DATA disk in it. This means DOS will only look for programs on the disk in Drive B for two disk drive users and in Drive A for hard disk users. Note that DOS did not show you any of the files on any other drive. It only looked on the default drive. Note that the internal command, `DIR`, did work or execute. It displayed the directory or table of contents for the default drive.

STEP 4: Do nothing.

STEP 4: Key in the following:

```
A>PATH; <Enter>
```

STEP 5: Key in the following:

```
B>FORMAT B:
```

```
B>FORMAT B:
Bad command or file name

B>_
```

STEP 5: Key in the following:

```
A>FORMAT A:
```

```
A>FORMAT A:
Bad command or file name

A>_
```

WHAT'S HAPPENING? Here is a system message. There are no files on the DATA disk just formatted. Thus, when DOS went to the DATA disk to find the external command `FORMAT`, so that this command could be loaded into memory and executed, it found no file by this name. In fact, it found no files. The message tells you that DOS could not do what you asked because it could not locate the file on the DATA disk. DOS is not smart enough to check any other disk for the command. Note the difference between internal and external commands. `DIR`, an internal command, worked regardless of which drive was the default, because internal commands are kept in memory once the system is booted. `FORMAT` did not load or work because DOS had to go to the disk to find the command, and it is external to the disk.

STEP 6: Key in the following:

```
B>A:  <Enter>
```

STEP 6: Key in the following:

```
A>C:  <Enter>
```

```
A>_
```

```
C>_
```

WHAT'S HAPPENING? You have changed the default drive back to the DOS System Disk.

4.5 FORMATTING A DISK WITH A VOLUME LABEL

There are also parameters you can use with the `FORMAT` command. You indicate an option by using a switch, the slash (/). In this case, the option you are going to use is putting a volume label on the disk you are formatting. A volume label is an electronic label. You are naming your disk. It is very much like labeling a file drawer so you know what it contains. The switch is `/V`, which tells the `FORMAT` command that not only is it to format a disk, but it is also to allow you to name the disk by placing an electronic volume label on the disk.

ACTIVITY 4.6 FORMATTING A DISK WITH A VOLUME LABEL: USING THE VOL COMMAND

NOTE: Two disk drive users will have the DOS System Disk in Drive A with the `A>` displayed and the DATA disk in Drive B. Hard disk users will be logged into the DOS System Disk on Drive C and have the `C>` displayed. The DATA disk will be in Drive A.

STEP 1: Key in the following:

`A>FORMAT B:/V <Enter>`

```
Insert new diskette in Drive B:
and strike ENTER when ready_
```

STEP 2: You should have the DATA disk in Drive B. Press `<Enter>`.

```
Formatting.....
```

STEP 1: Key in the following:

`C>FORMAT A:/V <Enter>`

```
Insert new diskette in Drive A:
and strike ENTER when ready_
```

STEP 2: You should have the DATA disk in Drive A. Press `<Enter>`.

```
Formatting.....
```

WHAT'S HAPPENING? You have begun the process of formatting the DATA disk. Do not do anything until the following is displayed:

```
Formatting...Format complete
Volume label (11 characters, enter for none)?_
```

```
Formatting...Format complete
Volume label (11 characters, enter for none)?_
```

WHAT'S HAPPENING? DOS first asks you a question: "Do you want to place a label on this disk (Volume label)?" It then, gives you the rules, which are that a volume label can be less than but no longer than 11 characters. If you have a label already and do not want a volume label on this disk, press **<Enter>** (enter for none). However, in this instance, you do want a volume label.

STEP 3: Key in the following:

SAMPLE DATA <Enter>

```
362496 bytes total disk space
362496 bytes available on disk

Format another (Y/N)?_
```

STEP 4: Key in the following:

N <Enter>

STEP 3: Key in the following:

SAMPLE DATA <Enter>

```
362496 bytes total disk space
362496 bytes available on disk

Format another (Y/N)?_
```

STEP 4: Key in the following.

N <Enter>

WHAT'S HAPPENING? You named your disk **SAMPLE DATA** because this disk is where you are going to try out samples. When you use a volume label, make it as meaningful as possible so that you do not have to look at all the files on the disk to know what is on the disk. A meaningful name (labels) might be DOS 3.1, telling you that this disk is your DOS System Disk or **INCOMETAXES** for a disk that contained your income tax data. There are two ways to see your volume label.

STEP 5: Key in the following:

A>DIR B: <Enter>

```
Volume in drive B is SAMPLE DATA
Directory of B:\

File not found

A>_
```

STEP 5: Key in the following:

C>DIR A: <Enter>

```
Volume in drive A is SAMPLE DATA
Directory of A:\

File not found

C>_
```

WHAT'S HAPPENING? In earlier directory displays, the message read "Volume in drive N has no label." N represents the letter of the drive where the disk is located. You can see displayed the label you entered, SAMPLE DATA. There is a command specifically for the volume label. It is VOL, an internal command, which allows you to look at the volume label on any disk, whether or not there is a label. By using this command, you can see quickly what is on a disk without having to run a directory command.

STEP 6: Key in the following:

```
A>VOL  <Enter>
```

```
 Volume in drive A has no label

A>_
```

WHAT'S HAPPENING? Since a volume label was never put on this disk, it gives a negative answer—no label. Note that when you used the VOL command, DOS only looked on Drive A, the default drive. To look at the the volume label on Drive B, you must be specific and request that DOS look on Drive B by giving VOL another parameter.

STEP 6: Key in the following:

```
C>VOL  <Enter>
```

```
 Volume in drive C is HARD DRIVE

C>_
```

WHAT'S HAPPENING? The volume label on your hard disk may well be different depending on whether a volume label was entered. If no volume label was placed on the hard disk drive, you will see a negative answer—"Volume in Drive C has no label." Note that when you used the VOL command, DOS only looked on Drive C, the default drive. To look at the the volume label on Drive A, you must specifically request that DOS look on Drive A by giving VOL another parameter.

STEP 7: Key in the following:

```
A>VOL B:  <Enter>
```

```
A>VOL B:

 Volume in drive B is SAMPLE DATA

A>_
```

STEP 7: Key in the following:

```
C>VOL A:  <Enter>
```

```
C>VOL A:

 Volume in drive A is SAMPLE DATA

C>_
```

WHAT'S HAPPENING? Here you placed a volume label on the DATA disk. As you can see, if a volume label is meaningful, it can help you know what files are on the disk. It is much like labeling a file cabinet drawer, so that when you are looking for a file, you do not have to open up every drawer to look at all the file folders in the drawer to know what is in the file cabinet.

4.7 BOOTABLE AND NONBOOTABLE DISKS

You have learned that in order to use a new disk, you must first prepare the disk by using the FORMAT command. In addition, you have learned to place an electronic label on your disk with the VOLUME (/V) parameter. There is another major parameter you can use with the FORMAT command. This parameter or option allows you to place the operating system on a disk, making it a bootable disk. What is a bootable disk? We have learned that in order for a computer to work, an operating system must be resident in memory. The computer has that operating system in memory because you booted the system with the DOS System Disk, which allowed the system to read the operating system files into memory. These critical files on the disk, or the actual operating system, are comprised of the hidden system files, IBMBIO.COM and IBMDOS.COM, and the COMMAND.COM file, which is not hidden. Why would you want to make a disk bootable? Sometimes you do not need all the utility programs. You will see later that you may want to copy application programs to a disk. You do not want to first load DOS as a separate disk; you want the ability to boot from the disk that has your application.

In the last activity, you formatted a disk, with a VOLUME label of SAMPLE DATA, but you did not put an operating system on the disk, making it a nonbootable or nonsystem disk. The following activity will show you what happens with a nonsystem disk.

ACTIVITY 4.8 TRYING TO BOOT WITH A NONSYSTEM DISK

STEP 1: Remove the DOS System Disk from Drive A.

STEP 2: Insert the disk, labeled with your name and DATA disk, into Drive A. Refer to this disk from now on as the DATA disk. Be sure the drive door is shut.

STEP 3: Reboot the system. To reboot the system, hold down the <Ctrl> key, the <Alt> key, and the <Del> key simultaneously.

```
Non-System disk or disk error
Replace and strike any key when ready
_
```

STEP 1: Do nothing.

STEP 2: The disk, labeled with your name and DATA disk is in Drive A. Refer to this disk from now on as the DATA disk.

STEP 3: Reboot the system. To reboot the system, hold down the <Ctrl> key, the <Alt> key, and the <Del> key simultaneously.

```
Non-System disk or disk error
Replace and strike any key when ready
_
```

WHAT'S HAPPENING? When you rebooted the system, you eliminated anything that was in memory. The system went through its startup routine and went to the disk in Drive A, looking for the boot record to load IBMBIO.COM,

IBMDOS.COM, and COMMAND.COM. Since the DATA disk did not have these system files stored on it, the computer could not locate them. Since there are no system files on the DATA disk in Drive A and, hence, no files to load into memory, nothing can happen. The boot record displayed the "disk error" message above.

STEP 4: Remove the DATA disk from Drive A. Insert the DATA disk in Drive B.

STEP 4: Open the door to Drive A.

STEP 5: Insert the DOS System Disk back into Drive A. Press any key, per the instructions on the screen.

STEP 5: Press any key, per the instructions on the screen.

STEP 6: You will see the date prompt. Enter the correct date and then enter the correct time at the prompt.

STEP 6: You will see the date prompt. Enter the correct date and then enter the correct time at the prompt.

```
A>_
```

```
C>_
```

WHAT'S HAPPENING? You have successfully booted the system. Because you now have the DOS System disk back in Drive A, the startup routine could find the files IBMBIO.COM, IBMDOS.COM, and COMMAND.COM on the disk in Drive A and could load these files into memory, thus booting the system.

WHAT'S HAPPENING? You have successfully booted the system. Opening the drive door is the equivalent of having nothing in the drive. When you rebooted the system, the startup routine went to the disk in Drive A looking for the system files. Since there was no disk in Drive A (the door was open), the system looked on the hard disk and found the files IBMBIO.COM, IBMDOS.COM, and COMMAND.COM on the hard drive. It could load these files into memory and, thus, boot the system.

STEP 7: Do nothing.

STEP 7: Close the drive door.

ACTIVITY 4.9 FORMATTING A DATA DISK WITH AN OPERATING SYSTEM

NOTE: Two disk drive users will have the DOS System Disk in Drive A with the A> displayed and the DATA disk in Drive B. Hard disk users will be logged into the DOS System Disk on Drive C and have the C> displayed. The DATA disk will be in Drive A.

STEP 1: Key in the following:

A>FORMAT B:/S <Enter>

```
A>FORMAT B:/S
Insert new diskette for drive B:
and strike ENTER when ready_
```

STEP 1: Key in the following (be sure you key in A:/S):

C>FORMAT A:/S <Enter>

```
C>FORMAT A:/S
Insert new diskette for drive A:
and strike ENTER when ready_
```

WHAT'S HAPPENING? You are asking that the program called FORMAT be loaded into memory and executed, which means the DATA disk is going to be formatted again. In addition, the /S parameter told the FORMAT command that you not only wanted the DATA DISK to be formatted, but that you also wanted the operating system entered on this disk so that your DATA disk will be bootable. The /S parameter will copy the hidden files IBMBIO.COM and IBMDOS.COM to the DATA disk as well as the file named COMMAND.COM.

STEP 2: Confirm that the DATA disk is in Drive B.

STEP 2: Confirm that the DATA disk is in Drive A.

STEP 3: Press <Enter>

```
Formatting....
```

STEP 3: Press <Enter>

```
Formatting....
```

WHAT'S HAPPENING? The message displayed tells you that the program is executing. Do not do anything until you see the following screen display:

```
Formatting....Format complete
System transferred

  362496 bytes total disk space
   62464 bytes used by system
  300032 bytes available on disk

Format another (Y/N)?_
```

```
Formatting....Format complete
System transferred

  362496 bytes total disk space
   62464 bytes used by system
  300032 bytes available on disk

Format another (Y/N)?_
```

STEP 4: Press n. Press <Enter>

STEP 4: Press n. Press <Enter>

WHAT'S HAPPENING? The DATA disk was formatted. However, because you added the parameter /S, the system was transferred. Note the "System transferred" message on the screen. This message tells you that the two hidden files and COMMAND.COM are now residing on the DATA disk. In addition, note that 62464 bytes are taken up by the system. This means you have only 300032 bytes left for data. If you had any unusable sectors, it would also be reported at this time.

STEP 5: Remove the DOS System Disk from Drive A. Remove the DATA disk from Drive B. Insert it into Drive A.

STEP 5: Do nothing.

STEP 6: Reboot the system (press <Ctrl>, <Alt>, and <Del> keys).

STEP 6: Reboot the system (press <Ctrl>, <Alt>, and <Del> keys).

WHAT'S HAPPENING? Note that the DATA disk booted the system. You did not get the message "`Non-system disk or disk error`" as you did in Activity 4.8. You know you booted the system because you got the date prompt.

STEP 7: Enter the correct date and time.

STEP 7: Enter the correct date and time.

```
A>_
```

```
A>_
```

STEP 8: Key in the following:

```
A>FORMAT B:  <Enter>
```

STEP 8: Key in the following:

```
A>FORMAT A:  <Enter>
```

```
A>FORMAT B:
Bad command or file name

A>_
```

```
A>FORMAT A:
Bad command or file name

A>_
```

WHAT'S HAPPENING? This message appeared because `FORMAT` is an external command or utility and is not on the disk in Drive A. When you formatted the DATA disk, you transferred the operating system to the disk. The operating system only consists of `IBMBIO.COM`, `IBMDOS.COM`, and `COMMAND.COM` and does not include the utility programs or external commands. The system files are mandatory to operating the system. The utilities or external commands, although extremely useful, do not need to be on the disk for you to use the computer.

STEP 9: Key in the following:

```
A>DIR  <Enter>
```

```
Volume in drive A has no label
Directory of A:\

COMMAND COM  23210 3-7-85 1:43p
   1 File(s)   300032 bytes free

A>_
```

STEP 9: Key in the following:

```
A>DIR  <Enter>
```

```
Volume in drive A has no label
Directory of A:\

COMMAND COM  23210 3-7-85 1:43p
   1 File(s)   300032 bytes free

A>_
```


WHAT'S HAPPENING? This command executed because `DIR` is an internal command, always resident in memory after the operating system is booted. Note that you do not see `FORMAT.COM` on this directory. That is why the operating system could not find it when you keyed in the `FORMAT` command in Step 8.

STEP 10: Remove the DATA disk from drive A. Insert it into Drive B.

STEP 10: Change the default drive back to `C>` by keying in the following:

```
A>C:  <Enter>
```

STEP 11: Insert the DOS System Disk in Drive A. Be sure the drive doors are shut.

STEP 11: Do nothing.

4.10 FORMATTING A DISK WITH /S AND /V

When you format a disk, you have the option of formatting it with (1) no operating system and no label (`FORMAT N:` where `N` represents the disk drive letter), (2) with an operating system and no label (`FORMAT N:/S`), or (3) with a label and no operating system (`FORMAT N:/V`). In the above activities, you used these options. However, there is one more option. You can have both a volume label and an operating system (`FORMAT N:/S/V`). This command, `FORMAT`, does not care about the order of `/V` and `/S`. Thus, `FORMAT N:/S/V` or `FORMAT N:/V/S` are both correct syntax.

ACTIVITY 4.11 FORMATTING A DATA DISK WITH /S AND /V

NOTE: Two disk drive users will have the DOS System Disk in Drive A with the `A>` displayed and the DATA disk in Drive B. Hard disk users will be logged into the DOS System Disk on Drive C with the `C>` displayed. The DATA disk will be in Drive A.

STEP 1: Key in the following:

`A>FORMAT B:/S/V  <Enter>`

```
A>FORMAT B:/S/V
Insert new diskette for drive B:
and strike ENTER when ready_
```

STEP 2: The DATA disk should be in Drive B.

Press `<Enter>`

```
Formatting..._
```

STEP 1: Key in the following (be sure to key in **A:**):

`C>FORMAT A:/S/V  <Enter>`

```
C>FORMAT A:/S/V
Insert new diskette for drive A:
and strike ENTER when ready_
```

STEP 2: The DATA disk should be in Drive A.

Press `<Enter>`

```
Formatting..._
```

WHAT'S HAPPENING? The message displayed tells you that the program is executing. Do not do anything until you see the following screen display:

```
Formatting....Format complete
System transferred

Volume label (11 characters, ENTER for none)?_
```

STEP 3: Key in the following at the volume prompt:

`SAMPLE DATA <Enter>`

```
362496 bytes total disk space
 62464 bytes used by system
300032 bytes available on disk

Format another (Y/N)?_
```

STEP 4: Key in the following:

Press `n`. Press `<Enter>`

```
Formatting....Format complete
System transferred

Volume label (11 characters, ENTER for none)?_
```

STEP 3: Key in the following at the volume prompt:

`SAMPLE DATA <Enter>`

```
362496 bytes total disk space
 62464 bytes used by system
300032 bytes available on disk

Format another (Y/N)?_
```

STEP 4: Key in the following:

Press `n`. Press `<Enter>`

WHAT'S HAPPENING? You have now formatted the DATA disk with a volume label and an operating system. This operating system makes this DATA disk bootable. However, should a disk be bootable and have a label, particularly if it is a disk that is only going to be used for data? This is a decision for the user. Some people believe that all disks should be bootable; others would rather not waste 62464 bytes if they are never going to boot the disk. Volume labels can be very useful and do not cost much space. It is the user who has to decide.

CHAPTER SUMMARY

1. The command processor is stored as a file called **COMMAND.COM**. It processes what the user keys in. When you boot the system, this file is one of the operating system files placed in RAM. **COMMAND.COM** has internal commands built into it that are resident in memory until the computer is turned off.
2. Disks are the means to store data and programs.
3. All disks must be formatted so that DOS can read and write data and programs to them.
4. DOS uses sections of a disk, be it a hard disk or a floppy disk. A disk is divided into concentric circles called tracks. Each track is divided into sectors. The number of tracks, sectors, and sides of a disk determine the capacity of the disk.
5. Each disk has a directory and File Allocation Table (FAT). The number of files that a disk can hold is based on the size of the directory.
6. When formatted, all disks have a boot record, a FAT, a directory, and data sectors.
7. A boot record has either the bootstrap routine to load DOS if it is a system disk or a message indicating that it is not a system disk.
8. The FAT (File Allocation Table) is a map of every track and sector on the disk and tells DOS where files are on the disk. The directory has information about the files including the file name and the file's starting cluster entry in the FAT.
9. The data sectors are where files are actually stored.
10. A disk is formatted with the **FORMAT** command, an external utility program. Parameters for the **FORMAT** command include the letter of the disk drive to format, **/V** to place a volume label on a disk, and **/S** to place the operating system files on the disk.

REVIEW QUESTIONS

1. What are the three system files that make up the operating system?
2. What purpose do disks serve?
3. Why must you format a disk?
4. Define tracks, sectors, and clusters.
5. What determines the size of the sectors on a disk?
6. Define the FAT. How is it used?

7. What information is in the directory sectors?
8. Define file attributes. Give at least two examples of file attributes.
9. What is a volume label?
10. What command allows you to see the volume label?
11. Why is FORMAT a dangerous command?
12. What does FORMAT /S do to a disk?
13. What is a bootable disk?
14. Define internal commands. What is another name for these commands?
15. Define external commands. What is another name for these commands?
16. Is FORMAT.COM part of the operating system?
17. Explain the message, "Bad command or file name."
18. What can you do when you see the message, "Bad command or file name"?
19. Who determines whether or not a disk is formatted with a system and/or a volume label, and why?
20. When a disk is formatted with no parameters, what files are on the disk?

TRUE/FALSE

1. The hidden system file is COMMAND.COM.
2. Both the DIR command and the VOL command will display the volume label on a disk.
3. DOS tries to write data in noncontiguous sectors.
4. A data disk must always be formatted before being used.
5. Only a system disk has a boot record.
6. The number of tracks, sectors, and sides determines the capacity of a disk.
7. FORMAT B: would format the disk in Drive A.
8. A volume label must not exceed 11 characters.
9. FORMAT A:/S/V will put a system and a volume label on the disk in Drive A.
10. DIR format.com will execute the command format and format a disk.

SUGGESTED ACTIVITIES

Remember—Be very careful in using the FORMAT command. Never issue the command C> FORMAT C: or C> FORMAT.

1. Format the DATA disk (two disk drive users, the disk that is in Drive B; hard disk users, the disk that is in Drive A). Put an operating system and a volume label on the DATA disk. The volume label will be DATADISK. When you have finished formatting the DATA disk, use the directory command to display what is on the DATA disk. Print the screen.
2. Clear the screen. Display the volume label of the DOS System Disk (two disk drive users, Drive A; hard disk users, Drive C). Do not use the DIR command to display the volume label.

USING INTERNAL COMMANDS: COPY and TYPE

CHAPTER

5

CHAPTER OBJECTIVES

This chapter discusses some essential internal commands that help to manage and manipulate files on a disk. After completing this chapter, you will:

Know the syntax of the COPY and TYPE commands.

Be able to copy files on the same disk.

Understand and be able to create dummy files.

Be able to display text files with the TYPE command.

Understand and be able to use wildcards with the COPY command.

Be able to copy text files to the printer.

5.0 MANAGING YOUR FILES WITH INTERNAL COMMANDS

Several major internal commands will help manage your files on disks: DIR, COPY, RENAME, DEL and TYPE. These commands are internal, meaning that once you have booted the system, you no longer need to have the DOS System disk with the utility files in any drive. The commands deal only with files as a whole; you are not working with the contents of the files, just manipulating the files. The commands allow you to see what files you have (DIR), move files from here to there (COPY), to change their names (RENAME), to throw files away (DEL) and to take a quick peek at what is inside the files (TYPE). This chapter will tell you how to use the COPY and TYPE commands.

5.1 MATERIALS NEEDED

1. Microcomputer
2. DOS System Disk
3. DATA disk

5.2 THE COPY COMMAND

COPY, one of the most frequently used internal commands, is used to copy files from one place to another. COPY does exactly what it says—it takes an original source file and makes an identical copy of it, then places the copy where you want it to go. In a sense it is similar to a photocopy machine. You place your original on the copy plate, hit the appropriate button, and receive a copy of your original document. Nothing has happened to your document. If it has a smudge on it, so does your copy. The same thing is true with the COPY command. It makes an exact copy of the file, and the original file remains the same. Copying a file does not alter the original file in any way.

Why might you want to copy files? You might want to copy a file from one disk to another. For example, you might create an inventory of all your household goods for your homeowner's insurance policy. It would be stored as a file on your disk. If your home burned down, so would your disk with your inventory file. Thus, it makes sense to copy this file onto another disk and store it somewhere else, perhaps in a safety deposit box.

You might want to make a second copy of an existing file on the same disk. Why would you want to do this? One of the advantages of computers is that you can minimize your labor. For instance, you are very interested in a particular political issue and wish to send letters to your government representatives expressing your views. The content of the letter is going to be the same, but the addresses will be different. One letter is for your senator, one is for your representative, and one is for the President. The letter you write is stored as a file on your disk. Rather than having to rekey or retype each letter, you can make copies of the letter and then change just the address block and the salutation.

You might want to copy a file to a device. One of the most common devices is the printer. You can copy a file to the printer to get a hard copy. In the example above, you are going to mail a letter to your representatives, not a disk. Therefore, you need a hard copy of the file; in other words, you copy the file to the printer. These are some of the uses of the COPY command.

COPY has a very specific syntax. Its syntax is always:

COPY source destination

COPY is the command or the work you want the system to do. The source is what you want copied or your original. The destination is where you want it copied.

5.3 CREATING TEXT FILES USING THE COPY COMMAND

The files that you have been dealing with were program files supplied by DOS or by the disk included with this text. You can create or make up your own files with your own data. These are not going to be program files. They are what are known as text files, text being data or information that you key in. One of the ways to make or create a file is to use the `COPY` command.

Until now, you did not have any "originals" that you created. In this example, the source—what you want to copy—is going to be a device. The device you are going to use is the console or `CON`, the device name. `CON` means that the source is going to be whatever you enter on the keyboard and display on the monitor. The destination is going to be a file that you will place on your DATA disk. You are going to name this file, which is analogous to making a file folder and pasting a name or label on the outside of the file folder. The contents, what is inside the file, will be what you key at the console.

5.4 REVIEW OF FILE-NAMING RULES

To name a file, you must follow the DOS rules. The file specification is comprised of two parts, the file name and the file extension. The file-naming rules are as follows:

1. All files on one disk must have a unique name.
2. All files must have a name that is no longer than eight characters.
3. File extensions are optional. An extension cannot be any longer than three characters.
4. All characters can be used in file names and file extensions except the following illegal or forbidden characters: `<space> ."/\ [ ] : ; | < > + = , * ?`

ACTIVITY 5.5 CREATING A TEXT FILE USING THE COPY COMMAND

NOTE: You are now going to create or name a file and then key in data for that file based on the file-naming rules. Please key in exactly what is shown below. If you make an error keying in data, you can use the `<Backspace>` to delete characters. However, once you advance a line by pressing `<Enter>`, you cannot go back to correct any typing errors. However, in this text typographical errors are not that important. This is not a class in typing.

STEP 1: The DOS System Disk is in Drive A with the `A>` displayed.

STEP 1: You are logged into the DOS System Disk on Drive C with the `C>` displayed.

STEP 2: Get the disk labeled DATA disk. Insert this disk in Drive B. You can use this disk because you formatted it in a prior exercise.

STEP 3: Key in the following:

```
A>DIR B:   <Enter>
```

```
Volume in drive B is DATADISK
Directory of B:\

COMMAND COM 23210 3-07-87 1:43p
   1 File(s)    300032 bytes free

A>_
```

STEP 2: Get the disk labeled DATA disk. Insert this disk in Drive A. You can use this disk because you formatted it in a prior exercise.

STEP 3: Key in the following:

```
C>DIR A:   <Enter>
```

```
Volume in drive A is DATADISK
Directory of A:\

COMMAND COM 23210 3-07-87 1:43p
   1 File(s)    300032 bytes free

C>_
```

WHAT'S HAPPENING? The formatted DATA disk has one visible file on it, `COMMAND.COM`, which was placed on the disk when you formatted it with a system in Chapter 4, Suggested Activity 1. There are no other files on this disk except the hidden system files.

STEP 4: Key in the following:

```
A>COPY CON B:exercise.txt <Enter>
```

STEP 4: Key in the following:

```
C>COPY CON A:exercise.txt <Enter>
```

WHAT'S HAPPENING? `COPY` is the command. `CON` is the source from which the data will come. `CON` is a device name, meaning that everything that is keyed in from the keyboard and displayed on the screen will be entered into the file. The designated drive and the file name is the destination. Two disk drive users, b: tells DOS that you want this file placed on the DATA disk in Drive B. Hard disk users, A: tells DOS that you want this file placed on the DATA disk in Drive A. The name of the file follows the file-naming rules. It is a unique name no longer than eight characters with no illegal characters. `.txt` is the file extension, no longer than three characters with no illegal characters. Note that you used a period to separate the file name from the file extension. This is not part of the file specification. It is a delimiter to DOS that says, "I'm done with the file name; get ready for the file extension." Once you have pressed `<Enter>`, you will see the cursor blinking directly below the command line. DOS is waiting for you to key in something. `<Enter>` at the end of a line means to press the `<Enter>` key. It indicates a carriage return, which moves you to the next line.

STEP 5: Key in the following on both floppy and hard disk systems:

```
Today's date <Enter>
<Enter>
This is a practice exercise in creating or <Enter>
making a text file. exercise is the <Enter>
file name. .txt is the selected file <Enter>
extension. All this data, starting with <Enter>
the date, is the data or text that is <Enter>
going to be inside the ''file folder'' named <Enter>
exercise.txt <Enter>
<Enter>
Your name <Enter>
```

WHAT'S HAPPENING? You have just keyed in some data that is going to go into this file. However, you need to tell DOS that you are finished keying in data. DOS has no way of knowing that you are done unless you tell it so. At this point, nothing has yet been written to the DATA disk. The way you tell DOS that you are ready to write this file to the disk is to give it a signal. The signal is to press the `<Ctrl>` key and hold down the letter Z. The computer notation for this is either `<Ctrl>-Z` or `^Z`. Remember that this means to hold down the control key and the letter Z, not to type or key in the word control and/or the letter Z. Your cursor should be under the first letter in your name.

STEP 6: Do the following: Press `<Ctrl>-Z`. Press `<Enter>`

STEP 6: Do the following: Press `<Ctrl>-Z`. Press `<Enter>`

```
November 23, 1987

This is a practice exercise in creating or
making a text file.  exercise is the
file name.  .txt is the selected file
extension.  All this data, starting with
the date, is the data or text that is
going to be inside the "file folder" named
exercise.txt

Carolyn Z. Gillay
^Z
                1 File(s) copied
```

WHAT'S HAPPENING? The date and name in your file will differ, obviously, from mine. Note the message, "`1 File(s) copied`." Here is what happened when you pressed `<Ctrl>-Z` and then `<Enter>`. DOS wrote the file you created to the DATA disk. Note that you now have the prompt displayed. (Two disk drive users have the `A>` displayed; hard disk users have the `C>` displayed.) DOS is ready for your next command. How do you know that the file you just created was written to the DATA disk?

STEP 7: Key in the following:

```
A>DIR B:  <Enter>
```

```
Volume in Drive B is DATADISK
Directory of B:\

COMMAND  COM 23210  3-07-85 1:43p
EXERCISE TXT   302 11-23-87 6:24p
    2 File(s) 299008 bytes free

A>_
```

STEP 7: Key in the following:

```
C>DIR A:  <Enter>
```

```
Volume in Drive A is DATADISK
Directory of A:\

COMMAND  COM 23210  3-07-85 1:43p
EXERCISE TXT   302 11-23-87 6:24p
    2 File(s) 299008 bytes free

C>_
```

WHAT'S HAPPENING? The bytes, date, and time in your display may vary. Using the `DIR` command, you now know that there is a file called `exercise.txt` located on the DATA disk. (Remember that the DATA disk is in Drive B for two disk drive users and in Drive A for hard disk users.) This does not tell you the contents of the file. It only says that there is a "file folder" named exercise.txt on the DATA disk.

5.6 THE TYPE COMMAND

The `DIR` command allowed you to determine that, indeed, there is a "file folder" named `exercise.txt` on the DATA disk. Using the `DIR` command is like opening up your file drawer (the disk) and looking at the labels on the file folders. `DIR` does not show you what there is in the file folder. An internal command called `TYPE` opens up the file folder and places the contents on the screen. The `TYPE` command displays the file on the screen without stopping. If the file is longer than one screen full, you can stop the scrolling by pressing `<Ctrl>-<Num Lock>`.

`TYPE` has a syntax. It is:

```
TYPE [d:][path]filename[.ext]
```

`TYPE` is the command or the work you want the system to do. The brackets `[ ]` indicate that what is between the brackets is optional. You do not key in the brackets, only what is inside them. `d:` represents the drive specifier. You do not key in `d:`, you must substitute the drive letter where the file is located (`A:`, `B:`, or `C:`). Another name for the drive specifier is designated disk drive. This tells DOS on which disk drive to look for the information it needs. `[path]` is the name of the path. You do not key in `path` but substitute the name of the path, as in `C:\DOS`. `filename.ext` is mandatory (no brackets) and is the parameter that the `TYPE` command expects. You can only display one file at a time on the screen. You may not use wildcards or global file specifications with the `TYPE` command. In addition, a file must be a text file to be readable.

ACTIVITY 5.7 DISPLAYING FILES USING THE TYPE COMMAND

NOTE: Two disk drive users will have the DOS System Disk in Drive A with the A> displayed and the DATA disk in Drive B. Hard disk users will be logged into the DOS System Disk on Drive C and have the C> displayed. The DATA disk will be in Drive A.

STEP 1: Key in the following:

```
A>TYPE <Enter>
```

```
A>TYPE
Invalid number of parameters

A>_
```

STEP 1: Key in the following:

```
C>TYPE <Enter>
```

```
C>TYPE
Invalid number of parameters

C>_
```

WHAT'S HAPPENING? The message displayed on the screen is telling you that TYPE does not know what to do. DOS is asking you, "TYPE" or display what? Since you did not give a file name, the parameter TYPE cannot show the contents of this file.

STEP 2: Key in the following:

```
A>TYPE more.com <Enter>
```

STEP 2: Key in the following:

```
C>TYPE more.com <Enter>
```

NOTE: The following display will appear on both floppy and hard disk systems, although hard disk systems will display the C>.

```
A>type more.com
ʕ0ɟ!à= s        ºüʕ      ɟ!ɟ Æçʕ&èºʕ    ɟ!30ʕEɟ!
                                             èʕ>ɟ!» ʕEɟ!üº
A>_
```

WHAT'S HAPPENING? What you see displayed on the screen is, indeed, the contents of a file named more.com. It is a program or executable code but it is in machine language and not meaningful to you. This should demonstrate to you that a program is not readable and is not a text file. Programs or executable code are recognized by their file extensions. If you see the file extension .EXE, .COM, .SYS, or .BAS, this tells you that the file is a program. EXE stands for executable code, COM stands for command file, SYS stands for system file, and BAS stands for a BASIC program. However, note that the TYPE command will do whatever you ask, even if it is displaying nonsense. A file must be a text file to be readable. You can see the text file you just created by using the TYPE command, the drive designator or disk drive where the file is located, and the file name.

STEP 3: Key in the following:

`A>TYPE B:exercise.txt <Enter>`

```
A>TYPE B:exercise.txt
November 23, 1987

This is a practice exercise in creating or
making a text file.  exercise is the
file name.  .txt is the selected file
extension.  All this data, starting with
the date, is the data or text that is
going to be inside the "file folder" named
exercise.txt

Carolyn Z. Gillay

A>_
```

STEP 3: Key in the following:

`C>TYPE A:exercise.txt <Enter>`

```
C>TYPE A:exercise.txt
November 23, 1987

This is a practice exercise in creating or
making a text file.  exercise is the
file name.  .txt is the selected file
extension.  All this data, starting with
the date, is the data or text that is
going to be inside the "file folder" named
exercise.txt

Carolyn Z. Gillay

C>_
```

WHAT'S HAPPENING? In this case, the above is a text file and, thus, you can read it. Using the `TYPE` command, you "opened" your file folder, `exercise.txt`, and saw the contents displayed on the screen. You needed to include the drive designator (`B:` for two disk drive users and `A:` for hard disk users) in front of the file name `exercise.txt` because that told DOS which disk drive to select. Had you not included the drive designator, DOS would have looked for the file `exercise.txt` on the default drive (in this case `A:` for two disk drive users and `C:` for hard disk users). Since the file was not on the default drive, you would have received a "`File not found`" message. Note that after DOS has executed the `TYPE` command, it returns to the system prompt, ready for the next command.

5.8 DUMMY FILES

You are going to create some **dummy files**. Dummy means that these files have no particular meaning. You can use these files as examples in file management techniques. The concept of dummy files and/or dummy data is common in data processing. Often data processing professionals wish to test different portions of systems or programs. For instance, if you were writing a program about employee benefits, rather than looking at every employee, you would create dummy files and data in order to have a smaller representative sample that is manageable and easily tested. The following activities allow you to do the same. Following the instructions, you create or make up the file names and contents using the `COPY` command. You then display the contents of the file on the screen with the `TYPE` command.

ACTIVITY 5.9 CREATING AND DISPLAYING DUMMY FILES WITH THE COPY AND TYPE COMMANDS

STEP 1: The DOS System Disk should be in Drive A; the disk labeled DATA disk should be in Drive B.

STEP 1: You are logged into the DOS System Disk on Drive C, and the disk labeled DATA disk should be in Drive A.

NOTE: Remember that `<Ctrl>-Z` means holding down the Control key and then pressing the letter Z. Do not key in the word `Ctrl`. However, there is an easier way to get the `<Ctrl>-Z`. You can press the function key F6. The F6 key is `<Ctrl>-Z`.

STEP 2: Key in the following:

```
A>B:  <Enter>
```

```
B>_
```

STEP 2: Key in the following:

```
C>A:  <Enter>
```

```
A>_
```

WHAT'S HAPPENING? You have changed the default drive so that all the activities will automatically occur or default to the DATA disk. Two disk drive users, the DATA disk is in Drive B. Hard disk users, the DATA disk is in Drive A.

STEP 3: Key in the following:

```
B>COPY CON january.txt  <Enter>
This is my January file.  <Enter>
It is my first dummy file. <Enter>
This is file 1.  <Enter>
Ctrl-Z  <Enter>
```

```
B>COPY CON january.txt
This is my January file.
It is my first dummy file.
This is file 1.
^Z
    1 File(s) copied

B>_
```

STEP 3: Key in the following:

```
A>COPY CON january.txt <Enter>
This is my January file.  <Enter>
It is my first dummy file. <Enter>
This is file 1.  <Enter>
Ctrl-Z  <Enter>
```

```
A>COPY CON january.txt
This is my January file.
It is my first dummy file.
This is file 1.
^Z
    1 File(s) copied

A>_
```

WHAT'S HAPPENING? What you are doing here is telling DOS what work you want to do by keying in the command (`COPY`). The source or what you want copied is going to come from what you key in on the keyboard and will be displayed on the screen (the source is `CON`). The destination is going to be a file that will be copied to the DATA disk. The file will be named `january.txt` (the destination is `january.txt`). `january` is the file name and `.txt` is the file extension. Note that you did not need to specify the letter of the drive prior to the file name. DOS will automatically write the file `january.txt` to the default drive unless told otherwise.

STEP 4: Key in the following:

```
B>DIR  <Enter>
```

```
B>DIR

Volume in drive B is DATADISK
Directory of B:\

COMMAND  COM 23210  3-07-85 1:43p
EXERCISE TXT   302 11-23-87 6:24p
JANUARY  TXT    71 11-23-87 7:35p
    3 File(s)  297984 bytes free

B>_
```

STEP 4: Key in the following:

```
A>DIR  <Enter>
```

```
A>DIR

Volume in drive A is DATADISK
Directory of A:\

COMMAND  COM 23210  3-07-85 1:43p
EXERCISE TXT   302 11-23-87 6:24p
JANUARY  TXT    71 11-23-87 7:35p
    3 File(s)  297984 bytes free

A>_
```

WHAT'S HAPPENING? You should see the new file you just created, named `january.txt`, listed in the directory or table of contents. Do not worry if the time and date are different. That time and date reflect when you created the file. In addition, the bytes can vary because if you enter even one extra character, the number of bytes can change. The directory listing just presents the name of the file, like a file folder label. It does not indicate the contents or the inside of the file folder. If you want to see what is inside the folder, you can display the contents of the file called `january.txt` on the screen by using the `TYPE` command.

STEP 5: Key in the following:

```
B>TYPE january.txt  <Enter>
```

```
B>TYPE january.txt
This is my January file.
It is my first dummy file.
This is file 1.

B>_
```

STEP 5: Key in the following:

```
A>TYPE january.txt  <Enter>
```

```
A>TYPE january.txt
This is my January file.
It is my first dummy file.
This is file 1.

A>_
```

WHAT'S HAPPENING? The `TYPE` command displayed the contents of the file on the screen, or what is inside the file called `january.txt`. Now you are going to create some more files.

NOTE: Each time you press the F6 key or <Ctrl>-Z, you will get a message on the screen saying "1 File(s) copied." This indicates that the file you created was written to the DATA disk.

STEP 6: Key in the following:

```
B>COPY CON february.txt <Enter>
This is my February file. <Enter>
It is my second dummy file.<Enter>
This is file 2.  <Enter>
<Ctrl>-Z  <Enter>
```

```
    1 File(s) copied
```

STEP 7: Key in the following:

```
B>COPY CON march.txt  <Enter>
This is my March file. <Enter>
It is my third dummy file.<Enter>
This is file 3.  <Enter>
<Ctrl>-Z  <Enter>
```

```
    1 File(s) copied
```

STEP 8: Key in the following:

```
B>COPY CON april.txt  <Enter>
This is my April file. <Enter>
It is my fourth dummy file.<Enter>
This is file 4.  <Enter>
<Ctrl>-Z  <Enter>
```

```
    1 File(s) copied
```

STEP 9: Key in the following:

```
B>DIR  <Enter>
```

STEP 6: Key in the following:

```
A>COPY CON february.txt <Enter>
This is my February file. <Enter>
It is my second dummy file.<Enter>
This is file 2.  <Enter>
<Ctrl>-Z  <Enter>
```

```
    1 File(s) copied
```

STEP 7: Key in the following:

```
A>COPY CON march.txt  <Enter>
This is my March file. <Enter>
It is my third dummy file.<Enter>
This is file 3.  <Enter>
<Ctrl>-Z  <Enter>
```

```
    1 File(s) copied
```

STEP 8: Key in the following:

```
A>COPY CON april.txt  <Enter>
This is my April file. <Enter>
It is my fourth dummy file.<Enter>
This is file 4.  <Enter>
<Ctrl>-Z  <Enter>
```

```
    1 File(s) copied
```

STEP 9: Key in the following:

```
A>DIR  <Enter>
```

```
B>DIR

Volume in drive B is DATADISK
Directory of B:\

COMMAND  COM 23210   3-07-85 1:43p
EXERCISE TXT   302 11-23-87 6:24p
JANUARY  TXT    71 11-23-87 7:35p
FEBRUARY TXT    73 11-23-87 7:42p
MARCH    TXT    69 11-23-87 7:43p
APRIL    TXT    70 11-23-87 7:44p
    6 File(s)  294912 bytes free

B>_
```

```
A>DIR

Volume in drive A is DATADISK
Directory of A:\

COMMAND  COM 23210   3-07-85 1:43p
EXERCISE TXT   302 11-23-87 6:24p
JANUARY  TXT    71 11-23-87 7:35p
FEBRUARY TXT    73 11-23-87 7:42p
MARCH    TXT    69 11-23-87 7:43p
APRIL    TXT    70 11-23-87 7:44p
    6 File(s)  294912 bytes free

A>_
```

WHAT'S HAPPENING? The directory display tells you that you have added four "file folders" to the DATA disk. The directory display only tells you that the files are on the disk. It does not tell you what, if anything, is inside the file folder. If you want to look at the inside of the file to see the contents, you must use the `TYPE` command.

STEP 10: Key in the following:

```
B>TYPE march.txt   <Enter>
```

STEP 10: Key in the following:

```
A>TYPE march.txt   <Enter>
```

```
B>TYPE march.txt
This is my March file.
It is my third dummy file.
This is file 3.

B>_
```

```
A>TYPE march.txt
This is my March file.
It is my third dummy file.
This is file 3.

A>_
```

WHAT'S HAPPENING? With this command, `TYPE march.txt`, you are telling DOS to display on the screen the contents of the file named `march.txt`. You can only display one file at a time. If you want to look at your other files, you need to use the `TYPE` command again, followed by the name of the file.

5.10 MAKING ADDITIONAL FILES ON THE SAME DISK

You often want to have extra copies of files on the same disk. A copy is exactly that—it is identical to the original. Often, you may wish to make copies of files created when you use other software application packages. You do this because you want to leave your original files intact and work with copies. Then, if you err, you will still have your originals. For instance, if you had a data base management package and created an extensive client list, and you needed to update the list, rather than working on the original file, you could rekey in the entire client list. If you made a mistake, you would still have your original list. However, an easier method would be to copy the client list, stored as a file, to a new file with a new name and edit the new file to make the changes. When you make a copy of a file on the same disk, you must give it a different name. Every file on a disk must have a unique name.

ACTIVITY 5.11 USING THE COPY COMMAND TO MAKE ADDITIONAL FILES ON THE SAME DISK

NOTE: Two disk drive users will have the DOS System Disk in Drive A with the `B>` displayed and the DATA disk in Drive B. Hard disk users will be logged into the DOS System Disk on Drive C and have the `A>` displayed. The DATA disk will be in Drive A.

STEP 1: Key in the following:

`B>COPY march.txt march.txt <Enter>`

```
B>COPY march.txt march.txt
File cannot be copied onto itself
    0 File(s) copied

B>_
```

STEP 1: Key in the following:

`A>COPY march.txt march.txt <Enter>`

```
A>COPY march.txt march.txt
File cannot be copied onto itself
    0 File(s) copied

A>_
```

WHAT'S HAPPENING? You must give new files on the same disk different names. Just as you would not label two file folders the same in a file drawer, you would not label two disk files the same. Remember, files must have unique names.

STEP 2: Key in the following:

`B>COPY january.txt jan.tmp <Enter>`

```
B>COPY january.txt jan.tmp
    1 File(s) copied

B>_
```

STEP 2: Key in the following:

`A>COPY january.txt jan.tmp <Enter>`

```
A>COPY january.txt jan.tmp
    1 File(s) copied

A>_
```

WHAT'S HAPPENING? Here you are making a copy of the contents of the file on the DATA disk called `january.txt`. Copy the contents to the DATA disk. Call this new file `jan.tmp`. Two disk drive users also could have keyed in `B>COPY B:january.txt B:jan.tmp`. Hard disk users could also have keyed in A>COPY A:january.txt A:jan.tmp. Either is correct, but it is not necessary to specify the disk drive since the default drive is assumed. For two disk drive users, the default drive is B: and for hard disk users, the default drive is A:.

STEP 3: Key in the following:

B>TYPE jan.tmp <Enter>

```
B>TYPE january.tmp
This is my January file.
It is my first dummy file.
This is file 1.

B>_
```

STEP 3: Key in the following:

A>TYPE jan.tmp <Enter>

```
A>TYPE january.tmp
This is my January file.
It is my first dummy file.
This is file 1.

A>_
```

STEP 4: Key in the following:

B>TYPE january.txt <Enter>

```
B>TYPE january.txt
This is my January file.
It is my first dummy file.
This is file 1.

B>_
```

STEP 4: Key in the following:

A>TYPE january.txt <Enter>

```
A>TYPE january.txt
This is my January file.
It is my first dummy file.
This is file 1.

A>_
```

WHAT'S HAPPENING? The contents of each file are identical even though the file names are different. The COPY command does not do anything to the original; the contents of the original file remain the same. As far as DOS is concerned, what makes the files different is the unique file name. january.txt and jan.tmp are unique, separate files to the operating system.

STEP 5: Key in the following:

B>COPY february.txt feb.tmp <Enter>

```
    1 File(s) copied
```

STEP 5: Key in the following:

A>COPY february.txt feb.tmp <Enter>

```
    1 File(s) copied
```

STEP 6: Key in the following:

```
B>COPY march.txt mar.tmp <Enter>
```

```
    1 File(s) copied
```

STEP 7: Key in the following:

```
B>COPY april.txt apr.tmp <Enter>
```

```
    1 File(s) copied
```

STEP 8: Key in the following:

```
B>DIR  <Enter>
```

```
B>DIR

Volume in drive B is DATADISK
Directory of B:\

COMMAND  COM 23210  3-07-85 1:43p
EXERCISE TXT   302 11-23-87 6:24p
JANUARY  TXT    71 11-23-87 7:35p
FEBRUARY TXT    73 11-23-87 7:42p
MARCH    TXT    69 11-23-87 7:43p
APRIL    TXT    70 11-23-87 7:44p
JAN      TMP    71 11-23-87 7:35p
FEB      TMP    73 11-23-87 7:42p
MAR      TMP    69 11-23-87 7:43p
APR      TMP    70 11-23-87 7:44p
    10 File(s)  290816 bytes free

B>_
```

STEP 6: Key in the following:

```
A>COPY march.txt mar.tmp <Enter>
```

```
    1 File(s) copied
```

STEP 7: Key in the following:

```
A>COPY april.txt apr.tmp <Enter>
```

```
    1 File(s) copied
```

STEP 8: Key in the following:

```
A>DIR  <Enter>
```

```
A>DIR

Volume in drive A is DATADISK
Directory of A:\

COMMAND  COM 23210  3-07-85 1:43p
EXERCISE TXT   302 11-23-87 6:24p
JANUARY  TXT    71 11-23-87 7:35p
FEBRUARY TXT    73 11-23-87 7:42p
MARCH    TXT    69 11-23-87 7:43p
APRIL    TXT    70 11-23-87 7:44p
JAN      TMP    71 11-23-87 7:35p
FEB      TMP    73 11-23-87 7:42p
MAR      TMP    69 11-23-87 7:43p
APR      TMP    70 11-23-87 7:44p
    10 File(s)  290816 bytes free

A>_
```

WHAT'S HAPPENING? You had four files with the extension `.txt`. You still have those files, but, in addition, you now have four more files that you just copied or "created" with the extension `.tmp`. DOS keeps track of the files.

5.12 USING WILDCARDS WITH THE COPY COMMAND

In Chapter 3, you used global file specifications or wildcards (* and ?) with the `DIR` command so that you could display a group of files. You can also use the wild cards to copy files on the same drive. In Activity 5.11 you copied one file at a time, for example, `COPY january.txt jan.tmp`. You then proceeded to key in a command line for each file you wanted copied. Since the files had their file extension, `.txt`, in common, instead of having to key in each source file and each destination file, you could have used the wildcards to key in one command line.

ACTIVITY 5.13 USING WILDCARDS WITH THE COPY COMMAND TO COPY FILES ON THE SAME DISK DRIVE

NOTE: Two disk drive users will have the DOS System Disk in Drive A with the `B>` displayed and the DATA disk in Drive B. Hard disk users will be logged into the DOS System Disk on Drive C with the `A>` displayed. The DATA disk will be in Drive A.

STEP 1: Key in the following:

```
B>COPY *.tmp *.new  <Enter>
```

STEP 1: Key in the following:

```
A>COPY *.tmp *.new  <Enter>
```

As each file is copied, it is displayed on the screen.

```
B>COPY *.tmp *.new
JAN.TMP
FEB.TMP
MAR.TMP
APR.TMP
    4 File(s) copied
B>_
```

```
A>COPY *.tmp *.new
JAN.TMP
FEB.TMP
MAR.TMP
APR.TMP
    4 File(s) copied
A>_
```

WHAT'S HAPPENING? Your command line says `COPY` any file on the DATA disk that has the file extension `.tmp`, regardless of its file name, to a new set of files that will have the same file name but a different extension, `.new`. These files will be copied onto the DATA disk. Two disk drive users also could have keyed in `B>COPY B:*.tmp B:*.new` and hard disk users could have keyed in `A>COPY A:*.tmp A:*.new`. Once again, it is unnecessary to specify the designated drive. Since you did not tell it otherwise, DOS assumed the system prompt was the default.

STEP 2: Key in the following:

```
B>DIR *.tmp  <Enter>
```

STEP 2: Key in the following:

```
A>DIR *.tmp  <Enter>
```

STEP 3: Key in the following:

```
B>DIR *.new  <Enter>
```

```
B>DIR *.tmp

  Volume in drive B is DATADISK
  Directory of B:\

JAN      TMP    71 11-23-87 7:35p
FEB      TMP    73 11-23-87 7:42p
MAR      TMP    69 11-23-87 7:43p
APR      TMP    70 11-23-87 7:44p
    4 File(s)  286720 bytes free

B>DIR *.new

  Volume in drive B is DATADISK
  Directory of B:\

JAN      NEW    71 11-23-87 7:35p
FEB      NEW    73 11-23-87 7:42p
MAR      NEW    69 11-23-87 7:43p
APR      NEW    70 11-23-87 7:44p
    4 File(s)  286720 bytes free

B>_
```

STEP 3: Key in the following:

```
A>DIR *.new  <Enter>
```

```
A>DIR *.tmp

  Volume in drive A is DATADISK
  Directory of A:\

JAN      TMP    71 11-23-87 7:35p
FEB      TMP    73 11-23-87 7:42p
MAR      TMP    69 11-23-87 7:43p
APR      TMP    70 11-23-87 7:44p
    4 File(s)  286720 bytes free

A>DIR *.new

  Volume in drive A is DATADISK
  Directory of A:\

JAN      NEW    71 11-23-87 7:35p
FEB      NEW    73 11-23-87 7:42p
MAR      NEW    69 11-23-87 7:43p
APR      NEW    70 11-23-87 7:44p
    4 File(s)  286720 bytes free

A>_
```

WHAT'S HAPPENING? You keyed in two separate commands, `DIR *.tmp` and `DIR *.new`. You used the wildcards to display the `.new` files and the `.tmp` files instead of getting the entire directory. You also used the wildcard, `*`, to make copies of the `.tmp` files. Note that the file names are identical but the extensions are different, as you requested. You successfully copied the four files with the extension `.tmp` to four new files with the extension `.new`. However, the directory display merely shows that the files are there. To see that the contents of the original files and copied files are the same, you may use the `TYPE` command.

STEP 4: Key in the following:

```
B>TYPE feb.tmp  <Enter>
```

STEP 5: Key in the following:

```
B>TYPE feb.new <Enter>
```

STEP 4: Key in the following:

```
A>TYPE feb.tmp  <Enter>
```

STEP 5: Key in the following:

```
A>TYPE feb.new <Enter>
```

```
B>TYPE feb.tmp
This is my February file.
It is my second dummy file.
This is file 2.

B>TYPE feb.new
This is my February file.
It is my second dummy file.
This is file 2.

B>_
```

```
A>TYPE feb.tmp
This is my February file.
It is my second dummy file.
This is file 2.

A>TYPE feb.new
This is my February file.
It is my second dummy file.
This is file 2.

A>_
```

WHAT'S HAPPENING? Note that the file contents are identical even though the file names are different. To display the two files, you keyed in two command lines, `TYPE feb.tmp` and then `TYPE feb.new`. Why not use wildcards with the `TYPE` command? You cannot use wild cards with the `TYPE` command because the syntax of the `TYPE` command is `TYPE filename` and `TYPE` can only display one file at a time.

STEP 6: Key in the following:

```
B>TYPE *.new  <Enter>
```

STEP 6: Key in the following:

```
A>TYPE *.new  <Enter>
```

```
B>TYPE *.new
Invalid file name or file not found

B>_
```

```
A>TYPE *.new
Invalid file name or file not found

A>_
```

WHAT'S HAPPENING? The message displayed on the screen tells you that the `TYPE` command was literally looking for a file called `*.new`. You have no files by that name (file not found) and, furthermore, it is an invalid file name because the `*` cannot be used when naming a file.

5.14 PRINTING FILES USING THE COPY COMMAND

You have used `COPY` with a device (`CON`) as the source. `COPY` is the command and `CON` is the source used to create dummy text files. You have also been using the `COPY` command to copy or make additional files on the same disk. You have used the `TYPE` command to display the contents of the text files that you created. So far, the only way you could get a hard copy of the contents of your file has been to use the `<Shift>` and `<PrtSc>` key, but this method of printing has several disadvantages. When you use the `<Shift>` and `<PrtSc>` keys, you get everything that is displayed on the screen or monitor—the prompts, the commands, as well as the contents of the file. So far your text files have been very short and have fit entirely on the screen, but what if the contents of the file were longer than the 24 lines displayed on the screen? You would continually have to freeze the screen with the Ctrl-Num Lock keys and have the contents of your file printed in sections, which is neither efficient nor attractive. There is an easier way to send or copy the contents of your file to the printer. As you copied **from** a device, the console, you can also copy **to** a device; in this case the device is the printer. Since the printer is a device, it has a reserved name: `PRN` for printer. You can also use `LPT1` for Line Printer 1. If you use `LPT1`, be sure to key in the letter L, the letter P, the letter T, and the number 1. You cannot use the letter l ("ell") as the number 1.

ACTIVITY 5.15 USING THE COPY COMMAND TO PRINT FILES

NOTE: Two disk drive users will have the DOS System Disk in Drive A with the `B>` displayed and the DATA disk in Drive B. Hard disk users will be logged into the DOS System Disk on Drive C with the `A>` displayed. The DATA disk will be in Drive A.

STEP 1: Turn on the printer.

STEP 2: Key in the following:

```
B>COPY january.txt PRN  <Enter>
```

STEP 1: Turn on the printer.

STEP 2: Key in the following:

```
A>COPY january.txt PRN  <Enter>
```

WHAT'S HAPPENING? Even though you are using a device, the syntax remains the same. `COPY` is the command, the work you want done. `january.txt` is the source, the file you want copied. You do not need to put a drive designator in front of the file name because DOS will assume the default. `PRN` is the device name for the printer. The printer is the destination, where you want the contents of the file to go. As soon as you press `<Enter>`, you should hear/see the printer begin to print. The hard copy or output is at the printer. Your screen will display the message `"1 File(s) copied."` You will see on the printer the following words:

```
-----------------------------------------------
o  This is my January file.                   o
o  It is my first dummy file.                 o
o  This is file 1.                            o
```

WHAT'S HAPPENING? Neither the file name nor the command line will be printed, only the contents of the file or what is inside the "file folder." You can use an alternate device name that is synonymous with `PRN`, called `LPT1`. Note that it is the letter L, the letter P, the letter T, and the number 1. DOS is very particular about device names. Only `LPT1` is correct. Do not substitute the lowercase letter l for the number 1.

STEP 3: Key in the following:

B>COPY march.txt LPT1 <Enter>

STEP 3: Key in the following:

A>COPY march.txt LPT1 <Enter>

```
-----------------------------------------------
| o  This is my March file.                 o |
| o  It is my third dummy file.             o |
| o  This is file 3.                        o |
```

WHAT'S HAPPENING? As you can see, DOS executed the command whether you used PRN or LPT1 as the destination. You cannot use the TYPE command to print files. TYPE january.txt PRN would be incorrect syntax. TYPE expects only one parameter. It is used for displaying text on the monitor, not for starting the printer.

5.16 PRINTING FILES USING THE COPY COMMAND AND WILDCARDS

You can also use wildcards when using COPY to print similarly named files. This allows you to use one command line to print several files.

ACTIVITY 5.17 USING THE COPY COMMAND AND WILDCARDS TO PRINT FILES

NOTE: Two disk drive users will have the DOS System Disk in Drive A with the B> displayed and the DATA disk in Drive B. Hard disk users will be logged into the DOS System Disk on Drive C with the A> displayed. The DATA disk will be in Drive A.

STEP 1: Key in the following:

```
B>COPY *.tmp PRN   <Enter>
```

STEP 1: Key in the following:

```
A>COPY *.tmp PRN   <Enter>
```

NOTE: You will see each file displayed on the screen as it is copied.

```
B>COPY *.tmp PRN
JAN.TMP
FEB.TMP
MAR.TMP
APR.TMP
   1 File(s) copied

B>_
```

```
A>COPY *.tmp PRN
JAN.TMP
FEB.TMP
MAR.TMP
APR.TMP
    1 File(s) copied

A>_
```

```
---------------------------------------------
o  This is my January file.              o
o  It is my first dummy file.            o
o  This is file 1.                       o
   This is my February file.
   It is my second dummy file.
   This is file 2.
   This is my March file.
   It is my third dummy file.
   This is file 3.
   This is my April file.
   It is my fourth dummy file.
   This is file 4.
```

WHAT'S HAPPENING? The hard copy or printout wrote the contents of one file right after another with no differentiation between the files. The printout does not print the file names, only the contents of the files. You actually printed the contents of four different files. As they were printed, the file names appeared on the screen. The reason the screen display only showed one file copied was that you only gave one destination, the printer.

NOTE: Your screen display and printout could vary if you created the files in a different order. When you use a wildcard, DOS finds the files on a first-come, first-served basis.

CHAPTER SUMMARY

1. The internal commands DIR, COPY, and TYPE allow you to manage the files on a disk.
2. DIR allows you to display the files on any disk on the screen.
3. TYPE allows you to display the contents of a file on the screen. The syntax is TYPE [d:][path]filename[ext].
4. COPY allows you to copy files selectively. You can copy files on the same disk; copy (create) files from a device, CON; and copy files to a device, PRN.
5. The syntax of the copy command is COPY [d:][path]source [d:][path]destination. Source is what you want to copy. Destination is where you want it copied.
6. The COPY command never changes the source.
7. When you name files, you must follow the DOS file-naming rules. Every file must have a unique file name that does not exceed eight characters. A file extension is optional but if included must not exceed three characters. File names usually refer to what is in the file and file extensions usually refer to the type of data in the file. Some application programs assign file extensions.
8. When naming files, it is best to stick with alphanumeric characters. Certain characters are illegal, such as the colon : and the <Space>.
9. A dummy file is a file usually created for test purposes. A dummy text file can be created using the COPY CON filename.ext command. This sets up the "file folder." Any text data keyed in after that becomes the contents of the file.
10. Wildcards may be used with the COPY command.

REVIEW QUESTIONS

1. What is the maximum number of characters that may be used when naming a file? A file extension?
2. What command will allow you to see the file names on your disk?
3. How can you create a text file?
4. How can you print your file? What are the advantages/disadvantages of each method?
5. What command allows you to see the contents of your file displayed on the screen?
6. What is the syntax for the DIR command?
7. What is the syntax for the COPY command?
8. What is the syntax for the TYPE command?
9. What makes internal commands significant?
10. What are the major internal commands?
11. Can you use wildcards with the COPY command? If yes, why would you use a wildcard?
12. Can you use wildcards with the DIR command? If yes, why would you use a wildcard?
13. Can you use wildcards with the TYPE command? If yes, why would you use a wildcard?
14. What are some examples of legal file names?
15. What are some characters that you cannot use in naming files?
16. Must file names be unique on a disk? Why or why not?

17. Is a file extension mandatory when naming a file?
18. Can you use the TYPE command to get a hard copy of a text file?
19. Can files with the extension .EXE or .COM be displayed on the screen with the TYPE command? What kind of display will you get?
20. Give two reasons for making a copy of file on the same disk.

TRUE/FALSE

1. Eight characters is the maximum number that can be used for a file name.
2. The wild card that substitutes for one character is the *.
3. Pressing the <Alt> key and the <PrtSc> key will print what is displayed on the screen.
4. When using COPY CON filename, it is not possible to correct errors in your lines of type after you have pressed <Enter>.
5. COPY is an unimportant internal command.
6. TYPE *.txt will display the contents of all the files with the file extension .txt.
7. TAXES.87 is a valid file name.
8. DISKCOPY is used to make identical copies of disks. COPY is used to make identical copies of files.
9. COPY new.fil PRINTER will copy the contents of new.fil to the printer.
10. COPY old.one new.one will create a new file called new.one and retain the old file called old.one on the disk.

SUGGESTED ACTIVITIES

NOTE: Two disk drive users will have the DOS System Disk in Drive A and the DATA disk in Drive B. Hard disk users will be logged into the DOS System Disk on Drive C. The DATA disk will be in Drive A.

1. Create a text file to be placed on the DATA disk. Name it homework.dat. Following are the contents of this file:

```
Today's date

I am learning how to create a text file.  I am using
the console as my source.  When I key in data, it is similar
to typing a document.  When I am done keying this in,
I will tell DOS that I am done by hitting Ctrl-Z.
DOS will then write this file to the DATA disk.

Your name
```

2. Clear the screen. Do a directory display of the DATA disk to display the file names. If the screen is scrolling, wait until the last screen is displayed. Print this screen.
3. Clear the screen. Display the contents of the file, homework.dat on the screen. Print this screen.

4. Create three more text files on the DATA disk using the `COPY CON` command. The first file will be called `employee.one`. The contents will be: This is the employee file one. The second file will be called `employee.two`. The contents of this file will be: This is the employee file two. The third file will be called `employee.thr`. The contents of the file will be: This is the employee file three. Use `DIR` to display all the employee file names. Print this screen.
5. Clear the screen. Display the contents of the file `employee.thr` on the screen. Print this screen.
6. Copy the contents of the file employee.one to the printer. Do not use the `<Shift>` and `<PrtSc>` keys.
7. Make copies of all the employee files on the DATA disk. The new file names will be `ditto` but the file extensions will remain the same. Use a wildcard. You will end up with three new files with `ditto` as a file name. Use the `DIR` command to display only the `ditto` file names on the DATA disk. Print this screen.
8. Copy the contents of all the `ditto` files to the printer. Do not use the `<Shift>` and `<PrtSc>` keys. Use a wildcard.
9. Make a copy of the `ditto.one` file. Call the new file `test.fil`. Use the `DIR` command to display only the `test.fil` name on the screen. Print this screen.
10. Print only the contents of the file `homework.dat`. Do not use the `<Shift>` and `<PrtSc>` keys.

EXPANDING THE USE OF THE COPY COMMAND

CHAPTER

6

CHAPTER OBJECTIVES

This chapter continues the discussion of the `COPY` command, introduces the concept of a path, and reinforces the use of the `DIR` and `TYPE` commands. After completing this chapter, you will:

Be able to copy files to other disk drives.

Set up and use a subdirectory (hard disk users).

Understand the concept of overwriting files.

Be able to overwrite files.

Understand and be able to concatenate text files.

Be able to verify that a file has been copied properly.

6.0 MATERIALS NEEDED

1. Microcomputer
2. DOS System Disk
3. DATA disk
4. ACTIVITIES disk

6.1 COPYING FILES TO ANOTHER DISK

The `COPY` command, introduced in Chapter 5, is an internal command. It is always there to use after you have booted the system. Internal commands remain in memory even if the DOS System Disk is not in any drive.

`COPY` is one of the most used commands. In Chapter 5, you used `COPY` to make duplicate copies of files. You also used wildcards to make copies of files and created some text files. In this chapter, you are going to explore the other uses for the `COPY` command. The important point to remember is that the syntax always is:

```
COPY source destination
```

or, in correct syntax:

```
COPY [d:][path]filename[.ext] [d:][path]filename[.ext]
```

When using any command, you must first enter the command to tell the system what work is to be done. Then you enter the parameters that the command requires. The parameters for the `COPY` command are the source (what you want to copy) and the destination (where you want the source copied to). You do not key in the brackets, only what is inside the brackets. Do not key in `d:`, which indicates the designated drive or drive specifier. You must substitute the letter of the drive you want.

Often you wish to copy files to another disk in order to make backup copies, copy a program file (external command) to another disk, or share data files with an associate. The following activities will demonstrate how to copy files from one disk to another.

You may have noticed a new parameter. You can specify not only which drive `[d:]` a file is on but also what **path** the `COPY` command should follow. Paths are used most commonly with hard disks. You substitute the specific path you are seeking for the command word `[path]`. However, you do not key in the brackets or the word "path."

6.2 A BRIEF INTRODUCTION TO SUBDIRECTORIES AND PATHS

A hard disk can be compared to a large office building under construction. Part of the completion process is to divide the large, open area into many separate offices. Life would be very difficult if you went into an office building for an appointment with an accounting firm and had to stop at every desk to ask if it was the accounting firm you sought.

Like an office building under construction, a hard disk is divided into subdirectories. The user does not have to look at every file on the hard disk in order to find a group of related files. Thus, all the accounting files and programs for your company would be placed into a **subdirectory** named accounting. To carry this analogy further, it would be very difficult to find a specific office without a guide. Most people really do not want to wander from office to office looking for an accounting firm. Thus, when they walk into the office building, they usually go to the directory to locate the room number of the office they seek. The directory is a list that indicates where the specific office is located. The term **path** serves the same function. You don't have to "wander" from subdirectory to subdirectory. You can tell DOS specifically where the "office" is by means of the path.

Just as an office building can add new offices or remove existing offices, a user can both make and remove subdirectories with the special commands MD and RD. However, in an office building, putting a sign on the door saying "Jones Accounting Firm" does not mean there is anything in that office yet. The accountants have to move in. The same is true for subdirectories. Creating subdirectories means creating an "office" where files can be placed. A subdirectory is created by the command MD (make directory), but until you copy files into the subdirectory, it is just a shell. In addition, in an office building, you are not limited to looking at a list of the offices. You can physically visit any office. Again, the same is true with subdirectories. Just as you can change the default drive, you can also change the default subdirectory by means of the CD command (current or change directory). Thus, you can physically place your arena of work in the specific subdirectory of interest so that it becomes the default.

To insure that hard disk users will be able to follow the instructions in the text, the following activity will set up a subdirectory on the hard disk and then copy the files from the ACTIVITIES disk into the hard disk subdirectory. Since many of the activities in the chapter will involve copying files from the ACTIVITIES disk to the DATA disk, creating a subdirectory will also eliminate floppy disk swapping for hard disk users. Two disk drive users have two disk drives, so they can place the ACTIVITIES disk in one drive and the DATA disk in the other. They do not have to create any subdirectories.

ACTIVITY 6.3 SETTING UP A SUBDIRECTORY—HARD DISK USERS ONLY

STEP 1: Be sure the system is booted with the C>. Insert the ACTIVITIES disk in Drive A.

STEP 2: Key in the following:

```
C>MD \junk  <Enter>
```

```
C>MD \junk

C>_
```

WHAT'S HAPPENING? With the MD \junk command, you have created a subdirectory on the hard disk called \junk. This is an area or shell you have created. It is like creating a new file cabinet called \junk. It is still empty. There are no files in \junk yet, but you now have a place to put files. \junk was selected as a name for the subdirectory since it is highly unlikely that this subdirectory name will conflict with any other subdirectory on the hard disk. You are now going to "fill" the file cabinet with all the files on the ACTIVITIES disk.

STEP 3: Key in the following:

```
C>COPY A:*.* \junk <Enter>
```

```
A:FEB.87
A:MAR.87
A:APR.87
A:FILE2.CZG
A:FILE3.CZG
A:FILE2.FP
A:FILE3.FP
A:FILE4.FP
A:FILE2.SWT
A:FILE3.SWT
A:RIGHT.RED
A:DRESS.UP
A:LEFT.RED
A:MIDDLE.RED
A:RIGHT.UP
A:MIDDLE.UP
A:BLUE.JAZ
A:GREEN.JAZ
A:ADDRESS.DAT
A:BYE.TXT
A:GOODBYE.TXT
A:TEST.TXT
    70 File(s) copied

C>_
```

WHAT'S HAPPENING? Note that this is the last screenful of files. The syntax of the COPY command was followed. C>COPY is the work you want to do. A:*.* is the source or what you want copied. A: is the physical disk drive you want DOS to look on. *.* means you want each and every file on the ACTIVITIES disk. As each file was found on the ACTIVITIES disk in Drive A, it was listed on the screen, until the COPY command had found every file. The destination is the subdirectory \junk of Drive C. Just as a disk drive has a name, like A: or B:, the name of the subdirectory is C:\junk or C:(backslash) junk. All the files that were on the ACTIVITIES disk are now also on the hard disk subdirectory called \junk.

STEP 4: Key in the following:

C>CD \junk <Enter>

```
C>CD \junk

C>_
```

WHAT'S HAPPENING? (Note: Your prompt could look like C:\junk> if your system setup includes a custom prompt.) What you have done is logged into the subdirectory \junk. This is the equivalent of changing logged drives. The default is now C:\junk. You are effectively on the ACTIVITIES disk. For the rest of this activity, your default is also the ACTIVITIES disk.

ACTIVITY 6.4 COPYING FILES TO ANOTHER DISK AND KEEPING THE SAME FILE NAME

STEP 1: Be sure the system is booted with the A> displayed on the screen.

STEP 1: Be sure you are logged into the subdirectory \junk on Drive C. You can be sure by keying in C>CD \junk <Enter>

STEP 2: Insert the disk labeled ACTIVITIES in Drive A. Insert the disk labeled DATA disk in Drive B.

STEP 2: Remove the ACTIVITIES disk from Drive A. Insert the disk labeled DATA disk in Drive A.

WHAT'S HAPPENING? The work you want to do now is to copy files from one disk to another. Since COPY is an internal command, you do not need the DOS System Disk. The internal commands are in memory or RAM until you power down. In order to copy files from one disk to another, you have to place the disks in the disk drives so that you can access the files you want to copy. In other words, you are setting up the work activity area. Two disk drive users want to copy files from the ACTIVITIES disk and hard disk users want to copy files from the subdirectory C:\junk, which has all the ACTIVITIES disk files. The destination will be the DATA disk. Hard disk users, for this activity, the ACTIVITIES disk is where you are logged in. The current default is subdirectory \junk. The COPY command must be able to locate the files before it can copy them.

STEP 3: Key in the following:

A>DIR hello.txt <Enter>

STEP 3: Key in the following:

C>DIR hello.txt <Enter>

```
A>DIR hello.txt

Volume in drive A is ACTIVITIES
Directory of A:\

HELLO  TXT    51  11-23-87  1:12p
    1 File(s)  173056 bytes free

A>_
```

```
C>DIR hello.txt

Volume in drive is HARD DRIVE
Directory of C:\JUNK

HELLO  TXT    51  11-23-87  1:12p
    1 File(s) 7593984 bytes free

C>_
```

WHAT'S HAPPENING? You asked DOS to see if you had a file called `hello.txt` on the ACTIVITIES disk. This confirms that the file you want to copy is on the default drive.

STEP 4: Key in the following:

```
A>DIR B:hello.txt  <Enter>
```

STEP 4: Key in the following:

```
C>DIR A:hello.txt  <Enter>
```

```
A>DIR B:hello.txt

Volume in Drive B is DATADISK
Directory of Drive B:\

File not found

A>_
```

```
C>DIR A:hello.txt

Volume in Drive A is DATADISK
Directory of Drive A:\

File not found

C>_
```

WHAT'S HAPPENING? You asked DOS to look for the file on the DATA disk. DOS came back and told you there is no file by that name on the DATA disk. Note that prior to the file name, `hello.txt`, you had to place a drive letter so that DOS would know which disk drive to look on.

STEP 5: Key in the following:

```
A>COPY hello.txt B:  <Enter>
```

STEP 5: Key in the following:

```
C>COPY hello.txt A:  <Enter>
```

```
A>COPY hello.txt B:
    1 File(s) copied

A>_
```

```
C>COPY hello.txt A:
    1 File(s) copied

C>_
```

WHAT'S HAPPENING? You said `COPY` (the command or the work you wanted done) the source (the file named `hello` with the file extension of `txt`, located on the ACTIVITIES disk) to the destination (the DATA disk). Since you did not supply a file name, how did DOS know what name to give the file on the DATA disk? The answer has to do with default values or assumptions. The command you keyed in is a "shorthand" version of the syntax for the `COPY` command. The "longhand" version or complete command would look as follows for two disk drive users:

```
COPY A:hello.txt  B:hello.txt
```

For hard disk users, the longhand version would look as follows:

```
COPY C:\junk\hello.txt  A:hello.txt
```

DOS makes certain assumptions if you do not key in all the information. You must always key in the command; in this case, the command is `COPY`. You must always key in a source. For two disk drive users, the source is A: or the physical disk drive you want DOS to look on. However, you do not need to include A: since the default drive is A. You gave DOS no other instructions so it assumes or defaults to the disk in Drive A. It is looking for the file called `hello.txt`. For hard disk users, the source is C:, the physical disk drive, but in addition, DOS also needs the path or subdirectory of `\junk`. This tells DOS where to look for this file. However, you did not need to include `C:\junk`. Since you gave DOS no other instructions it assumes or defaults to where you are logged in, which is `C:\junk`. It is looking for the file called `hello.txt` on the default. You must always have a destination or where you want the file copied to. Your destination in this case is the DATA disk which is in Drive B for two disk drive users and in Drive A for hard disk system users. You did not have to follow the drive designator letter with the file name `hello.txt`, because the assumption or default the DOS `COPY` command makes is that if you do not indicate the file specification, you wish to keep the same file name. Note that this is different from copying a file on the same disk. On the same disk, files may not have the same file specification—each file has to have a unique name. Since this is a different disk, you can use the same file name.

STEP 6: Key in the following:

```
A>DIR B:hello.txt  <Enter>
```

```
A>DIR B:hello.txt

Volume in Drive B is DATADISK
Directory of Drive B:\

HELLO   TXT    51   11-23-87   1:12p
    1 File(s)  277504 bytes free

A>_
```

STEP 6: Key in the following:

```
C>DIR A:hello.txt  <Enter>
```

```
C>DIR A:hello.txt

Volume in Drive A is DATADISK
Directory of Drive A:\

HELLO   TXT    51   11-23-87   1:12p
    1 File(s)  277504 bytes free

C>_
```

WHAT'S HAPPENING? By using the `DIR` command, you verified that the file called `hello.txt` was copied to the DATA disk. You can use the `TYPE` command to see if the contents of the files are identical.

STEP 7: Key in the following:

```
A>TYPE hello.txt  <Enter>
```

STEP 8: Key in the following:

```
A>TYPE B:hello.txt  <Enter>
```

```
A>TYPE hello.txt
HELLO EVERYONE.
HOW ARE YOU?
ISN'T THIS FUN???

A>TYPE B:hello.txt
HELLO EVERYONE.
HOW ARE YOU?
ISN'T THIS FUN???

A>_
```

STEP 7: Key in the following:

```
C>TYPE hello.txt  <Enter>
```

STEP 8: Key in the following:

```
C>TYPE A:hello.txt  <Enter>
```

```
C>TYPE hello.txt
HELLO EVERYONE.
HOW ARE YOU?
ISN'T THIS FUN???

C>TYPE A:hello.txt
HELLO EVERYONE.
HOW ARE YOU?
ISN'T THIS FUN???

C>_
```

WHAT'S HAPPENING? As you can see, you have successfully copied the file called `hello.txt` from the ACTIVITIES disk to the DATA disk. You kept the file names the same, and the contents of the two files are identical.

ACTIVITY 6.5 COPYING FILES TO ANOTHER DISK WITH ANOTHER FILE NAME

STEP 1: The ACTIVITIES disk should still be in Drive A and the DATA disk should be in Drive B.

STEP 2: Key in the following:

```
A>COPY hello.txt B:hi.txt <Enter>
```

```
A>COPY hello.txt B:hi.txt
    1 File(s) copied

A>_
```

STEP 1: You should be logged into the subdirectory `C:\junk`. You can be sure by keying in `C>CD \junk`. The DATA disk should be in Drive A.

STEP 2: Key in the following:

```
C>COPY hello.txt A:hi.txt <Enter>
```

```
C>COPY hello.txt A:hi.txt
    1 File(s) copied

C>_
```

WHAT'S HAPPENING? The syntax of the `COPY` command has not changed. You said `COPY` (the command or the work you wanted done) the source (the file named hello with the file extension of txt, located on the ACTIVITIES disk) to the destination (the DATA disk), followed by the "new" file name, `hi.txt`. Since you assigned a new file name, `hi.txt`, DOS will use it. The only default value DOS used is that it assumed that `hello.txt` is located on the ACTIVITIES disk. DOS did not use any default value for the new file name on the DATA disk because you supplied the file name you wanted DOS to use, in this case, `hi.txt`. Remember, a computer follows your instructions. It only uses default values if you do not tell it what to do. You now have two files on the DATA disk with the same file contents but different file names, `hello.txt` and `hi.txt`. DOS does not know that these file contents are identical.

STEP 3: Key in the following:

`A>TYPE B:hello.txt   <Enter>`

STEP 4: Key in the following:

`A>TYPE B:hi.txt   <Enter>`

```
A>TYPE B:hello.txt
HELLO EVERYONE.
HOW ARE YOU?
ISN'T THIS FUN???

A>TYPE B:hi.txt
HELLO EVERYONE.
HOW ARE YOU?
ISN'T THIS FUN???

A>_
```

STEP 3: Key in the following:

`C>TYPE A:hello.txt   <Enter>`

STEP 4: Key in the following:

`C>TYPE A:hi.txt   <Enter>`

```
C>TYPE A:hello.txt
HELLO EVERYONE.
HOW ARE YOU?
ISN'T THIS FUN???

C>TYPE A:hi.txt
HELLO EVERYONE.
HOW ARE YOU?
ISN'T THIS FUN???

C>_
```

WHAT'S HAPPENING? The contents of the file are identical; only the file names are different. You have always used the correct syntax, `COPY source destination`. As you can see, you can let the system use default values or you can provide the values you want.

6.6 HOW TO OVERWRITE FILES WITH THE COPY COMMAND

Because you have been making copies of files, you have been giving the files on the same disk unique names. One of the reasons for doing this is when you tried to use the same file name on the same disk, you got an error message, "`File cannot be copied onto itself, 0 File(s)  copied.`" DOS would not permit you to make that error. However, the rule of unique file names is only true if the files are on the same disk and subdirectory. If you are using more than one disk or more than one subdirectory, DOS will let you use the same file name on different disks or subdirectories. There have been no problems so far because when you copied the source file from one disk to the destination file on another disk, it was a new file on the destination disk. However, if you already had a file on the destination disk with the same file name, DOS would not give you an error message. It would merely overwrite the destination file with the contents of the source file. This also happens on the same disk if there is an existing destination file to which you write. The same rules apply to subdirectories. Overwrite means just what it says; it writes over or replaces what used to be in that file. Hence, if the contents of the Source file are different from the contents of the destination file, the destination and source file will now have not only the same file name but also the same file contents. The previous contents of the destination file will be gone.

This process seems dangerous because you could lose the data in a file. You may wonder why DOS does not protect you against this error as it does when you try to copy a file with the same name on the same disk. The programmers who wrote DOS do not protect you because to DOS it is not an error. In working with computers, typically, you do want to overwrite files.

Data, or what is inside the files, usually changes all the time. For example, if you have a customer list stored as a file named `customer.lst` on a disk, the information in the file or the data changes as you add customers, delete customers, and update information about customers. When you have completed your work for the day, you want to backup your file or copy it to another disk, because you are working with it on a daily basis. Thus, you have a file called `customer.lst` on your source disk and a file called `customer.lst` on your destination disk. `customer.lst` is a good, descriptive file name. You really do not want to create a new file name every time you copy the file to the destination disk because creating new file names and then tracking current files can be time-consuming and confusing. In addition, as you can see, if you are working with a file on a daily basis, you could end up with hundreds of file names. In reality, you do not care about last week's or yesterday's customer information, or the old file; you care about the current version and its backup version. Thus, when copying a file for backup purposes, you do want the source file to overwrite the destination file. To demonstrate how this process works, you are going to create two files on different disks with the same file name and then overwrite one file with another.

ACTIVITY 6.7 OVERWRITING FILES USING THE COPY COMMAND

STEP 1: The ACTIVITIES disk should still be in Drive A and the DATA disk should be in drive B.

STEP 1: You should be logged into the subdirectory `C:\junk`. You can be sure by keying in `C>CD \junk`. The DATA disk should be in Drive A.

STEP 2: Remember that `<Ctrl>-Z` means to press the Control key and then the letter Z. Key in the following:

```
A>COPY CON test.txt  <Enter>
This is a test file.  <Enter>
It will show how to <Enter>
overwrite a file. <Enter>
<Ctrl-Z>  <Enter>
```

STEP 3: Key in the following:

```
A>COPY CON B:test.txt  <Enter>
The contents of this  <Enter>
file will be  <Enter>
replaced by the  <Enter>
contents of the  <Enter>
file created on the  <Enter>
ACTIVITIES DISK.  <Enter>
<Ctrl-Z>  <Enter>
```

STEP 2: Remember that `<Ctrl>-Z` means to press the Control key and then the letter Z. Key in the following:

```
C>COPY CON test.txt  <Enter>
This is a test file.  <Enter>
It will show how to <Enter>
overwrite a file. <Enter>
<Ctrl-Z>  <Enter>
```

STEP 3: Key in the following:

```
C>COPY CON A:test.txt  <Enter>
The contents of this  <Enter>
file will be  <Enter>
replaced by the  <Enter>
contents of the  <Enter>
file created on the  <Enter>
ACTIVITIES DISK.  <Enter>
<Ctrl-Z>  <Enter>
```

WHAT'S HAPPENING? You have created two separate text files with `COPY` as the command, `CON` as the source, and `test.txt` as the destination. The file `test.txt`, however, was written to different disks on different drives. Each file has the same name but different contents.

STEP 4: Key in the following:

```
A>TYPE test.txt  <Enter>
```

STEP 5: Key in the following:

```
A>TYPE B:test.txt  <Enter>
```

```
A>TYPE test.txt
This is a test file.
It will show how to
overwrite a file.

A>TYPE B:test.txt
The contents of this
file will be
replaced by the
contents of the
file created on the
ACTIVITIES disk.

A>_
```

STEP 4: Key in the following:

```
C>TYPE test.txt  <Enter>
```

STEP 5: Key in the following:

```
C>TYPE A:test.txt  <Enter>
```

```
C>TYPE test.txt
This is a test file.
It will show how to
overwrite a file.

C>TYPE A:test.txt
The contents of this
file will be
replaced by the
contents of
file created on the
ACTIVITIES disk.

C>_
```

WHAT'S HAPPENING? Note that the contents of the files are different, even though the file names are the same and the files are on different disks.

STEP 6: Key in the following:

`A>COPY test.txt test.txt <Enter>`

```
A>COPY test.txt test.txt
File cannot be copied onto itself
    0 File(s) copied

A>_
```

STEP 6: Key in the following:

`C>COPY test.txt test.txt <Enter>`

```
C>COPY test.txt test.txt
File cannot be copied onto itself
    0 File(s) copied

C>_
```

WHAT'S HAPPENING? You tried to make a copy of a file with the same file name, on the same disk, and in the same disk drive (and for hard disk users, in the same subdirectory). DOS will not let you overwrite the file on the same disk. You already have a file called `test.txt` on the ACTIVITIES disk. Now you are going to copy the file with the same name from one disk to another.

STEP 7: Key in the following:

`A>COPY test.txt B:test.txt <Enter>`

```
A>COPY test.txt B:test.txt
    1 File(s) copied

A>_
```

STEP 7: Key in the following:

`C>COPY test.txt A:test.txt <Enter>`

```
C>COPY test.txt A:test.txt
    1 File(s) copied

C>_
```

WHAT'S HAPPENING? Two disk drive users also could have written the command as `COPY test.txt B:`. You did not need to key in `B:test.txt`. `COPY` is the command; `A:test.txt` is the source, but since you are in Drive A, DOS defaults to Drive A. `B:` is the destination, and DOS assumes that the file name is `test.txt` since you did not give instructions. Hard disk users also could have written the command as `COPY test.txt A:`. You did not need to key in `A:test.txt`. `COPY` is the command; `C:\junk\test.txt` is the source, but since you are in Drive `C:\junk`, DOS defaults to Drive `C:\junk`. `A:` is the destination, and DOS assumes that the file name is `test.txt` since you did not give instructions. Note that this time you did not get an error message. The file `test.txt` was successfully copied from the ACTIVITIES disk to the DATA disk. But what about the contents of the file? The files still have the same name. Did anything change?

STEP 8: Key in the following:

`A>TYPE test.txt <Enter>`

STEP 8: Key in the following:

`C>TYPE test.txt <Enter>`

STEP 9: Key in the following:

`A>TYPE B:test.txt <Enter>`

```
A>TYPE test.txt
This is a test file.
It will show how to
overwrite a file.

A>TYPE B:test.txt
This is a test file.
It will show how to
overwrite a file.

A>_
```

STEP 9: Key in the following:

`C>TYPE A:test.txt <Enter>`

```
C>TYPE test.txt
This is a test file.
It will show how to
overwrite a file.

C>TYPE A:test.txt
This is a test file.
It will show how to
overwrite a file.

C>_
```

WHAT'S HAPPENING? The file contents are identical. What used to be inside the file called `test.txt` located on the DATA disk has been overwritten or replaced (gone forever) by the contents of the file called `test.txt` located on the ACTIVITIES disk. You should be aware of how this procedure works so that you do not overwrite a file accidentally. Overwriting also occurs on the same disk or subdirectory if the source file and destination file have different names.

STEP 10: Key in the following:

`A>TYPE B:test.txt <Enter>`

STEP 11: Key in the following:

`A>TYPE B:hi.txt <Enter>`

```
A>TYPE B:test.txt
This is a test file.
It will show how to
overwrite a file.

A>TYPE B:hi.txt
HELLO EVERYONE.
HOW ARE YOU?
ISN'T THIS FUN???

A>_
```

STEP 10: Key in the following:

`C>TYPE A:test.txt <Enter>`

STEP 11: Key in the following:

`C>TYPE A:hi.txt <Enter>`

```
C>TYPE A:test.txt
This is a test file.
It will show how to
overwrite a file.

C>TYPE A:hi.txt
HELLO EVERYONE.
HOW ARE YOU?
ISN'T THIS FUN???

C>_
```

WHAT'S HAPPENING? You have displayed two separate files on the screen, `hi.txt` and `test.txt`, which are on the DATA disk. The file names are different and the file contents are different.

STEP 12: Key in the following:

```
A>COPY B:test.txt B:hi.txt <Enter>
```

```
A>COPY B:test.txt B:hi.txt
    1 File(s) copied

A>_
```

STEP 12: Key in the following:

```
C>COPY A:test.txt A:hi.txt <Enter>
```

```
C>COPY A:test.txt A:hi.txt
    1 File(s) copied

C>_
```

WHAT'S HAPPENING? You did not get an error message telling you that you already had an existing file called `hi.txt`. DOS just overwrote the contents of `hi.txt` with the contents of `test.txt`. You can prove that this occurred by using the `TYPE` command.

STEP 13: Key in the following:

```
A>TYPE B:test.txt <Enter>
```

STEP 14: Key in the following:

```
A>TYPE B:hi.txt  <Enter>
```

```
A>TYPE B:test.txt
This is a test file.
It will show how to
overwrite a file.

A>TYPE B:hi.txt
This is a test file.
It will show how to
overwrite a file.

A>_
```

STEP 13: Key in the following:

```
C>TYPE A:test.txt <Enter>
```

STEP 14: Key in the following:

```
C>TYPE A:hi.txt  <Enter>
```

```
C>TYPE A:test.txt
This is a test file.
It will show how to
overwrite a file.

C>TYPE A:hi.txt
This is a test file.
It will show how to
overwrite a file.

C>_
```

WHAT'S HAPPENING? The contents of the existing file `hi.txt` were overwritten by the contents of the file `test.txt`. Overwriting files is the norm. The only time you do not overwrite a file is when the source file and the destination file on the same disk and same subdirectory have exactly the same file specification.

6.8 USING WILDCARDS WITH THE COPY COMMAND TO COPY FILES TO DIFFERENT DRIVES

In this chapter, in order to copy files from one disk to another, you had to key in each file name as a source and each drive designator and file name as a destination. This process can become very tedious, particularly when you wish to copy a group of files. Usually, you do work with groups of files. There is a shortcut you can take, using the global file specifications (wildcards) of * or ? that you used to copy files on the same disk in Chapter 5. Rather than having to key in the entire file name, you look for a common denominator so that you can copy the files as a group. You use the drive designator (`A:` or `B:` or `C:`) so that the `COPY` command knows which disk drive to look on for the files to copy and if you are in a subdirectory, you include the path name (the source) and the disk drive the files are going to be copied to (the destination).

ACTIVITY 6.9 USING WILDCARDS TO COPY DATA FILES TO ANOTHER DISK

STEP 1: The ACTIVITIES disk should be in Drive A. The DATA disk should be in Drive B:

STEP 2: Key in the following:

```
A>DIR *.dos  <Enter>
```

```
Volume in drive A is ACTIVITIES
Directory of A:\

WILDONE DOS 179 11-23-87  1:59p
WILDTWO DOS 180 11-23-87  1:59p
WILDTHR DOS 179 11-23-87  2:01p
    3 File(s) 210944 bytes free

A>_
```

STEP 1: You should be logged into the subdirectory `C:\junk`. You can be sure by keying in `C>CD \junk`. The DATA disk should be in Drive A.

STEP 2: Key in the following:

```
C>DIR *.dos  <Enter>
```

```
Volume in drive C is HARD DRIVE
Directory of C:\JUNK

WILDONE DOS 179 11-23-87  1:59p
WILDTWO DOS 180 11-23-87  1:59p
WILDTHR DOS 179 11-23-87  2:01p
    3 File(s) 75939845 bytes free

C>_
```

WHAT'S HAPPENING? Since global file specifications are so "global," before you initiate any activity, it is always a good idea to verify what files you are really going to select with the parameters you chose. `DIR` is a good command to use to check things out because all `DIR` does is display the files you have selected. Files are not affected by just displaying them. Another good idea, if you are worried about overwriting files on the destination disk, is to use the `DIR` command on the DATA disk.

STEP 3: Key in the following:

```
A>DIR B:*.dos  <Enter>
```

```
A>DIR B:*.dos

Volume in drive B is DATADISK
Directory of B:\

File not found

A>_
```

STEP 3: Key in the following:

```
C>DIR A:*.dos  <Enter>
```

```
C>DIR A:*.dos

Volume in drive A is DATADISK
Directory of A:\

File not found

C>_
```

WHAT'S HAPPENING? You have verified which files you are going to select to copy, and you have verified that there are no files by those names on the DATA disk. Now you can do the work you intended.

STEP 4: Key in the following:

```
A>COPY *.dos B:  <Enter>
```

```
A>COPY *.dos B:
WILDONE.DOS
WILDTWO.DOS
WILDTHR.DOS
   3 File(s) copied

A>_
```

STEP 4: Key in the following:

```
C>COPY *.dos A:  <Enter>
```

```
C>COPY *.dos A:
WILDONE.DOS
WILDTWO.DOS
WILDTHR.DOS
   3 File(s) copied

C>_
```

WHAT'S HAPPENING? You asked DOS to copy the contents of all the files with any file name and the file extension of `.dos` on the ACTIVITIES disk to the DATA disk. You want all the file names on the DATA disk to be the same as they are on the ACTIVITIES disk. As the files are found on the ACTIVITIES disk and copied to the DATA disk, you will see their names displayed on the screen, one file at a time.

NOTE: If the file names appear in a different order on the screen, it is nothing to worry about. This has to do with which files DOS found first on the source disk. It does not affect the outcome of the `COPY` command. All the files with `.dos` as an extension on the ACTIVITIES disk remain there; you are simply making copies of these files on the DATA disk, which is no different than keying in `A>COPY wildone.dos B:`, then `A>COPY wildtwo.dos B:`, and `A>COPY wildthr.dos B:` for two disk drive users. Hard disk users would have to key in `C>COPY  wildone.dos A:`, then `C>COPY  wildtwo.dos A:`, and `C>COPY  wildthr.dos A:`. The wildcards save keystrokes. Were the files copied?

STEP 5: Key in the following:

A>DIR *.dos <Enter>

STEP 5: Key in the following:

C>DIR *.dos <Enter>

STEP 6: Key in the following:

A>DIR B:*.dos <Enter>

STEP 6: Key in the following:

C>DIR A:*.dos <Enter>

```
A>DIR *.dos

Volume in drive A is ACTIVITIES
Directory of A:\

WILDONE DOS 179 11-23-87  1:59p
WILDTWO DOS 180 11-23-87  1:59p
WILDTHR DOS 179 11-23-87  2:01p
    3 File(s) 173056 bytes free

A>DIR B:*.dos

Volume in drive B is DATADISK
Directory of B:\

WILDONE DOS 179 11-23-87  1:59p
WILDTWO DOS 180 11-23-87  1:59p
WILDTHR DOS 179 11-23-87  2:01p
    3 File(s) 272384 bytes free

A>_
```

```
C>DIR *.dos

Volume in drive C is HARD DRIVE
Directory of C:\JUNK

WILDONE DOS 179 11-23-87  1:59p
WILDTWO DOS 180 11-23-87  1:59p
WILDTHR DOS 179 11-23-87  2:01p
    3 File(s) 75939845 bytes free

C>DIR A:*.dos

Volume in drive A is DATADISK
Directory of A:\

WILDONE DOS 179 11-23-87  1:59p
WILDTWO DOS 180 11-23-87  1:59p
WILDTHR DOS 179 11-23-87  2:01p
    3 File(s) 272384 bytes free

C>_
```

WHAT'S HAPPENING? By doing a directory display of the specified files, you now know that the *.dos files are still on the ACTIVITIES disk and you have copies of these files on the DATA disk. You can also use combinations of the ? and the *.

STEP 7: Key in the following:

A>COPY wild?.* B: <Enter>

STEP 7: Key in the following:

C>COPY wild?.* A: <Enter>

```
A>COPY wild?.* B:
WILD1.XXX
WILD2.YYY
WILD3.ZZZ
    3 File(s) copied

A>_
```

```
C>COPY wild?.* A:
WILD1.XXX
WILD2.YYY
WILD3.ZZZ
    3 File(s) copied

C>_
```

WHAT'S HAPPENING? Again, do not be concerned if the files do not appear on the screen in the exact order shown above. Note that you copied a different set of files. `wild?.*` is completely different from `*.dos`, even though the `*.dos` files all started with the word `wild`. You asked DOS to copy all the files that had names starting with `wild` but were only five characters in length (`wild?`). That is why the `wildone`, `wildtwo`, and `wildthr` files were not selected. Their file names are longer than five characters. The * represented any file extension which is why you could get files that had extensions of `.xxx`, `.yyy`, and `.zzz`.

STEP 8: Key in the following:

`A>COPY w*.* B:  <Enter>`

```
A>COPY w*.* B:
WILDONE.DOS
WILDTWO.DOS
WILDTHR.DOS
WILD1.XXX
WILD2.YYY
WILD3.ZZZ
WILDONE
    7 File(s) copied

A>_
```

STEP 8: Key in the following:

`C>COPY w*.* A:  <Enter>`

```
C>COPY w*.* A:
WILDONE.DOS
WILDTWO.DOS
WILDTHR.DOS
WILD1.XXX
WILD2.YYY
WILD3.ZZZ
WILDONE
    7 File(s) copied

C>_
```

WHAT'S HAPPENING? You copied all the files on the ACTIVITIES disk that started with the letter w and had any file name and any or no file extension. Note that you copied a file called `wildone` that has no file extension. You did overwrite files, but that was your intent. You can also use wild cards to copy files and change the file names on the destination disk.

STEP 9: Key in the following:

`A>COPY *.dos B:*.aaa  <Enter>`

```
A>COPY *.dos B:*.aaa
WILDONE.DOS
WILDTWO.DOS
WILDTHR.DOS
    3 File(s) copied

A>_
```

STEP 9: Key in the following:

`C>COPY *.dos A:*.aaa  <Enter>`

```
C>COPY *.dos A:*.aaa
WILDONE.DOS
WILDTWO.DOS
WILDTHR.DOS
    3 File(s) copied

C>_
```

WHAT'S HAPPENING? In this example you created three more files on the DATA disk that do not have the `.dos` extension (the source). Instead, all the new files have the file extension of `.aaa`.

STEP 10: Key in the following:

`A>DIR B:w*.* <Enter>`

```
A>DIR B:w*.*

Volume in drive B is DATADISK
Directory of B:\

WILDONE  DOS 179 11-23-87   1:59p
WILDTWO  DOS 180 11-23-87   1:59p
WILDTHR  DOS 179 11-23-87   2:01p
WILD1    XXX  63 11-23-87   2:03p
WILD2    YYY  63 11-23-87   2:04p
WILD3    ZZZ  63 11-23-87   2:04p
WILDONE       85 11-23-87  12:06p
WILDONE  AAA 179 11-23-87   1:59p
WILDTWO  AAA 180 11-23-87   1:59p
WILDTHR  AAA 179 11-23-87   2:01p
     10 File(s) 265216 bytes free

A>_
```

STEP 10: Key in the following:

`C>DIR A:w*.* <Enter>`

```
C>DIR A:w*.*

Volume in drive A is DATADISK
Directory of A:\

WILDONE  DOS 179 11-23-87   1:59p
WILDTWO  DOS 180 11-23-87   1:59p
WILDTHR  DOS 179 11-23-87   2:01p
WILD1    XXX  63 11-23-87   2:03p
WILD2    YYY  63 11-23-87   2:04p
WILD3    ZZZ  63 11-23-87   2:04p
WILDONE       85 11-23-87  12:06p
WILDONE  AAA 179 11-23-87   1:59p
WILDTWO  AAA 180 11-23-87   1:59p
WILDTHR  AAA 179 11-23-87   2:01p
     10 File(s) 265216 bytes free

C>_
```

WHAT'S HAPPENING? You successfully copied the files named `*.dos` from the ACTIVITIES disk. Note that on the directory display of the DATA disk you have three new `wild` files with the `.aaa` file extension. Not only did you copy the `*.dos` files from the ACTIVITIES disk, but as you copied them to the DATA disk you also changed the file names.

6.10 COMBINING TEXT FILES WITH THE COPY COMMAND

Sometimes it is useful to combine the contents of two or more text files. This is also known as **concatenation of files**. Concatenation means to link together. You might wish to concatenate if you have several short documents that would be easier to work with if they were combined into one file. When you combine files, nothing happens to the original files; they remain intact. You just create another new file from the original files. The syntax never changes. It remains `COPY [d:][path]source [d:][path]destination`.

ACTIVITY 6.11 COMBINING THE CONTENTS OF FILES USING THE COPY COMMAND

STEP 1: Remove the ACTIVITIES disk from Drive A. Insert the DATA disk in Drive A. A> should be displayed on the screen.

STEP 1: Your DATA disk should be in Drive A. Change the default drive to A. A> should be displayed on the screen.

WHAT'S HAPPENING? You may have noticed that this text often has you change the default drive and/or reiterates which disk is in which drive. Is this necessary? Yes and no. Obviously, as long as you follow the syntax, you can choose to have any drive as the default drive. And there are reasons for changing the default drive. One is to simplify the instructional process, but a more important reason is that when you work with computers, it is best to train yourself to follow certain patterns in order to minimize careless errors. A good pattern to follow is to go from left to right or from Drive A to Drive B. A computer will do exactly what you tell it to do and will do it quickly. What sophisticated computer users find is that they can get into big trouble very quickly by being too sure they know what they are doing. More than one user has overwritten or deleted files that they should not have been overwritten or deleted, simply by not paying attention to the default drive. The default drive is very important. For hard disk users, the default subdirectory is also very important. It is also very important to know which disk is which. Pay attention to the prompt; it tells where the activity is occurring.

NOTE: The following activities assume you did Suggested Activity 4 in Chapter 5, where you created three text files called employee.one, employee.two, and employee.thr. If you do not have these three files on the DATA disk, go back to the Suggested Activities in Chapter 5 and create these three files.

STEP 2: Key in the following:

A>TYPE employee.one <Enter>

STEP 3: Key in the following:

A>TYPE employee.thr <Enter>

```
A>TYPE employee.one
This is the employee file one.

A>TYPE employee.thr
This is the employee file three.

A>_
```

STEP 2: Key in the following:

A>TYPE employee.one <Enter>

STEP 3: Key in the following:

A>TYPE employee.thr <Enter>

```
A>TYPE employee.one
This is the employee file one.

A>TYPE employee.thr
This is the employee file three.

A>_
```

WHAT'S HAPPENING? You have displayed the contents of two files on the screen. Each file is unique with a different file name and different file contents. You are going to place the contents of these two individual files into a new file that will consist of the contents of the first file, `employee.one`, followed by the contents of the second file, `employee.thr`. The command line is one line. Do not hit `<Enter>` at the end of the line; wait until you see `<Enter>`.

STEP 4: Key in the following:

```
A>COPY employee.one +
employee.thr
joined.sam  <Enter>
```

```
A>COPY employee.one + employee.thr joined.sam
EMPLOYEE.ONE
EMPLOYEE.THR
        1 File(s) copied
A>_
```

STEP 4: Key in the following:

```
A>COPY employee.one +
employee.thr
joined.sam  <Enter>
```

```
A>COPY employee.one + employee.thr joined.sam
EMPLOYEE.ONE
EMPLOYEE.THR
        1 File(s) copied
A>_
```


WHAT'S HAPPENING? Note that the message says "`1 file copied.`" It seems as if you have too many parameters because the syntax is `COPY source destination`. However, you are still following the correct syntax for the `COPY` command. You are making one destination file out of two source files. What you did here was to say `COPY` (the command) the contents of the file called `employee.one` and the contents of the file called `employee.thr` (source) to a new file called `joined.sam` (destination). The + (plus sign) told DOS that the source had more to it than just one file. It also told DOS that you are joining files. The destination file is the last file name on the command line that does not have a plus sign in front. Look at Step 4. `joined.sam` has a space in front of it, not a plus sign, making `joined.sam` the destination.

STEP 5: Key in the following:

```
A>TYPE joined.sam  <Enter>
```

```
A>TYPE joined.sam
This is the employee file one.
This is the employee file three.

A>_
```

STEP 5: Key in the following:

```
A>TYPE joined.sam  <Enter>
```

```
A>TYPE joined.sam
This is the employee file one.
This is the employee file three.

A>_
```


WHAT'S HAPPENING? The contents of the file `joined.sam` consist of the contents of the file `employee.one`, followed immediately by the contents of the file `employee.thr`. Note that the contents in `joined.sam` do not show any file names. You do not know where one file ended and the next began. `joined.sam` is a new file, but you did not destroy or in any way alter the two original source files, `employee.one` or `employee.thr`. You can prove this by using the `TYPE` command.

STEP 6: Key in the following:

```
A>TYPE employee.one  <Enter>
```

STEP 7: Key in the following:

```
A>TYPE employee.thr  <Enter>
```

```
A>TYPE employee.one
This is the employee file one.

A>TYPE employee.thr
This is the employee file three.

A>_
```

STEP 6: Key in the following:

A>TYPE employee.one <Enter>

STEP 7: Key in the following:

A>TYPE employee.thr <Enter>

A>TYPE employee.one
This is the employee file one.

A>TYPE employee.thr
This is the employee file three.

A_

WHAT'S HAPPENING? As you can see, the source files remain unchanged. You merely created a third file from the contents of two files. You can join many files with the plus sign. However, you can also use wildcards to join files or concatenate them, so you do not have to key in all the file names. If you wanted to join all the files with a `.tmp` file extension and place them into a new file called `months.sam`, you would have to key in `A>COPY  jan.tmp + feb.tmp + mar.tmp + apr.tmp months.sam`. You can save many keystrokes by using wildcards.

STEP 8: Key in the following:

```
A>COPY *.tmp months.sam <Enter>
```

```
A>COPY *.tmp months.sam
JAN.TMP
FEB.TMP
MAR.TMP
APR.TMP
   1 File(s) copied

A>_
```

STEP 8: Key in the following:

A>COPY *.tmp months.sam <Enter>

A>COPY *.tmp months.sam
JAN.TMP
FEB.TMP
MAR.TMP
APR.TMP
   1 File(s) copied

A>_

WHAT'S HAPPENING? Using the wildcard has the same effect as keying in all the file names and connecting the source files with plus signs. DOS found each file with a `.tmp` file extension and wrote the contents of those files to a new file called `months.sam`. However, there is a risk in using wildcards. When you use a wildcard, DOS does the order of selection based on the order of the files on the disk and you have no way of knowing what that order is. In fact, your display could be different if you created the files in a different order or if you did not follow all the text instructions in precisely the order given. The thing to remember is that if you must have files copied in a specific order, the plus sign will order the files the way you specify. If you use a wildcard, DOS will select the order the files are copied.

STEP 9: Key in the following:

```
A>TYPE months.sam   <Enter>
```

```
A>TYPE months.sam
This is my January file.
It is my first dummy file.
This is file 1.
This is my February file.
It is my second dummy file.
This is file 2.
This is my March file.
It is my third dummy file.
This is file 3.
This is my April file.
It is my fourth dummy file.
This is file 4.

A>_
```

STEP 9: Key in the following:

```
A>TYPE months.sam   <Enter>
```

```
A>TYPE months.sam
This is my January file.
It is my first dummy file.
This is file 1.
This is my February file.
It is my second dummy file.
This is file 2.
This is my March file.
It is my third dummy file.
This is file 3.
This is my April file.
It is my fourth dummy file.
This is file 4.

A>_
```


WHAT'S HAPPENING? As you can see, you have joined together the contents of all the `.tmp` files into a new file called `months.sam`. Your original `.tmp` files remain as they were. If your display is not exactly like the display above, do not be concerned. DOS selected the files based on how your DATA disk has been set up. You can also concatenate files from different drives or different subdirectories, provided you use the drive designator and the path in front of the file name. For example, if you wanted to combine a file from the disk in Drive A and a file from the disk in Drive B, you would write the command as `A>COPY file.one + B:file.two file.thr`. The source in this example is `file.one`, located on the disk in Drive A, but since the default drive is A you did not need to place `A:` in front of `file.one`. The other source file connected by the `+` is `B:file.two`. You would need to include the B: in front of `file.two` because otherwise DOS would look for `file.two` only on the disk in Drive A, the default. The destination file is going to be on Drive A since no other drive was specified. The destination file will be called `file.thr`. If you want to combine a file from a subdirectory called `junk` on Drive C and a file in Drive A, you would write the command as `A>COPY file.one + C:\junk\file.two file.thr`. The source in this example is `file.one`, located on the disk in Drive A, but since the default drive is A, you did not need to place `A:` in front of `file.one`. The other source file connected by the `+` is `C:\junk\file.two`, located on drive C in the subdirectory `junk`. You need to include the `C:\junk` in front of `file.two` because otherwise DOS would look for `file.two` only on Drive A, the default. The destination file, `file.thr` is going to be on Drive A since no other drive or subdirectory was specified.

6.12 UNDERSTANDING VERIFY WHEN USING THE COPY COMMAND

There is another parameter you can use for the COPY command. This parameter is /V for verify. When this parameter is added to the COPY command, the command checks to insure that the sectors that are written to the destination disk are recorded correctly. Errors when writing to a destination disk are very rare. However, if you have a critical file or program that you wish to doublecheck, you can use this option. Verify does cause the COPY command to run more slowly because of the additional work. The /V is only effective during the duration of the COPY command.

ACTIVITY 6.13 USING VERIFY WITH THE COPY COMMAND

STEP 1: The DATA disk should be in Drive A. The A> should be displayed.

STEP 2: Key in the following:

```
A>COPY joined.sam good.sam /V  <Enter
```

```
A>COPY joined.sam good.sam /V
     1 File(s) copied

A>_
```

STEP 1: The DATA disk should be in Drive A. The A> should be displayed.

STEP 2: Key in the following:

```
COPY joined.sam good.sam /V  <Enter>
```

```
A>COPY joined.sam good.sam /V
     1 File(s) copied

A>_
```

WHAT'S HAPPENING? You copied the file called joined.sam (source) located on the DATA disk in Drive A to a new file called good.sam (destination), also on the DATA disk on Drive A. The COPY command not only copied the source file joined.sam, but as it copied, it verified with the /V parameter, that the destination file good.sam was correctly copied.

CHAPTER SUMMARY

1. The syntax of the copy command is COPY [d:][path]source [d:][path]destination. d: represents any lettered drive. path represents any subdirectory location. Because d: and path are enclosed in brackets, they are optional.
2. The syntax of the TYPE command is TYPE [d:][path]filename[.ext].
3. A subdirectory is a means to divide up a hard disk into more manageable portions. A subdirectory has a name. To locate a file on a subdirectory, you use the path. The path indicates the subdirectory's name.

4. You can copy files from one disk to another, if you provide the disk drive letter and/or path so DOS knows where to look. If you do not provide the disk drive letter and the path name, DOS always assumes the default. The default is indicated by the prompt displayed on the screen.
5. Wildcards can be used to copy files to different disks, provided that the proper disk drive letter, path, and subdirectory name are supplied to DOS.
6. When using wildcards to copy files, first use the `DIR` command with the wildcard specifications to be sure you know which files will be selected to be copied.
7. If you use `*.*` with a command, it will find all the files. Thus, `DIR *.*` will display all the files on the default drive. `COPY *.* B:` would copy all the files on the default drive to `B:`.
8. Overwriting files with the `COPY` command is the process whereby the contents of the source file copies over the contents of the destination file. The only time you cannot overwrite a file is when there is already a file with the identical name on the same disk and/or subdirectory.
9. Concatenation means combining the contents of files with the `COPY` command. The syntax is still `COPY source destination` but the source files are connected by a plus sign and there is only one destination file.
10. `/V` is a parameter, used with the `COPY` command, that verifies that the source files are copied properly.

REVIEW QUESTIONS

1. Explain what a subdirectory is.
2. Why are subdirectories primarily used on hard drives?
3. What is a path? How is it used?
4. The syntax of the `COPY` command is:
   `COPY [d:][path]source.fil [d:][path]destination.fil`
   What do the brackets mean? What does `d:` mean? Is `d:` keyed in? What does path mean? Is path keyed in?
5. You are now in Drive A. How would you write a command line to create a text file called `left.one` on the disk in Drive B?
6. Your default drive is A. How would you write a command line to copy a file called `old.txt`, located on the disk in Drive A, to the disk in Drive B, without changing the file name?
7. Your default drive is A. How would you write a command line to copy a file called `old.txt`, located on the disk in Drive A, to the disk in Drive B, changing the file name to `new.txt`?
8. The default drive is A. How would you write a command line to copy a file called `address.txt`, located on Drive C in a subdirectory called `\personal`, to the disk in Drive A?
9. You have a group of files located on Drive C that have the file extension `.txt`. You want to copy these files to a disk in Drive A. How would you do it?
10. How would you combine the contents of two files?
11. What is the most efficient way to combine the contents of several files?
12. What does overwriting of files mean?
13. Why or why not should a computer user be aware of overwriting of files?

14. Why would you want to make one or more additional files and copy them to another disk?
15. Why would you want to make a copy of a file on the same disk?
16. What parameter allows you to verify that a file has been copied correctly?
17. Under what circumstances would you verify copying a file?
18. Before you use wildcards to make copies of files, is there anything you should do first? Why?
19. Why is the default drive an important concept?
20. Why would you want to concatenate files?

TRUE/FALSE

1. When copying files, a different name must be given to a file if copied to a different disk.
2. Concatenation is a way of linking the contents of files.
3. Wildcards cannot be used when you concatenate files.
4. The command `A>COPY *.txt B:` will copy all files on the disk in Drive A with the file extension `.txt` to the disk in Drive B and give the files the same name on the disk in Drive B.
5. When `COPY A:payroll.dbf B:` is keyed in, all files named payroll having any file extension will be copied to the disk in Drive B.
6. When `COPY CON B:customer.lst` is keyed in, the contents of the file can be keyed in from the console.
7. When you key in `TYPE B:january.txt`, the `TYPE` command must be located on the disk in the default drive.
8. When you see `C>` displayed on the screen, it means that the system is presently running a program named C.
9. When `DIR B:*.bas` is keyed in, a directory of all files on the disk in Drive B that have the file extension `.bas` will be displayed.
10. When `COPY feb.txt B:feb.tmp` is keyed in, the original file, `feb.txt`, remains on the default drive and a new file, `feb.tmp`, is created on the disk in Drive B.

SUGGESTED ACTIVITIES

Two disk drive users: Place the DOS System Disk in Drive A and the DATA disk in Drive B. To begin, have your default drive be `A>`. Hard disk users: Place the DATA disk in Drive A. To begin, change the default to the area where the DOS System programs are. It may require two steps if the DOS System Disk is in a subdirectory. First key in C: and then log into the correct subdirectory as `C>CD \DOS`.

1. Copy all the files that begin with the letter F from the DOS System Disk to the DATA disk. Keep the file names the same on the DATA disk. Do a directory display of all the file names on the DATA disk that begin with the letter F. You may display more file names than those you copied. Print the screen.
2. Copy all the files that begin with the letter F from the DOS System Disk to the DATA disk. Keep the file names the same on the DATA disk but change the file extension to `.eee`. Use the `DIR` command to display only the `.eee` file names. Print the screen.
3. You are going to concatenate some files. Find all the files on the DATA disk that have the file extension `.aaa`. Put the contents of these files into a new file, also on the DATA disk, called `together.ace`. Print the contents of this new file. Do not use the `<Shift>` and `<PrtSc>` keys.

4. Create three text files on the DATA disk. Call the files yoursa.lab, yoursb.lab, and yoursc.lab. The contents of yoursa.lab are "This is a silly thing to write once." The contents of yoursb.lab are "This is even sillier to write this twice." The contents of yoursc.lab are "Now I have to write this a third time." Copy these .lab files to the DOS System Disk. Remember, hard disk users, if your DOS System Disk is in a subdirectory, you must include the path name in your destination. Display only the .lab file names on the DOS System Disk using the DIR command. Print the screen.
5. Make copies of the .lab files on the DATA disk. Keep the file name the same but make the file extensions .kkk. Do a directory display of only the .kkk file names. Print the screen with the file names displayed.
6. Find all the files on the DATA disk that have the file extension .kkk. Place the contents of these files into one new file on the DATA disk called extra.abc. Print the contents of the file called extra.abc. You do not want the file name but the contents of the file. Do not use the <Shift> and <PrtSc> keys.
7. On the DATA disk, overwrite the file named extra.abc with the contents of the file called wildone. Use the TYPE command to display the contents of extra.abc on the screen after you have overwritten it. Then print the screen.
8. Copy all the files that have .fil as a file extension from the ACTIVITIES disk to the DATA disk. Hard disk users, remember that these files are in the subdirectory junk. The path name would therefore be C:\junk*.fil. After these files have been copied to the DATA disk, prove that they are there. Use the DIR command, locate any files that have .fil as a file extension on the directory of the DATA disk, and display the file names on the screen. Then print the screen.

FILE MAINTENANCE: Using ERASE, DEL and RENAME

CHAPTER

7

CHAPTER OBJECTIVES

This chapter continues the discussion of the essential internal commands that help you manage and manipulate your files on a disk. The major internal commands are DIR, COPY, TYPE, DEL, and RENAME. This chapter focuses on the DEL and RENAME commands and also explains how to back up data files. After completing this chapter, you will:

Understand the major internal commands.

Understand how to delete files.

Understand how to rename files.

Be able to back up data files.

7.0 MATERIALS NEEDED

1. DOS System Disk
2. ACTIVITIES disk
3. DATA disk
4. A new disk or a disk that you no longer need

7.1 GETTING RID OF FILES WITH THE ERASE AND DEL COMMANDS

In the various activities completed previously, you have created many files. Some have been copies of other files, and some you created as text files with the `COPY CON filename.ext` command. Your DATA disk began as a disk absent of files other than the system files. As you have been working, the number of files on the disk has increased dramatically, typical when working with computers. There is a kind of Murphy's Law that says you create as many files as you have disk space. However, you do not want to keep files forever. The more files and/or disks you have, the harder it is to keep track of what disks have which files and which files are the ones you need. If you have floppy disks, you end up with many floppies and you're never sure what files are where. Looking at a floppy disk tells little because a floppy disk's information is magnetically encoded; and if you have a hard disk, you can't even look at it because it's sealed. Thus, by keeping only the files you need on your disk, you decrease the number of files to manage.

Logic should tell you that if you can copy and create files, you should be able to eliminate files by deleting or erasing them. You can do these tasks with the `ERASE` or the `DEL` command. These commands are internal and always resident in memory. You do need to be careful with these commands. Once you hit `<Enter>` after the `ERASE` or `DEL` command, the file is gone, with no warning. DOS does not ask you if this is really the file you want to get rid of; it simply obeys your instructions.

A lost file cannot be recovered except by certain special utility programs, but they are chancy. Technically, what happens when you delete files is that DOS does not actually remove the file from the disk physically. It just removes the file entry from the FAT (File Allocation Table). The FAT "unallocates" the space that the data in the file occupied, even though, in fact, the data is still on the disk. When you create the next file, DOS sees that there is available space in the FAT and assigns the new file to that space. DOS then overwrites the old file with the new file. This is why some special utility programs such as Norton Utilities can occasionally help you recover deleted files, particularly if you realize immediately that you have inadvertently erased a file. However, once a file is overwritten by new data, nothing can recover the previous data. It is gone forever. When you use the DOS `ERASE` or `DEL` command, you cannot recover deleted files. There is no utility on the DOS System Disk that allows you to retrieve erased files.

The internal command to expunge files is either `ERASE` or `DEL`. What is the difference between these two commands? None. Both `ERASE` and `DEL` work precisely the same. There is no apparent reason for having two commands for getting rid of files. The syntax of the command is:

```
ERASE [d:][path]filename[.ext]
```

or

```
DEL [d:][path]filename[.ext]
```

Note that `ERASE` is spelled out and `DEL` is an abbreviation for delete. You can neither abbreviate `ERASE` as `ERA`, nor can you spell out `DELETE` for `DEL`. The commands must be used as they are specified. Most computer users key in `DEL` instead of `ERASE` for the simple reason that `DEL` has fewer characters. Computer users are big on saving keystrokes.

ACTIVITY 7.2 USING THE ERASE AND DEL COMMAND WITH INDIVIDUAL FILES ON THE SAME DISK

STEP 1: Place the DOS System Disk in Drive A. Boot the system. Be sure the **A>** is displayed.

STEP 1: Boot the System. Be sure **C>** is displayed on the screen.

STEP 2: Remove the DOS System Disk from Drive A. Insert the DATA disk in Drive A.

STEP 2: Insert the DATA disk in Drive A.

WHAT'S HAPPENING? The work you wish to do is to erase or delete files. Since **DEL** and **ERASE** are internal commands, two disk drive users no longer need the DOS System disk in Drive A. Hard disk users, when you booted the system from Drive C, you installed the operating system in memory. **DEL** and **ERASE** are commands in RAM. They will remain there until you turn off the power.

STEP 3: Do nothing.

```
A>_
```

STEP 3: Key in the following:

```
C>A:  <Enter>
```

```
A>_
```

WHAT'S HAPPENING? Hard disk users have changed the default drive to A. Two disk drive users already have the default drive as A.

NOTE: Two disk drive users will have the DATA disk in Drive A with the **A>** displayed. Hard disk users will also have the DATA disk in Drive A with the **A>** displayed.

STEP 4: Key in the following:

```
A>DIR wildone.aaa  <Enter>
```

```
Volume in drive A is DATADISK
Directory of A:\

WILDONE   AAA     179   11-23-87    1:59p
        1 File(s)     196608  bytes free.

A>_
```

STEP 4: Key in the following:

```
A>DIR wildone.aaa  <Enter>
```

```
Volume in drive A is DATADISK
Directory of A:\

WILDONE   AAA     179   11-23-87    1:59p
        1 File(s)     196608  bytes free.

A>_
```

WHAT'S HAPPENING? You are seeing if the file called `wildone.aaa` is located on the DATA disk in Drive A. You got a "yes" answer; this file is on the disk.

STEP 5: Key in the following:

A>ERASE wildone.aaa <Enter>

```
A>ERASE wildone.aaa

A>_
```

STEP 5: Key in the following:

A>ERASE wildone.aaa <Enter>

A>ERASE wildone.aaa

A>_

WHAT'S HAPPENING? You are asking DOS to `ERASE` the file called `wildone.aaa`, located on the DATA disk in Drive A. You did not need to include the `A:`, because DOS assumed the default and looked only for the file called `wildone.aaa` on the disk in Drive A. However, it appeared that nothing happened. All you got on the screen was the `A>`.

STEP 6: Key in the following:

A>DIR wildone.aaa <Enter>

```
Volume in drive A is DATADISK
Directory of A:\

File not found

A>_
```

STEP 6: Key in the following:

A>DIR wildone.aaa <Enter>

Volume in drive A is DATADISK
Directory of A:\

File not found

A>_

WHAT'S HAPPENING? The file is there and was displayed in Step 4. Now, however, the message says the file is no longer there. You now know that DOS executed the `ERASE` command and removed the file called `wildone.aaa`. It is no longer on the DATA disk.

STEP 7: Key in the following:

A>DIR wildtwo.aaa <Enter>

```
A>DIR wildtwo.aaa

Volume in drive A is DATADISK
Directory of A:\

WILDTWO     AAA       180    11-23-87    1:59p
        1 File(s)        197632 bytes free.

A>_
```

STEP 7: Key in the following:

A>DIR wildtwo.aaa <Enter>

A>DIR wildtwo.aaa

Volume in drive A is DATADISK
Directory of A:\

WILDTWO   AAA   180   11-23-87   1:59p
        1 File(s)   197632 bytes free.

A>_

WHAT'S HAPPENING? This screen display indicates that the file named `wildtwo.aaa` is on the DATA disk in Drive A. Before you delete a file, it is always a good practice to verify that the file is on the disk and that you really want to remove it.

STEP 8: Key in the following:

A>DEL wildtwo.aaa <Enter>

```
A>DEL wildtwo.aaa

A>_
```

STEP 8: Key in the following:

A>DEL wildtwo.aaa <Enter>

A>DEL wildtwo.aaa

A>_

WHAT'S HAPPENING? The `A>` is displayed on the screen, indicating that the file was deleted. This can be verified by using the `DIR` command.

STEP 9: Key in the following:

A>DIR wildtwo.aaa <Enter>

```
Volume in drive A is DATADISK
Directory of A:\

File not found

A>_
```

STEP 9: Key in the following:

A>DIR wildtwo.aaa <Enter>

Volume in drive A is DATADISK
Directory of A:\

File not found

A>_

WHAT'S HAPPENING? The file called `wildtwo.aaa` is gone from the DATA disk in Drive A. As you can see, the `ERASE` command and the `DEL` command do exactly the same thing.

What if the file you want to erase is not on the disk?

STEP 10: Key in the following:

A>DEL nofile.xxx <Enter>

```
A>DEL nofile.xxx
File not found

A>_
```

STEP 10: Key in the following:

A>DEL nofile.xxx <Enter>

A>DEL nofile.xxx
File not found

A>_

WHAT'S HAPPENING? In order for DOS to execute the command, `DEL`, it must be able to find the file to delete.

STEP 11: Key in the following:

A>DEL <Enter>

STEP 11: Key in the following:

A>DEL <Enter>

A>DEL
Invalid number of parameters

A>_

A>DEL
Invalid number of parameters

A>_

WHAT'S HAPPENING? Not only must DOS find the file, it must also have a file to find. Remember the syntax is DEL filename. The "Invalid number of parameters" message is the computer equivalent of "Get rid of what file?" Unless you tell DOS precisely what to do, it will not know what to do.

7.3 USING WILDCARDS WITH THE DEL COMMAND

You have been erasing or deleting individual files one file at a time. Often, however, you want to erase many files—cleaning up your disk. It is tedious to erase many files one at a time. Just as you can use the global file specifications with the DIR and COPY commands, you can also use the wildcards with the ERASE or DEL command. These allow you to erase a group of files with a one-line command. However, you should be exceedingly careful when using wildcards with the DEL command. Once again, the strength of wildcards is also their weakness. Global means global. You can eliminate many files very quickly. If you are not careful you could erase files you want to keep. In fact, you probably will one day. This is known as "Oh no, not those files gone." This does not mean you should not use wildcards. They are far too useful and powerful. It is just a warning to be careful.

ACTIVITY 7.4 USING THE ERASE AND DEL COMMAND WITH WILDCARDS ON THE SAME DISK

NOTE: Both two disk drive users and hard drive users should have the DATA disk in Drive A. The default drive should be Drive A with the A> displayed on the screen.

STEP 1: Key in the following:

A>DIR *.tmp <Enter>

STEP 1: Key in the following:

A>DIR *.tmp <Enter>

```
A>DIR *.tmp

Volume in drive A is DATADISK
Directory of A:\

JAN          TMP     71       11-23-8    7:35p
FEB          TMP     73       11-23-8    7:42p
MAR          TMP     69       11-23-87   7:43p
APR          TMP     70       11-23-8    7:44p
         4 Files(s)   198656 bytes free

A>_
```


```
A>DIR *.tmp

Volume in drive A is DATADISK
Directory of A:\

JAN          TMP     71       11-23-8    7:35p
FEB          TMP     73       11-23-8    7:42p
MAR          TMP     69       11-23-87   7:43p
APR          TMP     70       11-23-8    7:44p
         4 Files(s)   198656 bytes free

A>_
```


WHAT'S HAPPENING? You should see four files that have `.tmp` as a file extension displayed on the screen. Prior to a global erase, it is always wise and prudent to key in `DIR` with the global file specification you are going to erase. This process allows you to confirm visually that you are not going to erase a file you want to retain.

STEP 2: Key in the following:

```
A>DEL *.tmp  <Enter>
```

STEP 2: Key in the following:

```
A>DEL *.tmp  <Enter>
```


```
A>DEL *.tmp

A>_
```


```
A>DEL *.tmp

A>_
```


WHAT'S HAPPENING? You asked DOS to erase or delete **every** file on the DATA disk in Drive A that has any file name and has the file extension `.tmp`. Note that only `A>` appears on your screen. The `DEL` command executed and erased those `*.tmp` files quickly and permanently. To verify this, you can use the `DIR` command.

STEP 3: Key in the following:

```
A>DIR *.tmp <Enter>
```

STEP 3: Key in the following:

```
A>DIR *.tmp <Enter>
```


```
A>DIR *.tmp

Volume in drive A is DATADISK
Directory of A:\

File not found

A>_
```


```
A>DIR *.tmp

Volume in drive A is DATADISK
Directory of A:\

File not found

A>_
```

WHAT'S HAPPENING? Those `*.tmp` files are, indeed, gone from the DATA disk and therefore not recoverable. Again, let it be emphasized that before you use a wildcard to delete groups of files, you should use the `DIR` command to see what files you are going to delete. For instance, if you had a file called `test.tmp` that you had forgotten about, the directory display would include it as follows:

```
A>DIR *.tmp

Volume in drive A is DATADISK
Directory of A:\

JAN          TMP       71      11-23-8    7:35p
FEB          TMP       73      11-23-8    7:42p
MAR          TMP       69      11-23-87   7:43p
APR          TMP       70      11-23-8    7:44p
TEST         TMP     1222       6-15-87   6:20a
        5 File(s)    198656 bytes free

A>_
```

Using the `DIR` command with the wildcards and the `DEL` command will let you display on the screen all the files that have been selected by `*.tmp`, which includes the `test.tmp` file that you did not want to erase. If you had keyed in `DEL *.tmp`, all the above files would have been deleted. Remember, the computer does not come back and tell you that, "Oh, by the way, `test.tmp` is also included with the `*.tmp` files; did you want to erase that file?" The `DEL` command simply eliminates all the `.tmp` files because that is what you told it to do.

7.5 USING THE ERASE/DEL COMMAND ON ANOTHER DRIVE

Using the `DEL` command to eliminate files works exactly the same on other drives, with or without wildcards, as it did in the above activities. The syntax of the command remains `DEL filename`. The only difference is that you must specify which disk drive and which subdirectory DOS is going to look on prior to the file name. Once again, DOS follows your instructions exactly as keyed in; it does not check back with you to see if you are deleting the correct file. One of the most common mistakes computer users make is placing the drive designator or subdirectory in the wrong place, which completely changes the instructions you give DOS. Again, the syntax of the command is:

```
DEL [d:][path]filename[.ext]
```

`DEL` is the command. `d:` represents the designated drive. `path` represents any subdirectory. `filename.ext` represents the name of the file you wish to delete. If, for example, the file you want to delete is on Drive A, you would substitute `A:` for `d:`. If the file you want to delete is on Drive C, you would substitute `C:`

for the `d:`. If the path name was `\DOS`, you would substitute `\DOS` for `path`. `filename.ext` is the name of the file—the file specification. For example, if the default drive is `A>` and you want to delete a file on the disk in Drive B called `gone.fil`, a common error is to key in the command as:

```
A>DEL gone.fil B:
```

This is wrong because you did not use the proper syntax, `DEL d:filename.ext`. The command should have been keyed in as `DEL B:gone.fil`. Not only is the command wrong, it is also illogical, the equivalent of sending someone to throw away a file folder and not telling that person which file cabinet to look in. What are the results of incorrectly keying in the command? DOS will delete the file on the disk in Drive A, the default drive, and will not pay attention to the `B:`, which is in the wrong place. Remember to be aware of what the default drive is, and what the path is, and where the file is that you wish to delete.

ACTIVITY 7.6 USING THE ERASE AND DEL COMMAND ON ANOTHER DRIVE

STEP 1: Remove the DATA disk from Drive A. Insert it into Drive B.

STEP 1: Be sure the DATA disk is in Drive A.

STEP 2: Get the disk labeled ACTIVITIES. Insert it into Drive A.

STEP 2: Key in the following:

```
A>C: <Enter>
```

NOTE: The default for two disk drive users should be `A>`. The default for hard disk users should be `C>`.

STEP 3: Do nothing.

STEP 3: Key in the following:

```
C>COPY A:hello.txt  <Enter>
```

```
C>COPY A:hello.txt
        1 File(s) copied

C>_
```

WHAT'S HAPPENING? Two disk drive users did not have to do anything as the ACTIVITIES disk in Drive A already has a copy of the file called `hello.txt`. Hard disk users copied a file from the DATA disk in Drive A to Drive C, the hard disk. The purpose is to have two identically named files on different drives. The way the command is written may look incorrect because there is no apparent destination. The source is the DATA disk in Drive A and the file name is `hello.txt`. Here, the destination follows the default values. Since you did not key in a drive as a destination, DOS assumes the default or `C:`, and since you did not give it a new file name, DOS assumes the default or the same file name. The longhand version of the command is `C>COPY A:hello.txt C:hello.txt`. If the hard disk user was logged into a subdirectory called `\DOS`, the longhand version of the command would be `C>COPY A:hello.txt C:\DOS\hello.txt`. The default, in that case, is the disk drive and the subdirectory.

STEP 4: Key in the following:

`A>DIR hello.txt <Enter>`

```
A>DIR hello.txt

Volume in drive A is ACTIVITIES
Directory of A:\

HELLO   TXT    51 11-23-87    1:12p
    1 File(s)  173056 bytes free

A>_
```

STEP 5: Key in the following:

`A>DIR B:hello.txt <Enter>`

```
A>DIR B:hello.txt

Volume in drive B is DATADISK
Directory of B:\

HELLO   TXT 51 11-23-87    1:12p
    1 File(s)  202752 bytes free

A>_
```

STEP 4: Key in the following:

`C>DIR hello.txt <Enter>`

```
C>DIR hello.txt

Volume in drive C is HARD DRIVE
Directory of C:\

HELLO TXT 51 11-23-87   1:12p
   1 File(s)  7561216 bytes free

C>_
```

STEP 5: Key in the following:

`C>DIR A:hello.txt <Enter>`

```
C>DIR A:hello.txt

Volume in drive A is DATADISK
Directory of A:\

HELLO   TXT   51   11-23-87  1:12p
    1 File(s)  202752 bytes free

C>_
```

WHAT'S HAPPENING? You have two files called `hello.txt`. For two disk drive users one file is on the ACTIVITIES disk in Drive A. For hard disk users it is on the hard disk in Drive C. The other file is on the DATA disk in Drive B for two disk drive users or Drive A for hard disk users. You want to delete the file on the DATA disk, not on the ACTIVITIES disk or the hard disk.

STEP 6: Key in the following:

A>DEL B:hello.txt <Enter>

```
A>DEL B:hello.txt

A>_
```

STEP 6: Key in the following:

C>DEL A:hello.txt <Enter>

```
C>DEL A:hello.txt

C>_
```

WHAT'S HAPPENING? You have asked DOS to erase the file on the DATA disk called hello.txt. The file should be gone from the DATA disk but the file called hello.txt on the ACTIVITIES disk (two disk drive users) or Drive C (hard disk users) should still be there.

STEP 7: Key in the following:

A>DIR B:hello.txt <Enter>

STEP 8: Key in the following:

A>DIR hello.txt <Enter>

```
A>DIR B:hello.txt

Volume in drive B is DATADISK
Directory of B:\

File not found

A>DIR hello.txt

Volume in Drive A is ACTIVITIES
Directory of A:\

HELLO    TXT 51   11-23-87   1:12p
    1 File(s)  210944 bytes free

A>_
```

STEP 7: Key in the following:

C>DIR A:hello.txt <Enter>

STEP 8: Key in the following:

C>DIR hello.txt <Enter>

```
C>DIR A:hello.txt

Volume in drive A is DATADISK
Directory of A:\

File not found

C>DIR hello.txt

Volume in Drive C is HARD DRIVE
Directory of C:\

HELLO    TXT 51   11-23-87   1:12p
    1 File(s)  7561216 bytes free

C>_
```

WHAT'S HAPPENING? The file called hello.txt is still on the ACTIVITIES disk in Drive A (two disk drive users) or on the hard disk in Drive C (hard disk users), but the file called hello.txt on the DATA disk is gone. Had two disk drive users keyed in the command as A>DEL hello.txt or A>DEL hello.txt B:, the file would have been deleted on the ACTIVITIES disk in Drive A and not deleted on the DATA disk in Drive B. Had hard disk users keyed in the command as C>DEL hello.txt or C>DEL hello.txt A:, the file would have been deleted on the hard disk in Drive C and not deleted on the DATA disk in Drive A.

7.7 CHANGING THE NAMES OF FILES WITH THE RENAME COMMAND

Often, when you are working with various files, you find that you want to change a file name. For example, you may wish to indicate an older version of a file yet maintain the current version. `COPY` would not work because you would overwrite the file. Or you might think of a more descriptive file name. As the contents of a file change, the old name may no longer reflect the contents. Sometimes, the reason is that you made a typographical error when you first named the file. DOS supplies a way to change existing file names with the `RENAME` command. It is an internal command. `RENAME` does exactly what it says; it changes the name of a file, similar to relabeling a file folder. The contents of the file do not change, only the name of the file folder. Using `RENAME` is different from copying a file. When copying a file, you retain the original but make a copy; you start with one file and end with two. With the `RENAME` command you start with one file under one name and end up with the same file under a new name. The syntax for this command is:

```
RENAME [d:][path]oldfile[.ext] newfile[.ext]
```

or

```
REN [d:][path]oldfile[.ext] newfile[.ext]
```

Note that the `RENAME` command has two forms, `RENAME` or `REN`, with exactly the same syntax. Most computer users choose `REN`, simply because it has fewer keystrokes. The syntax is the command, `REN`; the first parameter, or the old file name; and the second parameter, or the new file name. Note that you are going from left to right.

ACTIVITY 7.8 USING THE RENAME COMMAND WITH INDIVIDUAL FILES ON THE SAME DISK

STEP 1: Remove the ACTIVITIES disk from Drive A. Insert the DATA disk in Drive A.

STEP 1: Be sure the DATA disk is in Drive A. Key in the following:

```
C>A:  <Enter>
```

```
A>_
```

WHAT'S HAPPENING? Hard disk users have changed the default drive to A. Two disk drive users already have the default as A.

NOTE: Both two disk drive users and hard disk users should have the DATA disk in Drive A. The default drive should be Drive A with the `A>` displayed on the screen.

STEP 2: Key in the following:

```
A>TYPE jan.new  <Enter>
```

```
A>TYPE jan.new
This is my January file.
It is my first dummy file.
This is file 1.

A>_
```

STEP 2: Key in the following:
A>TYPE jan.new <Enter>
A>TYPE jan.new
This is my January file.
It is my first dummy file.
This is file 1.
A>_

WHAT'S HAPPENING? You are displaying the contents of the file called `jan.new` located on the DATA disk in Drive A. You opened the file folder called `jan.new` and looked inside.

STEP 3: Key in the following:

```
A>REN jan.new jan.new  <Enter>
```

```
A>REN jan.new jan.new
Duplicate file name or File not found

A>_
```

STEP 3: Key in the following:
A>REN jan.new jan.new <Enter>
A>REN jan.new jan.new
Duplicate file name or File not found
A>_

WHAT'S HAPPENING? The message tells you that two files on the same disk cannot have the same name ("`Duplicate file name`") or DOS could not find a file called `jan.new` ("`File not found`"). In this example, the broken rule is "`Duplicate file name.`" You already have a file on the DATA disk called `jan.new`.

STEP 4: Key in the following:

```
A>REN jan.new newfile.tst <Enter>
```

```
A>REN jan.new newfile.tst

A>_
```

STEP 4: Key in the following:
A>REN jan.new newfile.tst <Enter>
A>REN jan.new newfile.tst
A>_

WHAT'S HAPPENING? Using the command REN, you asked to change the name of the file called jan.new to a new file name—newfile.tst. Since the default is Drive A, DOS will only look on the disk in Drive A for the file called jan.new. Once you pressed <Enter>, you got back only the A>. Did anything happen?

STEP 5: Key in the following:

A>DIR jan.new <Enter>

STEP 5: Key in the following:

A>DIR jan.new <Enter>

A>DIR jan.new

Volume in drive A is DATADISK
Directory of A:\

File not found

A>_

A>DIR jan.new

Volume in drive A is DATADISK
Directory of A:\

File not found

A>_

WHAT'S HAPPENING? Once you have renamed a file, it no longer exists under the old file name.

STEP 6: Key in the following:

A>DIR newfile.tst <Enter>

STEP 6: Key in the following:

A>DIR newfile.tst <Enter>

A>DIR newfile.tst

Volume in drive A is DATADISK
Directory of A:\

NEWFILE TST 71 11-23-87 7:35p
1 File(s) 203776 bytes free

A>_

A>DIR newfile.tst

Volume in drive A is DATADISK
Directory of A:\

NEWFILE TST 71 11-23-87 7:35p
1 File(s) 203776 bytes free

A>_

WHAT'S HAPPENING? The above display demonstrates that the file called newfile.tst is on the DATA disk. You know that the file named jan.new is no longer on the DATA disk. Are the contents of the file newfile.tst the same as the contents of the file jan.new?

STEP 7: Key in the following:

A>TYPE newfile.tst <Enter>

STEP 7: Key in the following:

A>TYPE newfile.tst <Enter>

```
A>TYPE newfile.tst
This is my January file.
It is my first dummy file.
This is file 1.

A>_
```


```
A>TYPE newfile.tst
This is my January file.
It is my first dummy file.
This is file 1.

A>_
```


WHAT'S HAPPENING? As you can see, you changed the file name from `jan.new` to `newfile.tst`, but the contents of the file did not change.

7.9 USING RENAME WITH WILDCARDS ON THE SAME DRIVE

When you wish to change the names of a group of files, you can use the **REN** or **RENAME** command with the wildcards, ? and *, allowing you to change many file names with a one-line command. The wildcards or global file specifications are so "global" that, prior to renaming files, it is wise to do a directory display with the wildcards you want to use so that you can see what files are going to be renamed. You do not want to rename a file accidentally. Once a file is renamed, you cannot find the file under its old name, ever. This has caused havoc for users because it seems that the file is lost. The file is still on the disk, but you can't find it unless you know the new name.

ACTIVITY 7.10 USING THE RENAME COMMAND WITH WILDCARDS ON THE SAME DRIVE

NOTE: Both two disk drive users and hard disk users should have the DATA disk in Drive A. The default drive should be Drive A with the A> displayed on the screen.

STEP 1: Key in the following:

```
A>DIR *.new   <Enter>
```

STEP 1: Key in the following:

```
A>DIR *.new   <Enter>
```


```
A>DIR *.new

Volume in drive A is DATADISK
Directory of A:\

FEB        NEW      73       11-23-87     7:42p
MAR        NEW      69       11-23-87     7:43p
APR        NEW      70       11-23-87     7:44p
         3 File(s)      203776 bytes free

A>_
```


```
A>DIR *.new

Volume in drive A is DATADISK
Directory of A:\

FEB        NEW      73       11-23-87     7:42p
MAR        NEW      69       11-23-87     7:43p
APR        NEW      70       11-23-87     7:44p
         3 File(s)      203776 bytes free

A>_
```

WHAT'S HAPPENING? You have three files with the extension `.new`. (Remember, `jan.new` was renamed `newfile.tst`.) Your objective is to retain these three files, keep their file names, and change the file extension from `.new` to `.87`. You could rename these files one at a time, `REN feb.new feb.87`, then `REN mar.new mar.87`, and `REN apr.new apr.87`. But this repetition becomes very tiresome. Using the wildcards allows you to rename these three files at one time.

STEP 2: Key in the following:

A>REN *.new *.87   <Enter>

STEP 2: Key in the following:

A>REN *.new *.87   <Enter>

```
A>REN *.new *.87

A>_
```

A>REN *.new *.87

A>_

WHAT'S HAPPENING? All that is displayed is the `A>`. Was the work done? Are the files renamed? To verify that you did rename these files, you can use the `DIR` command.

STEP 3: Key in the following:

A>DIR *.new   <Enter>

STEP 3: Key in the following:

A>DIR *.new   <Enter>

```
A>DIR *.new

Volume in drive A is DATADISK
Directory of A:\

File not found

A>_
```

A>DIR *.new

Volume in drive A is DATADISK
Directory of A:\

File not found

A>_

WHAT'S HAPPENING? Files with the extension `.new` no longer exist on the DATA disk.

STEP 4: Key in the following:

A>DIR *.87   <Enter>

STEP 4: Key in the following:

A>DIR *.87   <Enter>

```
A>DIR *.87

Volume in drive A is DATADISK
Directory of A:\

FEB      87      73      11-23-87    7:42p
MAR      87      69      11-23-87    7:43p
APR      87      70      11-23-87    7:44p
        3 File(s)     203776 bytes free

A>_
```

```
A>DIR *.87

Volume in drive A is DATADISK
Directory of A:\

FEB      87      73      11-23-87    7:42p
MAR      87      69      11-23-87    7:43p
APR      87      70      11-23-87    7:44p
        3 File(s)     203776 bytes free

A>_
```

WHAT'S HAPPENING? With the `REN` command and the use of the wildcards, you renamed three files with one command.

7.11 USING RENAME ON DIFFERENT DRIVES

Since `REN` is an internal command, you can use it at any time for any file in any drive. If you wish to rename a file on a different drive, you must specify on which drive the old file is located. In the syntax of `REN oldfile.ext newname.ext`, DOS looks only for `oldfile.ext` on the designated drive. If you do not preface `oldfile.ext` with a drive letter, DOS only looks on the default drive. When you key in the command as `REN B:oldfile.ext newfile.ext`, DOS will look only on the disk in Drive B for the file called `oldfile.ext`. If a subdirectory is involved, you must also include the subdirectory, so the command would be `REN C:\junk\oldfile.ext newfile.ext`.

In addition, there is a substantial difference between the `COPY` command and the `REN` command. With the `COPY` command, you can copy a file from one disk to another disk, ending up with two identical files on different disks. You cannot do this with the `REN` command because it only changes the names of files on one disk at a time. Remember, with `REN` you are changing the name of an existing file on a specific disk. `REN` finds a file on the designated disk and renames it. The `REN` command cannot and does not move a file from one disk to another. If, for example, you had a file cabinet (disk), and in this cabinet you had a file folder called oldfile (file) that you renamed newfile, that folder is still in the same file cabinet. It does not jump to another file cabinet by the mere act of changing the name.

ACTIVITY 7.12 USING THE RENAME COMMAND ON DIFFERENT DRIVES

STEP 1: Remove the DATA disk from Drive A. Insert the DATA disk in Drive B.

STEP 1: Be sure the DATA disk is in Drive A.

STEP 2: Insert the DOS System disk in Drive A. Be sure A is the default drive with the `A>` displayed on the screen.

STEP 2: Key in the following:

```
A>C:   <Enter>
```

```
C>_
```

WHAT'S HAPPENING? Hard disk users have changed the default drive to C. Two disk drive users have the DOS System Disk in Drive A. The default is Drive A where the DOS programs are located.

STEP 3: Key in the following:

```
A>DIR B:newfile.tst   <Enter>
```

```
A>DIR B:newfile.tst

Volume in drive B is DATADISK
Directory of B:\

NEWFILE  TST 71   11-23-87   7:35p
    1 File(s) 203776 bytes free

A>_
```

STEP 3: Key in the following:

```
C>DIR A:newfile.tst   <Enter>
```

```
C>DIR A:newfile.tst

Volume in drive A is DATADISK
Directory of A:\

NEWFILE  TST 71   11-23-87   7:35p
    1 File(s)   203776 bytes free

C>_
```

WHAT'S HAPPENING? The directory display tells you that the file called `newfile.tst` does exist on the DATA disk.

STEP 4: Key in the following:

```
A>TYPE B:newfile.tst   <Enter>
```

```
A>TYPE B:newfile.tst
This is my January file.
It is my first dummy file.
This is file 1.

A>_
```

STEP 4: Key in the following:

```
C>TYPE A:newfile.tst   <Enter>
```

```
C>TYPE A:newfile.tst
This is my January file.
It is my first dummy file.
This is file 1.

C>_
```

WHAT'S HAPPENING? You used the `TYPE` command to see the contents of the file called `newfile.tst`, located on the DATA disk.

STEP 5: Key in the following:

```
A>REN newfile.tst jan.87  <Enter>
```

```
A>REN newfile.tst jan.87

Duplicate file name or File not
    found

A>_
```

STEP 5: Key in the following:

```
C>REN newfile.tst jan.87  <Enter>
```

```
C>REN newfile.tst jan.87

Duplicate file name or File not
found

C>_
```

WHAT'S HAPPENING? The file called `newfile.tst` is on the DATA disk, which is in Drive B for two disk drive users and in Drive A for hard disk users. Since you did not preface `newfile.tst` with `B:` (two disk drive users) or `A:` (hard disk users), DOS only looked on the default drive, `A>` or `C>`, and because DOS could not find the file `newfile.tst`, it could not execute the `REN` command.

STEP 6: Key in the following:

```
A>REN B:newfile.tst B:jan.87 <Enter>
```

```
A>REN B:newfile.tst B:jan.87
Invalid parameter

A>_
```

STEP 6: Key in the following:

```
C>REN A:newfile.tst A:jan.87 <Enter>
```

```
C>REN A:newfile.tst A:jan.87
Invalid parameter

C>_
```

WHAT'S HAPPENING? The syntax of this command is:

```
REN [d:][path]oldfile[.ext] newfile[.ext].
```

Since DOS knows you cannot change a file name on any other disk except where the original file is located, it will not allow you to put a drive designator before the new file name.

STEP 7: Key in the following:

```
A>REN B:newfile.tst jan.87  <Enter>
```

```
A>REN B:newfile.tst jan.87

A>_
```

STEP 7: Key in the following:

```
C>REN A:newfile.tst jan.87<Enter>
```

```
C>REN A:newfile.tst jan.87

C>
```

WHAT'S HAPPENING? You see no messages because the syntax is correct. DOS could find the file called `newfile.tst` on the DATA disk. You are requesting that DOS change the name of the file on the DATA disk called `newfile.tst` to a new file name that is going to be `jan.87`.

STEP 8: Key in the following:

`A>DIR B:newfile.tst <Enter>`

```
A>DIR B:newfile.tst

Volume in drive B is DATADISK
Directory of B:\

File not found

A>_
```

STEP 8: Key in the following:

`C>DIR A:newfile.tst <Enter>`

```
C>DIR A:newfile.tst

Volume in drive A is DATADISK
Directory of A:\

File not found

C>_
```

WHAT'S HAPPENING? You get the message "`File not found`" because the file no longer exists under the file name `B:newfile.tst` (two disk drive users) or `A:newfile.tst` (hard disk users).

STEP 9: Key in the following:

`A>DIR B:jan.87 <Enter>`

```
A>DIR B:jan.87

Volume in drive B is DATADISK
Directory of B:\

JAN      87    71   11-23-87    7:35p
    1 File(s)    203776 bytes free

A>_
```

STEP 9: Key in the following:

`C>DIR A:jan.87 <Enter>`

```
C>DIR A:jan.87

Volume in drive A is DATADISK
Directory of A:\

JAN      87    71   11-23-87    7:35p
1 File(s)    203776 bytes free

C>_
```

WHAT'S HAPPENING? You have successfully renamed the file on the DATA disk from `newfile.tst` to `jan.87`. Does the file `jan.87` have the same contents as `newfile.tst`? It should, because renaming changes only the file name, not the contents. To verify this, you can use the `TYPE` command.

STEP 10: Key in the following:

`A>TYPE B:jan.87 <Enter>`

STEP 10: Key in the following:

`C>TYPE A:jan.87 <Enter>`

```
A>TYPE B:jan.87
This is my January file.
It is my first dummy file.
This is file 1.

A>_
```

```
C>TYPE A:jan.87
This is my January file.
It is my first dummy file.
This is file 1.

C>_
```

WHAT'S HAPPENING? If you check the screen display following Step 4, you will see that the file contents are identical.

7.13 BACKING UP YOUR DATA DISK

You should get into the habit of always backing up your disks so that if something happens to the original disks, you will have a copy of the original material. In data-processing circles, this is called Disaster and Recovery Planning. It means exactly what it says. If there is a disaster—fire, flood, power surge, theft, head crash, coffee spilled on a disk—what is your plan to recover your programs and data? Backing up programs on your application disks can be tricky, especially on copy-protected disks (which means you cannot back them up with regular DOS commands). You should never back up your program or software application disks until you understand how the application programs work. All application software comes with documentation that instructs you on how to back up the specific application program disk you own. Backing up a hard disk is a special circumstance, using special DOS commands. You cannot and should not back up the hard drive using the techniques that will be described here because the contents of a hard disk will not fit on one floppy disk.

However, you can and should back up all data disks with the following techniques. There are two ways to back up a data disk. One way is to use the `DISKCOPY` command, which makes an identical copy of a disk, track for track and sector for sector. Hard disk users, remember that `DISKCOPY` cannot be used to back up the hard disk.

You can also use the `COPY` command to back up some files. Typically, a data disk is backed up at the end of every work session to keep your data and files current. It is very important to acquire a regular backup routine so that it becomes an automatic process.

ACTIVITY 7.14 BACKING UP THE DATA DISK USING THE DISKCOPY COMMAND

STEP 1: You should have two disks, the DOS System Disk currently in Drive A and the DATA disk currrently in Drive B. The DOS System Disk is the program disk. The DATA disk has the files on which you have been working. You are going to back up the DATA disk, not the DOS System Disk or the program disk.

STEP 1: You should have the C> displayed and the DATA disk in Drive A. Remove the DATA disk from Drive A and insert the DOS System Disk in Drive A. This is the disk labeled DOS System Disk. This is the floppy disk that you made in Chapter 2. It is not the DOS installed on the hard disk. You should have two disks, the DOS System Disk currently in Drive A and the DATA disk outside the computer. The DOS System Disk is the program disk. The DATA disk has the files you have been using. You are going to be backing up the DATA disk, not the DOS System Disk or the program disk.

STEP 2: Get a blank disk, one that has not been used or one that you no longer want. Write Backup Data Disk on the label.

STEP 2: Same

STEP 3: The DOS System Disk should be in Drive A. Remove the DATA disk from Drive B and place it outside the computer.

STEP 3: The DOS System Disk should be in Drive A. Key in the following:

```
C>A:  <Enter>
```

```
A>_
```

WHAT'S HAPPENING? Hard disk users have changed the default drive to A> because you only want to work with the floppy disk drive. You cannot use DISKCOPY from the hard disk or Drive C. Two disk drive users already have the default as A>.

STEP 4: Be sure the default prompt is A>. Key in the following:

```
A>DISKCOPY  <Enter>
```

STEP 4: Be sure the default prompt is A>. Key in the following:

```
A>DISKCOPY  <Enter>
```

```
A>DISKCOPY

Insert SOURCE diskette in Drive A

Press any key when ready.....
```


A>DISKCOPY

Insert SOURCE diskette in Drive A

Press any key when ready.....

WHAT'S HAPPENING? Be very careful at this point. You have called the program or external command, `DISKCOPY`, from the DOS System Disk in Drive A and loaded it into memory. You do not want to press a key yet. Think about this. If you hit a key at this moment, what disk is in Drive A or the SOURCE? The DOS System Disk is in Drive A (the source) and would copy to the disk that will be the destination, which means you would have two copies of the DOS System Disk and no copies of the DATA disk. What disk do you want to copy? You want a copy of the DATA disk that is outside your computer. You want the DATA disk as the source and your new blank disk, labeled Backup Data Disk, as the destination.

STEP 5: Remove the DOS System Disk from Drive A. Insert the DATA disk into Drive A. You have now made the DATA disk the source disk or what you want copied. Since you are using the `DISKCOPY` command, you do not have to worry about formatting a new disk because the `DISKCOPY` command formats a disk and then copies it.

STEP 5: Remove the DOS System Disk from Drive A. Insert the DATA disk into Drive A. You have now made the DATA disk the source disk or what you want copied. Since you are using the DISKCOPY command, you do not have to worry about formatting a new disk because the DISKCOPY command formats a disk and then copies it.

STEP 6: Press `<Enter>`

STEP 6: Press <Enter>

```
A>DISKCOPY

Insert SOURCE diskette in Drive A:

Press any key when ready....

Copying 40 tracks
9 Sectors/Track, 2 Side(s)
```


A>DISKCOPY

Insert SOURCE diskette in Drive A:

Press any key when ready....

Copying 40 tracks
9 Sectors/Track, 2 Side(s)

STEP 7: Do not do anything until you see the following screen display:

```
A>DISKCOPY

Insert SOURCE diskette in Drive A:

Press any key when ready....

Copying 40 tracks
9 Sectors/Track, 2 Side(s)

Insert TARGET diskette in drive A:

Press any key when ready...
```

STEP 8: Remove the DATA disk from Drive A. This was your source. Insert your blank disk, labeled Backup Data Disk, into Drive A. This is your target disk or destination, where you want the source copied to.

STEP 9: Now you are ready to "`Press any key when ready.`" You have copied the source into RAM and now you are going to write to the Backup Data Disk in Drive A.

STEP 10: Press `<Enter>`

STEP 11: Do not do anything until you see the following message on the screen:

```
Copy another diskette (Y/N)?_
```

STEP 12: Key in the letter n.

```
Copy another diskette (Y/N)?n

A>_
```

STEP 7: Do not do anything until you see the following screen display:

```
A>DISKCOPY

Insert SOURCE diskette in Drive A:

Press any key when ready....

Copying 40 tracks
9 Sectors/Track, 2 Side(s)

Insert TARGET diskette in drive A:

Press any key when ready...
```

STEP 8: Remove the DATA disk from Drive A. This was your source. Insert your blank disk, labeled Backup Data Disk, into Drive A. This is your target disk or destination, where you want the source copied to.

STEP 9: Now you are ready to "`Press any key when ready.`" You have copied the source into RAM and now you are going to write to the Backup Data Disk in Drive A.

STEP 10: Press `<Enter>`

STEP 11: Do not do anything until you see the following message on the screen:

```
Copy another diskette (Y/N)?_
```

STEP 12: Key in the letter n.

```
Copy another diskette (Y/N)?n

A>_
```

WHAT'S HAPPENING? DOS has completed the DISKCOPY program. You now have two copies of the DATA disk and one copy of the DOS System Disk. At the end of each work session, you should follow these steps to back up your DATA disk so you remain current. You do not need a brand-new backup disk each time. Keep using the same disk over and over. You are merely keeping current by today's date; you do not need a historical or archival record of each day's work. Some organizations, however, such as banks or the IRS may need to recreate such records so they will have not only a Disaster and Recovery Plan but also archival data.

STEP 13: Remove the disk labeled Backup Data Disk and keep it in a safe place until you need it again.

STEP 13: Remove the disk labeled Backup Data Disk and keep it in a safe place until you need it again.

7.15 BACKING UP FILES WITH THE COPY COMMAND

The following material is informational and meant only to be read. It is not an activity to be done. Using the DISKCOPY command backs up an entire disk. Often, however, you only need to back up files. Remember that you can also use the COPY command to back up specific files at any time. The syntax does not change; it is:

```
COPY [d:][path]source.[fil]
     [d:][path]destination.[fil]
```

COPY is the command. d: represents the disk drive designator where the file is located. path is the subdirectory. source.fil is the name of the file that you wish to copy—the source. d: represents the disk drive designator where you want the file copied to. destination.fil is the name of the file that is to be copied—the destination.

There is also a way to back up all files with one COPY command. Be sure that the destination disk is already formatted, because COPY does not format a new disk as DISKCOPY does.

It is easier to use the COPY command with a two disk drive system. Put the source disk in Drive A and the destination disk in Drive B. You would key in:

```
A>COPY *.* B:
```

A> is the default drive. COPY is the command. *.* means every file with every file extension, since * represents any and all characters; the first * represents any file name; the second represents any file extension. DOS will go to the source disk to find each file. As it copies the source file, it will list the file on the screen. B: represents the destination disk. since you give no file names following B:, DOS assumes that you want the same file name on the destination disk. If there is a file with the same name on the destination disk, DOS will overwrite it. Hard disk users can also use this command to COPY individual subdirectories, if there are not too many files to fit on a floppy disk. If you wanted to back up the subdirectory \junk, the command would be keyed in as:

```
C>COPY C:\junk\*.* A:
```

The wildcard, `*.*`, is the most global of the global file specifications. It means all the files, since all file names match it. `*.*` can be used with any command that allows the use of wildcards. However, be careful with this wildcard because every file means every file.

Hard disk users must be very careful not to key in `C>COPY *.* B:` or `C>COPY *.* A:`. You cannot and must not copy all the files from a hard disk to a floppy disk with the `COPY` command. There are too many files on the hard disk and they will not fit on a floppy disk.

CHAPTER SUMMARY

1. `DEL` or `ERASE` eliminates files.
2. The syntax for the `DEL` and `ERASE` commands are:
   `ERASE [d:][path]filename[.ext]`
   or
   `DEL [d:][path]filename[.ext]`
3. Wildcards can be used with `DEL` or `ERASE`.
4. `DEL` or `ERASE` does not eliminate the data on the disk, only the entry in the File Allocation Table. In DOS, there is no way to recover a deleted file.
5. Before you use wildcards with `DEL` or `ERASE`, it is wise to use the `DIR` command to see what is going to be erased.
6. You can change the names of files with the `RENAME` or `REN` command.
7. The syntax for renaming files is:
   `REN [d:][path]oldfile[.ext] newfile[.ext]`
   or
   `RENAME [d:][path]oldfile[.ext] newfile[.ext]`
8. Renaming can only be done on one drive or subdirectory. `RENAME` does not move files.
9. Renaming just changes the file name; it does not change the contents of the file.
10. With the `REN` command, you start with one file and end up with the same file with a new name. It is not like the `COPY` command, where you start with one file and end up with two, the original and the copy.
11. Wildcards can be used with the `REN` command.
12. Before you use wildcards with the `REN` command, it is wise to use the `DIR` command to see what files are going to be affected by the renaming.
13. Once a file is renamed, it cannot be found under the old name.
14. It is wise to make backup copies of any data files so that if something happens, you have another source to recover from.
15. You can back up the DATA disk with the `DISKCOPY` command or you can back up files on your DATA disk using the `COPY` command. `*.*` allows you to back up all the files.

REVIEW QUESTIONS

1. What is the syntax of the `DEL` command?
2. What is the purpose of the `DEL` command?
3. What is the difference between `DEL` and `ERASE`?
4. Why might you want to get rid of files on a disk?
5. What is the syntax of the `REN` command?
6. What is the difference between `REN` and `RENAME`?
7. Why would you want to change the name of a file?
8. What process would you use to make a backup copy of an entire data disk?
9. How can you create text files on a disk?
10. Why do you make backup copies of disks?
11. What does `*.*` represent?
12. If you keyed in:
    `A>DEL file.one`
    and got the message "`Bad command or file name,`" what could be wrong and what steps could you take to solve this problem?
13. If you keyed in:
    `A>REN b:file.one c:file.two`
    and got the message "`Invalid parameter`", what could be wrong and what steps could you take to solve this problem?
14. If you keyed in:
    `A>DEL B:*.txt`
    what would be the impact of that command?
15. If you keyed in:
    `A>REN *.two *.fil`
    what would happen to all the files with the extension `.two`?

TRUE/FALSE

1. `DISKCOPY` does not require that the target disk be formatted since it formats the target disk while it copies.
2. Files that are deleted can be recovered with a program from the DOS System Disk.
3. It is possible for two files to have the same name, if they are not on the same disk.
4. Using the `RENAME` command does not affect the original file name.
5. Prior to deleting files with wildcards, it is a good idea to use the `DIR` command with the wildcard specification to see what files are going to be deleted.
6. `RENAME` is an external command.
7. `DEL` is an internal command.
8. When you key in `A>DEL B:one.two`, the file called `one.two` will be deleted from the default drive.
9. `ERASE` and `DEL` are identical commands.
10. When you use the global file specification of `*.*`, you are asking for every file.

SUGGESTED ACTIVITIES

Two disk drive users: Place the DATA disk in Drive A. Begin the activities by having the default drive be `A>`. All activities will occur on the DATA disk.

Hard disk users: Place the DATA disk in Drive A. Begin by having the default drive be `A>`. All activities will occur on the DATA disk.

1. On the DATA disk, rename the file `yoursa.lab` to `nofile.xyz`. Using the `DIR` command, look for the file called `yoursa.lab`. Then look for the file called `nofile.xyz`. Print the screen that displays the result of these commands.
2. On the DATA disk, rename the file `nofile.xyz` back to `yoursa.lab`. Using the `DIR` command, look for the file called `nofile.xyz`. Then look for the file called `yoursa.lab`. Print the screen that displays the results of this command.
3. Rename all the files on the DATA disk that have a file extension of `.lab` to the same file name but with your initials as the file extension. For example, since my initials are czg, `.czg` would be my file extension. Be sure to use a wildcard. Clear the screen. Display the names of these new files with your initials as file extensions and print the screen that displays the results of these commands.
4. Do a directory display of all the files with the extension of `.kkk`. Make copies of all these files on the DATA disk with the same file name but the file extension of `.rrr`. Display the names of these copies with `.rrr` and print the screen that displays the results of this command.
5. Concatenate all the files on the DATA disk with a file extension of `.kkk`. Call the new file `plusfil.ttt`. Send the output of `plusfil.ttt` to the printer. Do not use the `<Shift>` and `<PrtSc>` keys.
6. On the DATA disk, copy the file called `plusfil.ttt` to a new file called `plus2.ttt`. Display the contents of the file `plus2.ttt` on the screen. Print the screen that shows these contents.
7. On the DATA disk, delete the file called `plus2.ttt`. Prove that it is no longer on the DATA disk by using the `DIR` command to find it. Print the screen that displays the results of this command.
8. On the DATA disk, delete all the files with the file extension of your initials (the files you created in Suggested Activity 3). Use a wildcard. Prove that these files are no longer on the DATA disk by using the `DIR` command to them. Print the screen that displays the results of this command.
9. On the DATA disk, delete any file with the extension `.ttt`. Delete any file with the extension `.eee`. Delete the file called `extra.abc`. Delete the file called `hi.txt`. Delete any file name beginning with `fi` regardless of the rest of the file name or file extension. Delete any file whose file name begins with `fo` regardless of the rest of the file name or file extension. Delete any file that begins with `fd` regardless of the rest of the file name and the file extension. Delete any file whose file name is `ditto` with any file extension. Do a directory display using the wide parameter. Print the screen of the wide display.
10. Back up your DATA disk.

INFORMATIONAL COMMANDS: CHKDSK, COMP, VER and LABEL

CHAPTER

8

CHAPTER OBJECTIVES

This chapter discusses the ability of an operating system to monitor itself by conveying information to the user. By using the command CHKDSK, you can get statistical information about the disk; by using COMP you can get information about files; by using VER you can see which version of DOS you have; and with LABEL you can change the volume label on a disk. After completing this chapter, you will:

Be able to elicit and understand statistical information about disks and memory with CHKDSK.

Understand contiguous and noncontiguous file layouts.

Understand how DOS chains files on a disk.

Be able to compare files.

Understand the concept of different software versions and releases.

Be able to use VER to find out what version of DOS is loaded into memory.

Be able to change the volume label on a disk.

8.0 MATERIALS NEEDED

1. DOS System Disk
2. ACTIVITIES disk
3. DATA disk
4. Backup Data disk

8.1 CHECKING A DISK AND MEMORY

There is information about your disks you often need. You need to know how much room is left on the disk so that you can add a new file. You want to know if there are any bad spots on a disk which can mean the loss of a file. Bad spots can come from a variety of sources such as a mishandled disk or a manufacturing defect. You want to know if a disk has the operating system on it or if it is a system disk. Using the DIR command would not help you because the system files are hidden and do not display on the screen. Occasionally, you might want to know if the files are being stored efficiently on a disk. Maybe you installed extended memory and want to be sure that it is being used, or you may have installed such RAM-resident programs as SideKick and want to know how much RAM you have for a program.

None of these tasks can be accomplished by merely looking at a disk or at memory, but you can find out this information by using a utility program called the CHKDSK command, an external command located on the DOS System Disk. In addition to showing the system files, which lets you know that a disk is a system disk, CHKDSK also gives other statistical information about a disk and about computer memory as well. The CHKDSK command analyzes the directory on a disk, making sure that the directory entries match the location and lengths of files with the File Allocation Table on the default drive (or designated drive). The command then supplies a disk and memory status report. After checking the disk, CHKDSK will report any errors and give information about the disk's total capacity, how many files are on a disk, and how much space is taken. CHKDSK will establish the space left on the disk for additional files and display the size of the computer's memory in terms of memory bytes. You should run the CHKDSK command occasionally for each disk to insure that your file structures have integrity.

ACTIVITY 8.2 USING THE CHKDSK COMMAND

STEP 1: Place the DOS System Disk in Drive A. Be sure that the A> is displayed on the screen. The DATA disk should be in Drive B.

STEP 1: Be sure the C> is displayed on the screen and that you are logged into the DOS System Disk on Drive C. The DATA disk will be in Drive A.

STEP 2: Key in the following:

```
A>DIR chkdsk.com  <Enter>
```

```
A>DIR chkdsk.com

Volume in drive A has no label
Directory of A:\

CHKDSK     COM     9435    3-07-85    1:43p
    1 File(s)    58368 bytes free
A>_
```

STEP 2: Key in the following:

```
C>DIR chkdsk.com  <Enter>
```

```
C>DIR chkdsk.com

Volume in drive C is HARD DRIVE
Directory of C:\

CHKDSK     COM     9435    3-07-85    1:43p
    1 File(s)    7651216 bytes free
C>_
```

WHAT'S HAPPENING? The `DIR` command told you that the program `chkdsk.com` is stored as a file on the DOS System Disk. `CHKDSK` is an external command. In order to execute or run this program, DOS has to be able to find it on a disk, load it into memory, and run the program. By keying in `DIR chkdsk.com`, you have verified that the file is on the disk. However, to execute the command or program, you have to call it.

STEP 3: Key in the following:

```
A>CHKDSK  <Enter>
```

```
A>CHKDSK

362496 bytes total disk space
 38192 bytes in two hidden files
262144 bytes in 36 user files
 61440 bytes available on disk

655360 bytes total memory
618272 bytes free
A>_
```

STEP 3: Key in the following:

```
C>CHKDSK  <Enter>
```

```
C>CHKDSK

Volume HARD DRIVE created Jun 23, 1987 2:31p

21225472 bytes total disk space
   49152 bytes in three hidden files
 6520832 bytes in 381 user files
14557184 bytes available on disk

  655360 bytes total memory
  618272 bytes free
C>_
```

WHAT'S HAPPENING? Do not worry if you do not see the same numbers displayed on your screen. These numbers are related to how the disk was formatted, whether there is a hard drive, the size of the hard drive, and how much internal memory is installed on a specific computer. In addition, if you see the line "`nnnn bytes in nn directories`," it is not relevant at this point. What is important is what the status report is telling you. Let us look at this example, line for line.

The first line on the screen tells you that the disk in Drive A has "`362496 bytes total disk space`." If you are looking at Drive C, you have "`21225472 bytes total disk space`." This is the entire capacity of the specific disk. Suppose you have a two-drawer filing cabinet. No matter what you do, the filing cabinet will only hold two drawers full of files.

The second line on the screen display indicates to you that you have "`38192 bytes in two hidden files`." If you are looking at the hard drive, you have "`49152 bytes in three  hidden files`." What are hidden files? On a DOS System Disk or the DOS utility area, which you booted from, these hidden files are `IBMBIO.COM` and `IBMDOS.COM`. The hidden files message informs you that this is a system disk. If you have a third hidden file, it is a volume label that is stored as a hidden file.

The third line on the screen display tells you that you have "`262144 bytes in 36 user files`." If you are looking at Drive C, the third line tells you that you have "`6520832 bytes in 381 userfiles`." A user file is any file that is stored on the disk. It does not have to be a file that you, the user, created. In this example, user files are program files, including the program files that came with the DOS System Disk.

The fourth line on the screen display, "`61440 bytes available on disk`," establishes how much room remains on the disk in Drive A for new files or information. If you are looking at Drive C, the hard disk, it displays "`14557184 bytes available on disk`," disclosing how much room is left on this disk for new files or information. What does this mean to you? A byte is one character such as the letter b, the letter c, or the number 3, or the punctuation mark ?. To give you a rough idea of what this means, a page of a printed novel contains about 2000 characters. Thus, a disk with a total capacity of 360,000 bytes could hold or store a maximum of about 180 pages of a novel. On the floppy disk in Drive A, there would be room for approximately 30 more pages of text (61440 divided by 2000 gives you 30 remaining pages). If you had a 20 meg hard disk (one megabytes means one million bytes) it would hold approximately 20,000,000 bytes or 10,000 pages of text. You can see why people like the capacity of hard disks. In the hard disk example shown, another 7300 pages could be stored on this specific hard disk. This approximation, however, is not entirely accurate because it does not take into account such things as programs stored in binary. Yet, it does give you an idea of disk capacity in "human terms." As you work with computers, you become accustomed to thinking in bytes. From these four lines of statistics you have information about a disk capacity.

After the fourth line on the display screen there are two blank lines. Then the fifth and sixth lines of information appear. This second group of numbers discloses the internal memory or RAM of the particular personal computer you are using. Memory and disk space are measured in bytes. Bytes are expressed in the context of the binary numbering system, as 2^0, 2^1, 2^2, and so on. Rather than being stated individually, bytes are grouped in kilobytes (K). One kilobyte is 2^{10}, or 1024. The odd 24 per thousand is dropped to simplify calculations. For all practical purposes the value of K is equal to 1000. Thus, 64K technically speaking would be $64 \times 1024 = 65536$ ($2^6 \times 2^{10} = 2^{16}$). In user terms, 64K is translated as 64,000 bytes, even though a 64K memory would actually have room for 65,536 bytes. Some common internal memory sizes transpose as shown in Table 8.1.

Table 8.1 Computer Memory Sizes

System Memory	Actual Number of Bytes
64K	65,536
128K	131,072
256K	262,144
512K	524,288
640K	655,360

In this example, the computer has "655360 bytes total memory," or, in computerese, it is a 640K machine. Remember that memory refers to the work space of the computer, which holds the programs and data while they are processed. If this computer has 655,360 bytes of total memory, why are there only "618272 bytes free"? Free means that you have only 618272 bytes available for data and programs. You must have an operating system installed in RAM (or memory) to be able to use the computer. When you booted the system and loaded the operating system, you loaded it into memory where the bytes remain resident.

STEP 4: Key in the following:

A>CHKDSK B: <Enter>

```
A>CHKDSK B:

Volume DATADISK    created Nov 23, 1987 8:10p

   362496 bytes total disk space
    38912 bytes in three hidden files
    63480 bytes in 38 user files
   260096 bytes available on disk

   655360 bytes total memory
   618272 bytes free
A>_
```

STEP 4: Key in the following:

C>CHKDSK A: <Enter>

```
C>CHKDSK A:

Volume DATADISK    created Nov 23, 1987 8:10p

   362496 bytes total disk space
    38912 bytes in three hidden files
    63480 bytes in 38 user files
   260096 bytes available on disk

   655360 bytes total memory
   618272 bytes free
C>_
```

WHAT'S HAPPENING? In Step 3, CHKDSK checked out the disk on the default drive (Drive A for two disk drive users and Drive C for hard disk users). Since you wanted to know about the status of the DATA disk, located in Drive B for two disk drive users and in Drive A for hard disk users, you had to ask specifically for that information and tell DOS which disk to check. In other words, you added a parameter (the parameter B: for two disk drive users and the parameter A: for hard disk users). This display looks similar to the first screen display. You have "362496 total disk space" because this is a 360K disk (360 × 1024 = 368640, rounded off to 360K). However, three hidden files are shown. When you formatted the DATA disk you used the /S option, which placed an operating system on the disk. This explains two hidden files. When you formatted this disk you also used the **/V** option, which allowed you to enter a volume label which is stored as a hidden file and therefore is the third hidden file. User files and bytes available will vary based on what is on the DATA disk. The last two lines displayed on the screen do not change, because you are still using the same computer and the amount of internal memory (RAM) on a specific computer does not vary. However, the statistical information about the disk does change because you have asked for information about a different disk. If you placed another disk in Drive B or Drive A, you would get different information about the files and the room left on the disk.

8.3 UNDERSTANDING INTERNAL AND EXTERNAL COMMANDS

In previous chapters, you have used the major internal commands: **DIR**, **COPY**, **RENAME**, **DEL**, and **TYPE**. You have also used some minor internal commands: **CLS**, **DATE**, and **TIME**. All of these commands are installed in RAM when you boot the system. If you take out the DOS System Disk from Drive A (two disk drive users) and/or change the default drive from the DOS System Disk (both two disk drive and hard disk users), you still have access to and use of any internal command because it is resident in memory for as long as the computer is on. External commands, however, have to be found on a disk and loaded into memory before they can be used. If DOS cannot find the external command on a disk, it gives you the message "Bad command or file name."

You have used a few external commands, among them **FORMAT**, **DISKCOPY**, and **DISKCOMP**. **CHKDSK** is also an external command. The next activity will demonstrate the use and relationship of internal and external commands.

ACTIVITY 8.4 USING THE COPY AND CHKDSK COMMANDS TO UNDERSTAND EXTERNAL AND INTERNAL COMMANDS

NOTE: Two disk drive users will have the DOS System Disk in Drive A with the **A>** displayed and the DATA disk in Drive B. Hard disk users will be logged into the DOS System Disk on Drive C and have the **C>** displayed. The DATA disk will be in Drive A.

STEP 1: Key in the following:

```
A>CHKDSK  <Enter>
```

STEP 1: Key in the following:

```
C>CHKDSK  <Enter>
```

```
A>CHKDSK

362496 bytes total disk space
 38912 bytes in two hidden files
262144 bytes in 36 user files
 61440 bytes available on disk

655360 bytes total memory
618272 bytes free
A>_
```

```
C>CHKDSK

Volume HARD DRIVE created Jun 23, 1987 2:31p

21225472 bytes total disk space
   49152 bytes in three hidden files
 6520832 bytes in 381 user files
14557184 bytes available on disk

  655360 bytes total memory
  618272 bytes free
C>_
```

WHAT'S HAPPENING? The CHKDSK command is located on the DOS System Disk, which is in Drive A for two disk drive users or in the DOS System Disk in Drive C for hard disk users. To execute or run the program, you keyed in CHKDSK at the system prompt. DOS first looked in memory for this command. Since CHKDSK is not an internal command, DOS could not find the program in RAM. It then went to the default disk (in Drive A for two disk drive users or in Drive C for hard disk users), located the program, loaded it into memory, and executed the program, giving you the above results.

STEP 2: Key in the following:

```
A>B:  <Enter>
```

```
B>_
```

STEP 2: Key in the following:

```
C>A:  <Enter>
```

```
A>_
```

WHAT'S HAPPENING? You have changed the default drive to where the DATA disk is located. For two disk drive users it is the disk in Drive B. For hard disk system users, it is the disk in Drive A.

STEP 3: Key in the following:

```
B>CHKDSK  <Enter>
```

```
B>CHKDSK
Bad command or file name

B>_
```

STEP 3: Key in the following:

```
A>CHKDSK  <Enter>
```

```
A>CHKDSK
Bad command or file name

A>_
```

WHAT'S HAPPENING? Since you keyed in CHKDSK at the system prompt, you are treating it as a program. DOS looked in memory for the CHKDSK program. Since it is an external command, DOS could not locate it. DOS then went to the disk in the default drive (Drive B for two disk drive users and Drive A for hard disk users). However, CHKDSK is not stored as a file on the DATA disk. DOS is not smart enough to go to any other disk to locate and load the CHKDSK program. It simply tells you that it could not find the command or program you keyed in, which is why you got the message "Bad command or file name." How can you solve the problem? One thing you could do is change the default drive back to where the CHKDSK program is located. Two disk drive users would key in the command A>CHKDSK B:. Hard disk users would key in the command C>CHKDSK A:.

Often, however, you do not wish to be constantly changing the default drive just to use a command. There is another alternative. Two disk drive users can copy the program CHKDSK from the disk in Drive A to the disk in Drive B so that when DOS looks for the CHKDSK program on Drive B, it will find it, load it, and execute it. Hard disk users can copy the program CHKDSK from the disk in Drive C to the disk in Drive A so that when DOS looks for the CHKDSK program on Drive A, it will find it, load it, and execute it.

STEP 4: Key in the following:

```
B>COPY A:chkdsk.com   <Enter>
```

```
B>COPY A:chkdsk.com
    1 File(s) copied
B>_
```

STEP 4: Key in the following:

```
A>COPY C:chkdsk.com   <Enter>
```

```
A>COPY C:chkdsk.com
    1 File(s) copied
A>_
```

WHAT'S HAPPENING? You are using the internal command COPY. Note that since COPY is an internal command, it does not matter which drive is the default drive. COPY is resident in memory and thus can execute. You still followed the proper COPY syntax, COPY source destination.

For two disk drive users, COPY is the command. The source is A:chkdsk.com. Note that you had to place A: in front of the file name because you want DOS to go to the disk in Drive A to find the file. Note also that now the CHKDSK command is being treated as a file called chkdsk.com stored on the disk in Drive A. The destination is implied. Since no drive was specified, the default (B:) will take precedence and since no file name was specified, the old file name will take precedence. The longhand version of the command is:

B>COPY A:chkdsk.com B:chkdsk.com.

For hard disk users, it is much the same. COPY is the command. The source is C:chkdsk.com. Note that you had to place C: in front of the file name because you want DOS to go to the hard disk, which is Drive C, to find the file. Note also that now the CHKDSK command is being treated as a file called chkdsk.com stored on the hard disk, which is Drive C. The destination is implied. Since no drive was specified, the default (A:) will take precedence and since no file name was specified, the old file name will take precedence. The longhand version of the command is:

A>COPY C:chkdsk.com A:chkdsk.com.

If chkdsk.com was stored in a subdirectory on Drive C called \DOS, the longhand version of the command would be:

A>COPY C:\DOS\chkdsk.com A:chkdsk.com.

STEP 5: Key in the following:

B>CHKDSK <Enter>

```
B>CHKDSK

Volume DATADISK    created Nov 23, 1987 8:10p
   362496 bytes total disk space
    38912 bytes in three hidden files
    73728 bytes in 39 user files
   249856 bytes available on disk

   655360 bytes total memory
   618272 bytes free
B>_
```

STEP 5: Key in the following:

A>CHKDSK <Enter>

```
A>CHKDSK

Volume DATADISK    created Nov 23, 1987 8:10p
   362496 bytes total disk space
    38912 bytes in three hidden files
    73728 bytes in 39 user files
   249856 bytes available on disk

   655360 bytes total memory
   618272 bytes free
A>_
```

WHAT'S HAPPENING? You did not get an error message, "Bad command or file name," because you copied the program called chkdsk.com to the disk in the default drive (Drive B for two disk drive users and Drive A for hard disk users). When you keyed in CHKDSK at the system prompt, DOS still could not find the program in memory because CHKDSK is not an internal command, but it could find it on the default disk. Once DOS found the program, it could load it into memory and run the command CHKDSK.

8.5 THE VERBOSE PARAMETER WITH THE CHKDSK COMMAND

The CHKDSK command has an exceedingly useful parameter, /V, known as running in the "verbose" mode. This parameter, in conjunction with the CHKDSK command, not only gives the usual status report but also lists every file on the disk, including hidden files. An important thing to remember about parameters is that they are associated with specific commands and perform specific tasks for those commands. The same parameter does not do the same thing with different commands. For instance, the /V you use with the COPY command means to verify the file as it is copied. When you use /V with the CHKDSK command, it displays all the files on the disk.

ACTIVITY 8.6 USING THE /V PARAMETER WITH THE CHKDSK COMMAND

STEP 1: Remove the DOS System Disk from Drive A. Insert the DATA disk in Drive A. The **A>** should be displayed.

STEP 1: The DATA disk should be in Drive A. The **A>** should be displayed.

NOTE: When you key in Step 2, the screen display will scroll by very quickly. There is a way to stop a screen from scrolling by "freezing the display." Simply hold the `<Ctrl>` key down and press the `<NumLock>` key. This freezes the screen display. After you press `<Enter>` in Step 2, immediately press the `<Ctrl>` key and the `<NumLock>` key. If you don't get it right the first time and the screen scrolls by too quickly, you can key in the command again.

STEP 2: Key in the following:

`A>CHKDSK /V  <Enter>`

STEP 3: Press the `<Ctrl>` key and the `<NumLock>` key simultaneously.

STEP 2: Key in the following:

`A>CHKDSK /V  <Enter>`

STEP 3: Press the `<Ctrl>` key and the `<NumLock>` key simultaneously.

```
A>CHKDSK /V
Volume DATADISK      created Nov 23, 1987 8:10p
Directory A:\
     A:\IBMBIO.COM
     A:\IBMDOS.COM
     A:\COMMAND.COM
     A:\DATADISK
     A:\EXERCISE.TXT
     A:\JANUARY.TXT
     A:\FEBRUARY.TXT
     A:\MARCH.TXT
     A:\APRIL.TXT
     A:\YOURSA.RRR
     A:\YOURSB.RRR
     A:\YOURSC.RRR
     A:\CHKDSK.COM_
```

```
A>CHKDSK /V
Volume DATADISK      created Nov 23, 1987 8:10p
Directory A:\
A:\IBMBIO.COM
A:\IBMDOS.COM
A:\COMMAND.COM
A:\DATADISK
A:\EXERCISE.TXT
A:\JANUARY.TXT
A:\FEBRUARY.TXT
A:\MARCH.TXT
A:\APRIL.TXT
A:\YOURSA.RRR
A:\YOURSB.RRR
A:\YOURSC.RRR
A:\CHKDSK.COM_
```

WHAT'S HAPPENING? Your display might be slightly different, depending on when you pressed the `<Ctrl>` and `<NumLock>` keys and what files you have on the DATA disk. The important files to note are at the top of the display, **IBMBIO.COM** and **IBMDOS.COM**. These are the two hidden system files that you have never seen displayed on the screen with the **DIR** command. That tells you absolutely that this is a system or bootable disk. In addition, note the file called DATADISK, which is the volume label for the DATA disk stored as a file.

STEP 4: To continue the display and "unfreeze" the screen, press any key.

```
    A:\FRANK.FIL
    A:\STEVEN.FIL
    A:\PERSONAL.FIL

362496 bytes total disk space
 38912 bytes in 3 hidden files
 73728 bytes in 39 user files
249856 bytes available on disk

655360 bytes total memory
618272 bytes free

A>_
```

STEP 4: To continue the display and "unfreeze" the screen, press any key.

```
    A:\FRANK.FIL
    A:\STEVEN.FIL
    A:\PERSONAL.FIL

362496 bytes total disk space
 38912 bytes in 3 hidden files
 73728 bytes in 39 user files
249856 bytes available on disk

655360 bytes total memory
618272 bytes free

A>_
```

WHAT'S HAPPENING? When you pressed any key, you allowed the command to continue executing, so the display continued scrolling. You also got the statistical and memory information at the end of the display for all the files on the disk. You can specify another drive and use the **/V** parameter. For instance, you could key in **A>CHKDSK B:/V** or **A>CHKDSK C:/V**.

8.7 CONTIGUOUS AND NONCONTIGUOUS FILES OR FRAGMENTED FILES

Contiguous means being in contact or touching. What does this have to do with files? Well, DOS divides a disk into numbered blocks called clusters. Clusters on a floppy are made of two 512-byte sectors. The number of sectors that make up a cluster on a hard disk vary depending on the size of the hard disk and the version of DOS being used. The FAT (File Allocation Table) keeps a record of the cluster number each file occupies. As DOS begins to write files on a new disk, it makes an entry in the disk's directory for that file and updates the FAT with the cluster numbers used to store that file. DOS writes files based on next available space. As DOS begins to write files to a disk, it writes the files in adjacent clusters. The files are considered to be **contiguous**. For example, if you began writing a letter to your senator, it would be stored on your disk in the manner shown in Figure 8.1.

Figure 8.1 One File in Clusters

senator	senator	senator				
cluster 1	cluster 2	cluster 3	cluster 4	cluster 5	cluster 6	cluster 7
cluster 8	cluster 9	cluster 10	cluster 11	cluster 12	cluster 13	cluster 14

The clusters with nothing in them are simply empty spaces on the disk. Now you decide to write a letter to your mother. DOS would write this new file to the next adjacent sector, which would begin with cluster 4 as shown in Figure 8.2.

Figure 8.2 Contiguous Files in Clusters

senator	senator	senator	mother	mother	mother	
cluster 1	cluster 2	cluster 3	cluster 4	cluster 5	cluster 6	cluster 7
cluster 8	cluster 9	cluster 10	cluster 11	cluster 12	cluster 13	cluster 14

These two files, `senator` and `mother`, are contiguous. Each part of each file follows on the disk. Now you decide to add a comment to your senator letter, which will make the `senator` file bigger. When DOS goes to write the letter to the disk, it looks for the next empty cluster, which is cluster 7. It would appear as shown in Figure 8.3.

Figure 8.3 Noncontiguous Files in Clusters

senator	senator	senator	mother	mother	mother	senator
cluster 1	cluster 2	cluster 3	cluster 4	cluster 5	cluster 6	cluster 7
senator						
cluster 8	cluster 9	cluster 10	cluster 11	cluster 12	cluster 13	cluster 14

The parts of the file named senator are separated, making these files **non-contiguous** or **fragmented**. The process becomes more complicated as you add and delete files. For example, if you delete the file `senator`, the FAT marks clusters 1, 2, 3, 7 and 8 as available even though the data actually remains on the disk. You then decide to develop a phone file, shown in Figure 8.4.

Figure 8.4 Adding a File

phone	phone	senator	mother	mother	mother	senator
cluster 1	cluster 2	cluster 3	cluster 4	cluster 5	cluster 6	cluster 7
senator						
cluster 8	cluster 9	cluster 10	cluster 11	cluster 12	cluster 13	cluster 14

If you then decide to write a letter to your friend Joe and another letter to your friend Mary, and to add to the `phone` file and to the letter to your mother, the disk would look as like Figure 8.5.

Figure 8.5 Adding More Files

phone	phone	joe	mother	mother	mother	joe
cluster 1	cluster 2	cluster 3	cluster 4	cluster 5	cluster 6	cluster 7
mary	mary	phone	phone	mother		
cluster 8	cluster 9	cluster 10	cluster 11	cluster 12	cluster 13	cluster 14

Thus, the parts of these files are broken up and no longer stored in adjacent clusters. They are now known as noncontiguous files or a fragmented disk. DOS will take longer to read noncontiguous files because the read/write heads must move around the disk to find all the parts of a file. You can see if files are contiguous or noncontiguous by using another parameter with the `CHKDSK` command.

ACTIVITY 8.8 USING THE CHKDSK COMMAND TO SEE IF FILES ARE CONTIGUOUS

NOTE: Two disk drive users will have the DATA disk in Drive A with the `A>` displayed. Hard disk users will have the DATA disk in Drive A with the `A>` displayed.

STEP 1: Key in the following:

`A>CHKDSK april.txt <Enter>`

```
A>CHKDSK april.txt
Volume DATADISK    created Nov 23, 1987 8:10p

      362496 bytes total disk space
       38912 bytes in three hidden files
       73728 bytes in 39 user files
      249856 bytes available on disk

      655360 bytes total memory
      618272 bytes free
   All specified file(s) are contiguous.
   A>_
```

STEP 1: Key in the following:

`A>CHKDSK april.txt <Enter>`

```
A>CHKDSK april.txt
Volume DATADISK    created Nov 23, 1987 8:10p

      362496 bytes total disk space
       38912 bytes in three hidden files
       73728 bytes in 39 user files
      249856 bytes available on disk

      655360 bytes total memory
      618272 bytes free
   All specified file(s) are contiguous.
   A>_
```

WHAT'S HAPPENING? The screen display supplies all the statistical information about the disk in Drive A and about memory. In addition, the last line states, "`All specified file(s) are contiguous.`" By adding the parameter of the file name `april.txt` after the `CHKDSK` command, you asked DOS to not only check the disk but also to look at the file `april.txt` to see if all the parts of this specific file are next to one another on the DATA disk. Are they contiguous? The message said "yes."

STEP 2: Key in the following:

A>CHKDSK *.txt <Enter>

STEP 2: Key in the following:

A>CHKDSK *.txt <Enter>

```
A>CHKDSK *.txt
Volume DATADISK    created Nov 23, 1987 8:10p
    362496 bytes total disk space
     38912 bytes in three hidden files
     73728 bytes in 39 user files
    249856 bytes available on disk

    655360 bytes total memory
    618272 bytes free

    All specified file(s) are contiguous.
    A>_
```


```
A>CHKDSK *.txt
Volume DATADISK    created Nov 23, 1987 8:10p
    362496 bytes total disk space
     38912 bytes in three hidden files
     73728 bytes in 39 user files
    249856 bytes available on disk

    655360 bytes total memory
    618272 bytes free

    All specified file(s) are contiguous.
    A>
```


WHAT'S HAPPENING? The command asked CHKDSK not only to give you the usual statistical information but also to see if all the files that have .txt as an extension are contiguous. By using wildcards, you can check a group of files with a common denominator. In this case, the common denominator is the file extension .txt. The message displayed on the screen said "yes." All the files with the extension .txt are contiguous.

STEP 3: Key in the following:

A>CHKDSK *.* <Enter>

STEP 3: Key in the following:

A>CHKDSK *.* <Enter>

```
A>CHKDSK *.*
Volume DATADISK    created Nov 23, 1987 8:10p

    362496 bytes total disk space
     38912 bytes in three hidden files
     73728 bytes in 39 user files
    249856 bytes available on disk

    655360 bytes total memory
    618272 bytes free

    A:\CHKDSK.COM
       Contains 5 non-contiguous blocks.
    A>_
```


```
A>CHKDSK *.*
Volume DATADISK    created Nov 23, 1987 8:10p

    362496 bytes total disk space
     38912 bytes in three hidden files
     73728 bytes in 39 user files
    249856 bytes available on disk

    655360 bytes total memory
    618272 bytes free

    A:\CHKDSK.COM
       Contains 5 non-contiguous blocks.
    A>_
```


WHAT'S HAPPENING? Your screen display may vary. It may not show the same files as noncontiguous. You may have more noncontiguous files, or you may have none. In that case you would have received the message, "All specified file(s) are contiguous." The point is that the CHKDSK command, followed by star dot star (*.*), checked every single file on the disk in Drive A to see if all the files were contiguous. *.* represents all files on the disk. Remember, when the disk has any noncontiguous files, the screen display would look as follows:

```
A>CHKDSK *.*
 Volume DATADISK    created Jun 10, 1987 8:10p

362496 bytes total disk space
 38912 bytes in three hidden files
 73728 bytes in 39 user files
249856 bytes available on disk

655360 bytes total memory
618272 bytes free

A:\FILE2
  Contains 2 non-contiguous blocks
A:\FILE3
  Contains 1 non-contiguous blocks
A:\FILE4
  Contains 3 non-contiguous blocks.
A>_
```

WHAT'S HAPPENING? What difference does it make if files are contiguous or not? It matters to the extent that noncontiguous files or a fragmented disk can slow performance. In other words, if a file is contiguous, DOS can find all its parts quickly, minimizing the amount of time the head has to spend in reading/writing to the disk. If files are noncontiguous, DOS has to look more extensively for all the parts of the file, which causes the read/write heads to fly about the disk. The longer the disk is used, the more fragmented it becomes, slowing its performance. However, on a floppy-based system with no hard disk, it does not make too much difference in performance. But there is a way to solve the problem with a floppy-based system: format a new disk. Place the newly formatted disk in Drive B, the old, fragmented disk in Drive A, and key in `A>COPY *.* B:`. As DOS executes the command, it finds the first file, including all the associated clusters, on the disk in Drive A and copies that file contiguously to the disk in Drive B. Then it goes to the second file. This is why the disk in Drive B must be newly formatted and also why you do not use the `DISKCOPY` command. `DISKCOPY` makes an identical, track for track, cluster for cluster, sector for sector version of an old disk to a new disk.

Where you notice a decline in performance is on a hard drive system. This is not so easy to fix. You cannot use the `C>COPY *.* A:` command. You would need to back up the hard disk, using the special hard disk backup command. Then you would need to reformat the hard disk—not a task to be taken lightly—and then restore all the programs with the special hard disk restore command. However, that would not really solve the problem. This sounds complex, and it is. The solution most hard disk users opt for is to purchase a special type of program that is not present on the DOS System Disk, a program that rearranges the storage on the hard disk so that each file is stored in sequentially numbered clusters. This makes all files contiguous.

8.9 COMPARING FILES

In the preceding activities, you have made copies of many files. As you may have noticed, the number of files on the disk continues to grow. The more files you have, the harder it is to remember which file is which. Many times you will want to know if two files with different names or two files with the same name might have the same contents. One method of checking the contents is to use the `TYPE` command with each file name (`TYPE filename.ext`) and compare the contents visually on the screen. Another way is to send the contents of each file to the printer and compare the contents of these files visually. (`COPY filename.ext PRN`). This is not too difficult when dealing with the dummy files you have created, because the contents of these files are very brief, but this is not the norm.

Usually, file contents are extensive and either one of these visual checks would be time-consuming. In addition, it would be very easy to miss small differences. Also, many programs are in binary format, the "nonsense characters," and there is no way to compare these files visually. It would be useful to have a command that would allow you to compare files quickly. You have already used the `DISKCOMP` command. `DISKCOMP` compares an entire disk, track for track, sector for sector. As the name `DISKCOMP` implies, the command compares disks, not files. That is why the `COMP` command exists. It allows you to compare the contents of any two files very quickly. DOS does the work for you and compares the files to see if they are identical. If you compare files that are different or have been modified, even by one character, you will get an error message.

COMP is an external command. Its syntax is:

```
COMP [d:][path]filename1[.ext] [d:][path]filename2[.ext]
```

`filename1.ext` and `filename2.ext` are the file names of the two files that you wish to compare. DOS will look for the first file name and if it does not find it, it will not look for the second file name. `d:` is the designated drive. You substitute the lettered drive if the file is not on the default drive. `path` is the path name and you substitute the subdirectory if it is not the default path.

ACTIVITY 8.10 USING THE COMP COMMAND TO COMPARE DIFFERENT FILES

STEP 1. Remove the DATA disk from Drive A. Insert the ACTIVITIES disk in Drive A. Key in the following:

```
A>TYPE april.txt <Enter>
```

STEP 1. Remove the DATA disk from Drive A. Insert the ACTIVITIES disk in Drive A. Key in the following:

```
A>TYPE april.txt <Enter>
```

```
A>TYPE april.txt
This is my April file.
It is my fourth dummy file.
This is file 4.
A>_
```


```
A>TYPE april.txt
This is my April file.
It is my fourth dummy file.
This is file 4.
A>_
```


STEP 2: Key in the following:

STEP 2: Key in the following:

```
A>TYPE wildtwo.dos  <Enter>
```


```
A>TYPE wildtwo.dos  <Enter>
```


```
A>TYPE wildtwo.dos
This is a file created to demonstrate how to
use wildcards.  Wildcards allow me to copy a group
of files using the wildcards symbols, * and ?.
It is my second wildcard file.
A>_
```


```
A>TYPE wildtwo.dos
This is a file created to demonstrate how to
use wildcards.  Wildcards allow me to copy a group
of files using the wildcards symbols, * and ?.
It is my second wildcard file.
A>_
```


WHAT'S HAPPENING? The file names are different and the file contents are different. Remember, `COMP` compares the contents of the files.

STEP 3: Key in the following:

STEP 3: Key in the following:

```
A>COMP april.txt wildtwo.dos <Enter>
```


```
A>COMP april.txt wildtwo.dos <Enter>
```


WHAT'S HAPPENING? The syntax of the command is correct. You are asking DOS to compare the contents of two files located on the ACTIVITIES disk in Drive A. The first file name is `april.txt`. You want to compare the contents of this file to the contents of a second file called `wildtwo.dos`. Because the default drive is `A>`, you did not have to specify the disk drive for each file. DOS will only look on Drive A, the default drive, for the two files you wish to compare.

```
A>COMP april.txt wildtwo.dos
Bad command or file name
A>_
```


```
A>COMP april.txt wildtwo.dos
Bad command or file name
A>_
```


WHAT'S HAPPENING? What seems to be wrong? The syntax is correct and the files do exist. Remember, `COMP` is an external command. The program, called `comp.com`, is not on the ACTIVITIES disk. Since `COMP` is an external command, DOS could not find it in memory. It then went to the disk in Drive A to find the command, but it could not find the program on the default drive. It indicated "`Bad command or file name.`"

In order for two disk drive users to execute the `COMP` program, there are two choices. You can place the DOS System disk in Drive A and the ACTIVITIES disk in Drive B; then you can key in the command as `A>COMP B:april.txt B:wildtwo.dos`. Or you can copy `comp.com` from the DOS System Disk to the ACTIVITIES disk. You are going to copy the command, stored as the program comp.com, from the DOS System Disk to the ACTIVITIES disk.

Hard disk users also have two choices. You can change the default to C:, where the DOS System Disk is, and key in the command as C>COMP A:april.txt A:wildtwo.dos, or you can copy comp.com from the DOS System Disk on Drive C to the ACTIVITIES disk. You are going to copy the command, stored as the program comp.com, from the DOS System disk to the ACTIVITIES disk.

STEP 4: Remove the ACTIVITIES disk from Drive A. Insert the ACTIVITIES disk in Drive B. Insert the DOS System disk in Drive A. Key in the following:	STEP 4: Key in the following: [Remember, if it is in a subdirectory, you must include the path name C:\DOS\comp.com]
A>COPY comp.com B: <Enter>	A>COPY C:comp.com <Enter>

WHAT'S HAPPENING? You have copied the file comp.com from DOS to the ACTIVITIES disk. Since you wanted it to have the same file name on the ACTIVITIES disk, you did not have to include the file name as a destination. You can verify that the command comp.com was copied by using the DIR command.

STEP 5: Key in the following:	STEP 5: Key in the following:
A>DIR B:comp.com <Enter>	A>DIR comp.com <Enter>
STEP 6: Key in the following:	STEP 6: Key in the following:
A>COPY chkdsk.com B: <Enter>	C>COPY chkdsk.com A: <Enter>
STEP 7: Key in the following:	STEP 7: Key in the following:
A>COPY chkdsk.com B:ck.com <Enter>	C>COPY chkdsk.com A:ck.com <Enter>

WHAT'S HAPPENING? You have copied the file, chkdsk.com, from the DOS System Disk to the ACTIVITIES disk with the same name. You then copied the file, chkdsk.com, from the DOS System Disk to the ACTIVITIES disk but with a different name, ck.com.

STEP 8: Remove the DOS System Disk from Drive A. Insert the ACTIVITIES disk in Drive A.	STEP 8: Do nothing.

STEP 9: Key in the following:

```
A>COMP april.txt wildtwo.dos <Enter>
```

```
A>COMP april.txt wildtwo.dos

A:APRIL.TXT and A:WILDTWO.DOS

Files are different sizes

Compare more files (Y/N)?_
```

STEP 8: Key in the letter n. This will take you back to the A>.

STEP 9: Key in the following:

A>COMP april.txt wildtwo.dos <Enter>

A>COMP april.txt wildtwo.dos

A:APRIL.TXT and A:WILDTWO.DOS

Files are different sizes

Compare more files (Y/N)?_

STEP 8: Key in the letter n. This will take you back to the A>.

WHAT'S HAPPENING? Since you now have the command COMP on the ACTIVITIES disk, the program will execute. However, the message is telling you that the two files you asked COMP to compare, april.txt and wildtwo.dos, are different sizes. If they are different sizes, the files cannot be the same and there is no point in continuing. The COMP command will go no further.

ACTIVITY 8.11 USING THE COMP COMMAND TO COMPARE IDENTICAL FILES

NOTE: The ACTIVITIES disk should be in Drive A and the A> should be displayed for both two disk drive users and hard disk users.

STEP 1: Key in the following:

```
A>TYPE april.txt <Enter>
```

```
A>TYPE april.txt
This is my April file.
It is my fourth dummy file.
This is file 4.

A>_
```

STEP 1: Key in the following:

A>TYPE april.txt <Enter>

A>TYPE april.txt
This is my April file.
It is my fourth dummy file.
This is file 4.

A>_

STEP 2: Key in the following:

```
A>TYPE apr.87  <Enter>
```

```
A>TYPE apr.87
This is my April file.
It is my fourth dummy file.
This is file 4.

A>_
```

STEP 2: Key in the following:

```
A>TYPE apr.87  <Enter>
```

```
A>TYPE apr.87
This is my April file.
It is my fourth dummy file.
This is file 4.

A>_
```


WHAT'S HAPPENING? The file names are different, but the file contents are identical. Remember that `COMP` compares the contents of the files.

STEP 3: Key in the following:

```
A>COMP april.txt apr.87  <Enter>
```

```
A>COMP april.txt apr.87

Eof mark not found

Files compare ok

 Compare more files (Y/N)?_
```

STEP 3: Key in the following:

```
A>COMP april.txt apr.87  <Enter>
```

```
A>COMP april.txt apr.87

Eof mark not found

Files compare ok

Compare more files (Y/N)?_
```


WHAT'S HAPPENING? The `COMP` command first determined that the files were the same size. It compared the two files character by character and found them identical: "`Files compare ok`." Do not be concerned about the message "`Eof mark not found`." It simply means that DOS did not include the end-of-file marker as a character in the file. Remember that files are written to the disk in clusters. One cluster points to the next cluster that contains data in the same file. When there is no longer data in a file, the last cluster does not point to any more clusters. Observe the graphical representation of this concept of **linked** or **chained** files in Figure 8.6.

Figure 8.6 Linked or Chained Files

```
this        is       tex       t.
--------------------------------------
FFF1       FFF2     FFF3      FFF4
FFF2       FFF3     FFF4      FFFF
            ^         ^         ^
 |__________|    |____|   |_____|
```

In the figure, the top line represents the data that is actually in a file. The second line represents the actual cluster number. The bottom line approximates the way the FAT links the files (FFFF has to do with hexadecimal representation). The first cluster is FFFl. When the FAT sees FFF2 in cluster FFFl, that tells DOS to go to the next cluster, FFF2. Cluster FFFl is linked to cluster FFF2, and FFFl is pointing to the location FFF2, which tells DOS that there is another part of the file. DOS goes to cluster FFF2 and reads it. When the FAT sees FFF3 in cluster FFF2, it tells DOS to go to the next cluster, FFF3. Cluster FFF2 is linked to cluster FFF3, and FFF2 is pointing to the location FFF3, indicating to DOS that there is another part of the file. DOS goes to cluster FFF3 and reads it. When the FAT sees FFF4 in cluster FFF3, it tells DOS to go to the next cluster, FFF4. Cluster FFF4 is linked to cluster FFF3, and FFF3 is pointing to the location FFF4, which tells DOS that there is another part of the file. DOS goes to cluster FFF4 and reads it. When DOS sees the FFFF, that tells it that this is the end, there are no more clusters, the file ended.

Often programs will have a special symbol that DOS can recognize called an **end-of-file marker**. When DOS sees that symbol, it knows that the file is finished and it does not need to read any more of a cluster. However, note that the data in this file ended before the end of the cluster, a common occurrence. There was no special end-of-file marker. DOS had to continue to read the rest of the cluster, even though there was no more data. DOS knew that there were no more clusters to read because there were no more pointers. Thus, when the message "`Eof mark not found. Files compare ok`" appears, DOS is indicating that it found no "official" end of the file. It did, however, read all the clusters that made up the file and found the two files to be identical. Later versions of DOS will read the <Ctrl>-Z as an end-of-file marker and will just give you the message, "`Files compare ok`".

What if you wished to use the `COMP` command again?

STEP 4: Key in the letter `y`.

```
A>COMP april.txt apr.87

A:APRIL.TXT and A:APR.87

Eof mark not found

Files compare ok

Compare more files (Y/N)?y

Enter primary file name

_
```

STEP 4: Key in the letter `y`.

```
A>COMP april.txt apr.87

A:APRIL.TXT and A:APR.87

Eof mark not found

Files compare ok

Compare more files (Y/N)?y

Enter primary file name

_
```


WHAT'S HAPPENING? DOS knows that `COMP` is an external command. Before it "dumps" the command from memory, it asks you if you want to use `COMP` again; if so, you do not have to reload the command from the disk. Note how DOS prompts you.

STEP 5: Key in the following:

```
mar.87  <Enter>
```

```
Enter primary file name
mar.87

Enter 2nd file name or drive id
_
```

STEP 6: Key in the following:

```
march.txt  <Enter>
```

```
Enter primary file name
mar.87

Enter 2nd file name or drive id
march.txt

Eof mark not found

Files compare ok

Compare more files (Y/N)?_
```

STEP 7: Key in the letter n.

```
A>_
```

STEP 5: Key in the following:

```
mar.87  <Enter>
```

```
Enter primary file name
mar.87

Enter 2nd file name or drive id
_
```

STEP 6: Key in the following:

```
march.txt  <Enter>
```

```
Enter primary file name
mar.87

Enter 2nd file name or drive id
march.txt

Eof mark not found

Files compare ok

Compare more files (Y/N)?_
```

STEP 7: Key in the letter n.

```
A>_
```


WHAT'S HAPPENING? You have compared another set of identical files, `march.txt` and `mar.87`. However, what if the files were the same size but had different contents?

STEP 8: Key in the following:

```
A>TYPE file2.czg  <Enter>
```

```
A>TYPE file2.czg
This is file 2.
A>_
```

STEP 8: Key in the following:

```
A>TYPE file2.czg  <Enter>
```

```
A>TYPE file2.czg
This is file 2.
A>_
```

STEP 9: Key in the following:

```
A>TYPE file3.czg  <Enter>
```

```
A>TYPE file3.czg
This is file 3.

A>_
```

STEP 9: Key in the following:

```
A>TYPE file3.czg  <Enter>
```

```
A>TYPE file3.czg
This is file 3.

A>_
```


WHAT'S HAPPENING? Note that these two files are identical, except that one has a 3 and the other has a 2.

STEP 10: Key in the following:

```
A>COMP file2.czg file3.czg  <Enter>
```

```
A>COMP file2.czg file3.czg

Compare errors at OFFSET D
File 1 = 32

File 2 = 33

Compare more files (Y/N)?_
```

STEP 10: Key in the following:

```
A>COMP file2.czg file3.czg  <Enter>
```

```
A>COMP file2.czg file3.czg

Compare errors at OFFSET D
File 1 = 32

File 2 = 33

Compare more files (Y/N)?_
```


STEP 11: Press `n`. This should take you back to the `A>`.

STEP 11: Press `n`. This should take you back to the `A>`.

WHAT'S HAPPENING? The message discloses that the files were identical in size (otherwise there was no point in continuing to compare them). However, when the `COMP` command checked each character in each file, it found only two differences and it told you where the differences were located. (It is telling you this in the hexadecimal, base-16 number system. Do not worry. You do not need to know hexadecimal numbers.) What is important is that the message tells you the files are not the same, even though the only difference is that `file2.czg` has a 2 and `file3.czg` has a 3. `COMP` literally compares character to character. You have been comparing text files, but the `COMP` command will compare any two files, even binary or program files. There is a program file on the ACTIVITIES disk called `ck.com`. Is this the same as `CHKDSK.COM`?

STEP 12: Key in the following:

A>COMP chkdsk.com ck.com <Enter>

STEP 12: Key in the following:

A>COMP chkdsk.com ck.com <Enter>

```
A>COMP chkdsk.com ck.com

A:CHKDSK.COM and A:CK.COM

Eof mark not found

File(s) compare ok

Compare more files (Y/N)?_
```


```
A>COMP chkdsk.com ck.com

A:CHKDSK.COM and A:CK.COM

Eof mark not found

File(s) compare ok

Compare more files (Y/N)?_
```


WHAT'S HAPPENING? The two program files are identical.

STEP 13: Press n. This will take you back to A>.

STEP 13: Press n. This will take you back to A>.

ACTIVITY 8.12 USING THE COMP COMMAND WITH WILDCARDS

NOTE: Two disk drive users will have the ACTIVITIES disk in Drive A with the A> displayed. Hard disk users will also have the ACTIVITIES disk in Drive A with the A> displayed.

STEP 1: As with many commands, you can also use the wildcards * and ? with the COMP command. Key in the following:

A>COMP *.fp *.swt <Enter>

STEP 1: As with many commands, you can also use the wildcards * and ? with the COMP command. Key in the following:

A>COMP *.fp *.swt <Enter>

```
A>COMP *.fp *.swt

A:FILE2.FP and A:FILE2.SWT

Files compare ok

A:FILE3.FP and A:FILE3.SWT

Files compare ok

A:FILE4.FP and A:FILE4.SWT

A:FILE4.SWT - File not found

Compare more files (Y/N)?_
```

```
A>COMP *.fp *.swt

A:FILE2.FP and A:FILE2.SWT

Files compare ok

A:FILE3.FP and A:FILE4.SWT

Files compare ok

A:FILE4.FP and A:FILE4.SWT

A:FILE4.SWT - File not found

Compare more files (Y/N)?_
```

STEP 2: Press `n`. This will take you back to `A>`.

STEP 2: Press `n`. This will take you back to `A>`.

WHAT'S HAPPENING? You have three files with the the `.fp` extension, `file2.fp`, `file3.fp`, and `file4.fp`. Beginning at the top, you are asking DOS to take `file2.fp`, find a file that has an identical file name with the extension `.swt` (`file2.swt`), and compare the two files (`file2.fp` and `file2.swt`). When the comparison for those two files is complete, DOS will go to the next file, `file3.fp`, and do the same (`COMP file3.fp file3.swt`). DOS carries out the instructions. However, when it gets to `file4.fp`, it can find no corresponding file, `file4.swt`. Therefore, DOS cannot compare these files ("`FILE4.SWT not found`"). Since the files that did compare are identical, you get the message "`Files compare ok.`"

8.13 UNDERSTANDING VERSION NUMBERS

These is a common numbering scheme used with almost all software programs. Software is often revised or changed in order to add more commands, called **enhancements**; to repair errors in the programs (bugs); or to incorporate the new advances in hardware. To keep track of these **versions** or **releases**, they are numbered. If you have version 1.0, you have an early version. If you have 3.2, you have a later release. You must know which release or version of software you are working with so that you know what commands are available. In addition, application software packages often require a certain version of DOS. When you purchase a software package, it is not merely comprised of disks; it also comes with what is known as **documentation** or the instructions for the package. One section, called System Requirements, will specify how much memory you need to run this package, as well as the needed version of DOS.

Although it is system software, DOS is still software that has been revised several times and will be revised in the future. DOS releases typically are associated with new hardware advances. The first version was numbered 1.0. The numbering scheme means that if the number preceding the decimal changes, there were major changes or enhancements. If the number following the decimal changes, only minor changes were made. Thus the differences between DOS 3.1 and 3.2 are minor. However, the differences between DOS 1.0 and 3.2 are significant. DOS is upwardly compatible but not downwardly compatible, which means that if you are using DOS version 3.3, it could read disks created under DOS version 2.1. However, if you are using DOS 2.1, it may not be able to read a disk created under DOS version 3.3, and the new commands available under version 3.3 would not be available to users of version 2.1.

You can see that it is important to know which version of DOS was loaded into memory. Most external DOS commands work correctly only when they are used with the same version of DOS in which they were located. In other words, if you booted with DOS version 2.1 and then placed a version 3.3 disk in the drive to run the `CHKDSK` command, an external program available under both versions, you would get an error message saying "`Incorrect DOS version`." DOS has an internal command, `VER`, to use to verify which version you used.

ACTIVITY 8.14 USING THE VER COMMAND

STEP 1: Key in the following:

```
A>VER  <Enter>
```

```
A>VER

IBM Personal Computer DOS Version 3.10

A>_
```

STEP 1: Key in the following:

```
A>VER  <Enter>
```

```
A>VER

IBM Personal Computer DOS Version 3.10

A>_
```


WHAT'S HAPPENING? This says that the version of DOS in this computer is 3.1. If you have a different version of DOS, it will appear here.

8.15 UNDERSTANDING THE LABEL COMMAND

You have been able to change the names of files with the `RENAME` command. When you formatted your disk in Chapter 4, you put a volume label on your DATA disk: `DATADISK`. Often, the contents of your data disk change, so you need a new volume label to reflect that change. You cannot use the `RENAME` command because the volume label is stored as a hidden file. There is a way to change this situation, however, by using DOS version 3.0 or above. Prior to 3.0, there was no way to change the volume label. However, later releases of DOS offer an external command called `LABEL`. The syntax for the label command is: `LABEL [d:]`.

The brackets represent an option which means that `LABEL`, when used without parameters, will assume the default drive. For instance, `A>LABEL` would assume you want to change the volume label on the disk in Drive A, since `A:` is the default. `d:` is a parameter that allows you to specify on which disk you want to change the volume label. For instance, `A>LABEL B:` would allow you to change the volume label on the disk in Drive B and `A>LABEL C:` would allow you to change the label on Drive C.

ACTIVITY 8.16 USING THE LABEL COMMAND

NOTE: Both two disk drive users and hard disk users will have the ACTIVITIES disk in Drive A with the `A>` displayed.

STEP 1: Key in the following:

A>LABEL <Enter>

```
A>LABEL
Bad command or file name

A>_
```

STEP 1: Key in the following:

A>LABEL <Enter>

```
A>LABEL
Bad command or file name

A>_
```

WHAT'S HAPPENING? LABEL is an external command and not on the ACTIVITIES disk. Two disk drive users, to use this command you have to either copy it from the DOS System Disk to the ACTIVITIES disk or place the DOS System Disk in Drive A. Hard disk users, you either have to copy it from the DOS System Disk in Drive C to the ACTIVITIES disk or log on to Drive C to the DOS System Disk.

STEP 2: Remove the ACTIVITIES disk from Drive A. Insert the DOS System Disk in Drive A. Insert the ACTIVITIES disk in Drive B. The A> should be displayed.

STEP 2: Key in the following:

A>C: <Enter>

```
C>_
```

WHAT'S HAPPENING? The default drive is now C. You should be logged into the DOS System Disk on Drive C and have the C> displayed. Remember that if the DOS System Disk is in a subdirectory, be sure that you are in that subdirectory.

STEP 3: Key in the following:

A>LABEL B: <Enter>

```
A>LABEL B:

Volume in Drive B is ACTIVITIES

Volume label (11 characters, ENTER for none)?_
```

STEP 3: Key in the following:

C>LABEL A: <Enter>

```
C>LABEL A:

Volume in Drive A is ACTIVITIES

Volume label (11 characters, ENTER for none)?_
```

WHAT'S HAPPENING? You are not asking DOS to look at the volume label as you do with the VOL command; you are asking DOS to change the label on the ACTIVITIES disk. Note how similar this message is to formatting a disk with the FORMAT /V command.

STEP 4: Press <Enter>

```
LABEL B:

Volume in Drive B is ACTIVITIES

Volume label (11 characters, ENTER for none)?

Delete current volume label (Y/N)?_
```

STEP 4: Press <Enter>

```
LABEL A:

Volume in Drive A is ACTIVITIES

Volume label (11 characters, ENTER for none)?

Delete current volume label (Y/N)?_
```

WHAT'S HAPPENING? You pressed <Enter> for no, but this is different from using FORMAT B:/V. This is a "used disk," and there already is a volume label. When you pressed <Enter>, the LABEL command gave you the option of retaining the current volume label on the ACTIVITIES disk or deleting the volume label completely.

STEP 5: Press y <Enter>

```
A>_
```

STEP 5: Press y <Enter>

```
C>_
```

WHAT'S HAPPENING? You just deleted the volume label, ACTIVITIES. To verify that the label is gone, you can use the VOL command to display the label on the ACTIVITIES disk.

STEP 6: Key in the following:

A>VOL B: <Enter>

```
A>VOL B:

Volume in drive B has no label

A>_
```

STEP 6: Key in the following:

C>VOL A: <Enter>

```
C>VOL A:

Volume in drive A has no label

C>_
```

WHAT'S HAPPENING? You displayed, not changed, the volume label on the ACTIVITIES disk, proving that there is no longer a volume label on the ACTIVITIES disk.

STEP 7: Key in the following:

A>LABEL B: <Enter>

STEP 7: Key in the following:

C>LABEL A: <Enter>

```
A>LABEL B:

Volume in Drive B has no label

Volume label (11 characters, ENTER for none)?_
```

STEP 8: Where the cursor is blinking, key in the following:

`ACTIVITIES <Enter>`

```
A>LABEL B:

Volume in Drive B has no label

Volume label (11 characters, ENTER for none)?ACTIVITIES

A>_
```

```
C>LABEL A:

Volume in Drive A has no label

Volume label (11 characters, ENTER for none)?_
```

STEP 8: Where the cursor is blinking, key in the following:

`ACTIVITIES <Enter>`

```
C>LABEL A:

Volume in Drive A has no label

Volume label (11 characters, ENTER for none)?ACTIVITIES

C>_
```

WHAT'S HAPPENING? The system prompt is displayed. You can use the `VOL` command to verify that the volume label was changed.

STEP 9: Key in the following:

`A>VOL B: <Enter>`

```
A>VOL

Volume in drive B is ACTIVITIES

A>_
```

STEP 9: Key in the following:

`C>VOL A: <Enter>`

```
C>VOL

Volume in drive A is ACTIVITIES

C>_
```

WHAT'S HAPPENING? You changed the label of the disk. Remember, the `VOL` command displays the volume label and is an internal command. `LABEL` is an external command and lets you **change** the volume label.

CHAPTER SUMMARY

1. The `CHKDSK` command allows you to get statistical information about disks and memory.
2. `CHKDSK` will tell you whether or not the disk has hidden files, how much room is left on the disk in bytes, how many files are on the disk, if there are any bad spots on the disk, how much total memory is on the computer, and how much memory is available.

3. Files that are contiguous have been written to the disk in adjacent clusters. Noncontiguous files are those that have been written to the disk in nonadjacent clusters. This is also known as a fragmented disk. It can slow the access time to a file. Using a file parameter with the `CHKDSK` command will verify whether or not the specified files are contiguous.
4. Clusters are made up of sectors. Clusters are the smallest unit written to on a disk. The amount of sectors in a cluster can vary. Clusters on a double-sided disk are made of two 512-byte sectors. The number of sectors that make up a cluster on a hard disk can vary.
5. If you use the `/V` parameter with the `CHKDSK` command, it not only checks the disk but also lists all the files on that disk.
6. The `COMP` command compares the contents of files. Both text and program files can be compared.
7. When DOS writes files to the disk, it maps them in the File Allocation Table (FAT). One cluster points to the next cluster in a file until there is no more data in that file.
8. Software is released under a version number. This is for the purpose of fixing problems or adding enhancements. The higher the number, the later the release.
9. DOS has had several releases. The most current is version 3.3. To find out what version is in memory, you can use the `VER` command, an internal command.
10. If you have version 3.0 or above, you can change the volume label of a disk with the `LABEL` command. Earlier releases of DOS did not have this command.

REVIEW QUESTIONS

1. What does the `CHKDSK` command do? Why should you use it?
2. What is a fragmented disk?
3. How can you tell whether files are contiguous? Why does it matter if files are contiguous?
4. What does linked or chained files mean?
5. What is the verbose mode? What does it show the user?
6. What does the `COMP` command do?
7. Look at the following screen display:

```
362496 bytes total disk space
 38192 bytes in two hidden files
262144 bytes in 36 user files
 61440 bytes available on disk

655360 bytes total memory
618272 bytes free
```

What are the hidden files? What are the user files?

8. Why are you interested in the version number of DOS that you are using? How would you find out what version number you are using?
9. What is the difference between the `VOL` command and the `LABEL` command?
10. What does "`Eof mark not found, Files compare ok`" mean?

TRUE/FALSE

1. External commands reside on disks and must be read into the computer's memory in order to execute the command.
2. The CHKDSK command may be used to determine the size of your computer's memory.
3. The VER command verifies that the data written on a disk has been correctly recorded.
4. The VOL command determines the volume of bytes stored on a disk.
5. COMP and DISKCOMP do exactly the same thing.
6. COMP can compare any two files, text or binary.
7. You cannot use wild cards with the COMP command.
8. CHKDSK /V displays the names of all the files on a disk, including any hidden files.
9. The LABEL command allows you to change the volume label on a disk.
10. The VOL command allows you to change the volume label on a disk.

SUGGESTED ACTIVITIES

1. Display the volume label of the ACTIVITIES disk. Do not use the LABEL command. Print the screen.
2. Check the status of the ACTIVITIES disk. Print the screen.
3. Check to see if all the files with the extension .dat on the ACTIVITIES disk are contiguous. Print this screen.
4. Use the verbose mode with the CHKDSK command on the ACTIVITIES disk. After the display has stopped scrolling, print the screen.
5. On the ACTIVITIES disk, compare the files right.red and dress.up. After the command has executed and the results of the comparison are on the screen, print the screen.
6. On the ACTIVITIES disk, compare all the files with the extension .red to all the files with the extension .up. Use a wildcard. After the command has executed and the results of the comparison are on the screen, print the screen.
7. Display the volume label of the DATA disk. Print the screen.
8. Change the volume label on the DATA disk from DATADISK to LESSONS. Display the new volume label and print the screen.
9. Change the volume label on the DATA disk from LESSONS to DATADISK. Display the new volume label and print the screen.
10. On the DATA disk, using the COPY CON command, create two files. One called blue.jaz will have the following contents: "This is file 1." The other file will be called green.jaz and its contents will be "This is file 2." Compare these two files. After the command has executed and the results of the comparison are on the screen, print the screen.
11. Check to see if all the files on the DATA disk are contiguous. Print this screen.
12. Display the version number of DOS you are using. Print the screen.
13. Back up the DATA disk.

EDLIN, THE TEXT EDITOR

CHAPTER

9

CHAPTER OBJECTIVES

This chapter discusses how to create and edit text files with the utility program, EDLIN, that comes with DOS. After completing this chapter, you will:

Be able to create a text file.

Be able to insert and delete lines.

Be able to list a file.

Exit from EDLIN with or without changes to a file.

Be able to print text files.

Be able to use the editing keys to correct errors.

9.0 MATERIALS NEEDED

1. DOS System Disk
2. DATA disk
3. Backup Data disk

9.1 A LINE EDITOR

The DOS System Disk contains many utility programs or external commands such as FORMAT or CHKDSK that we studied in previous chapters. These commands have been oriented to one task. You keyed in the command name, and the program executed one task, and then brought you back to the system prompt. EDLIN is another utility program on the DOS System Disk that can be used by anyone working at the system level. However, EDLIN acts like an application program. When you load EDLIN, it takes you into a separate program with its own commands and syntax.

What is EDLIN? It is a **line-oriented text editor.** It is not a word processor. It does not offer features like word wrap, formatting, or document printing. You cannot use cursor keys to move up and down the screen. You work on one line at a time, which is why it is called a line editor. The reason why you would want to use this tool instead of a powerful word processor is that it is helpful when you are writing a short memo and do not want to load your word processing package. EDLIN generates text files that have no special characters, as do many word processing programs, and it is extremely important for writing batch files, which you will learn about later.

9.2 USING EDLIN

You have created text files with the COPY command (COPY CON d:filename). However, there are disadvantages to this method. You could neither go back to correct any lines that had errors, nor could you edit an existing file. With EDLIN, you can create and edit documents. Indeed, it will edit any text file, no matter how it was created. You can also use EDLIN to create and change files that consist of lines of text data. You use a series of commands that work only with EDLIN. DOS commands do not work in EDLIN, because it is a separate program.

When you are in EDLIN, you key in lines of data and press <Enter> after each line. EDLIN will save a file, if you wish. If you do save a file, you can return to it later to make any necessary changes. Since EDLIN is a line editor, you can add lines, delete lines, or change lines, one line at a time. Each line is automatically numbered by EDLIN. These line numbers are not part of the file; they are only reference numbers and therefore will not print. When you add or delete lines, all the remaining lines are automatically renumbered.

EDLIN has its own commands and prompt. Its prompt is the asterisk, *, instead of A> or B> or C>. Remember, EDLIN is an external program or command. The syntax is:

```
EDLIN [d:][path]filename[.ext]
```

ACTIVITY 9.3 CREATING A NEW FILE WITH EDLIN

STEP 1: Boot the system. The DOS System Disk should be in Drive A. Insert the DATA DISK in Drive B.

```
A>_
```

STEP 1: Boot the system. Insert the DATA disk in Drive A.

```
C>_
```

STEP 2: Key in the following:

```
A>B:  <Enter>
```

```
B>_
```

STEP 2: Key in the following:

```
C>A:  <Enter>
```

```
A>_
```

WHAT'S HAPPENING? You have changed the default drive.

STEP 3: Key in the following:

```
B>EDLIN myletter.txt  <Enter>
```

```
B>EDLIN myletter.txt
Bad command or file name

B>_
```

STEP 3: Key in the following:

```
A>EDLIN myletter.txt <Enter>
```

```
A>EDLIN myletter.txt
Bad command or file name

A>_
```

WHAT'S HAPPENING? `EDLIN` is an external program and therefore not on the DATA disk. You could change the default drive to where `EDLIN` is located: `A>` for two disk drive users or `C>` for hard disk users. Now you are going to copy the file called `edlin.com`, located on the DOS System Disk to the DATA disk.

STEP 4: Key in the following:

```
B>COPY A:edlin.com  <Enter>
```

```
B>COPY A:edlin.com

   1 File(s) copied
B>_
```

STEP 4: Key in the following [Remember, if DOS is in a subdirectory, you must include the path name as well as the drive (`C:\DOS\edlin.com`)]:

```
A>COPY C:edlin.com  <Enter>
```

```
A>COPY C:edlin.com

   1 File(s) copied
A>_
```

WHAT'S HAPPENING? You did not have to specify the destination or the file name because you wanted the file `edlin.com` copied to the default drive, the DATA disk, with the same file name.

STEP 5: Remove the DOS System Disk from Drive A. Remove the DATA disk from Drive B. Insert the DATA disk in Drive A. Change the default to A:. If you have a system configuration of one floppy high-capacity drive and one floppy 360K disk drive, do not change disks nor the default drive. Leave the DATA disk in Drive B. The only difference in the rest of the activities in Chapter 9 will be that instead of seeing `A>`, you will see `B>`.

STEP 5: Do nothing.

NOTE: Both two disk drive users and hard disk users should have the DATA disk in Drive A; therefore, the default drive will be Drive A. The `A>` should be displayed on the screen. The instructions for both two disk drive users and hard disk users will be the same for the rest of this chapter.

STEP 6: Key in the following:

```
A>EDLIN myletter.txt   <Enter>
```

```
A>EDLIN myletter.txt
New file
*_
```

WHAT'S HAPPENING? You want to write a text file called `myletter.txt` to the DATA disk in the default drive. On the screen, `EDLIN` tells you that this is a new file. Your prompt is now the `*`.

STEP 7: Key in the following:

```
CLS   <Enter>
```

```
*CLS
Entry error
*_
```

WHAT'S HAPPENING? `CLS` is a DOS internal command that clears the screen, but you got an error message, "`Entry error`." DOS commands, internal or external, do not work in `EDLIN`, which has its own set of commands. The `*` indicates that you are at the prompt level. You now need to tell `EDLIN` what work you want to do. Since you want to enter data or text, you use the `*` as the prompt and follow with the command `i` for insert. Line editors work in **modes,** so you have to indicate what mode you are in. In this case it is the insert mode. The `i` tells `EDLIN` that you are ready to enter data.

STEP 8: Key in the following:

```
i  <Enter>
```

```
*i
  1:*_
```

WHAT'S HAPPENING? The command was i which tells EDLIN you are ready to enter data. EDLIN obeyed your command and presented you with a blank, numbered line, ready for data.

STEP 9: Key in the following:

```
This is my first edlin text file.  <Enter>
```

```
1:*This is my first edlin text file.
2:*_
```

WHAT'S HAPPENING? Note how EDLIN presented you with a new blank, numbered line. Since you are still in the insert mode, EDLIN is assuming you want to enter more data and will keep presenting you with blank lines.

STEP 10: Key in the following lines. Include the errors. You will learn how to correct them later. After you press <Enter>, you will see the next line number displayed.

```
this is the sexxond line of this file.  <Enter>
this is the third line of my gile.  <Enter>
This is the fourth line of my file.  <Enter>
```

```
1:*This is my first edlin text file.
2:*this is the sexxond line of this file.
3:*this is the third line of my gile.
4:*This is the fourth line of my file.
5:*_
```

WHAT'S HAPPENING? Note how EDLIN has moved to line 5. Anything following a line number is treated as text by EDLIN, but now you have to tell EDLIN you are finished keying in data. In other words, you want to get out of the insert mode and return to the EDLIN prompt, *. To indicate that you are finished keying in data you must send a special signal to EDLIN.

STEP 11: Press the <Ctrl> key. While pressing the <Ctrl> key, press the letter C on the keyboard.

```
*i
    1:*This is my first edlin text file.
    2:*this is the sexxond line of this file.
    3:*this is the third line of my gile.
    4:*This is the fourth line of my file.
    5:*^C
*_
```

WHAT'S HAPPENING? You are now back at the EDLIN prompt. You have completed keying in the data for this text file.

9.4 SEEING THE FILE

You have created a text file. If you wish to display what you have keyed in, you must use another command. L for list is the command that shows the contents of any EDLIN file. Note that EDLIN utilizes one-letter commands.

ACTIVITY 9.5 LISTING A FILE IN EDLIN

NOTE: You should still be in the EDLIN myletter.txt. The DATA disk is in Drive A, but you should see the * prompt. If you see the A>, you should key in EDLIN myletter.txt at the A>.

STEP 1: Key in the following:

L <Enter>

```
*L
    1: This is my first edlin text file.
    2: this is the sexxond line of this file.
    3: this is the third line of my gile.
    4: This is the fourth line of my file.
*_
```

WHAT'S HAPPENING? The L that you keyed in at the * prompt shows you the file. L listed all the lines in the file. Since EDLIN is a line editor, you can work with line numbers. You can key in any displayed line number as your first line.

STEP 2: Key in the following:

```
2L <Enter>
```

```
*2L
    2: this is the sexxond line of this file.
    3: this is the third line of my gile.
    4: This is the fourth line of my file.
*_
```

WHAT'S HAPPENING? By placing the number 2 in front of the command L, you asked EDLIN to list the file starting with line 2. All you see displayed on the screen is the file from line 2 to line 4, the end in this case. You can also ask EDLIN to display a range of lines.

STEP 3: Key in the following:

```
2,3L <Enter>
```

```
*2,3L
    2: this is the sexxond line of this file.
    3: this is the third line of my gile.
*_
```

WHAT'S HAPPENING? You asked EDLIN to show only the beginning of line 2 to the end of line 3. You can also display one line at a time.

STEP 4: Key in the following:

```
4,4L <Enter>
```

```
*4,4L
    4: This is the fourth line of my file.
*_
```

WHAT'S HAPPENING? You asked EDLIN to show you the beginning of line 4 to the end of line 4. The range is thus 4,4. Note also that L, the list command, makes no changes in the file. It merely shows the file and takes you back to the EDLIN prompt.

9.6 USING EDLIN TO MAKE CORRECTIONS IN A FILE

So far, you have entered data and looked at what you have entered. However, the advantage of using an editor is that you can correct or edit the text. Because `EDLIN` is a line editor, you edit one line at a time. Simply key in the number of the line you wish to correct. That line then appears on the screen in edit mode, ready for any corrections.

ACTIVITY 9.7 EDITING LINES

NOTE: You should still be in the `EDLIN myletter.txt`. The DATA disk is in Drive A, but you should see the `*` prompt. If you see the `A>`, you should key in `EDLIN myletter.txt` at the `A>`.

STEP 1: Key in the following:

```
2 <Enter>
```

```
*2
    2:*this is the sexxond line of this file.
    2:*_
```

WHAT'S HAPPENING? Displayed on the screen are two lines prefaced by `2:` The first line indicates what line 2 currently contains. The second, blank line is where you make corrections. Whatever is keyed in on the second line will replace what is currently in the first line.

STEP 2: Key in the following:

```
This is the second line of the file. <Enter>
```

```
    2:*this is the sexxond line of this file.
    2:*This is the second line of the file.
*_
```

WHAT'S HAPPENING? Note that you are back at the `*` prompt. You can only edit one line at a time. To see that the edit took place, use the `L` command.

STEP 3: Key in the following:

```
L  <Enter>
```

```
*L
    1: This is my first edlin text file.
    2:*This is the second line of this file.
    3: this is the third line of my gile.
    4: This is the fourth line of my file.
*_
```

WHAT'S HAPPENING? Line 2 has been corrected. The original line was replaced by what you keyed in. There are two asterisks. The one at the lower lefthand corner is the prompt. The asterisk following the 2 (`2:*This`) is a place marker, indicating which line in the file you were on previously. You did not put that asterisk there, nor can you remove it.

STEP 4: Key in the following:

```
3  <Enter>
```

```
*3
    3:*this is the third line of my gile.
    3:*_
```

STEP 5: Key in the following:

```
This is the third line of my file.  <Enter>
```

WHAT'S HAPPENING? You have corrected line 3. Note how one line at a time is corrected. To return to the * prompt without making any changes, press `<Enter>`.

STEP 6: Key in the following:

```
4  <Enter>
```

```
*4
    4:*This is the fourth line of my file.
    4:*_
```

STEP 7: Press <Enter>.

```
*4
    4:*This is the fourth line of my file.
    4:*
*_
```

WHAT'S HAPPENING? You are back at the * prompt because you made no changes to line 4. If you had hit even one key, that would have replaced whatever was on line 4. To verify that you made no changes to line 4, you again use the L command.

STEP 8: Key in the following:

```
L  <Enter>
```

```
*L
    1: This is my first edlin text file.
    2: This is the second line of this file.
    3: This is the third line of my file.
    4:*This is the fourth line of my file.
*_
```

WHAT'S HAPPENING? Note that line 4 is unchanged.

9.8 EXITING FROM A PROGRAM

You have been working in a program called EDLIN and writing your data lines to memory. So far, nothing has been saved permanently. If you want this file, myletter.txt, stored on the disk, you must exit from the program and return to the DOS system level. You must exit any program properly. If you just turned off your computer without exiting in the proper way, you would lose what is in memory and, hence, you would lose the file. All programs have unique ways to end the work session or leave the program. To exit from EDLIN or end your editing session, you use the letter E.

ACTIVITY 9.9 EXITING FROM EDLIN

NOTE: You should still be in the EDLIN file myletter.txt. The DATA disk is in Drive A, but you should see the * prompt. If you see the A>, you should key in EDLIN myletter.txt at the A>.

STEP 1: You should be at the * prompt. Key in the following:

```
E <Enter>
```

```
    1: This is my first edlin text file.
    2: This is the second line of this file.
    3: This is the third line of my file.
    4:*This is the fourth line of my file.
*E

A>_
```

WHAT'S HAPPENING? Note that the E for end or exit must be at the * prompt. If you keyed in E after a line number, it would be treated as data. An EDLIN command only works at the * prompt.

9.10 EDITING AN EXISTING FILE

One of the advantages to using an editor is that you can always go back to a file you created to make changes. When you first created the file, you named it. Now you have to remember what you named it so you can call it back to the screen.

ACTIVITY 9.11 EDITING AN EXISTING EDLIN FILE

NOTE: The DATA disk should be in Drive A with the A> displayed for both two disk drive users and hard disk users.

STEP 1: Key in the following:

```
A>EDLIN myletter.txt  <Enter>
```

```
A>EDLIN myletter.txt
End of input file
*_
```

WHAT'S HAPPENING? You issued the command EDLIN at the system level prompt, A>, calling the file myletter.txt to be displayed. You have now called the EDLIN program because you have the * prompt displayed. In addition, you know that this is not a new file because the prompt says "End of input file" not "New file" as it did when you created the file. If you thought that you had asked for an existing file and you got the "New file" message, the chances are you probably made a typographical error. If there is even one different character, for example miletter.txt instead of myletter.txt, EDLIN will think that it is a new file and treat it as such. To prove that this is the file on which you have been working, you can use the L command.

STEP 2: Key in the following:

```
L <Enter>
```

```
*L
    1:*This is my first edlin text file.
    2: This is the second line of this file.
    3: This is the third line of my file.
    4: This is the fourth line of my file.
*_
```

9.12 ADDING TEXT TO AN EXISTING FILE

You created the file myletter.txt. With the line editor, EDLIN, not only can you change existing lines in the file, but you can also add new lines or more data to the file. You need to tell EDLIN that you are in an insert mode, not an edit mode. Insert means adding data to this file. Since this is a line editor, you also need to tell EDLIN at what line number you wish to start adding data.

ACTIVITY 9.13 ADDING/INSERTING NEW LINES TO AN EXISTING FILE

NOTE: You should still be in the EDLIN file myletter.txt. The DATA disk is in Drive A but you should see the * prompt. If you see the A>, you should key in EDLIN myletter.txt at the A>.

STEP 1: Key in the following:

```
5i  <Enter>
```

```
*5i
    5:*_
```

WHAT'S HAPPENING? EDLIN presents a blank line preceded by the line number that you selected. Line 5 was selected because line 4 was the last line in the existing file.

STEP 2: Key in the following:

```
This is my fifth line.  <Enter>
```

```
5:*This is my fifth line.
6:*_
```

WHAT'S HAPPENING? You are in insert mode because you gave the i command. EDLIN knows that you want to add more lines of data and gave you 6, a new line number. You will stay in the insert mode until you tell EDLIN you are done entering new data by keying in <Ctrl>-C.

STEP 3: Remember that <Ctrl>-C means pressing the Control key. Then while pressing the <Ctrl> key, press the letter C. Key in the following:

```
This is my sixth line.  <Enter>
<Ctrl>-C
```

```
    5:*This is my fifth line.
    6:*This is my sixth line.
    7:*^C
*_
```

STEP 4: Key in the following:

```
L  <Enter>
```

```
*L
    1: This is my first edlin text file.
    2: This is the second line of this file.
    3: This is the third line of my file.
    4: This is the fourth line of my file.
    5: This is my fifth line.
    6: This is my sixth line.
*_
```

WHAT'S HAPPENING? The original four lines of text are still there with the addition of new text, lines 5 and 6. When you began adding new lines of data, you keyed in `5i` so that the next text began at the end of the file. If you did not know the last line number of the current file or if you wish to go immediately to the end of the file, you can use the pound sign (#) with the insert command. The pound sign takes you to the bottom of the file, and the `i` says you wish to add data.

STEP 5: Key in the following:

```
#i  <Enter>
```

```
*#i
    7:*_
```

WHAT'S HAPPENING? Note how `EDLIN` immediately took you to the end of the file, line 7.

STEP 6: Key in the following:

```
This is my seventh line.  <Enter>
<Ctrl>-C
```

```
*#i
    7:*This is my seventh line.
    8:*^ C
*_
```

WHAT'S HAPPENING? You added a new line of text and are now back at the * prompt. You are not limited to adding new lines of text at the end of a file. You can insert them any place you choose.

STEP 7: Key in the following:

```
2i  <Enter>
```

```
*2i
    2:*_
```

WHAT'S HAPPENING? Because you keyed in `2i` you got a blank line for new data. If you had just keyed in 2, you would have gotten the existing line 2.

STEP 8: Key in the following:

```
THIS IS MY NEW LINE 2.  <Enter>
<Ctrl>-C
```

```
*2i
    2:*THIS IS MY NEW LINE 2.
    3:*^C
*_
```

WHAT'S HAPPENING? You have added a new line of text to the file and returned to the prompt.

STEP 9: Key in the following:

```
L  <Enter>
```

```
*L
    1: This is my first edlin text file.
    2: THIS IS MY NEW LINE 2.
    3:*This is the second line of this file.
    4: This is the third line of my file.
    5: This is the fourth line of my file.
    6: This is my fifth line.
    7: This is my sixth line.
    8: This is my seventh line.
*_
```

WHAT'S HAPPENING? Note how `EDLIN` inserted a new line number 2 and automatically renumbered the rest of the lines. What used to be line 2 is now line 3; line 3 is now line 4, and so on. `EDLIN` lets you add a line wherever you like.

Sometimes users wish to add a blank line, but this can cause confusion. A "blank" line is really not blank. When you want a blank line while using a typewriter, you hit the carriage return and the paper rolls up one line. The same thing is true for a line editor or word processor. Carriage return is a special signal telling the computer to move the carriage return one line. Thus, to get a blank line, you press the `<Enter>` key.

STEP 10: Key in the following:

```
3i  <Enter>
```

```
*3i
    3:*_
```

STEP 11: Press <Enter>

```
*3i
    3:*
    4:*_
```

WHAT'S HAPPENING? By pressing the <Enter> key on line 3, you have marked this line with a "carriage return." To leave the insert mode, you still use <Ctrl>-C.

STEP 12: Press <Ctrl>-C

```
*3i
    3:*
    4:*^C
*_
```

STEP 13: Key in the following:

L <Enter>

```
*L
    1: This is my first edlin text file.
    2: THIS IS MY NEW LINE 2.
    3:
    4:*This is the second line of this file.
    5: This is the third line of my file.
    6: This is the fourth line of my file.
    7: This is my fifth line.
    8: This is my sixth line.
    9: This is my seventh line.
*_
```

WHAT'S HAPPENING? A "blank" line was inserted on line 3. It is not really blank; it has a carriage return signal for that line. Note that all the rest of the lines have been renumbered.

9.14 DELETING LINES IN A FILE

You can delete entire lines with the D command. Tell EDLIN the line number you wish to delete and follow it with the letter D. In addition, you can delete ranges or a group of lines.

ACTIVITY 9.15 DELETING LINES

NOTE: You should still be in the EDLIN file myletter.txt. The DATA disk is in Drive A, but you should see the * prompt. If you see the A>, you should key in EDLIN myletter.txt at the A>.

STEP 1: To delete line 2, key in the following:

2D <Enter>

```
*2D
*_
```

WHAT'S HAPPENING? You are returned to the * prompt. To verify that line 2 is gone, you can list the file.

STEP 2: Key in the following:

L <Enter>

```
*L
     1: This is my first edlin text file.
     2:*
     3: This is the second line of this file.
     4: This is the third line of my file.
     5: This is the fourth line of my file.
     6: This is my fifth line.
     7: This is my sixth line.
     8: This is my seventh line.
*_
```

WHAT'S HAPPENING? Often users will look at the preceding display and say, "But line 2 is still there." The line number 2 is there, but EDLIN removed the contents of line 2 and automatically renumbered the remaining lines. What used to be line 3 is now line 2; what used to be line 4 is now line 3, and so on. You still have a line number 2, but the text of the line is different. You had a nine-line file; now you have an eight-line file. To check that out, you are going to delete the current line 2, which is a "blank line." When you have completed the delete command, line 2 will contain the current line 3 text, "This is the second line of this file."

STEP 3: Key in the following:

```
2D  <Enter>
```

STEP 4: Key in the following:

```
L  <Enter>
```

```
*L
     1: This is my first edlin text file.
     2:*This is the second line of this file.
     3: This is the third line of my file.
     4: This is the fourth line of my file.
     5: This is my fifth line.
     6: This is my sixth line.
     7: This is my seventh line.
*_
```

WHAT'S HAPPENING? The "blank" line 2 is gone, and line 3 became line 2. Furthermore, the remaining lines were renumbered. You can also delete a range or group of lines by giving EDLIN the range of numbers followed by D. A comma separates the numbers.

STEP 5: Key in the following:

```
5,7D  <Enter>
```

STEP 6: You will be back at the * prompt. Key in the following:

```
L  <Enter>
```

```
*L
     1: This is my first edlin text file.
     2: This is the second line of this file.
     3: This is the third line of my file.
     4: This is the fourth line of my file.
*_
```

WHAT'S HAPPENING? You deleted all of lines 5, 6, and 7, a range of numbers, using the D command. Remember, that if you had wanted to retain line 6 and delete lines 5 and 7, the 5,7D would have erased all these lines.

It is very helpful when using line editors to use the `L` or list command every time you make a change to the file, so you can observe the change. Since `EDLIN` automatically renumbers the lines every time a change is made, it can be difficult to keep track of the line number you are on. Hence, if you had a 15-line file and deleted lines 5 through 9, old line number 10 would now be line 5.

9.16 PRINTING AN EDLIN FILE

After you create and edit a file, you typically want a printed copy. Because `EDLIN` is a line editor, not a word processor, it has no print commands. Thus, you must leave `EDLIN` and print at the system level. You use the `COPY` command to print the file.

ACTIVITY 9.17 PRINTING THE FILE

NOTE: You should still be in the `EDLIN` file `myletter.txt`. The DATA disk is in Drive A but you should see the `*` prompt. If you see the `A>`, you should key in `EDLIN myletter.txt` at the `A>`.

STEP 1: Key in the following:

```
E  <Enter>
```

```
*E

A>_
```

WHAT'S HAPPENING? You have exited from the `EDLIN` program and are back at the `A>`, the system level. Be sure the printer is turned on. To print the file, use the `COPY` command.

STEP 2: Key in the following:

```
A>COPY myletter.txt PRN  <Enter>
```

WHAT'S HAPPENING? The file should be printing. Note how the printed copy has no line numbers. You can not set margin spacing in `EDLIN`. Remember, you cannot print a file in `EDLIN`. You must exit the program and print from the system level.

9.18 EDITING TEXT FILES

So far **EDLIN** was used to create files and edit them. You can edit any text file with **EDLIN**; if the file was created with **COPY CON filename** or with **COPY filename.one filename.two**, you can still use **EDLIN** to edit. The following exercise will demonstrate that any file can be edited with **EDLIN**. In addition, you will learn about **.bak** files.

ACTIVITY 9.19 EDITING EXISTING FILES WITH EDLIN

NOTE: Two disk drive users and hard disk users will have the DATA disk in Drive A with the **A>** displayed.

STEP 1: Key in the following:

```
A>DIR *.87  <Enter>
```

```
A>DIR *.87

Volume in drive A is DATADISK
Directory of A:\

JAN          87        71        11-23-8    7:35p
FEB          87        73        11-23-8    7:42p
MAR          87        69        11-23-8    7:43p
APR          87        70        11-23-87   7:44

             4 Files(s)    237568 bytes free

A>_
```

WHAT'S HAPPENING? These files were not created with **EDLIN**, but you can edit them with **EDLIN**.

STEP 2: Key in the following:

```
A>EDLIN feb.87  <Enter>
```

```
A>EDLIN feb.87
End of input file
*_
```

WHAT'S HAPPENING? `EDLIN` will allow you to edit any file no matter how it was created. You know this is an existing file because you got the message, "`End of input file`."

STEP 3: Key in the following:

```
L  <Enter
```

```
*L
    1:*This is my February file.
    2: It is my second dummy file.
    3: This is file 2.
*_
```

STEP 4: Key in the following:

```
4i  <Enter>
```

```
*4i
    4:*_
```

STEP 5: Remember that `<Ctrl>-C` means to press the `<Ctrl>` key. While pressing the `<Ctrl>` key, press the letter `C`. Key in the following:

```
I am adding a new line to  <Enter>
this file to change or  <Enter>
edit it.  <Enter>
<Ctrl>-C
```

```
*4i
    4:*I am adding a new line to
    5:*this file to change or
    6:*edit it.
    7:*^C
*_
```

STEP 6: Key in the following:

E <Enter>

```
*E

A>_
```

WHAT'S HAPPENING? You have added some text to the feb.87 file and, with the EDLIN command E, you are telling EDLIN to exit the program. This will return you to the A>.

STEP 7: Key in the following:

A>TYPE feb.87 <Enter>

```
A>TYPE feb.87
This is my February file.
It is my second dummy file.
This is file 2.
I am adding a new line to
this file to change or
edit it.

A>_
```

WHAT'S HAPPENING? The file reflects the changes that you made. Even though you did not create it with EDLIN, you made changes to the file with EDLIN.

STEP 8: Key in the following:

A>DIR feb.* <Enter>

```
A>DIR feb.*

Volume in drive A is DATADISK
Directory of A:\

FEB            BAK      73      11 23-87  7:42p
FEB            87      135      11-23-87  8:42p
         2 Files(s)  236544 bytes free
A>_
```

WHAT'S HAPPENING? Note that you now have two files with a file name of `feb`. You created the file `feb.87`. Who created `feb.bak`? `EDLIN` did. Some application software packages do this, and `EDLIN` is one of them. When you call up or edit an existing file, `EDLIN` makes a backup copy of the original file. When you began editing the existing file, `feb.87`, `EDLIN` really named it `feb.$$$`. The `.$$$` extension is a temporary file created by `EDLIN`. The original file you named `feb.87` is not touched. You are actually editing or making changes to the temporary file called `feb.$$$`. When you end your editing session with `EDLIN` by keying in `E`, you are writing your edited version to the disk. Here is what `EDLIN` does:

`feb.87` is named `feb.bak` by `EDLIN`
`feb.$$$` is named `feb.87` by `EDLIN`

STEP 9: Key in the following:

```
A>TYPE feb.87  <Enter>
```

STEP 10: Key in the following:

```
A>TYPE feb.bak  <Enter>
```

```
A>TYPE feb.87
This is my February file.
It is my second dummy file.
This is file 2.
I am adding a new line to
this file to change or
edit it.

A>TYPE feb.bak
This is my February file.
It is my second dummy file.
This is file 2.

A>_
```

WHAT'S HAPPENING? The file now called `feb.bak` contains the contents of the unedited version of your original file. The file now called `feb.87` contains the contents of the updated or edited file, the most current version of your document with all the latest changes.

STEP 11: Key in the following:

```
A>EDLIN feb.87  <Enter>
```

```
A>EDLIN feb.87
End of input file
*_
```

STEP 12: Key in the following:

```
L  <Enter>
```

```
*L
     1:*This is my February file.
     2: It is my second dummy file.
     3: This is file 2.
     4: I am adding a new line to
     5: this file to change or
     6: edit it.
*_
```

WHAT'S HAPPENING? Here is the most current version of the file `feb.87`. You are now going to add more data to the file.

STEP 13: Key in the following:

```
7i  <Enter>
```

STEP 14: Key in the following:

```
This is my latest change.  <Enter>
This is all I'm going to key in.  <Enter>
<Ctrl>-C
```

```
*7i
     7:*This is my latest change.
     8:*This is all I'm going to key in.
     9:*^C
*_
```

WHAT'S HAPPENING? You have added data and are back at the * prompt. Now end the editing session.

STEP 15: Key in the following:

```
E <Enter>
```

WHAT'S HAPPENING? You are back at the `A>` at the system level because you have exited from the `EDLIN` program.

STEP 16: Key in the following:

```
A>DIR feb.*  <Enter>
```

```
A>DIR feb.*

Volume in drive A is DATADISK
Directory of A:\

FEB           BAK     135      11-23-87  8:42p
FEB           87      196      11- 3-87  8:52p
         2 Files(s)   236544 bytes free

A>_
```

WHAT'S HAPPENING? You still have only two files, `feb.87` and `feb.bak`. What are the contents of the two files?

STEP 17: Key in the following:

```
A>TYPE feb.87  <Enter>
```

STEP 18: Key in the following:

```
A>TYPE feb.bak  <Enter>
```

```
A>TYPE feb.87
This is my February file.
It is my second dummy file.
This is file 2.
I am adding a new line to
this file to change or
edit it.
This is my latest change.
This is all I'm going to key in.

A>TYPE feb.bak
This is my February file.
It is my second dummy file.
This is file 2.
I am adding a new line to
this file to change or
edit it.

A>_
```

WHAT'S HAPPENING? `EDLIN` only keeps two copies of any file—the most current version and the version from which the most current version was edited. Your original file is gone. When you start a new editing session, `EDLIN`, without warning, erases the `.bak` file for that file name which, in this case, had the contents:

```
This is my February file.
It is my second dummy file.
This is file 2.
```

When you began your new editing session and called up feb.87 to edit, EDLIN really named it feb.$$$. The file with the .$$$ extension is a temporary file created by EDLIN. When you ended your editing session with EDLIN, you wrote your new or edited version to the disk. This is what EDLIN does:

feb.bak, the original file you created, is erased
feb.87, the first change, now is named feb.bak by EDLIN.
feb.$$$, the most current change, now is named feb.87 by EDLIN

Each time you enter an editing session with EDLIN, the scenario described above occurs. Thus, you always have only two copies of your text file, the one you are currently working on and the last version you were working on. In essence, you have the current file and the last version of the current file. You cannot edit any file in EDLIN that has .bak as a file extension.

STEP 19: Key in the following:

```
A>EDLIN feb.bak  <Enter>
```

```
A>EDLIN feb.bak
Cannot edit .BAK file--rename file

A>_
```

WHAT'S HAPPENING? As you can see, you cannot edit this file. However, if you did want to edit the .bak file, DOS tells you to rename the file.

9.20 LEAVING EDLIN WITHOUT MAKING CHANGES

You have been exiting from EDLIN with the E command. Each time you do that, you are telling EDLIN you want to write the file to the disk. Instead of using E, you can also use Q for Quit. Q says to EDLIN: Do not write this version of this file with changes to the disk. Keep the file as it was before it was edited.

ACTIVITY 9.21 QUITTING A FILE IN EDLIN

NOTE: Two disk drive users and hard disk users will have the DATA disk in Drive A with the A> displayed.

STEP 1: Key in the following:

```
A>EDLIN feb.87  <Enter>
```

```
A>EDLIN feb.87
End of input file

*_
```

WHAT'S HAPPENING? You have the file `feb.87` ready to delete some lines of text with `EDLIN`.

STEP 2: Key in the following:

```
1,6D  <Enter>
```

STEP 3: Key in the following:

```
L  <Enter>
```

```
*L
    1:*This is my latest change.
    2: This is all I'm going to key in.
*_
```

WHAT'S HAPPENING? You have deleted the first six lines of the file. However, if you erred, you can recover the lost lines.

STEP 4: Key in the following:

```
Q  <Enter>
```

```
*Q
Abort edit (Y/N)?_
```

WHAT'S HAPPENING? `EDLIN` is asking you whether or not you want to leave this editing session.

STEP 5: Press `Y` and you will be returned to the `A>`.

STEP 6: Key in the following:

```
A>TYPE feb.87  <Enter>
```

STEP 7: Key in the following:

```
A>TYPE feb.bak  <Enter>
```

```
A>TYPE feb.87
This is my February file.
It is my second dummy file.
This is file 2.
I am adding a new line to
this file to change or
edit it.
This is my latest change.
This is all I'm going to key in.

A>TYPE feb.bak
This is my February file.
It is my second dummy file.
This is file 2.
I am adding a new line to
this file to change or
edit it.

A>_
```

WHAT'S HAPPENING? As you can see, your files are the same as they were prior to the line deletion. The **Q** meant that changes were not written to the disk. No data was lost. You aborted the changed file, the file with lines 1 through 6 deleted, to disk. Thus, if you end an **EDLIN** editing session with **Q** and answer **Y** to "abort edit," no changes will be made to the file. If you use **E** for end, the changes will be written to the file.

9.22 USING EDITING KEYS IN EDLIN

So far, when you have been working at the **EDLIN** prompt command level, the only way you could change or edit a numbered line was to work with the entire line. You had to delete a line or key in an entire line to make a correction. Although **EDLIN** is not a word processor, it does have some editing keys that you can use to save keystrokes. These include the function keys, labeled **<F1>**, **<F3>**, and so forth, and the keys labeled **<Ins>** and **<Del>**.

ACTIVITY 9.23 USING THE FUNCTION KEYS, <F1> AND <F3>

NOTE: Two disk drive users and hard disk users will have the DATA disk in Drive A with the A> displayed.

STEP 1: Key in the following:

```
A>EDLIN sales.let  <Enter>
```

```
A>EDLIN sales.let
New file
*_
```

WHAT'S HAPPENING? You have created a new file that has no data. To put data in this file, you must use the i or insert command.

STEP 2: Key in the following:

```
i  <Enter>
```

```
*i
   1:*_
```

WHAT'S HAPPENING? You are now in the insert mode and can insert data into this file.

STEP 3: Key in the following text. Key in the errors because you are going to learn how to correct them.

```
Today's date  <Enter>
<Enter>
TO:  John Jones, Sales Manager  <Enter>
FROM:  Your name <Enter>
<Enter>
<Enter>
I am interested in setting up a meetin <Enter>
with your staff.  I have developed a <Enter>
new software product that I think you <Enter>
will finx of interest.  <Enter>
<Enter>
```

```
<Enter>
I have developed a new operation system <Enter>
for the microcomputer.  It is <Enter>
easier to run than DOS.  I would like <Enter>
to show it off to your staff. <Enter>
<Enter>
<Enter>
Please let me know when we could get <Enter>
together so I may demonstrate this <Enter>
product.  I think you will be really <Enter>
impressed.  James Smith would be <Enter>
happy to give me a recommendation.  <Enter>
I can be reached at (714) 582-8888.  <Enter>
I look forward to hearing from you.  <Enter>
<Ctrl>-C
```

WHAT'S HAPPENING? You have created a text file. Pressing `<Ctrl>-C` returned you to the * prompt. So far, to edit a line, you have keyed in the line number of what you wanted to edit.

STEP 4: Key in the following:

```
3  <Enter>
```

```
*3
   3:*TO:  John Jones, Sales Manager
   3:*_
```

WHAT'S HAPPENING? On the top line you have displayed what line 3 currently contains. The bottom line is ready for you to make changes. However, when you key in text, the text goes to two places. One is the screen. At the same time, an exact copy of your line is being made to the input buffer. A buffer holds data temporarily in memory. It is often used to compensate for differences in rates of data flow. Devices operate at different speeds. For instance, a printer, a mechanical device, is much slower than a computer. A buffer can be used to hold the data sent to the printer by the computer. Then the computer can quickly send data to the printer and the printer holds that data in a buffer until it can print it.

In this case, the system always retains the last line entered in a buffer. Whatever changes you make and see on the screen are also being reflected in the input buffer, which can be used as a template. When you press `<Enter>` after your changes are complete, your new line is written to your file, overwriting the old line. If you do not want to make changes to the line you called up to edit, you would press `<Enter>`. You would be returned to the * prompt and the original line would be retained. If you keyed in even one character (and remember that the

<Space> bar is a character), that would overwrite what is on the current line. Thus, if you want no changes in a line, you would press <Enter>. Since you do not want to change line 3, you will press <Enter>.

STEP 5: <Enter>

```
*3
    3:*TO:  John Jones, Sales Manager
    3:*
*_
```

STEP 6: Key in the following:

10 <Enter>

```
*10
    10:*will finx of interest.
    10:*_
```

WHAT'S HAPPENING? You have an error in this line. You want to change finx to find. To make this correction, EDLIN allows you to use the function keys, located on the left side of the alphanumeric keyboard or on the top row above the alphanumeric keyboard.

STEP 7: Press the <F1> key.

```
    10:*will finx of interest.
    10:*w_
```

WHAT'S HAPPENING? The w is written to the screen. Each time the <F1> key is pressed, one character from the buffer is copied to the screen.

STEP 8: Press the <F1> key again.

```
    10:*will finx of interest.
    10:*wi_
```

WHAT'S HAPPENING? Again, the <F1> key wrote the next letter to the screen. The right arrow key, 6, located on some computers on the numeric keypad to the right of the alpha keyboard and on other computers as a separate "arrow" keypad, works the same way as the <F1> key. Locate the key with the -> symbol.

STEP 9: Press the -> key.

```
10:*will finx of interest.
10:*wil_
```

WHAT'S HAPPENING? The right arrow key worked exactly like the <F1> key. (If the right arrow key is on the numeric keypad with the number 6 and you get the number 6 displayed on the screen, that means the <Num Lock> toggle switch is set to numbers. Hit the toggle switch to set it back to the arrow functions.)

STEP 10: Keep pressing either the <F1> key or the -> key until the cursor is under the x in "finx." Change the x to d.

STEP 11: Key in the letter d.

```
10:*will finx of interest.
10:*will find_
```

STEP 12: Continue pressing the <F1> or -> key until you reach the end of the line.

```
10:*will finx of interest.
10:*will find of interest.
```

STEP 13: Press <Enter>

WHAT'S HAPPENING? You have returned to the *. The corrected line is now written to the file.

STEP 14: Key in the following:

7 <Enter>

```
7:*I am interested in setting up a meetin
7:*_
```

WHAT'S HAPPENING? You need to add a `g` at the end of `meetin`. To make this correction, you would have to either key the entire line or repeatedly press the <F1> key. However, there is an easier way to do this. The key labeled <F3> will write the entire line, copying from the buffer the rest of line to the screen.

STEP 15: Press the <F3> key.

```
    7:*I am interested in setting up a meetin
    7:*I am interested in setting up a meetin_
```

STEP 16: Key in the letter `g` and press <Enter>. You will be returned to the * prompt.

```
    7:*I am interested in setting up a meetin
    7:*I am interested in setting up a meeting
*_
```

WHAT'S HAPPENING? As you see, it is much easier to use the function keys to make corrections to a line than to key in the entire line again. The <F1> key replaces one character at a time. The <F3> key replaces the entire line.

9.24 USING THE INSERT AND DELETE KEYS

The <F1> and <F3> keys are useful for replacing existing characters or existing lines. What if you wish to add or delete words or characters? <F1> and <F3> allow you to replace only what is already in the buffer. The <Del> key and the <Ins> key, located on the numeric keypad, will perform these functions.

ACTIVITY 9.25 THE <INS> AND <DEL> KEYS IN EDLIN

NOTE: You should still be in the `EDLIN` file `sales.let`. The DATA disk is in Drive A but you should see the * prompt. If you see the `A>`, you should key in `EDLIN sales.let` at the `A>`.

STEP 1: Key in the following:

8 <Enter>

```
*8
    8*with your staff.  I have developed a
    8*_
```

WHAT'S HAPPENING? Here you want to make a complicated line change, adding the word sales before staff so that the line will read "`with your sales staff. I have developed a`." In other words, you want to insert the word sales.

STEP 2: To demonstrate the shortcomings of the function keys, press the <F1> key until the cursor is under the `s` in `staff`.

```
    8*with your staff.  I have developed a
    8*with your _
```

STEP 3: Key in the following:

sales_

STEP 4: Press the <F3> key to get the rest of the line. Do not press <Enter>.

```
    8*with your staff.  I have developed a
    8*with your sales.  I have developed a_
```

WHAT'S HAPPENING? When you keyed in the word `sales` you overwrote the word `staff`. What you really wanted to do was retain the word `staff` and insert the word `sales`.

STEP 5: Press the left arrow key <- on the numeric keypad (it also has the number 4 on it, if you do not have a separate arrow keypad). Note that each time you press it, you are deleting a character to the left of the cursor. Keep pressing the <- key until the cursor is under the s in staff.

```
8*with your staff.  I have developed a
8*with your _
```

WHAT'S HAPPENING? You want to insert a word, not overwrite a word. To insert a word, you use the insert key, labeled <Ins> on the numeric keypad. This key tells EDLIN that you want to insert a word and push the remaining words/letters to the right.

STEP 6: Press the <Ins> key and key in the word sales. Include a space by hitting the <Space> bar after the word sales.

```
8*with your staff.  I have developed a
8*with your sales _
```

STEP 7: Press the <F3> key. Press <Enter>

```
8*with your staff.  I have developed a
8*with your sales staff.  I have developed a
*_
```

WHAT'S HAPPENING? Here you inserted the word sales and pushed the rest of the line over to the right to make room for the word. When you pressed <Enter> you wrote your edited line to the file. If you wanted to delete a word, the key labeled <Del> on the numeric keypad will serve this function.

STEP 8: Key in the following:

```
9 <Enter>
```

```
*9
    9:*new software product that I think you
    9:*_
```

WHAT'S HAPPENING? In this example, you want to delete the word `new` so the edited line will read "`software product that I think you`." Neither the `<F1>`, `<F3>`, or `<Ins>` keys will help you do this editing. However, each time you press the `<Del>` key, a single character will be deleted. You cannot see this occurring on the screen. You simply have to count each time you press the `<Del>` key.

STEP 9: Press the `<Del>` key four times (one press for each letter, and the fourth time for the space bar). Press the `<F3>` key for the rest of the line. Press `<Enter>` at the end of the line.

```
    9:*new software product that I think you
    9:*software product that I think you
*_
```

WHAT'S HAPPENING? The `<Del>` key allowed you to delete letters within a line. The `<Ins>` key, the `<Del>` key, the `<F1>` key, and the `<F3>` keys are basic editing tools you can use in `EDLIN`. To end the editing session and save the edited version of the file, you must use the `E` at the `*` prompt.

STEP 10: Key in the following:

```
E   <Enter>
```

```
    9:*new software product that I think you
    9:*software product that I think you
*E

A>_
```

WHAT'S HAPPENING? You saved the file to the DATA disk and you are back at the system level.

CHAPTER SUMMARY

1. EDLIN is a program that comes with the DOS System Disk. It is a utility program.
2. DOS commands, internal or external, do not work once you are in the EDLIN program.
3. EDLIN allows the user to edit any text file.
4. Because EDLIN is a line editor, only one line at a time can be edited.
5. The major EDLIN editing commands include i for insert, D for delete, a line number to edit any line, L to list the file, E to exit from the program and save the data and Q to quit the file and not save the data.
6. The <F1> key allows you to replace one character at a time.
7. The <F3> key allows you to replace the whole line.
8. The <Ins> and <Del> keys allow you to insert or delete data on a line.

REVIEW QUESTIONS

1. What symbol is the EDLIN prompt?
2. Once in insert mode, what keys do you press to return to the EDLIN prompt?
3. When would you use the E command? What does it do to a text file?
4. When would you use the Q command? What does it do to a text file?
5. How do you print a file created with EDLIN?
6. Why would you need a line editor such as EDLIN? How would you use it?
7. What is the difference between a word processor and a line editor such as EDLIN?
8. From the EDLIN prompt, can you delete more than one line at a time? If yes, how would you write the command to delete lines 10 through 20?
9. From the EDLIN prompt, how do you display the text file on the screen?
10. This appears on the screen:
    ```
    New file
    *_
    ```
    What do you enter to allow you to write lines in this file?
11. This appears on the screen:
    ```
    Abort edit(Y/N)?_
    ```
    If you type Y and press <Enter>, which of the following will you see?
    a. A>_
    b. *
    c. 3:*_
12. What command would you use to add new lines between lines 8 and 9 in an EDLIN file?
13. What command would you use to add lines to the end of an existing file?
14. What command will list lines 5, 6, 7, 8, and 9?
15. The following is displayed on the screen:
    ```
    5:*Microcomputers are very powerful tools.
    5:*_
    ```
    If you press <Enter>, what happens to line 5?
16. Which of the following statements is true when you can use the <Ins> and <Del> keys:
    a. Whenever you are entering a new line of text in a file.
    b. Whenever you are editing an existing line of text in a file.

17. What editing key allows you to add a new character and pushes the other characters to the right?
18. What key(s) do you press to copy one character from the buffer to the screen?
19. What key(s) do you press to copy the rest of the characters from the buffer to the screen?
20. The following is displayed on the screen:

```
     6:*Microcomputers are very powerful tools.
     7:*They are used in many business applications.
*_
```

How would you place a blank line between lines 6 and 7?

TRUE/FALSE

1. You can set whatever margins you need in EDLIN.
2. Pressing <Ctrl>-C while in an EDLIN file returns you to the EDLIN prompt.
3. Pressing E when the * symbol is displayed terminates EDLIN and returns the system to the DOS prompt.
4. Pressing E when 3:*_ is displayed terminates EDLIN and returns the system to the DOS prompt.
5. *1,10L will list lines 1 through 10 on the screen.
6. If you hit the <Del> key, it will delete the entire line at one time.
7. If you press Q at the * prompt, none of the changes made in the file will be written to disk.
8. *1,10D will delete lines 1 through 10 in the file.
9. EDLIN automatically renumbers lines as you are editing a file.
10. *#i will automatically take you to the bottom of the file.

SUGGESTED ACTIVITIES

Two disk drive users and hard disk users: Put all the applications on the DATA disk.

1. Edit the file called sales.let created in the chapter. Make the following changes:
   a. Locate the last line in the second paragraph and change it from "to show it off to your staff" to "to demonstrate it to your staff."
   b. In the third paragraph, change "James Smith" to "James Smythe."
   c. In the second paragraph, change "operation system" to "operating system."
   d. Make the last two lines of the third paragraph, starting with "I can be reached at" a new or fourth paragraph.
2. Exit from EDLIN and print this file. Do not use the <Shift> and <PrtSc> key.

3. Use EDLIN to create a new file called computer.app. Key in the following text at the * prompt. Remember that you have to be in the insert mode. **Note:** An <Enter> by itself creates a blank line.

```
Your name (use your own name) <Enter>
Your street address <Enter>
Your city, state, and zip code <Enter>
<Enter>
Micro Computer Store <Enter>
15000 Marguerite Parkway <Enter>
Mission Viejo, California 92692 <Enter>
<Enter>
Dear Sir:  <Enter>
<Enter>
I purchased an IBM clone from your store last  <Enter>
week. I was told that it would run any software <Enter>
application that would run on an IBM. It does not.<Enter>
<Enter>
I am going to return the computer I bought <Enter>
from your store. I need to bXX another computer<Enter>
that works with the software I have. <Enter>
<Enter>
Sincerely, <Enter>
<Enter>
<Enter>
<Enter>
Your name <Enter>
```

4. Exit from EDLIN and print this file. Do not use the <Shift> and <PrtSc> keys.
5. Edit the file computer.app that you just created. Make the following corrections:
   a. Change the name of the company to New Age, Inc.
   b. In the address block above New Age, Inc., insert "Mr. Bill Jones, President."
   c. Correct bxx in the second paragraph to buy.
   d. Add a new last paragraph that reads, "If I am not fully satisfied, I will report you to the Better Business Bureau."
6. Exit from EDLIN and print this file. Do not use the <Shift> and <PrtSc> keys.
7. Delete all the files with the .bak file extension. Prove that you have done this. Print this screen.
8. Back up your DATA disk.

MANAGING THE PRINTER WITH THE MODE AND PRINT COMMANDS

CHAPTER

10

CHAPTER OBJECTIVES

This chapter reviews the ways to print a text file. In addition, it introduces some new ways of managing your printer by the using the `PRINT` and `MODE` commands and discusses resident commands and foreground and background tasks. After completing this chapter, you will:

Be able to print text files using four methods: `<Shift>-<PrtSc>`, `<Ctrl>-<PrtSc>`, `COPY`, and `PRINT`.

Be able to describe and use background programs such as `PRINT`.

Be able to set printer characteristics using the `MODE` command.

10.0 MATERIALS NEEDED

1. DOS System Disk
2. ACTIVITIES disk
3. DATA disk
4. Back up Data disk

10.1 PRINTING TECHNIQUES

You have learned three techniques for printing text files. One is to press the `<Shift>` key and the `<PrtSc>` key. This is a screen print that prints a "snapshot" of what is on the screen at a specific moment. A second technique is to toggle the printer on by pressing the `<Ctrl>` key and the `<PrtSc>` key. This method of printing allows you to have a running dialogue with the computer. Everything that is displayed on the screen is printed simultaneously. The third method is to use the COPY command to copy files to a device, the printer. This method allows a hard copy of the contents of a file. You are going to review these techniques as well as learn some other ways to print files.

ACTIVITY 10.2 PRINTING USING THE <PrtSc> KEY AND THE <SHIFT> KEY

NOTE: Two disk drive users will have the DOS System Disk in Drive A with the A> displayed and the ACTIVITIES disk in Drive B. Hard disk users will be logged into the DOS System Disk on Drive C with the C> displayed. The ACTIVITIES disk will be in Drive A.

STEP 1: Turn on the printer.

STEP 2: Key in the following:

A>TYPE B:january.txt <Enter>

```
A>TYPE B:january.txt
This is my January file.
It is my first dummy file.
This is file 1.
A>_
```

STEP 3: Press the <Shift> key. While pressing the <Shift> key, press the <PrtSc> key.

STEP 1: Turn on the printer.

STEP 2: Key in the following:

C>TYPE A:january.txt <Enter>

```
C>TYPE A:january.txt
This is my January file.
It is my first dummy file.
This is file 1.
C>_
```

STEP 3: Press the <Shift> key. While pressing the <Shift> key, press the <PrtSc> key.

WHAT'S HAPPENING? After you hit these two keys, you will see the cursor moving along the screen and hear the printer printing those lines of text. When you use the <Shift> key and the <PrtSc> key in conjunction, you get a snapshot of whatever is on your screen at a specific time. This can be valuable for diagnostic purposes. If something went wrong, you could get a hard copy of the message displayed on the screen. Look at the hard copy or printout. Note that everything that was on the screen was printed, the prompt, the TYPE command, as well as all the blank lines. Thus, if you only wanted the contents of a file and not the prompt or the command, you could not do it with this technique. Furthermore, you also have only the capability of printing what is on the screen. This means that if the text of a file was longer than 24 lines, you could not print it using the <PrtSc> key and <Shift> key.

The file just printed was a short text file comprised of three lines of text. All lines of the file appeared on the screen. However, what if, the file was more than

24 lines? You could not use the <PrtSc> key and the <Shift> key to print the entire file. In addition, if you wanted to send out a letter or memo, you would not want the prompts and commands to appear. You would want only the contents of the file to be printed.

ACTIVITY 10.3 PRINTING TEXT FILES USING THE COPY COMMAND

NOTE: Two disk drive users will have the DOS System Disk in Drive A with the A> displayed and the ACTIVITIES disk in Drive B. Hard disk users will be logged into the DOS System Disk on Drive C and have the C> displayed. The ACTIVITIES disk will be in Drive A.

STEP 1: Do nothing.

STEP 1: Key in the following:

```
C>A:  <Enter>
```

```
A>_
```

WHAT'S HAPPENING? You have changed the default drive from C> to A>.

STEP 2: Key in the following:

```
A>TYPE B:personal.fil <Enter>
```

STEP 2: Key in the following:

```
A>TYPE personal.fil <Enter>
```

NOTE: The following display will appear on both floppy and hard disk systems.

```
Babchuk    Nicholas  13 Stratford  Sun City West  AZ   Professor
Babchuk    Bianca    13 Stratford  Sun City West  AZ   Professor
Begg       Leroy     20 Elm        Ontario        CA   Systems Analyst
Helm       Milton    333 Meadow    Sherman Oaks   CA   Consultant
Moselle    Carolyn   567 Abbey     Rochester      MI   Day Care Teacher
Markiw     Nicholas  354 Bell      Phoenix        AZ   Engineer
Markiw     Emily     10 Zion       Sun City West  AZ   Retired
Nyles      John      12 Brooks     Sun City West  AZ   Retired
Nyles      Sophie    12 Brooks     Sun City West  AZ   Retired
Markiw     Nick      10 Zion       Sun City West  AZ   Retired
Papay      Fred      345 Newport   Orange         CA   Manager
Jones      Steven    32 North      Phoenix        AZ   Buyer
Smith      David     120 Collins   Orange         CA   Chef
Babchuk    Walter    12 View       Thousand Oaks  CA   President
Babchuk    Deana     12 View       Thousand Oaks  CA   Housewife
Jones      Cleo      355 Second    Ann Arbor      MI   Clerk
Smith      Henry     40 Northern   Ontario        CA   Engineer
Jones      Jerry     244 East      Mission Viejo  CA   Systems Analyst
Low        Ophelia   1213 Wick     Phoenix        CA   Writer
Tally      William   15 Fourth     Santa Cruz     CA   Banker
Gibbs      Michael   134 Seventh   Ann Arbor      MI   Editor
Richards   James     56 Twin Leaf  Orange         CA   Artist
Markiw     Nicholas  12 Fifth      Glendale       AZ   Engineer
A>_
```

WHAT'S HAPPENING? This list is longer than 24 lines. It scrolls past on the screen. You cannot see the entire file on the screen. If you are only interested in the contents of the file, not the prompts and commands, using the `<Shift>` key and the `<PrtSc>` key would not work either. To print a hard copy or print out, you need another command.

STEP 3: Key in the following:

```
A>COPY B:personal.fil PRN  <Enter>
```

```
A>COPY B:personal.fil PRN
        1 File(s) copied
```

STEP 3: Key in the following:

```
A>COPY personal.fil PRN  <Enter>
```

```
A>COPY personal.fil PRN
        1 File(s) copied
```

WHAT'S HAPPENING? With this command, you have asked DOS to `COPY` the contents of the file called `personal.fil` (source), located on the ACTIVITIES disk, to a device `PRN` (destination). You will see the contents of this text file printed on the printer. The printout you should get is shown below. Note that you only get the contents of the file, not the prompt or any of the commands.

NOTE: The following display will appear on both floppy and hard disk systems.

```
Gillay     Carolyn   699 Lemon      Orange          CA  Professor
Panezich   Frank     688 Lake       Orange          CA  Teacher
Tuttle     Steven    356 Embassy    Mission Viejo   CA  Golf Pro
Maurdeff   Kathryn   550 Traver     Ann Arbor       MI  Teacher
Maurdeff   Sonia     550 Traver     Ann Arbor       MI  Student
Smith      Gregory   311 Orchard    Ann Arbor       MI  Engineer
Smith      Carolyn   311 Orchard    Ann Arbor       MI  Housewife
Winter     Jim       333 Pick       Garden Grove    CA  Key Grip
Winter     Linda     333 Pick       Garden Grove    CA  Teacher
Golden     Herbert   345 Lakeview   Orange          CA  Doctor
Golden     Jane      345 Lakeview   Orange          CA  Nurse
Brent      Wendy     356 Edgewood   Ann Arbor       MI  Librarian
Brogan     Lloyd     111 Miller     Santa Cruz      CA  Vice-President
Brogan     Sally     111 Miller     Santa Cruz      CA  Account Manager
Babchuk    Nicholas  13 Stratford   Sun City West   AZ  Professor
Babchuk    Bianca    13 Stratford   Sun City West   AZ  Professor
Begg       Leroy     20 Elm         Ontario         CA  Systems Analyst
Helm       Milton    333 Meadow     Sherman Oaks    CA  Consultant
Moselle    Carolyn   567 Abbey      Rochester       MI  Day Care Teacher
Markiw     Nicholas  354 Bell       Phoenix         AZ  Engineer
Markiw     Emily     10 Zion        Sun City West   AZ  Retired
Nyles      John      12 Brooks      Sun City West   AZ  Retired
Nyles      Sophie    12 Brooks      Sun City West   AZ  Retired
Markiw     Nick      10 Zion        Sun City West   AZ  Retired
Papay      Fred      345 Newport    Orange          CA  Manager
Jones      Steven    32 North       Phoenix         AZ  Buyer
Smith      David     120 Collins    Orange          CA  Chef
Babchuk    Walter    12 View        Thousand Oaks   CA  President
Babchuk    Deana     12 View        Thousand Oaks   CA  Housewife
Jones      Cleo      355 Second     Ann Arbor       MI  Clerk
Smith      Henry     40 Northern    Ontario         CA  Engineer
JONES      JERRY     244 East       Mission Viejo   CA  Systems Analyst
Low        Ophelia   1213 Wick      Phoenix         CA  Writer
Tally      William   15 Fourth      Santa Cruz      CA  Banker
Gibbs      Michael   134 Seventh    Ann Arbor       MI  Editor
Richards   James     56 Twin Leaf   Orange          CA  Artist
Markiw     Nicholas  12 Fifth       Glendale        AZ  Engineer
```

10.4 TOGGLING ON THE PRINTER

Using `COPY filename PRN` prints the contents of files. But what if you want to print the directory or table of contents of your disk? You cannot use the `<Shift>` key and `<PrtSc>` key if the directory is longer than a screenful—more than 24 files. Nor can you use the `COPY` command because `DIR` is a command, not a file. What you can do is give the printer a command, the `<Ctrl>` key and `<PrtSc>`. Now everything that scrolls by on the screen is printed on the printer simultaneously. This command works like a toggle switch. Press it once to turn it on, and press it again to turn it off.

ACTIVITY 10.5 PRINTING WITH THE <CTRL> KEY AND THE <PrtSc> KEY

NOTE: Two disk drive users will have the DOS System Disk in Drive A with the A> displayed and the ACTIVITIES disk in Drive B. Hard disk users will have the ACTIVITIES disk in Drive A and the A> displayed. Be sure the printer is turned on.

STEP 1: Key in the following:

A>DIR B: <Enter>

STEP 1: Key in the following:

A>DIR   <Enter>

NOTE: The following display will appear on both floppy and hard disk systems.

```
AP          87        71    11-27-87   1:19p
CHKDSK      COM     9435     3-07-85   1:43p
CK          COM     9435     3-07-85   1:43p
FILE2       CZG       18    11-23-87   2:51p
FILE3       CZG       18    11-23-87   2:51p
FILE2       FP        18    11-23-87   2:53p
FILE3       FP        18    11-23-87   2:53p
FILE4       FP        18    11-23-87   2:53p
FILE2       SWT       18    11-23-87   2:54p
FILE3       SWT       18    11-23-87   2:54p
RIGHT       RED       25    11-23-87   2:57p
DRESS       UP        25    11-23-87   2:57p
LEFT        RED       24    11-23-87   3:03p
MIDDLE      RED       28    11-23-87   3:04p
RIGHT       UP        25    11-23-87   2:57p
MIDDLE      UP        28    11-23-87   3:04p
BLUE        JAZ       17    11-23-87   3:07p
GREEN       JAZ       17    11-23-87   3:08p
ADDRESS     DAT      601    11-23-87   3:13p
BYE         TXT       44    11-23-87   3:14p
GOODBYE     TXT       33    11-23-87   3:15p
TEST        TXT       67    11-23-87   4:46p
           73 Files(s)   148480 bytes free

A>_
```

WHAT'S HAPPENING? The table of contents (the directory) for the ACTIVITIES disk scrolls by on the screen. As you can see, it is more than a screenful. Using the `<Shift>` key and the `<PrtSc>` key will only print what is currently displayed on the screen, not the entire table of contents of the ACTIVITIES disk.

STEP 2: Key in the following:

```
A>COPY B:dir PRN  <Enter>
```

```
A>COPY B:dir PRN
B:DIR File not found
    0 File(s) copied

A>_
```

STEP 2: Key in the following:

```
A>COPY dir PRN  <Enter>
```

```
A>COPY dir PRN
DIR File not found
    0 File(s) copied

A>_
```

WHAT'S HAPPENING? `DIR` is not a file. It is a command that displays the table of contents. DOS was looking for a file called `DIR` on the ACTIVITIES disk. How then can you get a printout of the table of contents of any disk?

STEP 3: While pressing the `<Ctrl>` key, press the `<PrtSc>` key. You have just turned on the toggle switch.

STEP 4: Key in the following:

```
A>DIR B:  <Enter>
```

STEP 3: While pressing the `<Ctrl>` key, press the `<PrtSc>` key. You have just turned on the toggle switch.

STEP 4: Key in the following:

```
A>DIR  <Enter>
```

WHAT'S HAPPENING? As the directory for the ACTIVITIES disk scrolls by on the screen, it is also printing on the printer. Toggling on the printer with the `<Ctrl>` key and `<PrtSc>` key prints everything that is displayed on the screen. This technique can be valuable as a diagnostic routine. You get a printed copy of all the commands and displays that transpired during a work session.

STEP 5: While pressing the `<Ctrl>` key, press the `<PrtSc>` key. You have just turned off the toggle switch. (Pressing the `<Ctrl>` key and the letter `P` also toggles the print switch on or off.)

STEP 5: While pressing the `<Ctrl>` key, press the `<PrtSc>` key. You have just turned off the toggle switch. (Pressing the `<Ctrl>` key and the letter `P` also toggles the print switch on or off.)

STEP 6: Key in the following:

```
A>DIR B:  <Enter>
```

STEP 6: Key in the following:

```
A>DIR  <Enter>
```

WHAT'S HAPPENING? The directory of the ACTIVITIES disk should be scrolling by on the screen, but it should no longer be printing. If it is, just press the `<Ctrl>` key and `<PrtSc>` key again.

10.6 RESIDENT PROGRAMS

We have discussed two categories of programs: internal commands and external commands. The internal commands are those programs that remain resident in memory, once the system is booted. They remain until the power is turned off. They are automatically loaded when the system is booted, as part of the file `COMMAND.COM`. External commands reside on a disk and are called into memory and executed each time they are used. When an external command is finished executing, DOS again takes control of the computer. When another external command is called, DOS will use that same area of memory to run the new program.

There is a third category of programs called **semi-resident commands**. These programs still have to be called into memory from the disk. However, when the semi-resident command is finished executing, it turns control back to DOS. It tells DOS not to reuse the memory area where a semi-resident command is located. This means that the next time you wish to use a resident command, it is still in memory. It does not have to be reloaded from the disk as external commands do. The semi-resident program, once called into memory, remains there until the power is turned off. Commercially available memory-resident programs include those such as SideKick. DOS supplies some of its own resident programs as part of the DOS utilities. One of these is the `PRINT` command.

10.7 THE PRINT COMMAND

There are disadvantages to each of the printing techniques you have learned. The `<Shift>` key and `<PrtSc>` key only allows you to print one screenful at a time, including the commands and messages. Although the `<Ctrl>` key and `<PrtSc>` key will print all the lines, they also print the commands and messages. Using `COPY filename PRN` prints only the contents of the file, but while files are printing, the computer (and hence you) can do nothing else. The file contents print one right after another. `COPY filename PRN` does not advance to the top of the form (start a new page) when a new file begins to print. Another disadvantage is that if the file names have nothing in common, a wildcard cannot be used to print files, so each file requires a separate `COPY filename PRN` command.

There is another way to print the contents of files: by using the `PRINT` command. This is an external, semi-resident command. The program is stored on the

DOS System Disk as `print.com`. This program acts as a **print spooler**. Spool is an acronym for simultaneous peripheral operations on-line.

A printer works much more slowly than the CPU. But a print spooler can print without tying up the entire CPU. This is a form of **multi-tasking**, a computer doing two or more things at the same time. Another term is **background program** or background printing. This means that the computer can be doing another task while printing, usually running another program. The other program takes most of the computer's time and is said to be in the **foreground**. A background program gets less of the computer's time.

At this time, microcomputers running under DOS are not true multi-tasking machines. DOS-based computers can do only one thing at a time. The `PRINT` program takes turns with whatever else is happening on the computer. The computer appears to be multi-tasking because it is so fast. DOS can switch tasks about 18 times per second. To the user, this is so quick it seems as if the computer is doing two things at the same time.

The `PRINT` command is more a print queue than a print spooler. Queue, a word commonly used in England to mean lining up, means the same thing in computerese. Queuing means keeping a list of files or "lining up" the files to be printed. `PRINT` keeps track of the list of files and prints them from the disk, instead of from memory. One advantage to using `PRINT` is that more than one file at a time can be printed regardless of their names. Another advantage is that files can be queued to print while you do other things. In addition, each time the `PRINT` command prints a new file, it will start on a new page.

Only text files should be printed. Programs or non-text data files have control characters. These characters appear as nonsense and can make the printer behave erratically. If you are unsure of what a text file is, a very simple test is to use the `TYPE` command. If the file displays on the screen in plain English, it can be printed with the `PRINT` command. The syntax is:

```
PRINT filenam1.ext filenam2.ext ... [/T] [/C]
```

`filenam1.ext` represents any file name. The ellipsis points represent any other files that would be queued to print. Up to 10 files can be queued up to print. Ten files is the default value for the queue. The command is loaded when it is first keyed in and does not have to be loaded into memory again. It remains in memory until the computer is turned off or rebooted. `PRINT` uses about 3K of memory.

ACTIVITY 10.8 USING THE PRINT COMMAND

STEP 1: The DOS System Disk should be in Drive A. The ACTIVITIES disk should be in Drive B.

STEP 1: The ACTIVITIES disk should be in Drive A. You need to be where the DOS system files or external commands are located. Be sure to be logged into the DOS System Disk on drive C. Key in the following:

```
A>C: <Enter>
```

STEP 2: Key in the following:

A>COPY B:*.87 PRN <Enter>

```
A>COPY B:*.87 PRN
B:JAN.87
B:FEB.87
B:MAR.87
B:APR.87
   1 File(s) copied

A>_
```

STEP 2: Key in the following:

C>COPY A:*.87 PRN <Enter>

```
C>COPY A:*.87 PRN
A:JAN.87
A:FEB.87
A:MAR.87
A:APR.87
   1 File(s) copied

C>_
```

WHAT'S HAPPENING? You are using the COPY command and asking DOS to copy all the files on the ACTIVITIES disk that have 87 as a file extension.

After the printer has stopped printing, look at the printout. It will look like the following:

NOTE: The following display will appear on both floppy and hard disk systems.

```
This is my January file.
It is my first dummy file.
This is file 1.
This is my February file.
It is my second dummy file.
This is file 2.
This is my March file.
It is my third dummy file.
This is file 3.
This is my April file.
It is my fourth dummy file.
This is file 4.
```

WHAT'S HAPPENING? These are four separate files. Note how they were printed one after another. The printout looks like one file.

STEP 3: Key in the following:

A>PRINT B:*.87 <Enter>

```
A>PRINT B:*.87
Name of list device [PRN]:_
```

STEP 3: Key in the following:

C>PRINT A:*.87 <Enter>

```
C>PRINT A:*.87 Name of list device
Name of list device [PRN]:_
```

WHAT'S HAPPENING? This is the first time that you have used the PRINT command. It is loaded into memory, as are all external commands. This command is asking for the name of the device that the output should be sent to. Once the command has this information, it will not ask for it again. The device you select will remain in memory. You cannot change the selected device, unless you reboot the system. **PRN** is synonymous with **LPT1**. You do not have to worry about other devices unless you have other devices on your system such as another printer (**LPT2:**) or a communications port (**COM1:**). Never assign a device that is not on your system. In this activity, it is assumed that there is only one printer attached to your system.

STEP 4: Press `<Enter>`

```
A>PRINT B:*.87
Name of list device [PRN]:
Resident part of PRINT installed
     B:\JAN.87 is currently being printed
     B:\FEB.87 is in queue
     B:\MAR.87 is in queue
     B:\APR.87 is in queue
A>_
```

STEP 4: Press `<Enter>`

```
C>PRINT A:*.87
Name of list device [PRN]:
Resident part of PRINT installed
     A:\JAN.87 is currently being printed
     A:\FEB.87 is in queue
     A:\MAR.87 is in queue
     A:\APR.87 is in queue
C>_
```

WHAT'S HAPPENING? Note the difference between this command and the **COPY *.87 PRN**. When you used **COPY *.87 PRN**, the prompt (**A>** or **C>**) did not appear until everything was printed. However, when using the **PRINT** command, note that you were immediately returned to the default prompt (**A>** or **C>**). In addition, your files are currently printing on the printer. After the printer has ceased printing, look at the printout. Instead of all the file contents being printed as one file, as in Step 2, the **PRINT** command advanced the paper to the top of the form after it printed the first file or began a new page for the next file in the queue. Each new file gets a separate page as it starts to print.

STEP 5: Key in the following:

```
A>PRINT B:personal.fil B:address.
dat B:*.87 <Enter>
```

```
A>PRINT B:personal.fil B:address.dat B:*.87
     B:\PERSONAL.FIL is currently being printed
     B:\ADDRESS.DAT is in queue
     B:\JAN.87 is in queue
     B:\FEB.87 is in queue
     B:\MAR.87 is in queue
     B:\APR.87 is in queue
A>_
```

STEP 5: Key in the following:

```
C>PRINT A:personal.fil A:address.
dat A:*.87 <Enter>
```

```
C>PRINT A:personal.fil A:address.dat A:*.87
     A:\PERSONAL.FIL is currently being printed
     A:\ADDRESS.DAT is in queue
     A:\JAN.87 is in queue
     A:\FEB.87 is in queue
     A:\MAR.87 is in queue
     A:\APR.87 is in queue
C>_
```

WHAT'S HAPPENING? Since this is a memory-resident program, it does not need to be read from the DOS System Disk. You did not get the message "`Name of list device [PRN]:`" as this was established when you first loaded the program. Note how you are returned to the system prompt after the **PRINT** command lists the files it is going to print. To prove that you can do two tasks almost simultaneously, you are going to execute another command while the printer is printing the listed files.

STEP 6: Key in the following:

```
A>DIR B:   <Enter>
```

```
APR             87         71      11-27-87     1:19p
CHKDSK          COM      9435       3-07-85     1:43p
CK              COM      9435       3-07-85     1:43p
FILE2           CZG        18      11-23-87     2:51p
FILE3           CZG        18      11-23-87     2:51p
FILE2           FP         18      11-23-87     2:53p
FILE3           FP         18      11-23-87     2:53p
FILE4           FP         18      11-23-87     2:53p
FILE2           SWT        18      11-23-87     2:54p
FILE3           SWT        18      11-23-87     2:54p
RIGHT           RED        25      11-23-87     2:57p
DRESS           UP         25      11-23-87     2:57p
LEFT            RED        24      11-23-87     3:03p
MIDDLE          RED        28      11-23-87     3:04p
RIGHT           UP         25      11-23-87     2:57p
MIDDLE          UP         28      11-23-87     3:04p
BLUE            JAZ        17      11-23-87     3:07p
GREEN           JAZ        17      11-23-87     3:08p
ADDRESS         DAT       601      11-23-87     3:13p
BYE             TXT        44      11-23-87     3:14p
GOODBYE         TXT        33      11-23-87     3:15p
TEST            TXT        67      11-23-87     4:46p
               73 Files(s)     148480 bytes free

A>_
```

STEP 6: Key in the following:

```
C>DIR A:   <Enter>
```

```
APR             87         71      11-27-87     1:19p
CHKDSK          COM      9435       3-07-85     1:43p
CK              COM      9435       3-07-85     1:43p
FILE2           CZG        18      11-23-87     2:51p
FILE3           CZG        18      11-23-87     2:51p
FILE2           FP         18      11-23-87     2:53p
FILE3           FP         18      11-23-87     2:53p
FILE4           FP         18      11-23-87     2:53p
FILE2           SWT        18      11-23-87     2:54p
FILE3           SWT        18      11-23-87     2:54p
RIGHT           RED        25      11-23-87     2:57p
DRESS           UP         25      11-23-87     2:57p
LEFT            RED        24      11-23-87     3:03p
MIDDLE          RED        28      11-23-87     3:04p
RIGHT           UP         25      11-23-87     2:57p
MIDDLE          UP         28      11-23-87     3:04p
BLUE            JAZ        17      11-23-87     3:07p
GREEN           JAZ        17      11-23-87     3:08p
ADDRESS         DAT       601      11-23-87     3:13p
BYE             TXT        44      11-23-87     3:14p
GOODBYE         TXT        33      11-23-87     3:15p
TEST            TXT        67      11-23-87     4:46p
               73 Files(s)     148480 bytes free

A>_
```

WHAT'S HAPPENING? Note how the printer pauses as the **DIR** command is being executed. Although the system will respond more slowly to the **DIR** command, it is both printing the files and displaying the directory of the ACTIVITIES disk. You could not do this using the **COPY** command. In addition, note how you could print several files with different names.

10.9 VIEWING AND TERMINATING THE PRINT QUEUE

You have been queuing up files to print with the **PRINT** command. However, there are some parameters you should be aware of. You should be able to see what is in the print queue, be able to stop printing all the files, and be able to cancel the printing of a file. If you key in **PRINT** by itself, it will display on the screen the files that are still in the queue. Some parameters allow you to interrupt the print queue. If you wish to stop or cancel the print job, you use the **PRINT /T** parameter (**/T** means to terminate). If you wish to terminate the printing of a specific file, you use **PRINT filename /C**. Please read the following activity all the way through before doing it so you know what you are going to do. If you are too slow in keying in the information, the printer will print all the files prior to your keying anything in. Also, some printers will not accept the **/T** command, and the printer will not stop printing. However, the best way to find out is to try it.

ACTIVITY 10.10 USING THE PRINT COMMAND PARAMETERS

NOTE: Two disk drive users will have the DOS System Disk in Drive A with the **A>** displayed and the ACTIVITIES disk in Drive B. Hard disk users will be logged into the DOS System Disk on Drive C and have the **C>** displayed. The ACTIVITIES disk will be in Drive A.

STEP 1: Key in the following:

```
A>PRINT B:*.txt  <Enter>
```

```
A>PRINT B:*.txt
     B:\HELLO.TXT is currently being printed
     B:\EXERCISE.TXT is in queue
     B:\JANUARY.TXT is in queue
     B:\FEBRUARY.TXT is in queue
     B:\MARCH.TXT is in queue
     B:\APRIL.TXT is in queue
     B:\DEMOS.TXT is in queue
     B:\HI.TXT is in queue
     B:\BYE.TXT is in queue
     B:\GOODBYE.TXT is in queue
A>_
```

STEP 2: Key in the following:

```
A>CLS  <Enter>
```

STEP 3: Key in the following:

```
A>PRINT  <Enter>
```

```
A>PRINT
     B:\JANUARY.TXT is currently being printed
     B:\FEBRUARY.TXT is in queue
     B:\MARCH.TXT is in queue
     B:\APRIL.TXT is in queue
     B:\DEMOS.TXT is in queue
     B:\HI.TXT is in queue
     B:\BYE.TXT is in queue
     B:\GOODBYE.TXT is in queue
A>_
```

STEP 1: Key in the following:

```
C>PRINT A:*.txt  <Enter>
```

```
C>PRINT A:*.txt
     A:\HELLO.TXT is currently being printed
     A:\EXERCISE.TXT is in queue
     A:\JANUARY.TXT is in queue
     A:\FEBRUARY.TXT is in queue
     A:\MARCH.TXT is in queue
     A:\APRIL.TXT is in queue
     A:\DEMOS.TXT is in queue
     A:\HI.TXT is in queue
     A:\BYE.TXT is in queue
     A:\GOODBYE.TXT is in queue
C>_
```

STEP 2: Key in the following:

```
C>CLS  <Enter>
```

STEP 3: Key in the following:

```
C>PRINT  <Enter>
```

```
C>PRINT
     A:\JANUARY.TXT is currently being printed
     A:\FEBRUARY.TXT is in queue
     A:\MARCH.TXT is in queue
     A:\APRIL.TXT is in queue
     A:\DEMOS.TXT is in queue
     A:\HI.TXT is in queue
     A:\BYE.TXT is in queue
     A:\GOODBYE.TXT is in queue
C>_
```

WHAT'S HAPPENING? Your screen may display fewer files, depending on the time that you keyed in the `PRINT` command. However, note that you could execute the `CLS` command and then display what was currently in line to print. The `HELLO.TXT` and `EXERCISE.TXT` files are no longer displayed since they have already been printed.

STEP 4: Key in the following:

```
A>PRINT /T  <Enter>
```

```
A>PRINT /T
PRINT queue is empty

A>_
```

STEP 4: Key in the following:

```
C>PRINT /T  <Enter>
```

```
C>PRINT /T
PRINT queue is empty

C>_
```

WHAT'S HAPPENING? It will take a little time for the system to respond. The printer will continue to print for a few seconds until it completes the print job it is currently doing. In fact, you will not see your command displayed on the screen for a few seconds even though you keyed it in. The printer will beep at you when it ceases printing. You will have printed about four or five files, depending on when you terminated the print job and if your printer will accept the `/T` parameter.

STEP 5: Key in the following:

```
A>PRINT B:*.fil B:*.txt <Enter>
```

```
A>PRINT B:*.fil B:*.txt
PRINT queue is full
     B:\CAROLYN.FIL is currently being printed
     B:\FRANK.FIL is in queue
     B:\STEVEN.FIL is in queue
     B:\PERSONAL.FIL is in queue
     B:\HELLO.TXT is currently being printed
     B:\EXERCISE.TXT is in queue
     B:\JANUARY.TXT is in queue
     B:\FEBRUARY.TXT is in queue
     B:\MARCH.TXT is in queue
     B:\APRIL.TXT is in queue
A>_
```

STEP 5: Key in the following:

```
C>PRINT A:*.fil A:*.txt <Enter>
```

```
C>PRINT A:*.fil A:*.txt
PRINT queue is full
     A:\CAROLYN.FIL is currently being printed
     A:\FRANK.FIL is in queue
     A:\STEVEN.FIL is in queue
     A:\PERSONAL.FIL is in queue
     A:\HELLO.TXT is currently being printed
     A:\EXERCISE.TXT is in queue
     A:\JANUARY.TXT is in queue
     A:\FEBRUARY.TXT is in queue
     A:\MARCH.TXT is in queue
     A:\APRIL.TXT is in queue
C>_
```

WHAT'S HAPPENING? Note the "`Print queue is full`" message on the screen. The queue's default value is 10 files. There are more than 10 files. The rest of the `*.txt` files will not be printed because they did not get into the queue.

STEP 6: Key in the following:

```
A>PRINT /T  <Enter>
```

```
A>PRINT /T
PRINT queue is empty

A>_
```

STEP 6: Key in the following:

```
C>PRINT /T  <Enter>
```

```
C>PRINT /T
PRINT queue is empty

C>_
```

WHAT'S HAPPENING? You have "killed the queue," or stopped printing. However, `PRINT /T` cancels the entire print job. What if you wanted to print all the files but one? You can selectively remove a file from the print queue with the `/C` parameter. The syntax is `PRINT filename.ext /C`. In the next steps, you are going to cancel printing the files `bye.txt` and `goodbye.txt`. Be sure to read through the following steps before you begin working.

STEP 7: Key in the following:

```
A>PRINT B:*.txt  <Enter>
```

```
B>PRINT B:*.txt
      B:\HELLO.TXT is currently being printed
      B:\EXERCISE.TXT is in queue
      B:\JANUARY.TXT is in queue
      B:\FEBRUARY.TXT is in queue
      B:\MARCH.TXT is in queue
      B:\APRIL.TXT is in queue
      B:\DEMOS.TXT is in queue
      B:\HI.TXT is in queue
      B:\BYE.TXT is in queue
      B:\GOODBYE.TXT is in queue
A>_
```

STEP 7: Key in the following:

```
C>PRINT A:*.txt  <Enter>
```

```
C>PRINT A:*.txt
      A:\HELLO.TXT is currently being printed
      A:\EXERCISE.TXT is in queue
      A:\JANUARY.TXT is in queue
      A:\FEBRUARY.TXT is in queue
      A:\MARCH.TXT is in queue
      A:\APRIL.TXT is in queue
      A:\DEMOS.TXT is in queue
      A:\HI.TXT is in queue
      A:\BYE.TXT is in queue
      A:\GOODBYE.TXT is in queue
C>_
```

STEP 8: Key in the following:

```
A>PRINT B:bye.txt /C <Enter>
```

```
A>PRINT B:bye.txt /C
      B:\EXERCISE.TXT is currently being printed
      B:\JANUARY.TXT is in queue
      B:\FEBRUARY.TXT is in queue
      B:\MARCH.TXT is in queue
      B:\DEMOS.TXT is in queue
      B:\APRIL.TXT is in queue
      B:\HI.TXT is in queue
      B:\GOODBYE.TXT is in queue
A>_
```

STEP 8: Key in the following:

```
C>PRINT A:bye.txt /C <Enter>
```

```
C>PRINT A:bye.txt /C
      A:\EXERCISE.TXT is currently being printed
      A:\JANUARY.TXT is in queue
      A:\FEBRUARY.TXT is in queue
      A:\MARCH.TXT is in queue
      A:\APRIL.TXT is in queue
      A:\DEMOS.TXT is in queue
      A:\HI.TXT is in queue
      A:\GOODBYE.TXT is in queue
C>
```

STEP 9: Key in the following:

```
A>PRINT B:goodbye.txt /C <Enter>
```

STEP 9: Key in the following:

```
C>PRINT A:goodbye.txt /C <Enter>
```

```
A>PRINT B:goodbye.txt /C
      B:\JANUARY.TXT is currently being printed
      B:\FEBRUARY.TXT is in queue
      B:\MARCH.TXT is in queue
      B:\APRIL.TXT is in queue
      B:\DEMOS.TXT is in queue
      B:\HI.TXT is in queue
A>_
```

```
C>PRINT A:goodbye.txt /C
      A:\JANUARY.TXT is currently being printed
      A:\FEBRUARY.TXT is in queue
      A:\MARCH.TXT is in queue
      A:\APRIL.TXT is in queue
      A:\DEMOS.TXT is in queue
      A:\HI.TXT is in queue
C>_
```

WHAT'S HAPPENING? Note that after you keyed in `PRINT filename.ext /C` for `bye.txt` and `goodbye.txt`, the screen display listing the queued files no longer displayed `bye.txt` or `goodbye.txt`.

STEP 10: Key in the following:

`A>PRINT /T  <Enter>`

STEP 10: Key in the following:

`C>PRINT /T  <Enter>`

```
A>PRINT /T
PRINT queue is empty

A>_
```

```
C>PRINT /T
PRINT queue is empty

C>_
```

WHAT'S HAPPENING? You have terminated the print job.

10.11 THE MODE COMMAND

Another resident command is the `MODE` command. It has several functions that allow you to alter the way some parts of the hardware operate. In other words, you can set the mode of operations for various devices. The `MODE` command handles printers (parallel ports); serial (asynchronous) adapters, commonly known as communication ports; and display adapters, commonly known as screen displays. A port is simply an input/output connection, like a plug, where you can connect other devices to a computer.

Devices include such things as the console, printers, a mouse (a device that allows you to move the cursor with a small box that wheels around on a flat surface), a light pen (a device to point to things or draw designs on a special display screen), or a modem (a device that allows computers to communicate over phone lines). There are other devices. DOS really is not concerned with the actual device, but with the method of interface. **Interface** means the hardware and/or software necessary to connect one system or device to another so that they can transmit and receive information. Thus, DOS defines **standard devices** as **serial ports** or **parallel ports**.

A **serial** or **asynchronous port** can transfer data at the rate of one bit at a time. A **parallel port** transfers data at the rate of one byte at a time (eight bits). The transfer of eight bits must be concurrent so that the byte (eight bits) looks the same on the receiving end as on the sending end. An IBM PC can have up to two serial ports and three parallel ports. You can add, or upgrade, the hardware to include more ports. Other brand names of computers will have varying numbers of serial and parallel ports. DOS has reserved names for each standard device. They are shown in Table 10.1.

Table 10.1 Reserved Names for Standard Devices

PORT NAME	DOS NAME	ALIAS	MEANING
Parallel port 1	LPT1:	PRN:	Line Printer 1
Parallel port 2	LPT2:		Line Printer 2
Parallel port 3	LPT3:		Line Printer 3
Serial port 1	COM1:	AUX:	Communications port 1 Auxiliary device
Serial port 2	COM2:		Communications port 2

This is a simplified overview of a rather complex subject. The `MODE` command is hardware-dependent; thus, it is difficult to demonstrate all aspects and use of this command. In the following activity, you are going to be using the `MODE` command in conjunction with the printer to change the style of the print. The `MODE` command works with the IBM and/or Epson FX/MX series of printers or one that acts like the Epson printer. If you do not have one of these IBM-like printers, this use of the `MODE` command will not work.

10.12 SETTING THE PRINTER CHARACTERISTICS WITH THE MODE COMMAND

With this command, you can customize your printing. `MODE` also provides the opportunity to use one of three printers. The default printer settings are 80 characters per line and 6 lines per inch. You can also print in a smaller or condensed mode where there are 132 characters per line. In addition, you can print 8 lines per inch.

`MODE` is an external resident command. When you set the `MODE` for the printer, it remains set at the parameters that you specified until you change the mode, turn off the printer, or turn off the computer. The syntax is:

```
MODE LPT#: CPI,LPI
```

The pound symbol (#) represents the number of the printer (1, 2, or 3). The expression `CPI` represents characters per inch based on a one-inch line. Options are 80 (10 characters per inch) or 132 (16.5 characters per inch). The expression `LPI` represents lines per inch, either 6 or 8. Since `MODE` is an external command, DOS has to be able to access it initially to load it. However, once the printing characteristics for the printer are set, they remain set regardless of which disk you print from.

ACTIVITY 10.13 PRINTING USING THE MODE COMMAND

STEP 1: The DOS System Disk should be in Drive A, with the A> displayed. The ACTIVITIES disk should be in Drive B. Be sure the printer is turned on.

STEP 2: Key in the following:

A>MODE LPT1: 132,8 <Enter>

```
A>MODE LPT1: 132,8

    LPT1: not rerouted

    LPT1: set for 132

    Printer lines per inch set

No retry on parallel printer time-out

A>_
```

STEP 1: The C> prompt should be displayed and you should be logged into the DOS System Disk. The ACTIVITIES disk should be in Drive A. Be sure the printer is turned on.

STEP 2: Key in the following:

C>MODE LPT1: 132,8 <Enter>

```
C>MODE LPT1: 132,8

    LPT1: not rerouted

    LPT1: set for 132

    Printer lines per inch set

    No retry on parallel printer time-out

C>_
```

WHAT'S HAPPENING? You have just set the printer so that it will print condensed, giving 132 characters per inch and 8 lines to the inch. Time-outs have to do with the computer looping internally to wait for the printer to be ready. You have set your printer mode. Any text file that you print will be printed in a condensed mode or small mode until you reset the printer.

STEP 3: Key in the following:

`A>COPY B:personal.fil PRN <Enter>`

STEP 3: Key in the following:

`C>COPY A:personal.fil PRN <Enter>`

NOTE: The following display will appear on both floppy and hard disk systems.

```
Gillay     Carolyn    699 Lemon      Orange          CA   Professor
Panezich   Frank      688 Lake       Orange          CA   Teacher
Tuttle     Steven     356 Embassy    Mission Viejo   CA   Golf Pro
Maurdeff   Kathryn    550 Traver     Ann Arbor       MI   Teacher
Maurdeff   Sonia      550 Traver     Ann Arbor       MI   Student
Smith      Gregory    311 Orchard    Ann Arbor       MI   Engineer
Smith      Carolyn    311 Orchard    Ann Arbor       MI   Housewife
Winter     Jim        333 Pick       Garden Grove    CA   Key Grip
Winter     Linda      333 Pick       Garden Grove    CA   Teacher
Golden     Herbert    345 Lakeview   Orange          CA   Doctor
Golden     Jane       345 Lakeview   Orange          CA   Nurse
Brent      Wendy      356 Edgewood   Ann Arbor       MI   Librarian
Brogan     Lloyd      111 Miller     Santa Cruz      CA   Vice-President
Brogan     Sally      111 Miller     Santa Cruz      CA   Account Manager
Babchuk    Nicholas   13 Stratford   Sun City West   AZ   Professor
Babchuk    Bianca     13 Stratford   Sun City West   AZ   Professor
Begg       Leroy      20 Elm         Ontario         CA   Systems Analyst
Helm       Milton     333 Meadow     Sherman Oaks    CA   Consultant
Moselle    Carolyn    567 Abbey      Rochester       MI   Day Care Teacher
Markiw     Nicholas   354 Bell       Phoenix         AZ   Engineer
Markiw     Emily      10 Zion        Sun City West   AZ   Retired
Nyles      John       12 Brooks      Sun City West   AZ   Retired
Nyles      Sophie     12 Brooks      Sun City West   AZ   Retired
Markiw     Nick       10 Zion        Sun City West   AZ   Retired
Papay      Fred       345 Newport    Orange          CA   Manager
Jones      Steven     32 North       Phoenix         AZ   Buyer
Smith      David      120 Collins    Orange          CA   Chef
Babchuk    Walter     12 View        Thousand Oaks   CA   President
Babchuk    Deana      12 View        Thousand Oaks   CA   Housewife
Jones      Cleo       355 Second     Ann Arbor       MI   Clerk
Smith      Henry      40 Northern    Ontario         CA   Engineer
Jones      Jerry      244 East       Mission Viejo   CA   Systems Analyst
Low        Ophelia    1213 Wick      Phoenix         CA   Writer
Tally      William    15 Fourth      Santa Cruz      CA   Banker
Gibbs      Michael    134 Seventh    Ann Arbor       MI   Editor
Richards   James      56 Twin Leaf   Orange          CA   Artist
Markiw     Nicholas   12 Fifth       Glendale        AZ   Engineer
```

WHAT'S HAPPENING? The file called `personal.fil` printed in a much smaller type style. You can have it print a little bigger.

STEP 4: Key in the following:

`A>MODE LPT1: 132,6 <Enter>`

STEP 4: Key in the following:

`C>MODE LPT1: 132,6 <Enter>`

```
A>MODE LPT1: 132,6
    LPT1: not rerouted
    LPT1: set for 132
    Printer lines per inch set
    No retry on parallel printer time-out
A>_
```

```
C>MODE LPT1: 132,6
    LPT1: not rerouted
    LPT1: set for 132
    Printer lines per inch set
    No retry on parallel printer time-out
C>_
```

WHAT'S HAPPENING? The printer is now set to print 132 characters per line but 6 lines per inch instead of 8, so it will not be as condensed.

STEP 5: Key in the following:

`A>COPY B:personal.fil PRN <Enter>`

STEP 5: Key in the following:

`C>COPY A:personal.fil PRN <Enter>`

```
Gillay     Carolyn   699 Lemon     Orange         CA  Professor
Panezich   Frank     688 Lake      Orange         CA  Teacher
Tuttle     Steven    356 Embassy   Mission Viejo  CA  Golf Pro
Maurdeff   Kathryn   550 Traver    Ann Arbor      MI  Teacher
Maurdeff   Sonia     550 Traver    Ann Arbor      MI  Student
Smith      Gregory   311 Orchard   Ann Arbor      MI  Engineer
Smith      Carolyn   311 Orchard   Ann Arbor      MI  Housewife
Winter     Jim       333 Pick      Garden Grove   CA  Key Grip
Winter     Linda     333 Pick      Garden Grove   CA  Teacher
Golden     Herbert   345 Lakeview  Orange         CA  Doctor
Golden     Jane      345 Lakeview  Orange         CA  Nurse
Brent      Wendy     356 Edgewood  Ann Arbor      MI  Librarian
Brogan     Lloyd     111 Miller    Santa Cruz     CA  Vice-President
Brogan     Sally     111 Miller    Santa Cruz     CA  Account Manager
Babchuk    Nicholas  13 Stratford  Sun City West  AZ  Professor
Babchuk    Bianca    13 Stratford  Sun City West  AZ  Professor
Begg       Leroy     20 Elm        Ontario        CA  Systems Analyst
Helm       Milton    333 Meadow    Sherman Oaks   CA  Consultant
Moselle    Carolyn   567 Abbey     Rochester      MI  Day Care Teacher
Markiw     Nicholas  354 Bell      Phoenix        AZ  Engineer
Markiw     Emily     10 Zion       Sun City West  AZ  Retired
Nyles      John      12 Brooks     Sun City West  AZ  Retired
Nyles      Sophie    12 Brooks     Sun City West  AZ  Retired
Markiw     Nick      10 Zion       Sun City West  AZ  Retired
Papay      Fred      345 Newport   Orange         CA  Manager
Jones      Steven    32 North      Phoenix        AZ  Buyer
Smith      David     120 Collins   Orange         CA  Chef
Babchuk    Walter    12 View       Thousand Oaks  CA  President
Babchuk    Deana     12 View       Thousand Oaks  CA  Housewife
Jones      Cleo      355 Second    Ann Arbor      MI  Clerk
Smith      Henry     40 Northern   Ontario        CA  Engineer
Jones      Jerry     244 East      Mission Viejo  CA  Systems Analyst
Low        Ophelia   1213 Wick     Phoenix        CA  Writer
Tally      William   15 Fourth     Santa Cruz     CA  Banker
Gibbs      Michael   134 Seventh   Ann Arbor      MI  Editor
Richards   James     56 Twin Leaf  Orange         CA  Artist
Markiw     Nicholas  12 Fifth      Glendale       AZ  Engineer
```

WHAT'S HAPPENING? Note how this printout differs in size from the previous printout.

STEP 6: Key in the following:

```
A>MODE LPT1: 80,6  <Enter>
```

```
A>MODE LPT1: 80,6

    LPT1: not rerouted

    LPT1: set for 80

    Printer lines per inch set

No retry on parallel printer time-out

A>_
```

STEP 6: Key in the following:

```
C>MODE LPT1: 80,6  <Enter>
```

```
C>MODE LPT1: 80,6

    LPT1: not rerouted

    LPT1: set for 80

    Printer lines per inch set

    No retry on parallel printer time-out

C>_
```

WHAT'S HAPPENING? You have set the printer back to the default values. Thus, your choices for printing styles are limited to `MODE LPT1: 132,8`; `132,6`; `80,6`; or `80,8`.

CHAPTER SUMMARY

1. Printing the screen can be accomplished by using the `<Shift>` key and the `<PrtSc>` key.
2. Printing all the dialogue between the user and the computer can be accomplished by using the `<Ctrl>` key and the `<PrtSc>` key as a toggle switch.
3. Text files can be printed using the `COPY filename.ext PRN` command.
4. `PRINT` is a semi-resident command that, once loaded into memory, remains there until the computer is turned off.
5. The `PRINT` command is useful for queuing or lining up files to print.
6. The `PRINT` command is a program that can perform in the background, allowing the user to accomplish some other task while files are being printed.
7. Printing one file while you are running another command is called background printing.
8. Running the program that takes most of the computer's time is putting it in the foreground.
9. Only text files should be printed with any of the above techniques.
10. Text files are those that, when using the `TYPE` command, print as common English characters.
11. A port is a connection for an input/output (I/O) device.
12. A serial port transfers data one bit at a time.

13. A parallel port transfers data one byte (eight bits) at a time.
14. The **MODE** command can set the mode of operation for various devices attached to the computer.
15. The **MODE** command can be used to alter the type style of an IBM-type printer.

REVIEW QUESTIONS

1. How can you use the **MODE** command?
2. Why would you use the **PRINT** command?
3. Describe a memory resident program.
4. When using the **PRINT** command, how can you terminate the entire print queue?
5. When using the **PRINT** command, how can you stop one file from printing?
6. What is an alias for **LPT1**?
7. What is an alias for **AUX**?
8. Describe the difference between foreground and background programs.
9. Define an interface.
10. Name two standard DOS devices.
11. What parameters can you use with the **MODE** command for setting up the printer?
12. What does each parameter do in the **MODE** command?
13. What keys do you press to toggle on the printer?
14. What command can change the print style?
15. How many files can be queued up with the **PRINT** command?
16. The screen displays the following:

```
A>MODE LPT1: 80,6
Bad command or file name
A>_
```

    What does this message tell you? How can you solve the problem?
17. What does queue mean?
18. What does multitasking mean?
19. Are current microcomputers multitasking machines?
20. Why does DOS have reserved names for devices?

TRUE/FALSE

1. Multitasking means that a computer can do more than one task at a time.
2. A modem allows computers to communicate over phone lines.
3. When the **<Ctrl>** key and the **<PrtSc>** key are toggled on, it causes each line displayed on the screen to be printed.
4. The **MODE** command can set the operation of the serial port.
5. Keying in **MODE LPT1: 132,8** sets up the printer to print double-spaced.
6. **LPT1** and **PRN** can be used interchangeably.
7. **PRINT /END** stops the printer from printing any files.
8. The **MODE** command will work with any brand of printer.

9. When the <Shift> Key and the <PrtSc> key are pressed, you get a printout of whatever is on the screen.
10. Keying in `COPY B:new.one B:old.fil B:last.txt PRN` enables you to print files with different names.

SUGGESTED ACTIVITIES

Two drive system users: The DOS System Disk should be in Drive A with the `A>` displayed. The DATA disk should be in Drive B:. Hard drive users: You should be logged into the DOS System Disk on Drive C with the `C>` displayed. The DATA disk should be in Drive A. If your printer will not change modes, write out the command as it should be by hand.

NOTE: The following exercises are not a test in typing. Don't worry if you make typographical errors or if the format is not quite perfect. You are creating the files in order to be able to print them.

All exercises will be on the DATA disk.

1. Create a new text file on the DATA disk called `lexicon1.abc`. The contents are as follows:

ANALOG	Hors d'oeuvre usually made from cheese and served at staff parties.
BINARY	Possessing the ability to have friends of both sexes.
BUG	Small living thing that small living boys throw on small living girls.
CPU	A juvenile way of telling your dog that it missed the paper.
CHIP	Small crunchy object often served with onion dip.
COMMAND	Statement presented by a human and accepted by a computer in such a manner as to make the human feel that he or she is in control.
CURSOR	An expert in four-letter words.

2. Create a new text file on the DATA disk called `lexicon2.def`. The contents are as follows:

DEBUG	The act of placing shoe leather against a small creeping creature.
DOWNTIME	Mental coffee breaks, lunches, or Fridays, in the office or school.
ERROR	Something that only humans can commit.
K	A term used in employment ads to disguise how much they are really willing to pay.

3. Create a new text file on the DATA disk called `lexicon3.mor`. The contents are as follows:

MODEM	A contraction, as in "Give me some modem cookies."
OUTPUT	What people who talk backwards do with their cat.
RAM	A male sheep.
ROM	A RAM after a delicate operation.

4. Display the contents of the file called `lexicon1.abc` on the screen. Print the screen.
5. Combine all three `lexicon` files into a new file on the DATA disk called `dictnry.tot`. Print all the `lexicon` files and the `dictnry.tot` file with the `PRINT` command. After the files have been printed, print the screen, displaying the `PRINT` command.
6. Print the directory of the DATA disk. Do not use the `<Shift>` key and the `<PrtSc>` key command.
7. Change the mode to 132 CPI and 8 LPI. Print the `lexicon3.mor` file.
8. Change the mode to 132 CPI and 6 LPI. Print the `lexicon2.def` file.
9. Change the mode to 80 CPI and 6 LPI. Print the `lexicon1.abc` file.
10. Change the mode to 80 CPI and 8 LPI. Print the `dictnry.tot` file.
11. Use the `PRINT` command to print all the files on the DATA disk with `.txt` as an extension. As soon as you issue the command, cancel the print job. Print the screen that shows the termination of files.
12. Back up your DATA disk.

INTRODUCTION TO BATCH FILES

CHAPTER

11

CHAPTER OBJECTIVES

This chapter begins the discussion of batch files. Much of what is done with an operating system such as DOS is repetitive. Batch files, which allow you to write your own commands, can automate these processes. After completing this chapter, you will:

Understand the differences between batch and interactive processing.

Understand the concept of batch files.

Be able to write and execute simple batch files.

Understand an `autoexec.bat` file.

Be able to write and execute an `autoexec.bat` file.

11.0 MATERIALS NEEDED

1. DOS System Disk
2. DATA disk
3. Backup Data disk

11.1 CONCEPTS OF BATCH AND INTERACTIVE PROCESSING

You have been using a variety of DOS commands throughout this text. These commands are programs that are executed or run when you key in the command name. If you wish to run more than one command, you need to key in each and every command at the system prompt. You can customize or automate the sequence of DOS commands by writing a command sequence that DOS will execute with a minimum number of keystrokes. This is called a batch file, batch command, or a macro. Any command that can be entered at the system prompt can be included in a batch file.

A batch file contains one or more DOS commands. To create this file of commands, you write a text file using `EDLIN` or any text editor. The file that you write and name will run any command that DOS will execute. This file must have the file extension `.bat`. Once you have written this command file, you execute or run it by simply keying in the name of the batch file, just as you key in the name of a DOS command such as `CHKDSK`. DOS reads and executes each line of the command file. It is as if you sat in front of the terminal and separately keyed in each command line. Once you start running a batch file, DOS does not need your attention or input until the batch file is finished executing.

Batch files are used for several reasons. They allow you to minimize your keystrokes. They also allow you the freedom to walk away from your computer when it runs a long series of programs. Batch files are also used to put together a complex sequence of commands and store them under an easily remembered name. They automate any frequent and/or consistent procedure that you always want to do in the same manner. In addition, you can execute your application programs by calling them with a batch file.

The term **batch** is an old data processing term. In the early days of computing, all work was done by submitting a job (or all the instructions needed to successfully run the job) to the data processing shop which would run these jobs in batches. There was no chance for anyone to interact with the program. The job was run and the output was delivered. Thus, when you run a batch job, you are running a computer routine without interruption. Batch jobs are still run today. An example of a batch job would be running a payroll or issuing paychecks. The computer program that calculates and prints paychecks is run all at once, with no interruption. The output or results are the paychecks. This job can be run at any time. If a company decides that payday will be Friday, the data processing department can run the payroll Thursday night. If the company decides payday will be on Monday, the data processing department can run the payroll on Sunday night.

Batch files are in contrast to an **interactive** mode of data processing. Interactive means that you are interacting directly with the computer. An example of this would be the automatic teller machines (ATM), the money machines that banks use so that you can withdraw or deposit money without human intervention. A bank needs instant update of its records. It can't wait until next week to run a batch job to find out how much money you have deposited or withdrawn. If you withdraw $100, the bank first wants to be sure that you have $100 in your account and then it wants the $100 subtracted immediately from your balance. You are dealing with the computer in an interactive, real-time mode. It matters, this instant, what is going on with your account. The information has to be processed immediately.

11.2 HOW DOS BATCH FILES WORK

With the operating system, you will be creating and executing batch files. By now you should know that everything, data and programs, is stored as files. How does

DOS know the difference between a data file and a program file? It knows the difference based on the file extension. There is a very specific order in which the command processor interprets what you key in. When you key in something at the prompt, DOS first checks in RAM to see if what you keyed in is an internal command. It compares what you keyed in to the internal table of DOS commands. If it matches, DOS executes that program. If what you keyed in doesn't match an internal command, DOS next "guesses" that what you keyed in has the file extension `.com`. It looks on the default drive for what you keyed in plus the file extension `.com`. If it finds a match, it loads the program and runs it. If not, DOS goes through the same process but "guesses" that the file extension is `.exe`. (This is how you load and execute not only the DOS utility programs but also most application software. Application software will usually have the file extension `.exe` such as `Lotus.exe`.) If what you keyed in does not match these scenarios, DOS's last "guess" is that the file extension is `.bat`. It looks on the default drive for what you keyed in plus the file extension `.bat`. If it finds a match, it loads and executes the batch file, one line at a time. If what you keyed in does not match any of the above criteria, DOS sends back a message, "`Bad command or file name`."

An example of this is the format command that is stored as a file called `format.com`. At the `A>` or `C>`, you key in `FORMAT`. DOS does not find format in the internal table. It then "guesses" that the file is called `format.com`, which it is. DOS can find the program on the disk, load it, and execute it. What if you had files on a disk called (which you should never do) `format.com`, `format.exe`, and `format.bat`? How would DOS know which program to load and execute? DOS follows the rules. It would find and load the program with the `.com` file extension first and never even get to the other files.

Remember that the `.bat` file must be on the default disk when you invoke it. In addition, any programs, DOS or otherwise, that you wish to use must also be on the default disk or you will get an error message. Each line in a batch file must contain only one command.

11.3 EDLIN AS A TOOL TO WRITE BATCH FILES

You need a mechanism to write or create batch files. A batch file is a text file. You could use `COPY CON filename.bat`, but you cannot correct errors or edit a file created in this manner. You could also use a word processing program if it has a nondocument or text mode. However, most word processing programs are quite large and often need their own separate disks. Having a small, simple text editor is so important that DOS includes `EDLIN` as one of the utility programs on the DOS System Disk. The advantage of using `EDLIN` is that it is simple to use and small enough to fit onto almost any program disk. `EDLIN` is also universal. Everyone who has DOS has `EDLIN`.

You are going to write some batch files using `EDLIN`. Remember, `EDLIN` only creates the file, it does not run or execute it. You will execute the file. A batch file must be named with `.bat` as the file extension.

ACTIVITY 11.4 WRITING AND EXECUTING A BATCH FILE

STEP 1: The DOS System Disk should be in Drive A with the `A>` displayed. The DATA disk should be Drive B.

STEP 1: You should be booted into the DOS System Disk on Drive C with the `C>` displayed. The DATA disk should be in Drive A.

STEP 2: Key in the following:

```
A>B:  <Enter>
```

STEP 2: Key in the following:

```
C>A:  <Enter>
```

WHAT'S HAPPENING? You have changed the default drive to where the DATA disk is located.

STEP 3: Key in the following:

```
B>EDLIN example.bat  <Enter>
```

STEP 3: Key in the following:

```
A>EDLIN example.bat  <Enter>
```

```
B>EDLIN example.bat
New file
*_
```

```
A>EDLIN example.bat
New file
*_
```

WHAT'S HAPPENING? You are now using the `EDLIN` line editor. You are going to create a batch file named `example`. Note that the file extension is `.bat`.

STEP 4: At the * prompt, key in the following:

```
i  <Enter>
```

STEP 4: At the * prompt, key in the following:

```
i  <Enter>
```

```
EDLIN example.bat
New file
*i
    1:_
```

```
EDLIN example.bat
New file
*i
    1:_
```

STEP 5: Key in the following:

```
DIR *.dos  <Enter>
DIR A:*.dos  <Enter>
CHKDSK  <Enter>
<Ctrl>-C
```

STEP 5: Key in the following:

```
DIR *.dos  <Enter>
DIR C:*.dos  <Enter>
CHKDSK  <Enter>
<Ctrl>-C
```

STEP 6: You will be back at the * prompt. Key in the following:

```
L   <Enter>
```

```
*L
     1:*DIR *.dos
     2:*DIR A:*.dos
     3:*CHKDSK
*_
```

STEP 6: You will be back at the * prompt. Key in the following:

```
L   <Enter>
```

```
*L
     1:*DIR *.dos
     2:*DIR C:*.dos
     3:*CHKDSK
*_
```

WHAT'S HAPPENING? Look at this file line by line. Each numbered line is a legitimate and separate DOS command that could be keyed in at the prompt. Each command is on a separate line. Line 1 asks for a listing of all the files on the disk in the default drive that have the file extension `.dos`. Line 2 asks for all the files on a specified disk (A: or C:) that have the file extension `.dos`. Line 3 then asks DOS to load and execute the `CHKDSK` command from the default drive and check the disk in the default drive. At this point, all that has been done is to write or create the batch file. You need to exit `EDLIN` by keying in `E` at the * prompt.

STEP 7: Key in the following:

```
E   <Enter>
```

```
*L
     1:*DIR *.dos
     2:*DIR A:*.dos
     3:*CHKDSK
*E

B>_
```

STEP 7: Key in the following:

```
E   <Enter>
```

```
*L
     1:*DIR *.dos
     2:*DIR C:*.dos
     3:*CHKDSK
*E

A>_
```

STEP 8: Key in the following:

```
B>DIR example.bat   <Enter>
```

```
B>DIR example.bat

Volume in drive B is DATADISK
Directory of B:\

EXAMPLE      BAT    33    11-23-87   3:04p
          1 File(s)   230400 bytes free
B>_
```

STEP 8: Key in the following:

```
A>DIR example.bat   <Enter>
```

```
A>DIR example.bat

Volume in drive A is DATADISK
Directory of A:\

EXAMPLE      BAT    33    11-23-87   3:04p
          1 File(s)   230400 bytes free
A>_
```

WHAT'S HAPPENING? You exited the `EDLIN` program and returned to the system prompt. The `DIR example.bat` command shows that there is a file on the DATA disk called `example.bat`. It is a file like any other file. How do you make DOS treat it like a program file? To run or execute this batch file, you key in the name of the file at the prompt. DOS will then look for a file in its internal table called `example`. It will not find it. It will look for a file called `example.com` on the default disk, the DATA disk. No file exists called `example.com`. DOS looks for a file on the default disk called `example.exe`. No file exists called `example.exe`. DOS then looks for a file called `example.bat` on the default disk. It does find a file by this name. It loads it into memory and executes each line. Thus, to execute the batch file called `example`, key in the name of the file at the prompt. Watch what happens on the screen after you key in the file name. The display will scroll by.

STEP 9: Key in the following:

```
B>EXAMPLE   <Enter>
```

```
B>EXAMPLE

B>DIR *.dos

Volume in drive B is DATADISK
Directory of B:\

WILDONE     DOS     179     11-23-87    1:59p
WILDTWO     DOS     180     11-23-87    1:59p
WILDTHR     DOS     179     11-23-87    2:01p
    3 Files(s)    230400 bytes free

B>DIR A:*.dos

Volume in drive A has no label
Directory of A:\

File not found

B>CHKDSK
Volume DATADISK   created Nov 23, 1987    8:10p

     362496 bytes total disk space
      38912 bytes in 3 hidden files
      93814 bytes in 50 user files
     230400 bytes available on disk

     655360 bytes total memory
     535824 bytes free
B>_
```

STEP 9: Key in the following:

```
A>EXAMPLE   <Enter>
```

```
A>EXAMPLE

A>DIR *.dos

Volume in drive A is DATADISK
Directory of A:\

WILDONE     DOS     179     11-23-87    1:59p
WILDTWO     DOS     180     11-23-87    1:59p
WILDTHR     DOS     179     11-23-87    2:01p
    3 Files(s)    230400 bytes free

A>DIR C:*.dos

Volume in drive C is HARD DRIVE
Directory of C:\

File not found

A>CHKDSK
Volume DATADISK   created Nov 23, 1987    8:10p

     362496 bytes total disk space
      38912 bytes in 3 hidden files
      93814 bytes in 50 user files
     230400 bytes available on disk

     655360 bytes total memory
     535824 bytes free
A>_
```

WHAT'S HAPPENING? DOS read and executed each line of the batch file you wrote, one line at a time. The screen displayed each command line and the results of the command line as it executed. Note how each line executed as if you had sat in front of the keyboard and keyed in each command individually. You did key in the commands when you wrote the batch file, but you only had to key them in one time. By keying in `example` at the prompt, each command was executed automatically. The first line was "`DIR *.dos`." When DOS read that line, it executed it and showed on the screen all three files on the DATA disk with the file extension `.dos`. It read the next line of the `example` file and looked on the System Disk for any file that had the file extension `.dos`. Since there were no files on the System Disk with the extension `.dos`, it gave the message, "`File not found`." It then read the next command line, `CHKDSK`, executed that command, and displayed the statistics for the DATA disk. Now that you have written the file `example.bat`, you can execute this batch file `example` over and over again by keying in `example` at the prompt. By keying in one command, you can execute three DOS commands.

11.5 WRITING AND EXECUTING A BATCH FILE TO SAVE KEYSTROKES

The example above was a sample to show you how to write and execute a batch file. However, that file is not terribly useful. The next batch file to be written will allow you to key in only one keystroke instead of nine. When you want a directory listing of the A drive or C drive that uses the parameter `/P`, you need to key in `DIR A:/P` or `DIR C:/P`. That is eight keystrokes, and you have to use the shift key to access the colon instead of the semicolon. With a batch file, you can do the same task but you only have to press one key.

ACTIVITY 11.6 WRITING AND EXECUTING A ONE-LETTER BATCH FILE

NOTE: Two disk drive users will have the DOS System Disk in Drive A. The DATA disk will be in Drive B with the `B>` displayed. Hard disk users will have `A>` displayed. The DATA disk will be in Drive A.

STEP 1: Key in the following:

`B>EDLIN a.bat <Enter>`

```
B>EDLIN a.bat
New file
*_
```

STEP 1: Key in the following:

`A>EDLIN c.bat <Enter>`

```
A>EDLIN c.bat
New file
*_
```

STEP 2: Key in the following:

```
I   <Enter>
     1:*DIR A:/P  <Enter>
     2:*Ctrl-C
L <Enter>
```

```
*I
    1:*DIR A:/P
    2:*^C
*L
    1: DIR A:/P
*_
```

STEP 3: Key in the following:

```
E   <Enter>
```

```
*E
B>_
```

STEP 2: Key in the following:

```
I   <Enter>
     1:*DIR C:/P   <Enter>
     2:*Ctrl-C
L   <Enter>
```

```
*I
    1:*DIR C:/P  <Enter>
    2:*^C
*L
    1: DIR C:/P
*_
```

STEP 3: Key in the following:

```
E   <Enter>
```

```
*E
A>__
```

WHAT'S HAPPENING? You have written a one-line batch file. You exited `EDLIN` and are back at the system prompt. Now, whenever you want to see a list that pauses of the table of contents of the disk in Drive A (two disk drive users) or Drive C (hard disk users), you only have to key in one letter to execute this command.

STEP 4: Key in the following:

```
B>A   <Enter>
```

```
ANSI     SYS      1651   3-07-85    1:43p
ASSIGN   COM      1509   3-07-85    1:43p
ATTRIB   EXE     15091   3-07-85    1:43p
BACKUP   COM      5577   3-07-85    1:43p
BASIC    COM     17792   3-07-85    1:43p
BASICA   COM     27520   3-07-85    1:43p
CHKDSK   COM      9435   3-07-85    1:43p
COMMAND  COM     23210   3-07-85    1:43p
COMP     COM      3664   3-07-85    1:43p
DISKCOMP COM      4073   3-07-85    1:43p
DISKCOPY COM      4329   3-07-85    1:43p
EDLIN    COM      7261   3-07-85    1:43p
FDISK    COM      8173   3-07-85    1:43p
FIND     EXE      6403   3-07-85    1:43p
FORMAT   COM      9398   3-07-85    1:43p
GRAFTABL COM      1169   3-07-85    1:43p
GRAPHICS COM      3111   3-07-85    1:43p
JOIN     EXE     15971   3-07-85    1:43p
KEYBFR   COM      2473   4-12-85    4:22p
KEYBGR   COM      2418   4-12-85    4:23p
KEYBIT   COM      2361   4-12-85    4:25p
KEYBSP   COM      2451   4-12-85    4:24p
KEYBUK   COM      2348   4-12-85    4:26p
Strike a key when ready..._
```

STEP 4: Key in the following:

```
A>C   <Enter>
```

```
ANSI     SYS      1651   3-07-85    1:43p
ASSIGN   COM      1509   3-07-85    1:43p
ATTRIB   EXE     15091   3-07-85    1:43p
BACKUP   COM      5577   3-07-85    1:43p
BASIC    COM     17792   3-07-85    1:43p
BASICA   COM     27520   3-07-85    1:43p
CHKDSK   COM      9435   3-07-85    1:43p
COMMAND  COM     23210   3-07-85    1:43p
COMP     COM      3664   3-07-85    1:43p
DISKCOMP COM      4073   3-07-85    1:43p
DISKCOPY COM      4329   3-07-85    1:43p
EDLIN    COM      7261   3-07-85    1:43p
FDISK    COM      8173   3-07-85    1:43p
FIND     EXE      6403   3-07-85    1:43p
FORMAT   COM      9398   3-07-85    1:43p
GRAFTABL COM      1169   3-07-85    1:43p
GRAPHICS COM      3111   3-07-85    1:43p
JOIN     EXE     15971   3-07-85    1:43p
KEYBFR   COM      2473   4-12-85    4:22p
KEYBGR   COM      2418   4-12-85    4:23p
KEYBIT   COM      2361   4-12-85    4:25p
KEYBSP   COM      2451   4-12-85    4:24p
KEYBUK   COM      2348   4-12-85    4:26p
Strike a key when ready..._
```

WHAT'S HAPPENING? (Hard disk users—Your display may vary based on what is installed on the hard disk.) As you can see, you set up a command sequence in a batch file called `a.bat` or `c.bat`. You can run this batch file over and over again, simply by keying in the name of the batch file at the system prompt.

STEP 5: Press any key until the default prompt `B>` is displayed.

STEP 5: Press any key until the default prompt `A>` is displayed.

11.7 THE PROMPT COMMAND

The system prompt that you are familiar with is a letter of the alphabet designating the assigned or default drive, followed by the greater than sign, i.e., `A>`, `B>`, or `C>`. This is what the system always defaults to when it is booted. But the prompt can be changed because `PROMPT` is also an internal command. In other words, you can set the prompt. The syntax is:

```
PROMPT [any text]
```

`PROMPT` also has some characters that mean very specific things. These are called meta-strings. They always have the syntax `$c` where `c` represents any of the following list:

- `$` The dollar sign
- `t` The time
- `d` The date
- `p` The current directory of the default drive
- `v` The version number
- `n` The default drive letter
- `g` The greater than sign >
- `l` The less than sign <
- `b` The pipe sign ¦
- `h` A backspace; the previous character is erased
- `e` The escape character
- `_` The underscore, which is a CR-LF sequence (carriage return line feed) meaning go to the beginning of a new line on the screen

The following activity will allow you to change the prompt and use a meta-string. `PROMPT` keyed in without any parameters returns the prompt to the default (`A>`, `B>`, or `C>`).

ACTIVITY 11.8 CHANGING THE PROMPT

STEP 1: The DATA disk is in Drive B with the B> displayed. Key in the following:

B>PROMPT Hello there $g <Enter>

```
B>PROMPT Hello there $g

Hello there >_
```

STEP 1: The DATA disk is in Drive A with the A> displayed. Key in the following:

A>PROMPT Hello there $g <Enter>

```
A>PROMPT Hello there $g

Hello there >_
```

WHAT'S HAPPENING? You have changed the prompt. You no longer see B> or A> but what you supplied, Hello there >. The greater than symbol appeared because you used one of the meta-strings, $g.

STEP 2: Press <Enter> three times.

```
Hello there >
Hello there >
Hello there >
Hello there >_
```

STEP 2: Press <Enter> three times.

```
Hello there >
Hello there >
Hello there >
Hello there >_
```

WHAT'S HAPPENING? The function of the prompt has not changed, only its appearance. The new prompt works just as if the A> or B> or C> was displayed. Any command keyed in will work the same way.

STEP 3: Key in the following:

Hello there >TYPE mar.87 <Enter>

```
Hello there >TYPE mar.87
There is my March file.
It is my third dummy file.
This is file 3.

Hello there >_
```

STEP 3: Key in the following:

Hello there >TYPE mar.87 <Enter>

```
Hello there >TYPE mar.87
There is my March file.
It is my third dummy file.
This is file 3.

Hello there >_
```

WHAT'S HAPPENING? The TYPE command works as usual. What happens if you change drives?

STEP 4: Key in the following:

```
Hello there >A:  <Enter>
```

```
Hello there> A:

Hello there >_
```

STEP 4: Key in the following:

```
Hello there >C:  <Enter>
```

```
Hello there> C:

Hello there >_
```

WHAT'S HAPPENING? You changed the default drive from `B>` to `A>` (two disk drive users) and from `A>` to `C>` (hard disk users). But, as you can see, the prompt no longer displays the drive letter on the screen. You have no way of knowing which drive you are in.

STEP 5: Key in the following:

```
Hello there >VOL <Enter>
```

```
Hello there >VOL

 Volume in drive A has no label

Hello there >_
```

STEP 5: Key in the following:

```
Hello there >VOL <Enter>
```

```
Hello there >VOL

 Volume in drive C is HARD DRIVE

Hello there >_
```

WHAT'S HAPPENING? You did change the designated drive. You can see, however, that having the default drive letter displayed on the screen is very important.

STEP 6: Key in the following:

```
Hello there >PROMPT Hi $n$g <Enter>
```

```
Hello there >PROMPT Hi $n$g

Hi A>_
```

STEP 6: Key in the following:

```
Hello there >PROMPT Hi $n$g <Enter>
```

```
Hello there >PROMPT Hi $n$g

Hi C>_
```

WHAT'S HAPPENING? The meta-string `$n` displays the drive letter and the meta-string `$g` displays the greater-than sign.

STEP 7: Key in the following:

```
Hi A>PROMPT  <Enter>
```

STEP 7: Key in the following:

```
Hi C>PROMPT  <Enter>
```

```
Hi A>PROMPT

A>_
```

```
Hi C>PROMPT

C>_
```

WHAT'S HAPPENING? By using the PROMPT command with no parameters or meta-strings, the prompt becomes the usual A> or C>. You can always key in PROMPT to return to the default prompt.

STEP 8: Key in the following:

```
A>B:  <Enter>
```

STEP 8: Key in the following:

```
C>A:  <Enter>
```

WHAT'S HAPPENING? Your default drive is now where the DATA disk is.

11.9 A BATCH FILE USING THE PROMPT COMMAND

Now that you see how the PROMPT command works, you are going to write a batch file changing the prompt. It is hard to remember all the meta-strings. Typically, one looks them up. But by putting the information into a batch file, you only need to look up the information once and just remember the batch file name. The next batch file is going to put the system date above the letter prompt.

ACTIVITY 11.10 WRITING BATCH FILES USING THE PROMPT COMMAND

NOTE: Two disk drive users will have the DOS System Disk in Drive A. The DATA disk will be in Drive B and the B> will be displayed. Hard disk users will have the DATA disk in Drive A with the A> displayed.

STEP 1: Key in the following:

```
B>EDLIN dispdate.bat  <Enter>
```

```
B>EDLIN dispdate.bat
New file
*_
```

STEP 1: Key in the following:

```
A>EDLIN dispdate.bat  <Enter>
```

```
A>EDLIN dispdate.bat
New file
*_
```

WHAT'S HAPPENING? This file could be named anything with the extension `.bat`. However, it is helpful to select a file name that will indicate the purpose of the batch file. `dispdate` stands for "display the date above the prompt." Step 2 requires that the data be keyed in exactly as shown. The line reads "`PROMPT $d$_$n$g`" Following `$d$` is an underscore, which must be keyed in. `$d$` means display the date; _ means go to the next line; `$n` means display the default drive; and `$g` means display the > symbol.

STEP 2: Key in the following:

```
i   <Enter>
    PROMPT $d$_$n$g   <Enter>
    <Ctrl>-C
e   <Enter>
```

STEP 2: Key in the following:

```
i   <Enter>
    PROMPT $d$_$n$g   <Enter>
    <Ctrl>-C
e   <Enter>
```

WHAT'S HAPPENING? A batch file called `dispdate.bat` was written using `EDLIN`. `EDLIN` was exited and you are back at the system prompt. At this point, a new batch file exists. But it must be executed before it can carry out its commands.

STEP 3: Key in the following:

```
B>DISPDATE   <Enter>
```

```
B>DISPDATE

PROMPT $d$_$n$g

Mon 11-23-1987
B>
Mon 11-23-1987
B>_
```

STEP 3: Key in the following:

```
A>DISPDATE   <Enter>
```

```
B>DISPDATE

PROMPT $d$_$n$g

Mon 11-23-1987
A>
Mon 11-23-1987
A>_
```

WHAT'S HAPPENING? The date displayed will vary, based on the date that was keyed in when the system was booted. By keying in the name of the batch file at the prompt, `dispdate`, the new prompt was set so that the system date is displayed above the regular letter prompt. The reason that the date and drive letter prompt appear twice is that the first time it appears, `dispdate` is being executed. The second time you are returned to the operating system, or the new system prompt.

STEP 4: Key in the following:

```
Mon  11-23-1987
B>CLS  <Enter>
```

```
Mon  11-23-1987
B>_
```

STEP 4: Key in the following:

```
Mon  11-23-1987
A>CLS  <Enter>
```

```
Mon  11-23-1987
A>_
```

WHAT'S HAPPENING? CLS refreshed the screen and returned the prompt to the upper lefthand corner. Now, whenever you want the current date displayed along with the prompt, all you need to do is key in the batch file called dispdate. You no longer need to remember or look up the meta-strings. You have automated the process. When the system is booted, the default prompt is always A> or C>. To return to the default prompt is a matter of keying in PROMPT without any parameters.

STEP 5: Key in the following:

```
Mon  11-23-1987
B>PROMPT  <Enter>
```

```
Mon  11-23-1987
B>PROMPT

B>_
```

STEP 5: Key in the following:

```
Mon  11-23-1987
A>PROMPT  <Enter>
```

```
Mon 11-23-1987
A>PROMPT

A>_
```

WHAT'S HAPPENING? The default prompt is displayed. There are other things you can do with the PROMPT command. The next batch file will allow you to automate the setting of printer characteristics.

11.11 SETTING UP THE PRINTER IN CONDENSED MODE WITH A BATCH FILE

In Chapter 10, you learned how to set up the printer with the MODE command so that it printed in a condensed mode. This is another example of what you might put in a batch file. Rather than having to look up the necessary command and parameters each time, you look it up once and write the commands in a batch file. Then when you need to set your printer to condensed mode, you execute the batch file. (Remember, if MODE does not work with your printer, putting it in a batch file still isn't going to make it work.)

ACTIVITY 11.12 WRITING A PRINTER BATCH FILE

NOTE: Two disk drive users will have the DOS System Disk in Drive A. The DATA disk will be in Drive B with the `B>` displayed. Hard disk users will have the DATA disk in Drive A with the `A>` displayed.

STEP 1: Key in the following:

```
B>EDLIN smallprt.bat  <Enter>
```

STEP 1: Key in the following:

```
A>EDLIN smallprt.bat  <Enter>
```

```
B>EDLIN smallprt.bat
New file
*_
```

```
A>EDLIN smallprt.bat
New file
*_
```

WHAT'S HAPPENING? You are creating another batch file using `EDLIN`. Again, you could have named this file anything. `smallprt.bat` seemed a good name as it stands for small print.

STEP 2: Key in the following:

```
i   <Enter>
    MODE LPT1: 132,8  <Enter>
    <Ctrl>-C
E   <Enter>
```

STEP 2: Key in the following:

```
i   <Enter>
    MODE LPT1: 132,8  <Enter>
    <Ctrl>-C
E   <Enter>
```

WHAT'S HAPPENING? You keyed in the appropriate `MODE` command parameters to set the print 132 CPI and 8 LPI. You exited the program and returned to the system prompt. The printer is not set with the new characteristics until you execute the program.

STEP 3: Key in the following:

```
B>smallprt  <Enter>
```

STEP 3: Key in the following:

```
A>smallprt  <Enter>
```

```
B>smallprt

B>MODE LPT1:132,8
Bad command or file name

B>
B>_
```

```
A>smallprt

A>MODE LPT1:132,8
Bad command or file name

A>
A>_
```

WHAT'S HAPPENING? What went wrong? What is wrong with the batch file called `smallprt.bat`? Nothing is wrong with the batch file. DOS went to the DATA disk on the default drive and found the batch file `smallprt`. DOS loaded it and began to execute `smallprt`. You see the command line on the screen, `MODE LPT1:132,8`. DOS read the first line and went to find the `MODE` command on the default disk, the DATA disk. The `MODE` command, an external program DOS needs to load, is not on the default drive—thus the "`Bad command`" message. Not only must the batch file be on the default disk, but so must any commands or programs that the batch file is going to call. To fix this problem, the batch file `smallprt.bat` could be copied to where the `MODE` program is, or the `MODE` program could be copied to the DATA disk. There is a third alternative.

STEP 4: Key in the following:

```
B>EDLIN smallprt.bat   <Enter>
1i   <Enter>
     A:   <Enter>
     <Ctrl>-C
3i   <Enter>
     B:   <Enter>
     <Ctrl>-C
L    <Enter>
```

```
*L
    1: A:
    2: MODE LPT1:132,8
    3: B:
*_
```

STEP 4: Key in the following:

```
A>EDLIN smallprt.bat   <Enter>
1i   <Enter>
     C:   <Enter>
     <Ctrl>-C
3i   <Enter>
     A:   <Enter>
     <Ctrl>-C
L    <Enter>
```

```
*L
    1: C:
    2: MODE LPT1:132,8
    3: A:
*_
```

WHAT'S HAPPENING? What are you doing here? You are changing the default drive to the system area where the `MODE` command program is located. (Hard disk users, if the DOS programs are in a subdirectory, you must include the path such as `C:\DOS`). DOS can then find the `MODE` command and load it with the proper parameters to change the printer output. Then the default drive is changed to the drive that has the DATA disk and the files.

STEP 5: Key in the following:

```
E   <Enter>
```

```
*E

B>_
```

STEP 5: Key in the following:

```
E   <Enter>
```

```
*E

A>_
```

STEP 6: Turn on the printer. Key in the following:

B>smallprt <Enter>

```
B>smallprt

B>A:

A>MODE LPT1:132,8

LPT1: not rerouted

LPT1: set for 132

Printer lines per inch set

No retry on parallel printer time-out

A>B:

B>
B>_
```

STEP 6: Turn on the printer. Key in the following:

A>smallprt <Enter>

```
A>smallprt

A>C:

C>MODE LPT1:132,8

LPT1: not rerouted

LPT1: set for 132

Printer lines per inch set

No retry on parallel printer time-out

C>A:

A>
A>_
```

WHAT'S HAPPENING? The printer is now set in the condensed mode. The default drive is still where the DATA disk is without the bother of having to copy files from disk to disk. To set the printer back, the MODE command can be issued with the 80,6 parameters.

There is another way to cancel the settings and set the printer back to the default settings. Turning off the printer and turning it on again resets the printer to the default settings.

STEP 7: Turn off the printer. Turn on the printer.

STEP 7: Turn off the printer. Turn on the printer.

11.13 UNDERSTANDING AUTOEXEC.BAT FILES

There is a unique batch file that has a special name, autoexec.bat, that stands for automatically execute. When the system is booted and the operating system is loaded into memory, one of the last things DOS does, prior to displaying the date/time prompt, is to look for a file called autoexec.bat on the booting disk. If DOS finds it, this file takes precedence, and DOS automatically runs it. The autoexec.bat file is just a batch file. The only thing special about it is the time it is run. It is only run when you boot the system. Thus, only one autoexec.bat file can be on any one disk. But in order for autoexec.bat to be automatic, it must be on the booting disk, Drive A or Drive C.

This file is typically used for start-up routines. An `autoexec.bat` file contains commands that a specific user is interested in having run. In other words, it is a custom program.

Both hard disk users and two disk drive users are going to create an `autoexec` batch file on the DOS System Disk in Drive A and then boot from that disk. Hard disk users may already have an `autoexec.bat` file on their hard disk and will not want to overwrite that file. Because of that, the `autoexec.bat` file is going to be written on the DATA disk and then both hard disk users and two disk drive users will boot from the DATA disk. The `autoexec.bat` file is going to see if you have a file `example.bat` on the DATA disk, ask you for the system date, and run the `dispdate.bat` file created in Activity 11.10.

ACTIVITY 11.14 WRITING AND USING AN AUTOEXEC.BAT FILE

STEP 1. Change the default drive to `A>`.

STEP 1: Change the default drive to `A>`. The DATA disk should be in Drive A.

NOTE: Two disk drive users will have the DOS System Disk in Drive A with the `A>` displayed and the DATA disk in Drive B. Hard disk users will have the DATA disk in Drive A with the `A>` displayed on the screen.

STEP 2: Key in the following:

```
A>EDLIN autoexec.bat  <Enter>
```

```
A>EDLIN autoexec.bat
New file
*_
```

STEP 2: Key in the following:

```
A>EDLIN autoexec.bat  <Enter>
```

```
A>EDLIN autoexec.bat
New file
*_
```

STEP 3: Key in the following:

```
i   <Enter>
    DATE  <Enter>
    DIR B:example.bat <Enter>
    B:dispdate  <Enter>
    <Ctrl>-C
E   <Enter>
```

```
A>EDLIN autoexec.bat
New file
*i
     1:*DATE
     2:*DIR B:example.bat
     3:*B:dispdate
     4:*^C
*E
A>_
```

STEP 3: Key in the following:

```
i   <Enter>
    DATE  <Enter>
    DIR example.bat <Enter>
    dispdate  <Enter>
    <Ctrl>-C
E   <Enter>
```

```
A>EDLIN autoexec.bat
New file
*i
     1:*DATE
     2:*DIR example.bat
     3:*dispdate
     4:*^C
*E
A>_
```

WHAT'S HAPPENING? You have written a batch file named `autoexec.bat` using `EDLIN`. When you completed the batch file, you exited `EDLIN` and returned to the system prompt. This file, when executed, will run the `DATE` command. An `autoexec.bat` file will bypass the `DATE` and `TIME` command if they are not expressly in the `autoexec.bat` file. It then will execute the next line, which asks if the DATA disk has a file named `example.bat`. It calls the `dispdate.bat` file written in the last activity. `dispdate` is a custom prompt. It is included in this example to demonstrate that you can call another batch file from a batch file. The last command in a batch file can be another batch file, which allows you to chain one file to another. You could execute this file by keying in `autoexec` at the `A>`. What makes it unique is that it executes automatically when you boot the system.

STEP 4: Reboot the system by pressing the <Ctrl>, <Alt>, and <Del> keys. You will see the following:

```
A>DATE
Current date is Tue 1-01-1980
Enter new date (mm-dd-yy):_
```

STEP 4: Reboot the system by pressing the <Ctrl>, <Alt>, and <Del> keys. You will see the following:

```
A>DATE
Current date is Tue 1-01-1980
Enter new date (mm-dd-yy):_
```

WHAT'S HAPPENING? Note that the first command, the `DATE`, is being executed.

STEP 5: Key in today's date and press <Enter>.

```
A>DIR example.bat
  Volume in Drive B is DATADISK
  Directory of B:\

EXAMPLE    BAT    33      11-23-87    3:04P
     1 File(s)        252280 bytes free

B>dispdate

A>PROMPT $d$_$n$g

Mon 11-23-1987
A>
Mon 11-23-1987
A>_
```

STEP 5: Key in today's date and press <Enter>.

```
A>DIR example.bat
  Volume in Drive A is DATADISK
  Directory of A:\

EXAMPLE    BAT    33      11-23-87    3:04P
     1 File(s)        252280 bytes free

A>dispdate

A>PROMPT $d$_$n$g

Mon 11-23-1987
A>
Mon 11-23-1987
A>_
```

WHAT'S HAPPENING? You did not have to key in the file name to execute this program because it automatically executed when you booted the system. It ran the command `DIR example.bat` and showed you that you do have this file on the DATA disk. The custom prompt is not displayed twice. The first date and `A>`

prompt displayed are the result of executing the `PROMPT` command. The second date and `A>` indicate that the batch file has finished executing and you are back at the system level prompt waiting for the next command.

STEP 6: Key in the following:

```
A>PROMPT  <Enter>
```

STEP 7: Key in the following:

```
A>REN autoexec.bat auto.bat <Enter>
```

STEP 6: Key in the following:

```
A>PROMPT  <Enter>
```

STEP 7: Key in the following:

```
A>REN autoexec.bat auto.bat<Enter>
```


WHAT'S HAPPENING? In Step 6, you returned to the default system prompt. In Step 7, you renamed the `autoexec.bat` file to `auto.bat`. Now `auto.bat` is just another batch file and will not automatically execute when the system is booted. Remember that the name of the file that automatically boots is `AUTOEXEC.BAT`.

CHAPTER SUMMARY

1. Batch processing means to run a series of instructions without interruption.
2. Interactive processing allows the user to interface directly with the computer and update records immediately.
3. Batch files allow a user to put together a string of commands and execute them with one command.
4. Batch files must have the `.bat` file extension.
5. DOS first looks internally for a command, then a `.com` file extension, then an `.exe` file extension, and finally a `.bat` file extension.
6. The `PROMPT` command, an internal command, allows the prompt to be changed to suit the user.
7. The `PROMPT` command makes use of meta-strings that have predefined meanings to DOS.
8. The default prompt is always `A>` or `C>`.
9. `EDLIN` is a text editor used to write batch files.
10. A word processor, if it outputs in text, can be used to write batch files.
11. Batch files must be in text format.
12. Batch files are executed from the system prompt by keying in the batch file name.
13. A batch file called `autoexec.bat` can be created.
14. An `autoexec.bat` file will execute automatically when the system is booted.
15. There can only be one `autoexec.bat` file per booting disk.

REVIEW QUESTIONS

1. Give two reasons for writing a batch file.
2. Describe the differences between batch and interactive processing.
3. You have a batch file called `check.bat`. You key in `B>check`. What and where does DOS look for?
4. A batch file called `check.bat` is executing. You get the following display:

```
B>check
B>DIR *.com
Volume in Drive B is DATADISK
Directory of B:\

File not found

B>CHKDSK
Bad command or file name

B>
B>_
```

   Why did you get the "`Bad command`" message? How can you solve the problem?
5. How can the prompt be changed from `A>` to `Good morning`?
6. Define meta-strings.
7. How and why would you use meta-strings?
8. What does an `autoexec.bat` file do?
9. How many `autoexec.bat` files can be on a disk?
10. What tools can you use to write a batch file?
11. What commands can be put in a batch file?
12. The following is a line in batch file:

```
DIR *.tmp, DIR *.exe, DIR *.txt
```

   What would happen when DOS read that line?

TRUE/FALSE

1. It is possible to customize the prompt.
2. An `autoexec.bat` file is executed at the time of booting the system.
3. A batch file can call another batch file.
4. A batch file may have any file extension.
5. `PROMPT Hello $n$g` will change the prompt to read: `Hello B>`.
6. Batch files always contain text.
7. A batch file called `b.bat` that has the following line:

```
DIR B:/W
```

   will allow the user to get a wide display of the directory on Drive B with one keystroke.
8. Batch files are not very useful.
9. Running a batch file is as if a user sat in front of the keyboard and keyed in each command line.
10. A batch file called `new.bat` is executed by keying in `new` at the system prompt.

SUGGESTED ACTIVITIES

All tasks will be done on the DATA DISK.

Two disk drive users: Place the DATA disk in Drive B. Hard disk users: Place the DATA disk in Drive A.

1. Create a batch file named `extra.bat` using DOS commands:

   Clear the screen.
   Display the directory of the DATA disk for any file that has `.txt` as a file extension.
   Make a copy of the file called `wildone` and call the copy `tv.cat`.
   Copy the file called `tv.cat` to the printer.
   Erase the file called `tv.cat`.

   Execute or run your batch file to be sure it works.
2. Copy the batch file `extra.bat` to the printer—the contents of the file you just created, not the output or screen results. Do not turn in any output from running the batch file, just the actual contents of the batch file.
3. Set your printer using the batch file you created, `smallprt.bat`, to have the printer output in a condensed mode. Print the file called `sales.let` in condensed mode. If your printer will not run in a condensed mode, just print the file `smallprt.bat` and indicate that your printer cannot be changed with the `MODE` command.
4. Write a batch file called `regprt.bat` for the default printer characteristics `CPI 80` and `LPI 6`. Using this batch file, print a copy of the file `personal.fil` in regular print mode. If your printer will not accept the `MODE` command, print `personal.fil` and indicate that your printer cannot be changed with the `MODE` command.
5. Copy the contents of the file called `regprt.bat` to the printer.
6. Write an `autoexec.bat` file that gives a wide display of the default directory and then checks the disk. Copy the contents of this file to the printer. If you no longer wish this file to boot automatically, rename it `happy.day`.
7. Write a batch file called `newpmpt.bat`. In the file, change the prompt so that the prompt will be:

   ```
   Good day Drive B>
   ```

   B represents any drive letter. Execute this new prompt. When it is on the screen, print it.
8. Delete any files with the extension `.bak` on the DATA disk.
9. Do a directory display to prove all the `.bak` files are gone from the DATA disk. Print this screen.
10. Do a directory display of all the batch files on the DATA disk. Print this screen.

CUSTOMIZED BATCH FILES

CHAPTER

12

CHAPTER OBJECTIVES

This chapter continues the discussion of batch files. It introduces some special batch file commands and the use of dummy parameters. After completing this chapter, you will:

Be able to explain and demonstrate the use of special batch file commands such as `REM` and `PAUSE`.

Be able to stop executing a batch file.

Understand the concept of dummy parameters in batch files.

Be able to write batch files using dummy parameters.

12.0 MATERIALS NEEDED

1. DOS System Disk
2. DATA disk
3. Backup Data disk

12.1 SPECIAL BATCH FILE COMMANDS

There are more commands that are specially designed to be used in batch files. These commands can make batch files extremely versatile. They include `REM` and `PAUSE`.

12.2 THE REM COMMAND

The `REM` command, which stands for remarks, is a special command used only in batch files. It allows the user to key in explanatory text that will be displayed on the screen. Nothing else happens. `REM` does not cause DOS to take any action, but it is very useful. When DOS sees **REM**, it knows that anything following the **REM** is not a command and thus is not supposed to be executed, just displayed on the screen. **REM** allows a batch file to be **documented.** In a data processing environment, to document means to give an explanation about the purpose of the batch file. This can be very important when there are many batch files on a disk and when someone who did not write the batch file would like to use it.

ACTIVITY 12.3 USING THE REM COMMAND IN A BATCH FILE

NOTE: Two disk drive users will have the DATA disk in Drive B with the B> displayed. Hard disk users will have the DATA disk in Drive A and have the A> displayed.

STEP 1: Key in the following:

B>EDLIN dispdate.bat <Enter>

```
B>EDLIN dispdate.bat
End of input file
*_
```

STEP 1: Key in the following:

A>EDLIN dispdate.bat <Enter>

```
A>EDLIN dispdate.bat
End of input file
*_
```

WHAT'S HAPPENING? You are going to edit the batch file that you created in Chapter 11.

STEP 2: Key in the following:

```
1i<Enter>
REM The purpose of this file  <Enter>
REM is to display the system  <Enter>
REM or current date above the  <Enter>
REM usual system prompt.  <Enter>
<Ctrl>-C
```

STEP 2: Key in the following:

```
1i<Enter>
REM The purpose of this file  <Enter>
REM is to display the system  <Enter>
REM or current date above the  <Enter>
REM usual system prompt.  <Enter>
<Ctrl>-C
```

WHAT'S HAPPENING? The * prompt is displayed. You have inserted some new text with the **REM** preceding each new line. List your file with the L command at the * prompt.

STEP 3: Key in the following:

```
L <Enter>
```

```
*L
  1: REM The purpose of this file
  2: REM is to display the system
  3: REM or current date above the
  4: REM usual system prompt.
  5:*PROMPT $d$_$n$g
*_
```

STEP 3: Key in the following:

```
L <Enter>
```

```
*L
  1: REM The purpose of this file
  2: REM is to display the system
  3: REM or current date above the
  4: REM usual system prompt.
  5:*PROMPT $d$_$n$g
*_
```

WHAT'S HAPPENING? This batch file was created to display the system date above the prompt. The remarks just added explain the purpose of this batch file.

STEP 4: Key in the following:

```
*E  <Enter>
```

```
*E

B>_
```

STEP 4: Key in the following:

```
*E  <Enter>
```

```
*E

A>_
```

WHAT'S HAPPENING? The changes were made to the `dispdate.bat` file. You then returned to the system prompt. However, to execute this `dispdate` batch file, you must call it.

STEP 5: Key in the following:

```
B>dispdate  <Enter>
```

```
B>dispdate

B>REM The purpose of this file

B>REM is to display the system

B>REM or current date above the

B>REM usual system prompt.

B>PROMPT $d$_$n$g

Mon 11-23-1987
B>
Mon 11-23-1987
B>_
```

STEP 5: Key in the following:

```
A>dispdate  <Enter>
```

```
A>dispdate

A>REM The purpose of this file

A>REM is to display the system

A>REM or current date above the

A>REM usual system prompt.

A>PROMPT $d$_$n$g

Mon 11-23-1987
A>
Mon 11-23-1987
A>_
```

WHAT'S HAPPENING? The date displayed will vary depending on the date keyed in when the system was booted. By keying in `dispdate` the batch file was executed. DOS read the first line of the batch file, `REM The purpose of this file`. DOS knew that it was supposed to do nothing but display the text following `REM` on the screen. It then read the next line in the batch file, `REM is to display the system` and did the same. DOS kept reading and displaying the `REM` lines until it got to the `PROMPT`. `PROMPT` is a command. DOS then executed or ran the `PROMPT` program. The prompt now consists of the system prompt as well as the system date displayed above the lettered drive. The purpose of `REM` is to provide explanatory remarks about the batch file, not to execute text.

STEP 6: Key in the following:

```
Mon 11-23-1987
B>PROMPT  <Enter>
```

```
Mon 11-23-1987
B>PROMPT

B>_
```

STEP 6: Key in the following:

```
Mon 11-23-1987
A>PROMPT  <Enter>
```

```
Mon 11-23-1987
A>PROMPT

A>_
```

WHAT'S HAPPENING? The prompt has been set back to the default. Only the system prompt, the lettered drive, will be displayed without any date above it.

12.4 THE PAUSE COMMAND

Another batch file command is `PAUSE`. `PAUSE` does exactly what it sounds like: it tells the batch file to stop executing until the user takes some action. No other batch command will be executed until a key is pressed. `PAUSE` requires user intervention.

ACTIVITY 12.5 USING THE PAUSE COMMAND IN A BATCH FILE

NOTE: Two disk drive users will have the DATA disk in Drive B with the `B>` displayed. Hard disk users will have the DATA disk in Drive A with the `A>` displayed.

STEP 1: Key in the following:

```
B>EDLIN test.bat  <Enter>
```

```
B>EDLIN test.bat
New file
*_
```

STEP 1: Key in the following:

```
A>EDLIN test.bat  <Enter>
```

```
A>EDLIN test.bat
New file
*_
```

STEP 2: Key in the following:

```
i <Enter>
REM This is a test file <Enter>
REM to see how the <Enter>
REM pause command works. <Enter>
DIR *.87 <Enter>
COPY mar.87 august.tmp <Enter>
PAUSE Is the printer turned on? <Enter>
COPY august.tmp PRN <Enter>
ERASE august.tmp <Enter>
<Ctrl>-C
```

STEP 2: Key in the following:

```
i <Enter>
REM This is a test file <Enter>
REM to see how the <Enter>
REM pause command works. <Enter>
DIR *.87 <Enter>
COPY mar.87 august.tmp <Enter>
PAUSE Is the printer turned on? <Enter>
COPY august.tmp PRN <Enter>
ERASE august.tmp <Enter>
<Ctrl>-C
```


WHAT'S HAPPENING? A batch file called `test.bat` has been created. When the file is executed, the first three lines of the file, the `REM` statements, tell the purpose of the file. `test.bat` then displays on the screen all the files with the extension of `.87` (`DIR *.87`). It copies the file `mar.87` to a new file, `august.tmp` (`COPY mar.87 august.tmp`). The `PAUSE` statement gives the user a chance to make sure the printer is turned on before sending output to the printer. After the user takes action, the file `august.tmp` is copied to the printer (`COPY august.tmp PRN`). Last, the file `august.tmp` is erased.

STEP 3: Key in the following:

```
E <Enter>
```

```
*E

B>_
```

STEP 3: Key in the following:

```
E <Enter>
```


```
*E

A>_
```

STEP 4: To execute `test.bat`, key in the following:

```
B>test <Enter>
```

STEP 4: To execute `test.bat`, key in the following:

```
A>test <Enter>
```

```
B>test

B>REM This is a test file

B>REM to see how the

B>REM pause command works.

B>DIR *.87

   Volume in drive B is DATADISK
   Directory of B:\

JAN      87        71       11-23-87     7:35p
FEB      87       196       11-23-87     2:21p
MAR      87        70       11-23-87     7:44p
APR      87        70       11-23-87     7:44p
      4 File(s)  220160 bytes free

B>COPY mar.87 august.tmp
        1 File(s) copied

B>PAUSE Is the printer turned on?
Strike a key when ready.....
```

```
A>test

A>REM This is a test file

A>REM to see how the

A>REM pause command works.

A>DIR *.87

   Volume in drive A is DATADISK
   Directory of A:\

JAN      87        71       11-23-87     7:35p
FEB      87       196       11-23-87     2:21p
MAR      87        70       11-23-87     7:44p
APR      87        70       11-23-87     7:44p
      4 File(s)  220160 bytes free

A>COPY mar.87 august.tmp
        1 File(s) copied

A>PAUSE Is the printer turned on?
Strike a key when ready.....
```

WHAT'S HAPPENING? The batch file `test` has stopped running, or "paused." It has halted execution until some action is taken. At this point there is a reminder to check to see if the printer is on.

STEP 5: To continue executing the rest of the instructions in the batch file, press any key.

STEP 5: To continue executing the rest of the instructions in the batch file, press any key.

```
B>COPY august.tmp PRN
        1 File(s) copied

B>ERASE august.tmp

B>
B>_
```

```
A>COPY august.tmp PRN
        1 File(s) copied

A>ERASE august.tmp

A>
A>_
```

WHAT'S HAPPENING? The batch file did continue executing all the steps. There should be a printout of the file called `august.tmp`. But since `august.tmp` was deleted, it should not be on the directory of the DATA disk.

STEP 6: Key in the following:

B>DIR august.tmp <Enter>

```
B>DIR august.tmp

Volume in Drive B is DATADISK
Directory of B:\

File not found

B>_
```

STEP 6: Key in the following:

A>DIR august.tmp <Enter>

```
A>DIR august.tmp

Volume in Drive A is DATADISK
Directory of A:\

File not found

A>_
```

12.6 STOPPING A BATCH FILE FROM EXECUTING

In the above activity, a key was pressed after the PAUSE command displayed. The batch file continued to execute. What if you did want to stop running the batch file? You can interrupt or exit from a batch file. You do this by pressing the <Ctrl>key and while pressing the <Ctrl> key, pressing the letter C (<Ctrl>-C or <Ctrl>-<break>). At whatever point <Ctrl>-C is pressed, the batch file is left. You return to the system prompt at the point where the file was interrupted. The rest of the lines in the batch file do not execute.

ACTIVITY 12.7 QUITTING A BATCH FILE

NOTE: Two disk drive users will have the DATA disk in Drive B with the B> displayed. Hard disk users will have the DATA disk in Drive A and with the A> displayed.

STEP 1: Key in the following:

B>EDLIN test.bat <Enter>

```
B>EDLIN test.bat
End of input file
*_
```

STEP 1: Key in the following:

A>EDLIN test.bat <Enter>

```
A>EDLIN test.bat
End of input file
*_
```

STEP 2: Key in the following for both floppy and hard disk systems:

```
4D  <Enter>
7i  <Enter>
PAUSE Do you want to erase august.tmp?  <Enter>
<Ctrl>-C
L  <Enter>
```

```
*4D
*7i
     7:*PAUSE Do you want to erase august.tmp?
     8:*^C
*L
     1: REM This is a test file
     2: REM to see how the
     3: REM pause command works.
     4: COPY mar.87 august.tmp
     5: PAUSE Is the printer turned on?
     6: COPY august.tmp PRN
     7: PAUSE Do you want to erase august.tmp?
     8:*ERASE august.tmp
*_
```

```
*4D
*7i
     7:*PAUSE Do you want to erase august.tmp?
     8:*^C
*L
     1: REM This is a test file
     2: REM to see how the
     3: REM pause command works.
     4: COPY mar.87 august.tmp
     5: PAUSE Is the printer turned on?
     6: COPY august.tmp PRN
     7: PAUSE Do you want to erase august.tmp?
     8:*ERASE august.tmp
*_
```

WHAT'S HAPPENING? In this edited batch file, lines 1-3 tell what this file is about (with the `REM` statements). Line 4 copies the file `mar.87` to a new file called `august.tmp`. The line 5 `PAUSE` statement gives time to check if the printer is on. Line 6 copies `august.tmp` to the printer. The line 7 `PAUSE` statement allows the user an opportunity not to erase the file `august.tmp`. Line 8 erases the file `august.tmp`.

STEP 3: Key in the following:

```
E  <Enter>
```

STEP 4: Key in the following:

```
B>test  <Enter>
```

```
B>test

B>REM This is a test file

B>REM to see how the

B>REM pause command works.

B>COPY mar.87 august.tmp
        1 File(s) copied

B>PAUSE Is the printer turned on?
Strike a key when ready.....
```

STEP 3: Key in the following:

```
E  <Enter>
```

STEP 4: Key in the following:

```
A>test  <Enter>
```

```
A>test

A>REM This is a test file

A>REM to see how the

A>REM pause command works.

A>COPY mar.87 august.tmp
        1 File(s) copied

A>PAUSE Is the printer turned on?
Strike a key when ready.....
```

WHAT'S HAPPENING? The batch file `test` has stopped running, or paused. It has halted execution until some action is taken. At this point, there is a reminder to check to see if the printer is on.

STEP 5: Be sure the printer is on. To continue executing the batch file, press any key.

```
B>COPY august.tmp PRN
        1 File(s) copied

B>PAUSE Do you want to erase august.tmp?
Strike any key when ready....
```

STEP 5: Be sure the printer is on. To continue executing the batch file, press any key.

```
A>COPY august.tmp PRN
        1 File(s) copied

A>PAUSE Do you want to erase august.tmp?
Strike any key when ready....
```

WHAT'S HAPPENING? The batch file has reached the second `PAUSE` command. It has stopped running. You don't want to erase `august.tmp`, but you want the batch file to cease operation. Previous experience with the `PAUSE` command showed that pressing any key would continue running the program. If any key were pressed here, the next line in the file, `ERASE august.tmp`, would execute and the file `august.tmp` would be erased. To stop this from happening, another action must be taken to interrupt the batch file processing.

STEP 6: While pressing the <Ctrl> key, press the letter C.

```
B>PAUSE Do you want to erase august.tmp?
Strike a key when ready. . .^C

Terminate batch job (Y/N)?_
```

STEP 6: While pressing the <Ctrl> key, press the letter C.

```
A>PAUSE Do you want to erase august.tmp?
Strike a key when ready. . .^C

Terminate batch job (Y/N)?_
```

WHAT'S HAPPENING? The message is giving you a choice: stop the batch file from running (Y for yes) or continue on with the batch file (N for no). If you key in Y for yes, the last line in the batch file, `ERASE august.tmp`, will not execute.

STEP 7: Press Y

```
Terminate batch job (Y/N)? Y
B>_
```

STEP 7: Press Y

```
Terminate batch job (Y/N)? Y
A>_
```

WHAT'S HAPPENING? The system prompt is displayed. If the batch job was interrupted properly, `august.tmp` should not have been deleted or the line `ERASE august.tmp` should not have been executed.

STEP 8: Key in the following:

B>DIR august.tmp <Enter>

```
B>DIR august.tmp

Volume in Drive B is DATADISK
Directory of B:\

AUGUST   TMP    69   11-23-87   7:43p

B>_
```

STEP 8: Key in the following:

A>DIR august.tmp <Enter>

```
A>DIR august.tmp

Volume in Drive A is DATADISK
Directory of A:\

AUGUST   TMP    69   11-23-87   7:43p

A>_
```

WHAT'S HAPPENING? The file august.tmp is still on the DATA disk. Pressing the <Ctrl>-C at the line PAUSE Do you want to erase august.tmp? broke into the batch file test.bat and stopped it from running. Since test.bat stopped executing and returned you to the system prompt, it never got to the command line, ERASE august.tmp. That is why the file august.tmp is still on the DATA disk.

12.8 DUMMY PARAMETERS IN BATCH FILES

Replaceable parameters are used in many DOS commands. Parameters are information that you key in when you run the command. For instance, TYPE requires one parameter, file name. The command, TYPE, remains the same, but the parameter will vary. TYPE uses the parameter that you keyed in to choose the file to display on the screen.

Batch files can also use replaceable parameters, usually called **dummy parameters.** When you key in the name of the batch file to execute it, you can also key in additional information that your batch file can use. When you write the batch file, you supply the markers or place holders to let the batch file know that something, a variable, will be keyed in with the batch file name. The place holders, or blank parameters, used in batch files are the percent sign (%) followed by a number from 1 to 9.

The batch files that you have written so far deal with specific commands and specific file names. But the real power of batch files is their ability to use dummy parameters. You are going to write a batch file in the usual way with specific file names and then change the batch file to see how dummy parameters work.

ACTIVITY 12.9 USING DUMMY PARAMETERS IN BATCH FILES

NOTE: Two disk drive users will have the DATA disk in Drive B with the B> displayed. Hard disk users will have the DATA disk in Drive A with the A> displayed.

STEP 1: Key in the following:

```
B>EDLIN practice.bat  <Enter>
i  <Enter>
DIR A:auto.bat  <Enter>
TYPE A:auto.bat  <Enter>
COPY A:auto.bat PRN <Enter>
<Ctrl>-C
E  <Enter>
```

```
B>EDLIN practice.bat
New file
*i  <Enter>
     1:*DIR auto.bat
     2:*TYPE auto.bat
     3:*COPY auto.bat PRN
     4:*^C
*E

B>_
```

STEP 1: Key in the following:

```
A>EDLIN practice.bat  <Enter>
i  <Enter>
DIR auto.bat  <Enter>
TYPE auto.bat  <Enter>
COPY auto.bat PRN <Enter>
<Ctrl>-C
E  <Enter>
```

```
A>EDLIN practice.bat
New file
*i  <Enter>
     1:*DIR auto.bat
     2:*TYPE auto.bat
     3:*COPY auto.bat PRN
     4:*^C
*E

A>_
```

WHAT'S HAPPENING? You have created a simple batch file that shows you if the file `auto.bat` is on the DATA disk. (`auto.bat` was the file that was renamed from `autoexec.bat` in Chapter 11.) Then you will look at the contents of the file called `auto.bat` on the screen with the `TYPE` command and then you will copy `auto.bat` to the printer. Be sure the printer is on before you execute the batch file. To execute this batch file, you must call it.

STEP 2: Key in the following:

```
B>practice <Enter>
```

```
B>practice

B>DIR A:auto.bat

Volume in drive A has no label
Directory of A:\

AUTO     BAT      34      11-23-87    4:24p
     1 File(s)     217088 bytes free

B>TYPE A:auto.bat
DATE
DIR B:example.bat
B:dispdate

B>COPY A:auto.bat PRN
        1 File(s) copied

B>
B>_
```

STEP 2: Key in the following:

```
A>practice <Enter>
```

```
A>practice

A>DIR auto.bat

Volume in drive A is DATADISK
Directory of A:\

AUTO     BAT      34      11-23-87    4:24p
     1 File(s)     217088 bytes free

A>TYPE auto.bat
DATE
DIR example.bat
dispdate

A>COPY auto.bat PRN
        1 File(s) copied

A>
A>_
```

WHAT'S HAPPENING? The batch file called `practice` ran successfully. However, it can only be used for the file called `auto.bat`. What if you wanted to do the same sequence of commands for a file called `jan.tmp` or `personal.fil` or any other file on the disk? Until now, you would create another batch file using `jan.tmp` instead of `auto.bat`. For `personal.fil`, you would write another batch file using `personal.fil`. As you can see, you can quickly clutter up your disks with many batch files, all doing the same thing but using different file names. An easier way to do this is to have one batch file that does the same steps. When you execute it, you supply the parameter or file name in which you are specifically interested.

You are going to write a batch file with the same commands as `practice.bat`, only this time you will use dummy parameters. Be sure to use the percent sign (`%`), then the number `1`. Note that there is no space between the `%` and the number `1`. Be sure you use the number `1`, not the letter `l`.

STEP 3: Key in the following:

```
B>EDLIN prac.bat  <Enter>
I  <Enter>
DIR %1  <Enter>
TYPE %1  <Enter>
COPY %1 PRN  <Enter>
<Ctrl>-C
E  <Enter>
```

```
B>EDLIN prac.bat
New file
*I
     1:*DIR %1
     2:*TYPE %1
     3:*COPY %1 PRN
     4:*^C
*E
B>_
```

STEP 3: Key in the following:

```
A>EDLIN prac.bat  <Enter>
I  <Enter>
DIR %1  <Enter>
TYPE %1  <Enter>
COPY %1 PRN  <Enter>
<Ctrl>-C
E  <Enter>
```

```
A>EDLIN prac.bat
New file
*I
     1:*DIR %1
     2:*TYPE %1
     3:*COPY %1 PRN
     4:*^C
*E
A>_
```

WHAT'S HAPPENING? By using `%1`, instead of a specific file name, you are saying that you don't know yet what file name (`%1`) you want these commands to apply to. When you run the batch file `prac`, you will provide a value or parameter that the batch file will substitute for `%1`. Be sure the printer is turned on.

STEP 4: Key in the following:

```
B>prac jan.87  <Enter>
```

```
B>prac jan.87

B>DIR jan.87

Volume in drive B is DATADISK
Directory of B:\

JAN      87        71    11-23-87   7:35p
     1 File(s)      216064 bytes free

B>TYPE jan.87
This is my January file.
It is my first dummy file.
This is file 1.

B>COPY jan.87 PRN
     1 File(s) copied
B>
B>_
```

STEP 4: Key in the following:

```
A>prac jan.87  <Enter>
```

```
A>prac jan.87

A>DIR jan.87

Volume in drive A is DATADISK
Directory of A:\

JAN      87        71    11-23-87   7:35p
     1 File(s)      216064 bytes free

A>TYPE jan.87
This is my January file.
It is my first dummy file.
This is file 1.

A>COPY jan.87 PRN
     1 File(s) copied
A>
A>_
```

WHAT'S HAPPENING? Note what happened. The batch file `prac` executed each command line. However, when it found `%1` in the command line, it looked for what you keyed in after `prac`, which was `jan.87`. It substituted `jan.87` every time it found `%1`. As you can see, you have written a generic or "plain wrap" batch file that allows you to use the same batch file over and over. You just have to supply a value or parameter after the batch file name. Thus, you could key in `prac business.app`, `prac sales.let`, `prac feb.87`, or any other file name. The batch file will do the same commands over and over, using the parameter (the file name) you keyed in after the batch file name.

12.10 MULTIPLE DUMMY PARAMETERS IN BATCH FILES

In the above example, you used one dummy parameter. What happens if you need more than one parameter? For instance, if you want to include the `COPY` command in a batch file, `COPY` needs two parameters, source and destination. There are many commands that require more than one parameter. You may also use multiple parameters in batch files. You can have up to nine dummy parameters (`%1` through `%9`). The parameters are used in order from left to right. The next activity will allow you to create a batch file with multiple dummy parameters. This batch file allows you to create a command that DOS does not have. It will "move" a file (or copy it) from one place to another, then delete the original file.

ACTIVITY 12.11 USING MULTIPLE DUMMY PARAMETERS OR WRITING YOUR OWN COMMANDS

NOTE: Two disk drive users will have the DATA disk in Drive B with the **B>** displayed. Hard disk users will have the DATA disk in Drive A and with the **A>** displayed.

STEP 1: Key in the following for both floppy and hard disk systems:

```
B>EDLIN move.bat  <Enter>
New file
i   <Enter>
    DIR %1 <Enter>
    COPY %1 %2  <Enter>
    DIR %2  <Enter>
    REM Do you want to erase %1?  <Enter>
    REM If you DO NOT want to delete %1 <Enter>
    REM Press Ctrl C NOW  <Enter>
    PAUSE Else strike any key to erase %1  <Enter>
    DEL %1  <Enter>
    <Ctrl>-C
E   <Enter>
```

```
B>EDLIN move.bat
New file
*i
     1:*DIR %1
     2:*COPY %1 %2
     3:*DIR %2
     4:*REM Do you want to erase %1?
     5:*REM If you DO NOT want to delete %1
     6:*REM Press Ctrl C NOW
     7:*PAUSE Else strike any key to erase %1
     8:*DEL %1
     9:*^C
*E
B>_
```

```
A>EDLIN move.bat
New file
*i
     1:*DIR %1
     2:*COPY %1 %2
     3:*DIR %2
     4:*REM Do you want to erase %1?
     5:*REM If you DO NOT want to delete %1
     6:*REM Press Ctrl C NOW
     7:*PAUSE Else strike any key to erase %1
     8:*DEL %1
     9:*^C
*E
A>_
```

STEP 2: Key in the following:

```
B>MOVE jan.87 november.tst <Enter>
```

```
B>MOVE jan.87 november.tst
A>DIR jan.87
  Volume in Drive B is DATADISK
  Directory of B:\

JAN      87        71   11-23-87    7:35p
     1 File(s)    215040 bytes free

B>COPY jan.87 november.tst
     1 File(s) copied

B>DIR november.tst
  Volume in drive B is DATADISK
  Directory of B:\

NOVEMBER   TST     71   11-23-87    7:35p
     1 File(s)   214016 bytes free

B>REM  Do you want to erase jan.87

B>REM  If you do not NOT wish to erase jan.87

B>REM  Press Ctrl C NOW

A>PAUSE Else strike any key to erase jan.87
Strike a key when ready.....
```

NOTE: Since you do want to erase the file, strike a key. The batch file will continue executing.

```
B>DEL jan.87
B>
B>_
```

STEP 2: Key in the following:

```
A>MOVE jan.87 november.tst <Enter>
```

```
A>MOVE jan.87 november.tst
A>DIR jan.87
  Volume in Drive A is DATADISK
  Directory of A:\

JAN      87        71   11-23-87    7:35p
     1 File(s)    215040 bytes free

A>COPY jan.87 november.tst
  1 File(s) copied

A>DIR november.tst
  Volume in drive A is DATADISK
  Directory of A:\

NOVEMBER   TST     71 11-23-87      7:35p
     1 File(s)    214016 bytes free

A>REM  Do you want to erase jan.87

A>REM  If you do not NOT wish to erase jan.87

A>REM  Press Ctrl-C NOW

A>PAUSE Else strike any key to erase jan.87
Strike a key when ready.....
```

NOTE: Since you do want to erase the file, strike a key. The batch file will continue executing.

```
A>DEL jan.87
A>
A>_
```

WHAT'S HAPPENING? You ran the batch file called `MOVE`. You substituted or provided the values, `jan.87` (`%1`) and `november.tst` (`%2`), when you ran the batch file `MOVE` (`MOVE jan.87 november.tst`). To DOS, the command sequence or string of commands looked like this:

```
DIR jan.87
COPY jan.87 november.tst
DIR november.tst
REM Do you want to erase jan.87?
REM If you DO NOT want to erase jan.87
REM Press Ctrl C NOW
PAUSE Else strike any key to erase jan.87
DEL jan.87
```

Let's explain this command line by command line. When you keyed in `MOVE jan.87 november.tst`, you asked DOS to load the batch file called `MOVE.bat` and execute the first line, which is:

1. `DIR jan.87`. This line asked DOS to see if a file called `jan.87` was on the default directory. DOS knew it should substitute `jan.87` for `%1` because `jan.87` is the first parameter keyed in after `MOVE`.
2. `COPY jan.87 november.tst`. This line says to copy the file named `jan.87` (`%1`) to a new file to be called `november.tst` (`%2`). DOS knew which file was `%1` and could substitute `jan.87` for `%1` because `jan.87` was the first thing keyed in after the command `MOVE`. It knew what file was `%2` and could substitute `november.tst` for `%2` because `november.tst` was the second parameter keyed in after `jan.87`.
3. `DIR november.tst`. This line says do a directory search for the file called `november.tst` (`%2`). Again, DOS knew which file was `%2` because `november.tst` was in the second position. The reason that you included a directory search is to be sure that the file `jan.87` was copied to a new file called `november.tst` before you erased `jan.87`.
4. `REM Do you want to erase jan.87`. This line is just a remark to let the user know what is going to happen. The file called `jan.87` is about to be erased. DOS knew it was `jan.87` because it was indicated as `%1`.
5. `REM If you DO NOT want to erase jan.87`. This line is a remark to give the user a chance to back out and not erase `jan.87`. Again, DOS knew it should substitute `jan.87` for `%1`.
6. `REM Press Ctrl C NOW`. This line tells the user how not to delete the file.
7. `PAUSE Else strike any key to erase jan.87`. This command line forces the user to take action. DOS knew what file name to substitute for `%1`. This line is in the batch file so preventive action can be taken if the file (`%1`, or `jan.87`) was not copied to a file (`%2`, or `november.tst`), or if the user did not, after all, want to erase the file (`%1`, or `jan.87`). By pressing the Ctrl key and the letter C, the batch file is terminated and will not execute the last line of the file.
8. `DEL jan.87`. This command line will erase the file called `jan.87` (`%1`). Again, DOS knew which file to substitute for `%1`. The file `%1` or `jan.87` is now deleted. This command, which you just wrote as a batch file with dummy parameters, can be very useful. You can use it to copy files from one disk to another and then erase the file from the source disk so that you do not end up with multiple files on multiple disks. You do not need to take separate steps as all the steps are included in the batch file. If you are copying from drive to drive, you must include the drive designator and the path, if appropriate. For example, if you wanted to move a file from the disk in Drive A to the disk in drive B and then delete it from Drive A, you would key in the following:

    ```
    A>MOVE aug.old B:august.new
    ```

If you wanted to move a file from Drive C to Drive A, you would key in the following:

```
A>MOVE C:august.old august.new
```

If you wanted to move a file from Drive C in the subdirectory \junk to Drive A, you would key in the following:

```
A>MOVE C:\junk\august.old august.new
```

CHAPTER SUMMARY

1. There are special commands only used in batch files.
2. REM allows the user to document a batch file.
3. To document means to explain the purpose a file serves.
4. When DOS sees REM, it displays on the screen whatever text follows the REM, but does not execute it as a command.
5. PAUSE allows the user to take some action before the batch file continues to execute.
6. PAUSE does not force the user to do anything. The batch file just stops running until the user presses a key.
7. Dummy parameters allow the user to write batch files that can be used with many different parameters. The dummy parameters act as place holders for values that the user will substitute when executing the batch file.
8. Dummy parameters are sometimes called replaceable or substitute parameters.
9. The percent (%) sign followed by a numerical value, 1 to 9, indicates a dummy parameter in a batch file.
10. To stop a batch file from executing, press the <Ctrl> key and the letter C (<Ctrl>-C).

REVIEW QUESTIONS

1. Once a batch file is running, how would you stop it from continuing to run?
2. What does documenting mean in data processing?
3. Why would you want to document a batch file?
4. What happens when DOS sees REM in a file?
5. To have a batch file stop at a specific point so a user can take some action, what command would you use?
6. What is a dummy parameter? Describe how it might be used.
7. A batch file has the following commands:

   ```
   TYPE myfile.txt
   COPY myfile.txt PRN
   ```

   How could this batch file be changed to TYPE and COPY any file?
8. Is there any limit to the number of dummy parameters that can be used in a batch file?
9. What indicates to DOS that there is a dummy parameter in a file?

10. There is a batch file called `twice.bat`. Its commands are:
    ```
    COPY %1 %2
    COPY %2 PRN
    ```
    How would you execute this batch file if you wanted to copy `myfile.txt` to `happy.day` and then copy `happy.day` to the printer?

TRUE/FALSE

1. Dummy parameters are used in batch files.
2. Once a batch file begins executing, there is no way to stop it from running.
3. The `REM` command in a batch file is used for documenting a file.
4. The `REM` command in a batch file is used to remove text from a batch file.
5. When `PAUSE` appears on the screen, the user has five seconds to take any action or the batch file will continue to execute.
6. The pound sign (#) indicates to DOS that there is a dummy parameter in the batch file.
7. Dummy parameters allow the user to write a file that can accept values that the user will give it at a later time.
8. `PAUSE` forces the user to turn on the printer.

SUGGESTED ACTIVITIES

Two disk drive users and hard disk users: All activities will take place on the DATA disk.

1. Edit the file called `extra.bat` created in Chapter 11. Include some new lines that will pause so that the user can see what files there are with the extension of `.txt`. Be sure that the user has to pause prior to printing the file to see if the printer is turned on. Allow the user an opportunity to break out of the program prior to erasing the file `tv.cat`. Put in remarks wherever it seems appropriate. After you are done editing the `extra.bat` file, copy the contents of `extra.bat` to the printer.
2. Write a batch file called `check.bat` that will check the disk in the default drive. It will then do a wide display of the default directory. Include remarks to explain to the user what is going on. When the batch file is completed, copy the batch file `check.bat` to the printer.
3. Write a batch file called `prt.bat` using dummy parameters. The batch file should include the following commands:
   a. Clear the screen.
   b. Display the file name of a file that is to be copied.
   c. Copy one file to another file name.
   d. Have the batch file pause prior to printing so the user can see if the printer is turned on.
   e. Copy the new file to the printer.

   When the batch file is completed, copy the batch file, `prt.bat` to the printer.

4. Write another batch file called `gone.bat` using dummy parameters. The purpose of this file is to allow you to make backup copies of one or many files. You then want to display the files to be sure the copies were made. You want to erase the original files but first you want to verify what files are going to be erased. You also want to give yourself a chance to cancel the `erase` command. The commands should include:
   a. Clear the screen.
   b. Display any file names that will be copied.
   c. Copy the files from one name to another name.
   d. Display the file names of the newly created files.
   e. Display the file names of the files to be deleted.
   f. Inform the user what is happening.
   g. Instruct the user how to break out of the program if he or she does not wish to erase the files.
   h. Erase the original files.

NOTE: It is helpful to make a set of files on which to practice using `gone.bat`. For instance, copy all the `*.87` files to `*.gon` and use the `*.gon` files to practice on. When `gone.bat` works properly, copy `gone.bat` to the printer.

5. Write a batch file called `typelots.bat`. Use dummy parameters so that you can display the contents of three files instead of just one file that the `TYPE` command allows. When the batch file is completed, copy the batch file `typelots.bat` to the printer.
6. Write a batch file called `setprt.bat` using dummy parameters that will allow the user to set the printer to whatever `MODE` values he or she needs. When the batch file is completed, copy the batch file `setprt.bat` to the printer.
7. Delete any files with the extension `.bak` on the DATA disk.
8. Do a directory display to prove all the `.bak` files are gone from the DATA disk. Print this screen.
9. Do a directory display of all the batch files on the DATA disk. Print this screen.
10. Back up the DATA disk.

SUBDIRECTORIES

CHAPTER

13

CHAPTER OBJECTIVES

This chapter demonstrates the uses of subdirectories and introduces the subdirectory commands. After completing this chapter, you will:

Be able to explain the concepts of paths and subdirectories.

Be able to use the subdirectory commands.

Be able to use the `PATH` command.

Be able to use the `DOS` commands in conjunction with subdirectories.

13.0 MATERIALS NEEDED

1. DOS System Disk
2. DATA disk
3. Backup Data disk

13.1 DIRECTORIES AND SUBDIRECTORIES: THE HIERARCHICAL FILING SYSTEM OR TREE-STRUCTURED DIRECTORIES

Every disk must be formatted before it can be used. When you format a disk, a directory known as the **root directory** is always created automatically. Every disk must have a root directory so that files can be located on the disk. The directory is the area of the disk that contains information about what is stored on that specific disk. However, there is a limit to the number of files or entries that can be placed in the root directory of a disk. A single-sided disk has a maximum of 64 entries, a double-sided disk has a maximum of 112 entries, a high-capacity disk has a maximum of 224 entries, and a hard disk has a maximum of 512 entries.

For a floppy disk, 112 directory entries is usually sufficient. However, if you have many small files, 112 files is insufficient. Or, if you have a 10 or 20 megabyte hard disk, 512 files is not sufficient. In addition, scrolling through even 112 entries, looking for a specific file is not efficient. Normally, people work more efficiently when they logically group files and programs that belong together, for example, putting all accounting programs and accounting files in the same place. DOS version 2.0 and above gives you the capability of "fooling" the system to create as many file entries as you need. The only limitation is the size or capacity of the disk.

This capability is the **hierarchical** or **tree-structured** filing system. In this system the directory can not only have entries for files, but for other directories called **subdirectories**. Unlike the root directory, subdirectories can contain any number of entries.

When any disk is formatted, a single directory called the root directory is always created. The root directory is represented by a backslash. (Note: Do not confuse the backslash \ key with the slash / key.) All directories, other than the root directory, are called subdirectories. Unlike the root directory, the subdirectories are not limited to specific number of files. Subdirectories may have subdirectories of their own. The subdirectories divide up the disk into different areas which you can treat like completely separate disks. The directory structure of a disk is like an inverted tree with the root directory at the top and the subdirectories branching off from the root. It is much like a family tree, especially because of the dependent nature of subdirectories. For instance, the example on the left in Figure 13.1 is a family tree showing a mother who has two children; the one on the right is a root directory with two subdirectories. The two subdirectories will contain all the files and programs that have to do with sales and accounting.

Figure 13.1 A Directory Is Like a Family Tree

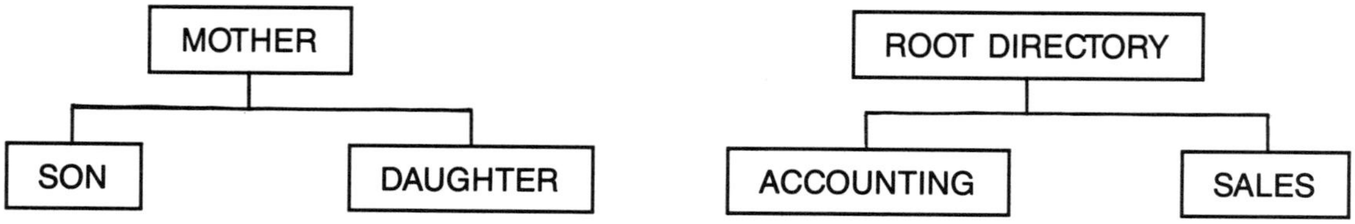

A child can have only one biological mother, but a child can become a parent and have children. Those children can also become parents and have children. Likewise, accounting can be a "child" of the root directory but also a "parent" to subdirectories beneath it (See Figure 13.2).

Figure 13.2 Hierarchical Structure of a Directory

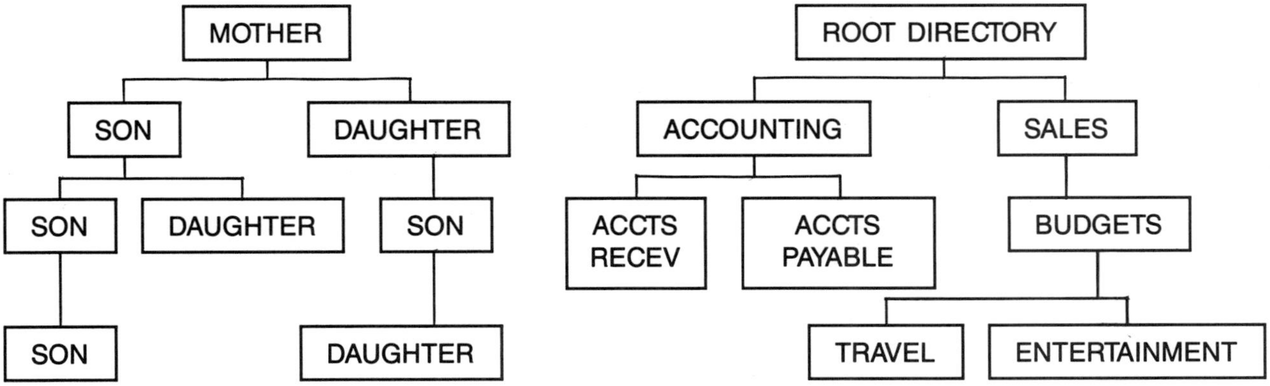

The children are dependent on the parent above. Each subdirectory is listed in its parent directory but not in any directory above the parent. Note the absolute **hierarchical structure**. You cannot skip a subdirectory any more than you can have a grandfather with a grandson and no father in between (See Figure 13.3). You move around in the directories via the path that tells DOS where to go for a particular file.

Figure 13.3 "Parents" and "Children" in a Directory

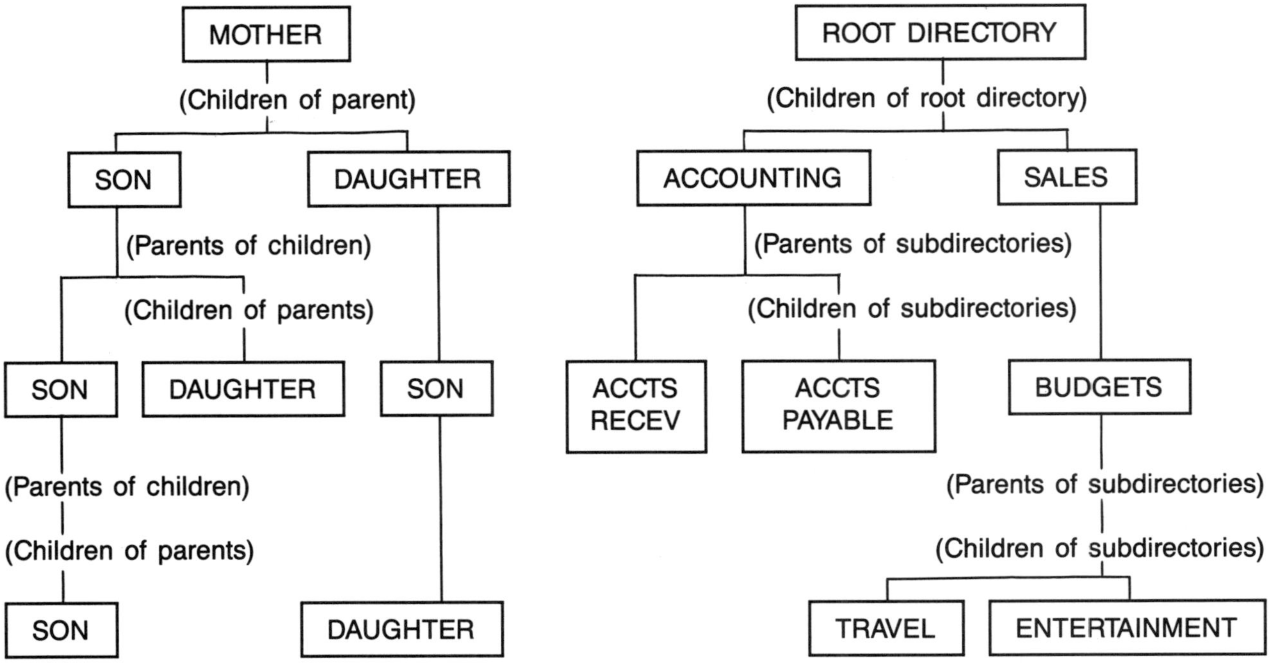

Using subdirectories is like setting up and using a file cabinet (or a separate floppy disk). The subdirectory is a shell or a place to put files. When you move around and use subdirectories, you are changing your work area, much like using another file cabinet or separate floppy disk. Subdirectories have names that you choose with the exception of the root directory, which is always known as \ or backslash. Subdirectories follow the same naming conventions as files: a maximum of eight characters for the file name, a period, and a maximum of three characters for the file extension. Although DOS treats subdirectories as files, the subdirectories themselves cannot be manipulated with the standard file manipulation commands such as **COPY** or TYPE.

Table 13.1 gives a list of the tree-structured management commands.

Table 13.1 Directory Management Commands

COMMAND	**FUNCTION**
CHDIR or CD	Change the directory
MKDIR or MD	Make or create a directory
RMDIR or RD	Remove or erase a directory
PATH	Display or set the path(s)

13.2 CREATING SUBDIRECTORIES

When you create a subdirectory, you are setting up a shell where files can be stored. There is nothing in the subdirectory to begin with. The internal **MD** command creates a subdirectory much like setting up a separate disk. When you format a disk, you are preparing it to hold files. When you set up a subdirectory, you are also setting it up to hold files. The syntax of the command is:

```
MD [d:][path] subdirectory.name
```

In the following activity, you will set up two subdirectories under the root directory. These subdirectories will be for two classes, one in DOS and one in word processing.

ACTIVITY 13.3 CREATING SUBDIRECTORIES

NOTE: Both two disk drive and hard disk users will have the DATA disk in Drive A with the **A>** displayed on the screen. The instructions for both two disk drive users and hard disk users will be the same for the rest of this activity. If you have a system configuration of one floppy high-capacity disk drive and one floppy 360K disk drive, do not change disks nor the default drive. Leave the DATA disk in Drive B. The only difference in ACTIVITIES 13.2 through 13.19 in Chapter 13 will be that instead of seeing **A:\>**, you will see **B:\>**.

STEP 1: Key in the following:

```
A>MD classdos <Enter>
```

STEP 2: Key in the following:

```
A>MD classwps  <Enter>
```

```
A>MD classdos

A>MD classwps
A>_
```

WHAT'S HAPPENING? You have created two subdirectories called `classdos` and `classwps` under the root directory. `Classdos` will hold all the files that involve a class in DOS and `classwps` will hold files that involve a class in word processing. Right now you have created the subdirectories to hold the files. These subdirectories are "empty" file cabinets. After you used the `MD` command, all you saw on the screen was the `A>`. How do you know that you created subdirectories? You can see the subdirectories you just created by using the `DIR` command.

STEP 3: Key in the following:

```
A>DIR cl*.*  <Enter>
```

```
A>DIR cl*.*

 Volume in drive A: is DATADISK
 Directory of A:\

CLASSDOS         <DIR>      11-24-87       9:00a
CLASSWPS         <DIR>      11-24-87       9:00a
       2 File(s)       209920 bytes free
A>_
```

WHAT'S HAPPENING? The `DIR` command identifies the files, not just as files called `classdos` and `classwps` but as subdirectories by displaying `<DIR>` after each file name. Note the line that reads `Directory of A:\`. The `\` after the `A:` indicates the root directory of the disk. Since `classdos` is a subdirectory, not just a file, you can display the contents of the directory with the `DIR` command much as you can display the directory of another disk.

STEP 4: Key in the following:

```
A>DIR classdos <Enter>
```

```
A>DIR classdos

 Volume in drive A: is DATADISK
 Directory of A:\CLASSDOS

.            <DIR>      11-24-87     9:00a
..           <DIR>      11-24-87     9:00a
     2 File(s)      209920 bytes free

A>_
```

WHAT'S HAPPENING? Now note the line that reads `Directory of A:\CLASSDOS`. This line is telling you the **path**. You are looking from the root directory into the subdirectory called `classdos`. Even though you just created the subdirectory `classdos`, it seems to have two subdirectories in it, one period (`.`) and two periods (`..`) followed by `<DIR>`. Every subdirectory that is created always has two named dummy subdirectories. The subdirectory named `.` is another name or abbreviation for `\classdos`. The subdirectory name `..` is an abbreviation for the parent directory, in this case the root directory `\`.

STEP 5: Key in the following:

```
A>DIR classwps  <Enter>
```

```
A>DIR classwps

 Volume in drive A: is DATADISK
 Directory of A:\CLASSWPS

.            <DIR>      11-24-87     9:00a
..           <DIR>      11-24-87     9:00a
     2 File(s)      209920 bytes free

A>_
```

WHAT'S HAPPENING? Now note the line that reads `Directory of A:\CLASSWPS`. This line is telling you the path. You are looking from the root directory into the subdirectory called `classwps`. This is the same way it worked when you asked for a directory on another drive. If, for instance, you had asked for a directory of the disk in Drive B, that line would have read, `Directory of B:\`. It tells you what you are looking at.

13.4 THE CURRENT DIRECTORY

Just as DOS keeps track of the default drive with `A>`, `B>` or `C>`, it also keeps track of the current or default directory. When you boot the system, the default drive is the drive where you loaded DOS and the default directory is the root directory of the default drive. You can change the directory just as you can change the drive designator so that you can make a specific subdirectory the default.

The change directory (`CHDIR` or `CD`) command has two purposes. If you key in `CD` with no parameters, DOS will display the name of the current directory. If you include a parameter, the name of a directory after the `CD`, it will change the directory to the directory that you requested and make it the default. This process is similar to changing drives by keying in the desired drive letter followed by a colon, i.e., `A:`, `B:`, `C:` The syntax is:

```
CD [d:][path][subdirectory.name]
```

ACTIVITY 13.5 USING THE CURRENT DIRECTORY COMMAND

NOTE: Both two disk drive and hard disk users will have the DATA disk in Drive A with the `A>` displayed on the screen. The instructions for both two disk drive users and hard disk users will be the same for the rest of this activity.

STEP 1: Key in the following:

```
A>CD <Enter>
```

```
A>CD
A:\

A>_
```

WHAT'S HAPPENING? This display tells you that you are in the root directory of the disk in Drive A, the DATA disk, and that any command you enter will apply only to this root directory, which is the default directory.

STEP 2: Key in the following:

```
A>DIR cl*.*  <Enter>
```

```
A>DIR cl*.*

 Volume in drive A: is DATADISK
 Directory of A:\

CLASSDOS        <DIR>      11-24-87     9:00a
CLASSWPS        <DIR>      11-24-87     9:00a
     2 File(s)        209920 bytes free
A>_
```

WHAT'S HAPPENING? Since you did not specify any parameters other than files that begin with `cl`, the `DIR` command found the files on the DATA disk in Drive A in the root directory (the default) and displayed those files. You can change the default subdirectory. You are going to go to the subdirectory called `classdos`.

STEP 3: Key in the following:

```
A>CD classdos  <Enter>
```

STEP 4: Key in the following:

```
A>CD  <Enter>
```

```
A>CD classdos

A>CD
A:\CLASSDOS
A>_
```

WHAT'S HAPPENING? In Step 3, `CD` followed by the name of the subdirectory, `classdos`, changed the default from the root directory to the subdirectory, `classdos`. However, all you saw on the screen was the `A>`. To confirm that you had indeed changed the default directory, in Step 4 you keyed in `CD`, which displayed `A:\CLASSDOS`. This tells you that you are in the subdirectory `\CLASSDOS` on the DATA disk in Drive A and that any command you enter will apply only to this directory. You can think of the command this way: `CD` with no parameters shows you the current directory; `CD` followed by a subdirectory name (parameter) changes the subdirectory.

STEP 5: Key in the following:

```
A>DIR
```

```
A>DIR

 Volume in drive A: is DATADISK
 Directory of A:\CLASSDOS

.            <DIR>      11-24-87     9:00a
..           <DIR>      11-24-87     9:00a
        2 File(s)     209920 bytes free

A>_
```

WHAT'S HAPPENING? Note that you are displaying the default directory, but the default is now the directory of `\CLASSDOS` rather than the root directory.

13.6 USING SUBDIRECTORIES

Figure 13.4 Structure of the DATA disk

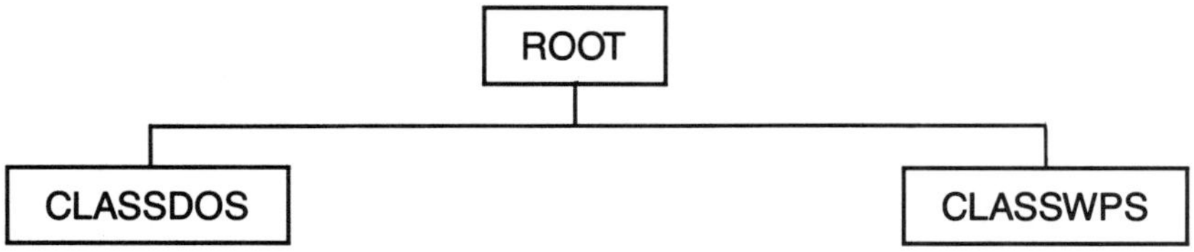

The DATA disk in Drive A is structured as shown in Figure 13.4. You can use each of these directories as if it were a separate disk but instead of just a lettered drive, you must also give the path. The path tells DOS what route to follow to look for files. You can use any DOS command. You can copy files, delete files, display files, rename files. Remember that as long as you follow the syntax, you can use any DOS command with subdirectories. The next activity will demonstrate the use of the `COPY` command with subdirectories. You are going to create a file in the root directory and then make copies to various subdirectories.

ACTIVITY 13.7 COPYING FROM ONE DIRECTORY TO ANOTHER

NOTE: Both two disk drive users and hard disk users will have the DATA disk in Drive A with the `A>` displayed on the screen. Both two disk drive users and hard disk users should be in the subdirectory `\classdos`. To be sure you are in the right subdirectory, you can key in `A>CD \classdos`. The instructions for both two disk drive users and hard disk users will be the same for the rest of this activity.

STEP 1: Key in the following:

```
A>COPY CON \master.fil <Enter>
Gillay, Carolyn  <Enter>
Smith, John  <Enter>
Jones, James  <Enter>
Jones, John  <Enter>
Tuttle, Steven  <Enter>
Panezich, Frank  <Enter>
<Ctrl>-Z
```

```
A>COPY CON \master.fil
Gillay, Carolyn
Smith, John
Jones, James
Jones, John
Tuttle, Steven
Panezich, Frank
^Z
     1 File(s) copied
A>_
```

WHAT'S HAPPENING? The syntax for the copy command remained the same (`COPY [d:][path]source [d:][path]destination`. You keyed in the command, `COPY`. Then you keyed in the source, `CON`. The destination was a file you called `master.fil`. Note, however, that you keyed in the \ or backslash to indicate that you wanted that file written to the root directory. Since the default directory is now `classdos`, had you not included the \, the file would have been written to the default subdirectory, `classdos`.

STEP 2: Key in the following:

`A>DIR \master.fil  <Enter>`

```
A>DIR \master.fil

Volume in drive A: is DATADISK
Directory of A:\

MASTER   FIL       90   11-24-87        9:29a
         1 File(s)      208896 bytes free
A>_
```

WHAT'S HAPPENING? The root directory indicated by the \ contains a file named `master.fil`. Since a subdirectory can be treated as if it were a separate disk, you can copy from one directory to another. The copy syntax is the same but you must include your directory name (path).

STEP 3: Key in the following:

`A>COPY \master.fil class.lst  <Enter>`

```
A>COPY \master.fil class.lst
        1 File(s) copied
A>_
```

WHAT'S HAPPENING? You just copied the file called master.fil located on the disk in Drive A in the root directory (\). You copied it to a new file called class.lst located in the subdirectory classdos. Since you did not specify otherwise, DOS assumed you wanted the file copied to the subdirectory you are currently in.

The longhand version of the command would be:

```
A>COPY A:\master.fil A:\classdos\class.lst
```

All you needed to key in on the destination was class.lst. The A:\classdos was assumed because it is the default.

STEP 4: Key in the following:

```
A>DIR  <Enter>
```

```
A>DIR
 Volume in drive A: is DATADISK
 Directory of A:\CLASSDOS

.              <DIR>        11-24-87       9:00a
..             <DIR>        11-24-87       9:00a
CLASS     LST          90   11-24-87       9:29a
     3 File(s)         207872 bytes free
A>_
```

WHAT'S HAPPENING? Note that you are looking at the directory for the subdirectory, \classdos, and that the file called master.fil has been copied to the subdirectory but is now called class.lst.

STEP 5: Key in the following:

```
A>DIR \class.lst <Enter>
```

```
A>DIR \class.lst

  Volume in Drive A is DATADISK
  Directory of A:\

File not found

A>_
```

WHAT'S HAPPENING? Note that the file called class.lst does not show on the root directory. It is only found inside the subdirectory, classdos. Just as you can copy a file with the same name to another disk, you can also copy a file with the same name to another directory.

STEP 6: Key in the following:

```
A>COPY class.lst \classwps <Enter>
```

```
A>COPY class.lst \classwps
     1 File(s) copied
A>_
```

WHAT'S HAPPENING? The copy syntax remained the same: the command, `COPY`; the source, `class.lst` from the default subdirectory, `classdos`; the destination, the subdirectory `\classwps`. That is to say, you were copying the file to the subdirectory `\classwps` with the same file name. There are now two files with the same name on the disk, but in different directories. Had you not used "computer shorthand," you would have keyed in what is shown in Figure 13.5. (Do not key it in. This is an example and the spacing is incorrect).

Figure 13.5 COPY Command Syntax

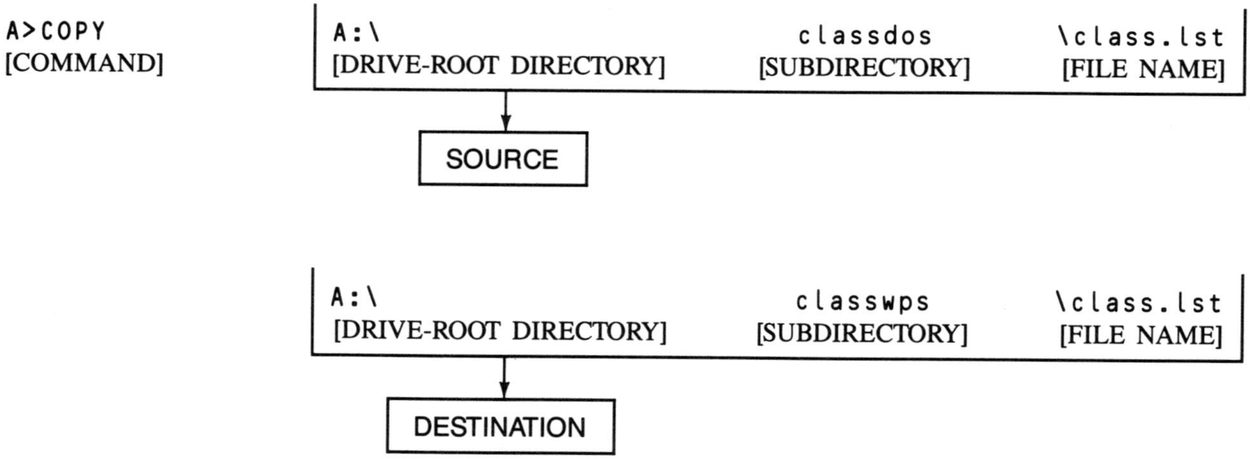

Figure 13.5 shows the "path" that the `COPY` command follows. A path leads either to a file or to an area of the tree that contains files and more directories. The path is the list of names of the directories starting with the root directory, continuing through all the subdirectories that lead you through the right areas of the tree, and ending with the directory that has the file you are interested in. The directory and file names in a path are separated by the backslash.

STEP 7: Key in the following:

```
A>DIR <Enter>
```

STEP 8: Key in the following:

```
A>DIR \classwps <Enter>
```

```
A>DIR
 Volume in drive A: is DATADISK
 Directory of A:\CLASSDOS
.             <DIR>        11-24-87      9:00a
..            <DIR>        11-24-87      9:00a
CLASS    LST          90   11-24-87      9:29a
     3 File(s)       206848 bytes free

A>DIR \classwps
 Volume in drive A: is DATADISK
 Directory of A:\CLASSWPS
.             <DIR>         11-24-87      9:00a
..            <DIR>         11-24-87      9:00a
CLASS    LST          90    11-24-87      9:29a
     3 File(s)       206848 bytes free
A>_
```

WHAT'S HAPPENING? Each subdirectory has a file with the same name, `class.lst`. This supposedly violates the unique file name for each disk. But these files names are unique. One file name is actually `A:\classdos\class.lst` and the other is `A:\classwps\class.lst`. This is the same idea as `A:\class.lst` and `B:\class.lst`. Any DOS internal command will work the same way as long as you use the proper syntax and specify where you are and where you are going.

13.8 ADDING SUBDIRECTORIES

Figure 13.6 Directory with Subdirectories

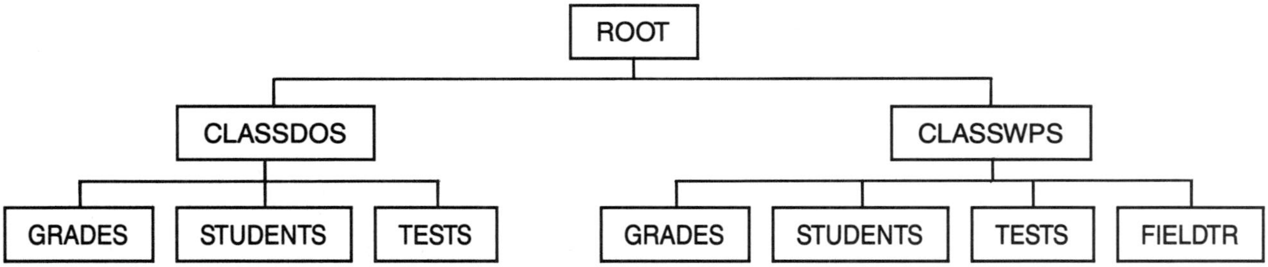

You are going to add additional subdirectories to the tree structure so that the levels will look like those in Figure 13.6. To create these additional subdirectories, you use the MD or make directory command (MKDIR or MD), which creates subdirectories. This command syntax is:

```
MD [drive] [path] subdirectory.name
```

The drive is the letter of the drive that contains the disk on which the subdirectory is to be created (such as A:, B: or C:). If you omit the drive designator, DOS creates the subdirectory on the default or current drive. The path is the path name of the directory in which the subdirectory is to be created. If you omit the path name, the subdirectory is created in the default or current subdirectory.

ACTIVITY 13.9 CREATING MORE SUBDIRECTORIES

NOTE: Both two disk drive users and hard disk users will have the DATA disk in Drive A with the A> displayed on the screen. Both two disk drive users and hard disk users should be in the subdirectory \classdos. To be sure you are in the right subdirectory, you can key in A>CD \classdos. The instructions for both two disk drive users and hard disk users will be the same for the rest of this activity.

STEP 1: Key in the following:

```
A>CD  <Enter>
```

```
A>CD
A:\CLASSDOS

A>_
```

WHAT'S HAPPENING? The default directory is \classdos. (Note: If \classdos is not displayed, key in CD \classdos.) To create three subdirectories in \classdos, you will use the MD command along with the subdirectory names. The subdirectories will be called students, grades, and tests.

STEP 2: Key in the following:

```
A>MD students  <Enter>
```

STEP 3: Key in the following:

```
A>MD grades  <Enter>
```

STEP 4: Key in the following:

```
A>MD tests  <Enter>
```

STEP 5: Key in the following:

```
A>DIR  <Enter>
```

```
A>DIR
  Volume in drive A is DATADISK
  Directory of A:\CLASSDOS
.            <DIR>       11-24-87     9:00a
..           <DIR>       11-24-87     9:00a
CLASS    LST          90 11-24-87     9:29a
STUDENTS     <DIR>       11-24-87     9:30a
GRADES       <DIR>       11-24-87     9:30a
TESTS        <DIR>       11-24-87     9:30a
        6 File(s)     200776 bytes free
A>_
```

WHAT'S HAPPENING? The file `class.lst` is displayed as well as the three subdirectories just created. Remember, there are no files in the newly created subdirectories yet. You have made room for files. You can also create subdirectories in the other subdirectory, `classwps`, as long as the proper path is included.

STEP 6: Key in the following:

```
A>MD \classwps\students  <Enter>
```

```
A>MD \classwps\students
A>_
```

WHAT'S HAPPENING? Since the default or current directory at this time is `classdos`, you first had to include the path (`\classwps`) or the directory where you wanted the subdirectory `students` placed. The make directory command does not change the current or default directory. You can verify that you created the subdirectory `students` in the subdirectory `\classwps` by using the `DIR` command with the path parameter.

STEP 7: Key in the following:

```
A>DIR \classwps  <Enter>
```

```
A>DIR  \classwps
  Volume in drive A is DATADISK
  Directory of A:\CLASSWPS
.             <DIR>          11-24-87      9:00a
..            <DIR>          11-24-87      9:00a
CLASS    LST            90   11-24-87      9:29a
STUDENTS      <DIR>          11-24-87      9:33a
         4 File(s)  202752 bytes free
A>_
```

WHAT'S HAPPENING? The subdirectory `classwps` is displayed with the students subdirectory listed. Note that to get to the directory of `classwps`, you had to specify `DIR \classwps` to tell DOS which directory you wanted to see.

13.10 KNOWING THE DEFAULT DIRECTORY

Since DOS always uses the default unless you specify otherwise, knowing the default is very important. Recognizing the default drive is easy as the screen displays the prompt or disk drive letter, `A>` or `B>` or `C>`. Knowing the default subdirectory is not as easy. As you can see, keeping track of the default subdirectory can be a complex process. You can always key in the `CD` command, which will display the default or current drive and directory you are in. But it would be easier if you could display the default subdirectory as well as the default drive. You can do this with the `PROMPT` command and the meta-string for subdirectory.

ACTIVITY 13.11 CHANGING THE PROMPT

NOTE: Both two disk drive users and hard disk users will have the DATA disk in Drive A with the `A>` displayed on the screen. Both two disk drive users and hard disk users should be in the subdirectory `\classdos`. To be sure you are in the right subdirectory, you can key in `A>CD \classdos`. The instructions for both two disk drive users and hard disk users will be the same for the rest of this activity.

STEP 1: Key in exactly the following:

```
A>PROMPT $p$g  <Enter>
```

```
A>PROMPT $p$g
A:\CLASSDOS>_
```

WHAT'S HAPPENING? You have changed the prompt to display not only the default disk drive but also the default subdirectory (`$p$g`). This is an ideal command to place in an `autoexec.bat` file.

13.12 SUBDIRECTORY MARKERS

The single `.` (one period) in a subdirectory is the subdirectory name. The `..` (two periods) represents the directory that contains the current directory or the parent directory. The parent is the directory immediately above the subdirectory. You can use the `..` as a shorthand version of the parent directory name to move up the tree structure. You can move UP the hierarchy because a child always has one parent. You cannot use the `..` to move down the hierarchy as a parent can have many children.

ACTIVITY 13.13 USING THE SUBDIRECTORY MARKERS

NOTE: Both two disk drive users and hard disk users will have the DATA disk in Drive A with the `A>` displayed on the screen. Both two disk drive users and hard disk users should be in the subdirectory `\classdos`. To be sure you are in the right subdirectory, you can key in `A>CD \classdos`. The instructions for both two disk drive users and hard disk users will be the same for the rest of this activity.

STEP 1: Key in the following:

`A:\CLASSDOS>CD ..   <Enter>`

```
A:\CLASSDOS>CD ..
A:\>_
```

WHAT'S HAPPENING? You used the `..` to move up to the root or main directory. The root directory is the parent of the subdirectory `\CLASSDOS`.

13.14 COMPLETING YOUR TREE

To exemplify a disk divided up into subdirectories, you are going to create more subdirectories and then copy files into the subdirectories.

ACTIVITY 13.15 MAKING MORE SUBDIRECTORIES

NOTE: Both two disk drive users and hard disk users will have the DATA disk in Drive A with the A> displayed on the screen. Both two disk drive users and hard disk users should be in the root directory \. To be sure you are in the right directory, you can key in A>CD \. The instructions for both two disk drive users and hard disk users will be the same for the rest of this activity.

STEP 1: Key in the following:

A:\>MD \classwps\grades <Enter>

```
A:\>MD \classwps\grades
A:\>_
```

WHAT'S HAPPENING? You created a subdirectory called grades under the subdirectory called classwps. Since you were at the root directory, you had to include the entire path name, \classwps\grades. You did not need to include the drive letter, as A: is the default drive. Had you keyed in MD \grades, the grades subdirectory would have been created in the root directory as the root directory is the default directory. You do not need to include the path name if you change directories and make \classwps the default directory.

STEP 2: Key in the following:

A:\>CD classwps <Enter>

```
A:\>CD classwps
A:\CLASSWPS>_
```

WHAT'S HAPPENING? \Classwps is now the default directory. Any activity that occurs will automatically default to this directory unless otherwise specified.

STEP 3: Key in the following:

A:\CLASSWPS>MD tests <Enter>

STEP 4: Key in the following:

A:\CLASSWPS>MD fieldtr <Enter>

```
A:\CLASSWPS>MD tests
A:\CLASSWPS>MD fieldtr
A:\CLASSWPS>_
```

WHAT'S HAPPENING? You have created two more directories, tests and fieldtr, in the parent subdirectory classwps. You did not need to include the entire path name (A:\classwps\tests or A:\classwps\fieldtr) because \classwps is the default. You can see the subdirectories you just created by using the DIR command.

STEP 5: Key in the following:

A:\CLASSWPS>DIR <Enter>

```
A:\CLASSWPS>DIR
  Volume in drive A is DATADISK
  Directory of A:\CLASSWPS
.              <DIR>        11-24-87   9:00a
..             <DIR>        11-24-87   9:00a
CLASS    LST          90    11-24-87   9:29a
STUDENTS       <DIR>        11-24-87   9:33a
GRADES         <DIR>        11-24-87   9:39a
TESTS          <DIR>        11-24-87   9:41a
FIELDTR        <DIR>        11-24-87   9:41a
         7 File(s)     199680 bytes free
A:\CLASSWPS>_
```

WHAT'S HAPPENING? You created the directories tests and fieldtr in the subdirectory classwps. Note that of the seven files in the subdirectory \classwps, six are subdirectories. You know they are subdirectories because you see <DIR> after the file name.

Note the entry CLASS LST. It is a "regular" file because it does not have <DIR> after its file name. You have now created nine subdirectories. Each subdirectory can be used as if it were a separate disk. A pictorial representation is shown in Figure 13.7.

Figure 13.7 Directory Structure

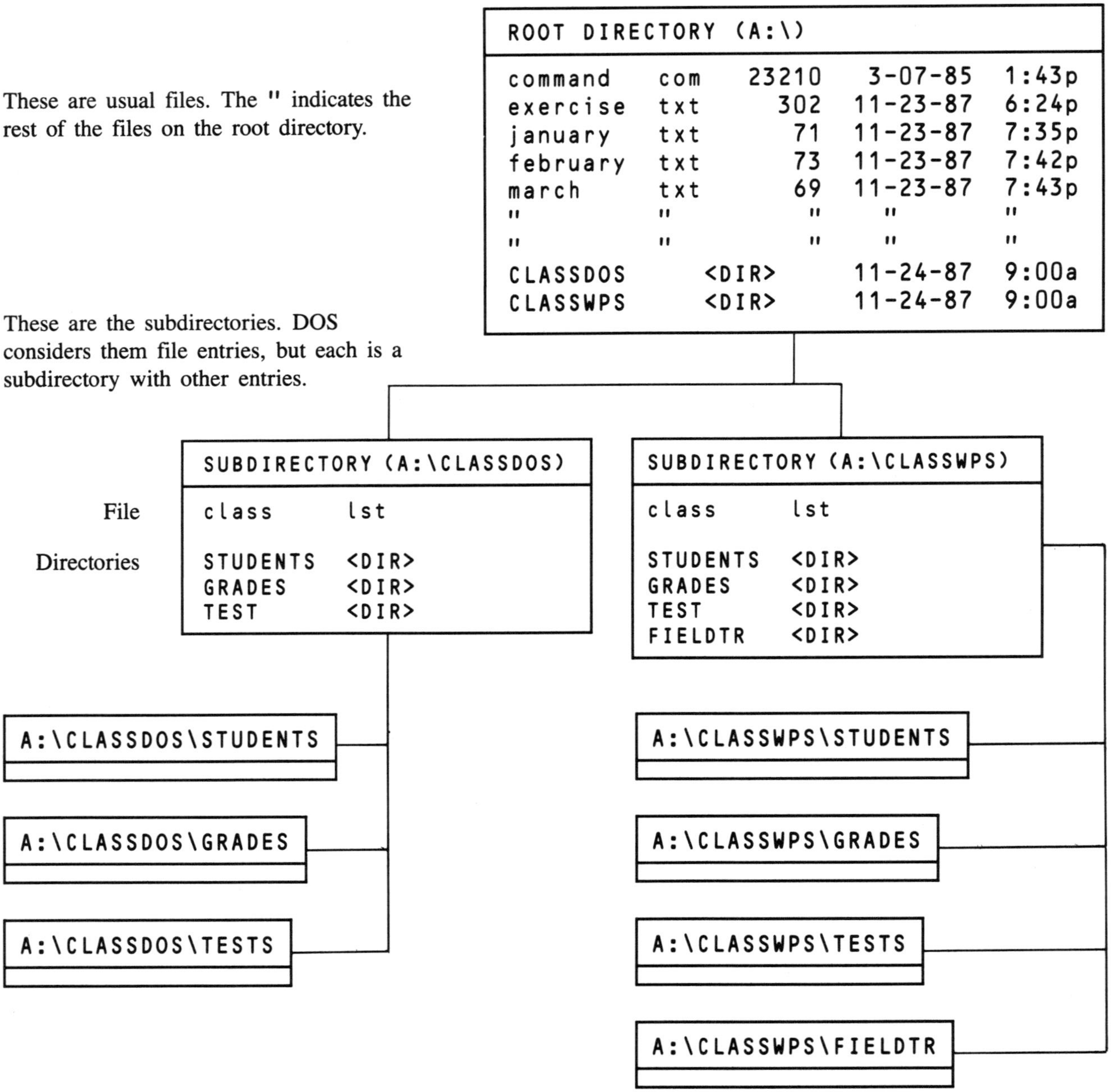

Another pictorial representation of the subdirectory structure is shown in Figure 13.8.

Figure 13.8 Subdirectory Structure

```
                              ROOT DIRECTORY (A:\)
file 1
file 2
"    "
                             ┌── A:\CLASSDOS\STUDENTS
A:\CLASSDOS: ────────────────┼── A:\CLASSDOS\GRADES
                             └── A:\CLASSDOS\TESTS

                             ┌── A:\CLASSWPS\STUDENTS
A:\CLASSWPS ─────────────────┼── A:\CLASSWPS\GRADES
                             ├── A:\CLASSWPS\TESTS
                             └── A:\CLASSWPS\FIELDTR
```

13.16 USING COMMANDS WITH SUBDIRECTORIES

These subdirectories that you created can be used as if they were separate disks. The DOS commands work as usual but you must include the path name to tell DOS what you want done with the files. These subdirectories are currently empty of files. You are going to see how the DOS commands work with subdirectories, using the `COPY` command to put files in the subdirectories.

In Figure 13.9, uppercase letters will indicate subdirectories; lowercase letters will indicate file names. After you complete the next activity, the final tree structure will look like the one in Figure 13.9.

Figure 13.9 Tree Structure

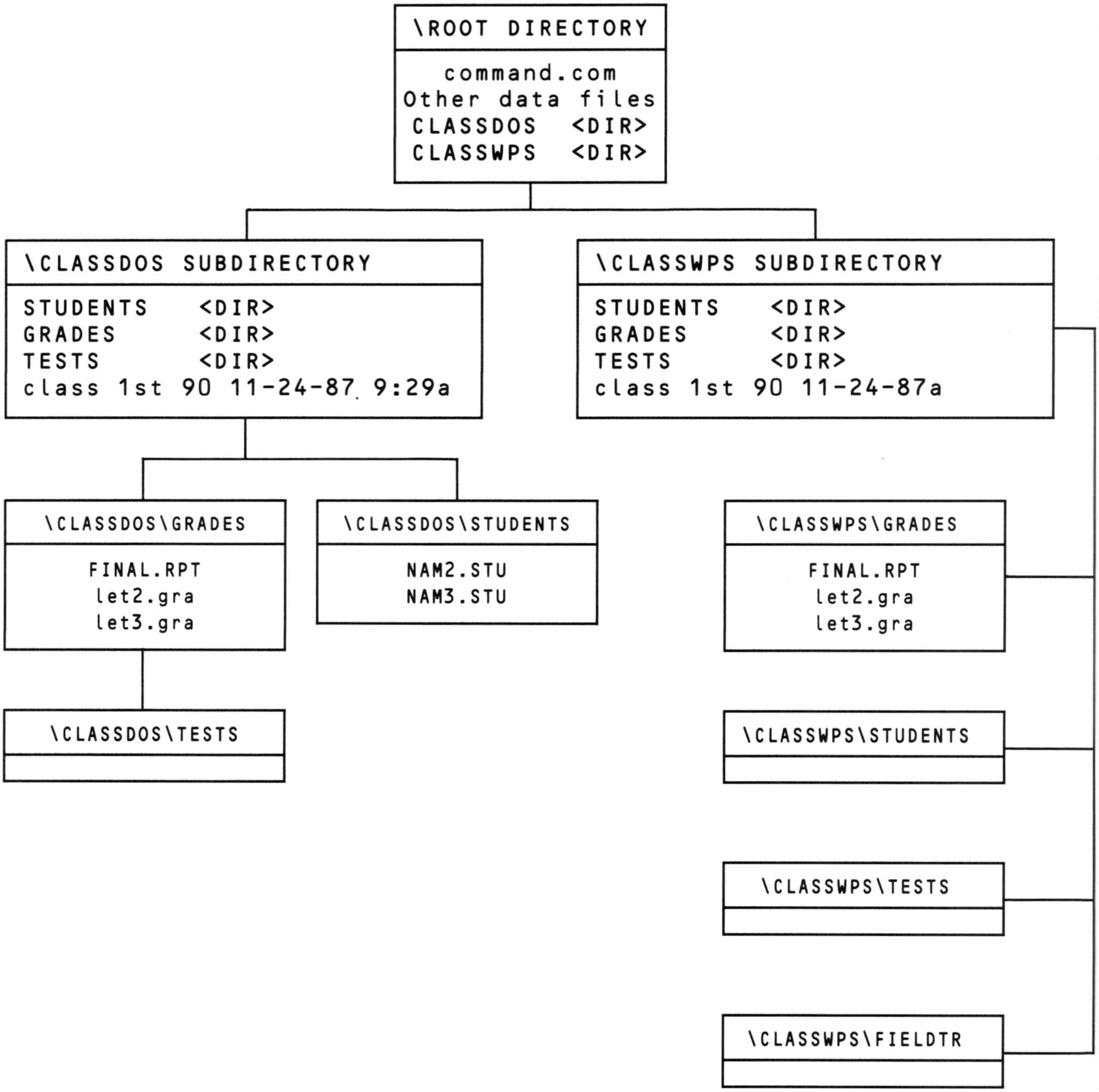

ACTIVITY 13.17 USING THE COPY COMMAND WITH SUBDIRECTORIES

NOTE: Two disk drive users and hard disk users will have the DATA disk in Drive A. You should be in the subdirectory `A:\classwps`. To get there from the root, you would key in `A>CD \classwps`. For clarity, commands and subdirectory names appear in uppercase; filenames are in lower case.

STEP 1: You are going to copy existing files to various subdirectories. The current directory is `A:\CLASSWPS`. You are going to move or go down one more level to the subdirectory `\GRADES`. The path is `A:\CLASSWPS\GRADES`. Key in the following:

```
A:\CLASSWPS>CD GRADES  <Enter>
```

```
A:\CLASSWPS>CD GRADES

A:\CLASSWPS\GRADES>_
```

WHAT'S HAPPENING? The prompt line now displays `A:\CLASSWPS\GRADES` as the current directory or the default directory. All activities will occur in this subdirectory unless you specify another path.

STEP 2: Key in the following:

```
A:\CLASSWPS\GRADES>COPY \CLASSDOS\class.lst final.rpt
<Enter>
```

```
A:\CLASSWPS\GRADES>COPY \CLASSDOS\class.lst final.rpt
          1 File(s) copied
A:\CLASSWPS\GRADES>_
```

WHAT'S HAPPENING? The file called `class.lst` that is in the subdirectory `\CLASSDOS` was successfully copied to the subdirectory `\CLASSWPS\GRADES` but is now called `final.rpt`. The syntax of the `COPY` command remained the same—`COPY source destination`. First you issued the command, `COPY`. But it was not enough to list just the file name, `class.lst`, as the source. You had to include the path so that DOS knew in which subdirectory the file was located. Hence the source was `\CLASSDOS\class.lst`. The destination is a file called `final.rpt`. But you did not have to key in the path for the destination because the default (`\CLASSWPS\GRADES`) was assumed. The longhand version of the command is:

```
COPY A:\CLASSDOS\class.lst A:\CLASSWPS\GRADES\final.rpt
```

If you had keyed in COPY class.lst final.rpt, you would have received the error message, "File not found." This is because DOS would have looked in the the current or default directory (A:\CLASSWPS\GRADES) for the file and would not have found it.

STEP 3: You are going to make a copy in the current directory so you do not need to include the path. Key in the following:

```
A:\CLASSWPS\GRADES>COPY final.rpt let2.gra  <Enter>
```

STEP 4: Key in the following:

```
A:\CLASSWPS\GRADES>COPY final.rpt let3.gra  <Enter>
```

```
A:\CLASSWPS\GRADES>COPY final.rpt let2.gra
          1 File(s) copied

A:\CLASSWPS\GRADES>COPY final.rpt let3.gra
          1 File(s) copied

A:\CLASSWPS\GRADES>_
```

WHAT'S HAPPENING? You copied two files. You did not have to include the path as the default was assumed. Technically, the commands looked like this:

```
COPY A:\CLASSWPS\GRADES\final.rpt A:\CLASSWPS\GRADES\let2.gra
COPY A:\CLASSWPS\GRADES\final.rpt A:\CLASSWPS\GRADES\let3.gra
```

STEP 5: Key in the following:

```
A:\CLASSWPS\GRADES>DIR  <enter>
```

```
A:\CLASSWPS\GRADES>DIR
Volume in drive A is DATADISK
  Directory of A:\CLASSWPS\GRADES
.             <DIR>         11-24-87     9:39a
..            <DIR>         11-24-87     9:39a
FINAL    RPT           90   11-24-87     9:39a
LET2     GRA           90   11-24-87     9:39a
LET3     GRA           90   11-24-87     9:39a
     5 File(s)         196608 bytes free
A:\CLASSWPS\GRADES>_
```

WHAT'S HAPPENING? Note that you see only the files that are in the default subdirectory.

STEP 6: You can also use wild cards with subdirectories. Key in the following:

```
A:\CLASSWPS\GRADES>COPY *.* \CLASSDOS\GRADES <Enter>
```

```
A:\CLASSWPS\GRADES>COPY *.* \CLASSDOS\GRADES
FINAL.RPT
LET2.GRA
LET3.GRA
     3 File(s) copied
A:\CLASSWPS\GRADES>_
```

WHAT'S HAPPENING? As the files were copied, they were listed on the screen. Again, the syntax is the same: the command, `COPY`; the source, `*.*` (all the files in the default subdirectory `\CLASSWPS\GRADES`); to the destination, `\CLASSDOS\GRADES`. You had to include the path name in the destination. Since you wanted to give the files the same name in the subdirectory, `\CLASSDOS\GRADES`, you did not have to specify the file names. DOS assumed or defaulted to the current file names.

STEP 7: Key in the following:

```
A:\CLASSWPS\GRADES>DIR \CLASSDOS\GRADES  <Enter>
```

```
A:\CLASSWPS\GRADES>DIR \CLASSDOS\GRADES
  Volume in drive A is DATADISK
  Directory of A:\CLASSDOS\GRADES
.             <DIR>          11-24-87      9:30a
..            <DIR>          11-24-87      9:30a
FINAL     RPT           90   11-24-87      9:39a
LET2      GRA           90   11-24-87      9:39a
LET3      GRA           90   11-24-87      9:39a
     5 File(s)         193536 bytes free
 A:\CLASSWPS\GRADES>_
```

WHAT'S HAPPENING? You can `COPY` files from anywhere to anywhere provided you give the path. Be aware of what the default subdirectory is and what the path is. Changing the prompt to display the subdirectory is very valuable.

STEP 8: Key in the following (Because the command line is so long in this example, it breaks into two lines even though you key it in as one line. Just keep on keying in the line as indicated and do not hit `<Enter>` until you reach `<Enter>` at the end of the line):

```
A:\CLASSWPS\GRADES>COPY \CLASSDOS\GRADES\let?.gra
    \CLASSDOS\STUDENTS\nam?.stu  <Enter>
```

```
A:\CLASSWPS\GRADES>COPY \CLASSDOS\GRADES\let?.gra \CLASSDOS\STUDENTS\nam?.stu
A:\CLASSDOS\GRADES\LET2.GRA
A:\CLASSDOS\GRADES\LET3.GRA
        2 File(s) copied
A:\CLASSWPS\GRADES>_
```

WHAT'S HAPPENING? Note how DOS displayed the entire path name as it copied the files. Here you copied all the `let` files from the subdirectory `\CLASSDOS\GRADES` to the subdirectory `\CLASSDOS\STUDENTS` with new file names that are called `nam?.stu`. To see that the files were copied correctly, you can use the `DIR` command.

STEP 9: Key in the following:

```
A:\CLASSWPS\GRADES>DIR \CLASSDOS\STUDENTS  <Enter>
```

```
A:\CLASSWPS\GRADES>DIR \CLASSDOS\STUDENTS
  Volume in drive A is DATADISK
  Directory of A:\CLASSDOS\STUDENTS

.            <DIR>         11-24-87     9:30a
..           <DIR>         11-24-87     9:30a
NAM2     STU          90   11-24-87     9:39a
NAM3     STU          90   11-24-87     9:39a
     4 File(s)           191488 bytes free

A:\CLASSWPS\GRADES>_
```

WHAT'S HAPPENING? You successfully copied the files because you used the proper path name. You have been using the `COPY` and `DIR` commands. Any DOS command will work if you use the proper syntax and use the proper path.

13.18 REMOVING DIRECTORIES

If a disk can be cluttered with files, you can imagine how a disk can be even more cluttered with subdirectories. The `ERASE` or `DEL` commands are used to get rid of files. You cannot use these commands to eliminate subdirectories. There is a special command to remove subdirectories, the remove directory command (RD or RMDIR). If a subdirectory has files in it, you cannot remove the subdirectory. This prevents you from accidentally wiping out not only a directory but all the files inside it. Thus, if a subdirectory has files in it, you must first DEL any files, then remove the subdirectory. The remove directory command syntax is:

```
RMDIR [d:] [path] subdirectory.name
RD [d:] [path] subdirectory.name
```

If you do not include the drive designator, DOS will use the default drive. The remove directory command will not remove the directory you are currently in or the current directory. It also will never remove the root directory.

ACTIVITY 13.19 USING THE RD COMMAND

NOTE: Both two disk drive users and hard disk users will have the DATA disk in Drive A with the A> displayed on the screen. Both two disk drive users and hard disk users should be in the subdirectory \classwps\grades. To be sure you are in the right subdirectory, you can key in A>CD \classwps\grades. The instructions for both two disk drive users and hard disk users will be the same for the rest of this activity.

STEP 1: Key in the following:

A:\CLASSWPS\GRADES>RD \CLASSDOS\STUDENTS <Enter>

```
A:\CLASSWPS\GRADES>RD \CLASSDOS\STUDENTS
Invalid path, not directory,
or directory not empty
A:\CLASSWPS\GRADES>_
```

WHAT'S HAPPENING? RD did not remove the directory \CLASSDOS\STUDENTS because, in this case, the directory was not empty. It contains the files nam2.stu and nam3.stu. Thus, to remove the directory, you must first delete the files in the directory. ERASE or DEL is for eliminating files, RD is for eliminating directories.

STEP 2: Key in the following:

A:\CLASSWPS\GRADES>DEL \CLASSDOS\STUDENTS*.* <Enter>

```
A:\CLASSWPS\GRADES>DEL \CLASSDOS\STUDENTS\*.*
Are you sure (Y/N)?_
```

WHAT'S HAPPENING? Since you asked to delete all the files (`*.*`), DOS is confirming that you really want to do this. Remember, you are deleting only the files in the subdirectory `\CLASSDOS\STUDENTS`, not all the files on the DATA disk.

STEP 3: Key in the following:

```
Y<Enter>
```

```
A:\CLASSWPS\GRADES>_
Are you sure (Y/N)?Y

A:\CLASSWPS\GRADES>_
```

WHAT'S HAPPENING? Since you responded Y for yes, the files are deleted. Now that the subdirectory `\CLASSDOS\STUDENTS` is empty of files, you can remove the directory with the `RD` command.

STEP 4: Key in the following:

```
A:\CLASSWPS\GRADES>RD \CLASSDOS\STUDENTS  <Enter>
```

```
A:\CLASSWPS\GRADES>RD \CLASSDOS\STUDENTS

A:\CLASSWPS\GRADES>_
```

WHAT'S HAPPENING? You removed the directory. But you see no message to confirm that you did remove it.

STEP 5: Key in the following:

```
A:\CLASSWPS\GRADES>DIR \CLASSDOS  <Enter>
```

```
A:\CLASSWPS\GRADES>DIR \CLASSDOS
  Volume in drive A is DATADISK
  Directory of A:\CLASSDOS
.             <DIR>         11-24-87      9:00a
..            <DIR>         11-24-87      9:00a
CLASS    LST          90    11-24-87      9:29a
GRADES        <DIR>         11-24-87      9:30a
TESTS         <DIR>         11-24-87      9:30a
        5 File(s)      194560 bytes free
A:\CLASSWPS\GRADES>_
```

WHAT'S HAPPENING? The subdirectory, `STUDENTS <DIR>` is not displayed. You did indeed remove it.

13.20 SETTING THE PATH

As you use subdirectories, you will be changing the current or default subdirectory. Often you will also want to use the DOS external commands or have DOS look for command files in other than the current subdirectory. Since a subdirectory is like a separate disk, DOS will give you the message "`File not found.`" In the past, you have copied the needed file to the disk. However, typically you do not want to have to copy DOS external commands to every subdirectory, nor do you want to copy all program files to all subdirectories. To eliminate this problem, there is a `PATH` command. `PATH`, an internal command, tells DOS where to look for a command file if it is not in the current directory. `PATH` only looks for files that can be executed, such as `.COM`, `.EXE`, or `.BAT`. DOS will not locate any files with any other file extensions. You can set up the `PATH` for command files any way you wish, to another subdirectory or to any disk drive.

The PATH command syntax is:

```
PATH [[d:][path] ; [d:][path]...]
```

`PATH` is the command. `PATH` with no parameters displays the current path. Drive indicates which drive designator you want the path to follow. If you omit the drive designator, DOS will use the default drive. `[path]` is the path name of the subdirectory that contains the command files. You can have DOS search more than one path but you use the semicolon (`;`) to indicate another drive and path. The semicolon (`;`) used without the drive or path cancels any paths you have created.

ACTIVITY 13.21 USING THE PATH COMMAND

STEP 1: Remove the DATA disk from Drive A. Insert the DATA disk into Drive B. Insert the DOS System Disk in Drive A.

STEP 1: Do nothing. The DATA disk should be in Drive A.

STEP 2: Key in the following:

STEP 2: Do nothing.

```
A:\>B:  <Enter>
```

```
A:\>B:

B:\>_
```

WHAT'S HAPPENING? You have changed the default drive to B:.

STEP 3: Key in the following:

```
B:\>CD \CLASSWPS  <Enter>
```

```
B:\>CD \CLASSWPS

B:\CLASSWPS>_
```

STEP 3: Key in the following:

```
A:\>CD \CLASSWPS  <Enter>
```

```
A:\>CD \CLASSWPS

A:\CLASSWPS>_
```

STEP 4: Key in the following:

```
B:\CLASSWPS>CHKDSK  <Enter>
```

```
B:\CLASSWPS>CHKDSK
Bad command or file name

B:\CLASSWPS>_
```

STEP 4: Key in the following:

```
A:\CLASSWPS>CHKDSK  <Enter>
```

```
A:\CLASSWPS>CHKDSK
Bad command or file name

A:\CLASSWPS>_
```

WHAT'S HAPPENING? DOS could not execute the external command because chkdsk.com is not stored as a file in the subdirectory \CLASSWPS. Rather than having to copy the file chkdsk.com to the subdirectory, you can use the PATH command. It tells DOS that if it does not find CHKDSK in the current subdirectory, to look for that file on the path that is set.

STEP 5: Key in the following:

```
B:\CLASSWPS>PATH A:\ <Enter>
```

```
B:\CLASSWPS>PATH A:\

B:\CLASSWPS>_
```

STEP 5: Key in the following:

```
A:\CLASSWPS>PATH C:\ <Enter>
```

NOTE: Hard disk system users, if the DOS utility programs are in a subdirectory on the hard disk, you must include the entire path name, i.e., PATH C:\DOS.

```
A:\CLASSWPS>PATH C:\

A:\CLASSWPS>_
```

WHAT'S HAPPENING? It appears that nothing has happened. But it has. You have set the path DOS will search. If it does not find the command in the default subdirectory (two disk drive users, it will go to the path set—the root directory of the DOS System Disk in Drive A. For hard disk users, it will go to the path set—the root directory of Drive C or the subdirectory where the DOS System Disk in Drive C:).

STEP 6: Key in the following:

`B:\CLASSWPS>CHKDSK <Enter>`

STEP 6: Key in the following:

`A:\CLASSWPS>CHKDSK <Enter>`

NOTE: The following display will appear on both floppy and hard disk systems.

```
Volume DATADISK  created Aug 24, 1987  2:49p
     362496 bytes total disk space
      38912 bytes in 3 hidden files
       8192 bytes in 8 directories
     120832 bytes in 77 user files
     194560 bytes available on disk

     655360 bytes total memory
     535824 bytes free
```

WHAT'S HAPPENING? You did not get the message "`Bad command or file name`" this time. When DOS could not find the file `chkdsk.com` in the subdirectory, `\CLASSWPS`, it searched the path that was set. When it searched the path, it found the file, loaded it into memory, and executed it.

STEP 7: Key in the following:

`B:\CLASSWPS>PATH <Enter>`

STEP 7: Key in the following:

`A:\CLASSWPS>PATH <Enter>`

```
B:\CLASSWPS>PATH
PATH=A:\

B:\CLASSWPS>_
```

```
A:\CLASSWPS>PATH
PATH=C:\

A:\CLASSWPS>_
```

WHAT'S HAPPENING? Note that `PATH` keyed in by itself displays the current path.

STEP 8: Key in the following:

`B:\CLASSWPS>PATH ; <Enter>`

STEP 8: Key in the following:

`A:\CLASSWPS>PATH ; <Enter>`

STEP 9: Key in the following:

`B:\CLASSWPS>PATH <Enter>`

STEP 9: Key in the following:

`A:\CLASSWPS>PATH <Enter>`

```
B:\CLASSWPS>PATH ;

B:\CLASSWPS>PATH
No Path

B:\CLASSWPS>_
```

```
A:\CLASSWPS>PATH ;

A:\CLASSWPS>PATH
No Path

A:\CLASSWPS>_
```

WHAT'S HAPPENING? PATH followed by the semicolon (;) cancels the currently set path. This was demonstrated by the response "No Path." As you can see, the PATH command saves you the trouble of copying program files from disk to disk or subdirectory to subdirectory. Instead, you can set the path.

CHAPTER SUMMARY

1. Subdirectories are created to help organize a disk as well as to defeat the file limitation of the root directory.
2. MD is an internal command that allows the user to create a subdirectory.
3. Subdirectory naming conventions follow DOS file naming conventions, i.e., a limit of eight characters in the file name and three characters in the file extension.
4. <DIR> following a file name indicates that it is a subdirectory.
5. CD is an internal command that when keyed in by itself will display the current or default subdirectory.
6. CD followed by a subdirectory name will change the current directory to the named directory.
7. RD is an internal command to eliminate subdirectories.
8. Subdirectories must be empty of files prior to using the RD command.
9. The root directory can never be eliminated.
10. In using subdirectories and file names, the backslash is the delimiter that separates the names.
11. The PATH command is an internal command that allows the user to tell DOS what disk and drive to search for command files.
12. DOS will only search the path for executable files, those having the file extension .EXE, .COM, or .BAT.
13. PATH keyed in by itself will display the current path.
14. PATH followed by a semicolon will cancel the path.
15. PROMPT pg will set the prompt to display the default drive and default subdirectory.

REVIEW QUESTIONS

1. What is the directory that is always created when a disk is formatted?
2. Define a subdirectory.
3. Why would you want to create a subdirectory?
4. The following message is displayed on the screen after the command is keyed in:

```
B:\CLASS>COPY myfile \NEW
Invalid directory.
```

   What is the problem? Can it be corrected?

5. The following message is displayed on the screen after the command is keyed in:

```
B:\CLASS>RD \NEWONE
Invalid path, not directory,
or directory not empty.
```

   What is the problem? How could it be corrected?

6. You are in the subdirectory CLASS. You key in COMP file2 file3. The error message says "Bad command or file name." In what two ways could you solve this problem so that you could use the COMP command?
7. What DOS commands can be used in a subdirectory?
8. What are the the subdirectory commands? Are they internal or external commands?
9. Define a path. How do you create a path? How do you cancel a path?
10. You are in the root directory. You have a subdirectory \CLASS. You want to create a subdirectory called \GRADES under the subdirectory \CLASS. What two ways could you write the command?
11. The following is the structure of a disk:

```
\
myfile.ext
CLASS <DIR>
```

```
\CLASS
.  <DIR>
.. <DIR>
new.fil
STUDENTS <DIR>
```

   Name the parent and children directories.

12. Using the example in question 11, how would you copy the file myfile.ext to the subdirectory STUDENTS from the root directory?
13. Using the example in question 11, how would you delete the file new.fil in the subdirectory CLASS from the root directory?
14. In the subdirectory CLASS, you see the entries:

```
.    <DIR>
..   <DIR>
```

   What do the dots mean?

15. In the above question, in what way could you use the dots?

TRUE/FALSE

1. The command to delete a subdirectory called \NEW is DEL \NEW.
2. The command used to change the current directory is MODE.
3. DOS only searches a path for executable files, those with the file extension .EXE, .COM, or .BAT.
4. Another name for a parent directory of a subdirectory is .. and it can be accessed by using the two periods.
5. You can use any DOS internal command in a subdirectory.
6. CD will display the default subdirectory.

7. The prompt command can be changed to display not only the disk drive but the subdirectory.
8. A subdirectory can only hold a maximum of 64 files.

SUGGESTED ACTIVITIES

Two disk drive system users: The DATA disk should be in Drive B. The DOS System Disk should be in Drive A. You should begin in the root directory of the DATA disk.

Hard disk system users: The DATA disk should be in Drive A. You should begin in the root directory of the DATA disk.

1. Create three subdirectories on the DATA disk called **BATCH**, **DATABASE**, and **SPRDSHT** in the root directory. Be sure you are not in a subdirectory. Using the **DIR** command, display these subdirectories on the screen and print the screen.
2. Create two subdirectories under **SPRDSHT** called **BUDGETS** and **TRAVEL**. Display the directory of the subdirectory **SPRDSHT** on the screen and print this screen.
3. Create two subdirectories under **DATABASE** called **REPORTS** and **LETTERS**. Display the directory of the subdirectory **DATABASE** and print this screen.
4. Create two subdirectories in the **\SPRDSHT\BUDGETS** subdirectory called **PERSONAL** and **WORK**. Copy the files called **let2.gra** and **let3.gra** from the subdirectory **\CLASSWPS\GRADES** to both the **PERSONAL** and **WORK** subdirectories. Do not change the file names. When the files have been copied, print the screen with the **COPY** command displayed.
5. Copy the files called **let2.gra** and **let3.gra** from the **\CLASSWPS\GRADES** subdirectory to the **\DATABASE\REPORTS** subdirectory. Call the files in the **\DATABASE\REPORTS** subdirectory **let2.rpt** and **let3.rpt**. Do a directory display of the subdirectory **\DATABASE\REPORTS** and print the screen.
6. Copy all the files in the root directory with the file extension **.bat** to the subdirectory **\BATCH**. Delete all the files in the root directory with the file extension **.bat**. Do a directory display of the **\BATCH** subdirectory. Print this screen.
7. Prove that files with the extension .bat are no longer in the root directory. Print this screen.
8. Remove the subdirectory **\SPRDSHT\BUDGETS\PERSONAL**. Do a directory display of **\SPRDSHT\BUDGETS** to demonstrate that the subdirectory **PERSONAL** is no longer there. Print this screen.
9. Display the current path. Print this screen.
10. Set the path to the DOS System Disk. Display the path. Print this screen.

APPENDIX A: BACKUP AND RESTORE

A1.0 UNDERSTANDING BACKUP AND RESTORE

Backing up data and programs is extremely important. A hard disk cannot be backed up with the DISKCOPY or the COPY commands. Instead, the DOS System disk provides two utility programs, BACKUP and RESTORE, which are specifically designed to back up the hard disk files and then restore the files when needed. The BACKUP command is different from the COPY or DISKCOPY command. It will prompt you to insert disks so all of the hard disk can be copied to floppy disks. Backing up the hard disk is not a trivial task. First of all, it requires formatted disks. To entirely back up a 10 Meg hard disk, takes about 30 360K floppy disks. A 20 Meg hard disk takes about 60 disks. Backing up takes a lot of time. You sit in front of the computer and insert each floppy when DOS instructs you to do so. DOS automatically numbers the disks in the proper order but you are well advised to pre-number the disks on the external label before getting started. Backup floppies are not usable by themselves. If you wish to use them, you make them usable with the RESTORE command.

Backups are insurance. You back up the hard disk for archival purposes and just in case of software or hardware failures. In other words, you usually do not need the backups unless there is a problem with the hard disk. Usually it is something terrible, like the hard disk "crashes" or you lose an important data file. That is when you RESTORE the files. However, it is extremely important and prudent to make backing up the hard disk a regular routine. In addition, it is wise to have more than one backup. How often you backup is dependent on how long it would take you to "rekey in" or recover the information. This means that if you update files daily, back them up daily. If you update files weekly, back them up weekly. A good daily routine is:

HARD DISK	HARD DISK	HARD DISK	HARD DISK	HARD DISK
Monday	Tuesday	Wednesday	Thursday	Friday
Floppies	Floppies	Floppies	Floppies	Floppies

This may seem like a lot of floppy disks, and it is. Which is one reason why many business people go to a tape based backup system. But the reason you backup so often is because of the following scenario. It is Friday. The hard disk crashes. You go to restore the hard disk from Thursday's floppy backup disks. Thursday's disks are bad. (Murphy's law—when things are bad, they are awful.) So if you only have one day's backup you are out of luck. But you are prepared. You have Wednesday's floppy disks. All you have lost is Thursday's work instead of all the work.

You should have at least two sets of backup floppy disks.

If there is a power failure or a hardware problem prior to the completion of the backup routine, all the backup files are useless because **BACKUP** deletes everything on the floppy disks. Thus if **BACKUP** is interrupted, the previous backup is destroyed prior to the new backup being completed.

A1.1 BACKING UP A HARD DISK WITH BACKUP

Be sure to have enough formatted floppy disks. You cannot interrupt the **BACKUP** program to format disks. Version 2.x only allows you to backup the hard disk to floppies. Version 3.x allows you to backup from or to any valid DOS medium. The source disk must not be write protected and if you are on a network, backup will not archive programs you do not have access to. The syntax for the command is:

```
BACKUP source destination
```

or

```
BACKUP d:[path][filename] d:[/S][/M][/A][/D:mm-dd-yy]
```

ACTIVITY A1.2 DOING A FULL BACKUP

NOTE: Do not do this unless you have enough floppy disks and are prepared to backup your entire hard disk. In addition, if you have any copy protected programs on the hard disk, first read the documentation for each application package. Sometimes you must uninstall an application package prior to using the **BACKUP** command.

STEP 1: Key in the following:

```
C>BACKUP C:\*.* A:/S  <Enter>
```

```
C>BACKUP C: A:/S

Insert backup diskette 01 in drive A:

Warning! Files in the target drive
A:\ root directory will be erased
Strike any key when ready

_
```

WHAT'S HAPPENING? You are asking the system to `BACKUP` all the files from Drive C in the root directory (`C:\*.*`) and all the files in any subdirectories on the hard disk (`/S`) to the disk in Drive A. Note that the `/S` parameter for subdirectories comes AFTER the destination or `A:`.

STEP 2: Insert a formatted disk in Drive A. Press `<Enter>` to begin backing up the hard disk.

```
***Backing up files to drive A:***
Diskette number: 01

\IBMBIO.COM
\IBMDOS.COM
\COMMAND
......
......
```

WHAT'S HAPPENING? "`......`" represents all the files as they are found. Each file, as it is copied from the hard disk to the disk in Drive A, is listed on the screen. If one disk will not take all the files, the following message will appear:

```
Insert backup diskette 02 in drive A:

Warning! Files in the target drive
A:\ root directory will be erased
Strike any key when ready

_
```

WHAT'S HAPPENING? You continue to insert disks until the hard disk is backed up. Each disk is numbered sequentially by DOS. When you have completed the process, you can look at the directory on `A:` and you will see a file named `BACKUPID@@@`. This file is on each disk you backup and obviously supplies the **backup id** number.

A1.3 INCREMENTAL BACKUPS

You can back up the hard disk in increments. You can back up individual files, a subdirectory, only those files that have been modified since the last backup, and back up files that have been created or modified since a certain date. Remember when you use a disk for backup, whatever was on that disk is gone. The following activities can be done, using the subdirectory `\junk` that was created in the text.

ACTIVITY A1.4 BACKING UP A FILE

STEP 1: Key in the following:

`C>BACKUP C:\junk\jan.tmp  A:  <Enter>`

```
C>BACKUP C:\junk\jan.tmp A:

Insert backup diskette 01 in drive A:

Warning! Files in the target drive
A:\ root directory will be erased
Strike any key when ready

_
```

WHAT'S HAPPENING? You are going to backup one file from the subdirectory `\junk` on Drive C called `jan.tmp` to the disk in Drive A.

STEP 2: Insert a formatted disk in Drive A. Press `<Enter>` to back up the file called `C:\junk\jan.tmp`.

```
***Backing up files to drive A:***
Diskette number: 01

\JUNK\JAN.TMP

C>_
```

WHAT'S HAPPENING? Since you only backed up one file, the process is complete.

ACTIVITY A1.5 BACKING UP A SUBDIRECTORY

STEP 1: Key in the following:

`C>BACKUP C:\junk A:`

```
C>BACKUP C:\junk A:

Insert backup diskette 01 in drive A:

Warning! Files in the target drive
A:\ root directory will be erased
Strike any key when ready

_
```

WHAT'S HAPPENING? You are asking the system to BACKUP all the files from Drive C in the subdirectory called \junk to the disk in Drive A.

STEP 2: Insert a formatted disk in Drive A. Press <Enter> to begin backing up the hard disk.

```
***Backing up files to drive A:***
Diskette number: 01

\JUNK\EXP87JAN.DAT
\JUNK\EXP87FEB.DAT
\JUNK\EXP87MAR.DAT
......
......
```

WHAT'S HAPPENING? "......" represents all the rest of the files in the subdirectory \JUNK as they are found. Each file, as it is copied from the hard disk to the disk in Drive A, is listed on the screen. If one disk will not take all the files, the following message will appear:

```
Insert backup diskette 02 in drive A:

Warning! Files in the target drive
A:\ root directory will be erased
Strike any key when ready
_
```

WHAT'S HAPPENING? You continue to insert disks until the subdirectory is backed up. Each disk is numbered sequentially by DOS. When you have completed the process, you can look at the directory on A: and you will see a file named BACKUPID@@@. This file is on each disk you backup and, obviously, supplies the backup id number.

ACTIVITY A1.6 BACKING UP SELECTED FILES IN A SUBDIRECTORY

STEP 1: Key in the following:

C>BACKUP C:\junk*.87 A:

```
C>BACKUP C:\junk\*.87  A:

Insert backup diskette 01 in drive A:

Warning! Files in the target drive
A:\ root directory will be erased
Strike any key when ready
_
```

WHAT'S HAPPENING? You are asking the system to BACKUP from Drive C the files that have the file extension .87 in the subdirectory called \junk to the disk in Drive A.

STEP 2: Insert a formatted disk in Drive A. Press <Enter> to begin backing up the hard disk.

```
***Backing up files to drive A:***
Diskette number: 01

\JUNK\JAN.87
\JUNK\FEB.87
\JUNK\MAR.87
\JUNK\APR.87

C>
```

WHAT'S HAPPENING? There were only four files with the extension .87 in the subdirectory \junk. Each file, as it is copied from the hard disk to the disk in Drive A, is listed on the screen. In this case, all the files fit onto one disk. However, if one disk would not take all the files, the following message would appear:

```
Insert backup diskette 02 in drive A:

Warning! Files in the target drive
A:\ root directory will be erased
Strike any key when ready
_
```

WHAT'S HAPPENING? You continue to insert disks until the subdirectory is backed up. Each disk is numbered sequentially by DOS. When you have completed the process, you can look at the directory on A: and you will see a file named BACKUPID@@@. This file is on each disk you backup and obviously supplies the backup id number.

STEP 3: Key in the following:

```
C>DIR A:  <Enter>
```

```
C>DIR A:

Volume in drive A has no label
Directory of A:\

BACKUPID   @@@       128    11-23-87     12:52p
JAN        87        200    11-23-87      1:18p
FEB        87        202    11-23-87      1:19p
MAR        87        198    11-23-87      1:19p
APR        87        199    11-23-87      1:19p
        5 File(s)        357376 bytes free

C>_
```

WHAT'S HAPPENING? Note the BACKUPID and the .87 files you backed up.

ACTIVITY A1.7 BACKING UP FILES THAT HAVE BEEN MODIFIED SINCE THE LAST BACKUP

STEP 1: Key in the following:

```
C>COPY CON C:\junk\change.87  <Enter>
This is my change document to  <Enter>
demonstrate how the /M parameter works.  <Enter>
<Ctrl>-Z
```

```
C>COPY CON C:\junk\change.87
This is my change document to
demonstrate how the /M parameter works.
^Z

C>_
```

WHAT'S HAPPENING? You have created a file that has been changed.

STEP 2: Key in the following:

```
C>BACKUP C:\junk\*.87  A:/M
```

```
C>BACKUP C:\junk\*.87  A:/M

Insert backup diskette 01 in drive A:

Warning! Files in the target drive
A:\ root directory will be erased
Strike any key when ready

_
```

WHAT'S HAPPENING? You created a new file, one that has been modified since the last backup. You then asked the system to **BACKUP** from Drive C only the files that have the file extension **.87** in the subdirectory called **\junk** to the disk in Drive A.

STEP 3: Insert the disk you used in Activity A1.6. Press **<Enter>** to begin backing up the modified files.

```
***Backing up files to drive A:***
Diskette number: 01

\JUNK\CHANGE.87

C>_
```

WHAT'S HAPPENING? The file, as it is copied from the hard disk to the disk in Drive A, is listed on the screen. Note that only one file has changed since the last back up.

STEP 4: Key in the following:

```
C>DIR A:
```

```
C>DIR A:

Volume in drive A has no label
Directory of A:\

BACKUPID   @@@        128     11-23-87       1:04p
CHANGE      87        200     11-23-87       1:02p
        1 File(s)          360448 bytes free

C>_
```

WHAT'S HAPPENING? Note that only the file that has been modified is backed up to the disk in Drive A. All the other files are gone.

ACTIVITY A1.8 BACKING UP SELECTED FILES BY DATE

STEP 1: Key in the following:

```
C>DATE 11/23/95  <Enter>
```

STEP 2: Key in the following:

```
C>COPY CON \junk\new.87  <Enter>
This is a new file to  <Enter>
show how the BACKUP command will  <Enter>
backup by a certain date.  <Enter>
<Ctrl>-Z
```

```
C>DATE 11/23/95

C>COPY CON new.87
This is a new file to
show how the BACKUP command will
backup by a certain date.
^Z

C>_
```

WHAT'S HAPPENING? You changed the date to a date in the future. Then you created a file based on that date so that you could test the `/M` option of the `BACKUP` command.

STEP 3: Key in the following:

```
C>BACKUP C:\junk\*.87 A:/D:11/22/95
```

```
C>BACKUP C:\junk\*.87  A:/D:11/22/95

Insert backup diskette 01 in drive A:

Warning! Files in the target drive
A:\ root directory will be erased
Strike any key when ready

_
```

WHAT'S HAPPENING? You have asked the system to `BACKUP` from Drive C the files with the extension `.87` that have been created or modified on or after November 23, 1995 in the subdirectory `\junk` to the disk in Drive A. Note that the `/D:` parameter follows the destination drive.

STEP 4: Insert the disk you used in Activity A1.7. Press `<Enter>` to begin backing up the files dated after 11/22/95.

```
***Backing up files to drive A:***
Diskette number: 01

\JUNK\new.87

C>_
```

WHAT'S HAPPENING? Only `\junk\new.87` was modified after November 22, 1985 in the subdirectory `\junk`. It was listed on the screen as it was copied from the hard disk to the disk in Drive A.

STEP 5: Key in the following:

```
C>DIR A:
```

```
C>DIR A:

Volume in drive A has no label
Directory of A:\

BACKUPID   @@@       128    11-23-95      1:14p
NEW        87        211    11-23-95      1:12p
         1 File(s)        360440 bytes free

C>_
```

WHAT'S HAPPENING? Note that only the file that has a date after 11/22/95 was backed up to the disk in Drive A. All the other files are gone.

ACTIVITY A1.9 ADDING FILES TO A BACK UP DISK

STEP 1: Insert the disk you used in Activity A1.8 into Drive A.

STEP 2: Key in the following:

```
C>BACKUP C:\junk\*.87 A:/A
```

```
C>BACKUP C:\junk\*.87  A:/A

***Backing up files to drive A:***
Diskette number: 01

\JUNK\JAN.87
\JUNK\FEB.87
\JUNK\MAR.87
\JUNK\APR.87
\JUNK\CHANGE.87
\JUNK\NEW.87

C>_
```

WHAT'S HAPPENING? All the files, in subdirectory `\junk` with the extension `.87`, are listed on the screen as they are copied from the hard disk to the disk in Drive A.

STEP 3: Key in the following:

C>DIR A:

```
C>DIR A:

Volume in drive A has no label
Directory of A:\

BACKUPID    @@@       128    11-23-95     1:14p
NEW         87        211    11-23-95     1:12p
JAN         87        200    11-23-87     1:18p
FEB         87        202    11-23-87     1:19p
MAR         87        198    11-23-87     1:19p
APR         87        199    11-23-87     1:19p
CHANGE      87        200    11-23-87     1:02p
NEW         @01       211    11-23-95     1:12p
   8 File(s)        354304 bytes free

C>_
```

WHAT'S HAPPENING? Note that this time the disk was not erased prior to adding the additional backup files. Since `new.87` is the same file, the `BACKUP` command named the second copy of the same file with the `@01` file extension.

A2.0 RESTORING A HARD DISK WITH RESTORE

You restore the hard disk using the disks that you backed up the file with by invoking the **RESTORE** command. The syntax for the command is:

```
RESTORE source destination
```

or

```
RESTORE d:  [d:][path][filename][ext] [/S][/P]
```

The first **d:** represents the source drive, usually Drive A. The second drive and path represent where you want the files to be restored. You can selectively restore individual files by using specific file names. The **/S** restores all the subdirectories below the path specified. The **/P** will prompt you before restoring files that have been changed since that last backup or files that are marked Read-Only.

ACTIVITY A2.1 DOING A FULL RESTORE

DANGER: Do not attempt this unless you really want to restore the hard disk. This is particularly true if you have any copy protected programs on the hard disk. Before you do a complete backup, read the instructions with any software you have installed on the hard disk. Be sure you have all the floppy disks that you used with the **BACKUP** command. **RESTORE** will only restore the files on the **BACKUP** disks. Hence, if you did not do a full **BACKUP**, **RESTORE** will not erase the files on the hard disk before copying backup files from the floppy disks.

STEP 1: Key in the following:

```
C>RESTORE A: C:\S  <Enter>
```

```
C>RESTORE A: C:\S

Insert backup disk 01 in drive A:
Strike any key when ready
```

STEP 2: You would insert the properly numbered disk and strike any key.

```
*** Files were backed up 11/23/1995 ***

*** Restoring files from drive A: ***
Diskette: 01
\JUNK\NEW.87
......
......
```

WHAT'S HAPPENING? "......" represents all the files as they are found. Each file, as it is copied from the floppy disk to the hard disk, is listed on the screen. If more than one floppy disk was required for the BACKUP, the following message will appear:

```
Insert backup diskette 02 in drive A:
Strike any key when ready
```

WHAT'S HAPPENING? You continue to insert disks in the proper order until the hard disk is restored.

A2.2 INCREMENTAL RESTORES

You can restore from the floppy disks to the hard disk in increments. You can restore individual files, a group of files, or a subdirectory. In the next activity, you are going to restore all the files you backed up in Activity A1.9

ACTIVITY A2.3 RESTORING SELECTED FILES IN A SUBDIRECTORY

STEP 1: Key in the following:

```
C>RESTORE A: C:\junk\*.87  <Enter>
```

```
C>RESTORE A: C:\junk\*.87

Insert backup diskette 01 in drive A:
Strike any key when ready...
```

STEP 2: Insert the backup disk from Activity A1.9 in Drive A. Press <Enter>.

```
*** Restoring files from drive A ***
Diskette: 01
\JUNK\NEW.87
\JUNK\JAN.87
\JUNK\FEB.87
\JUNK\MAR.87
\JUNK\APR.87
\JUNK\CHANGE.87
\JUNK\NEW.87

C>_
```

WHAT'S HAPPENING? Each file, as it is found on the backup disk, is restored to the hard disk. Note, however, that since you had two files with the name `new.87`, the second file overwrote the first `new.87`. If the backup had used more than one disk, DOS would have prompted you to insert the next numbered disk.

A2.4 CHOOSING TO RESTORE A FILE WITH THE /P PARAMETER

Sometimes you will update a file on the hard disk, but not back it up. Therefore, when you restore the hard disk, you do not want to restore the old version of the file. The `/P` parameter will prompt you and ask if you want this file restored.

ACTIVITY A2.5 CHANGING A FILE AND THEN RESTORING IT

STEP 1: Key in the following:

```
C>COPY CON \junk\change.87  <Enter>
This is the changed file.  <Enter>
<Ctrl>-Z
C>_
```

```
C>COPY CON \junk\change.87
This is the changed file.
^Z
1 File(s) copied

C>_
```

WHAT'S HAPPENING? The file, `change.87`, is now different from the one that is on the floppy disk.

STEP 2: Insert the disk backed up in Activity A1.9. Key in the following:

```
C>RESTORE A: C:\junk\*.87 /P  <Enter>
```

```
C>RESTORE A: C:\junk\*.87 /P

Insert backup diskette 01 in drive A:
Strike any key...
```

STEP 3: Press <Enter>.

```
Warning!  File \JUNK\CHANGE.87
was changed after it was backed up
Replace this file (Y/N)?

\JUNK\NEW.87

C>_
```

WHAT'S HAPPENING? Now you have the option of restoring the older file or keeping the new version.

STEP 4: Press N. Press <Enter>

```
Warning!  File \JUNK\CHANGE.87
was changed after it was backed up
Replace this file (Y/N)?N

\JUNK\NEW.87

C>_
```

WHAT'S HAPPENING? You did not restore the file change.87, but retained the current version. If you had keyed in Y for yes, the file on the floppy disk would have replaced the file on the hard disk.

A3.0 CONCEPTS OF TRANSFERRING SYSTEM FILES

When you format a disk with the /S option (FORMAT [d]:/S), you make the disk bootable. You have put the operating system, comprised of the two hidden files (IBMBIO.COM and IBMDOS.COM) and the COMMAND.COM file, on the first sectors and tracks of the disk. The FORMAT command with the /S parameter, however, not only puts the system files on the disk, it also erases everything else that is on the disk. There is an external command, SYS, that allows you to transfer only the hidden system files. SYS does not erase or format the disk. However the disk you wish to transfer the system files to must already have the space available to transfer the files or be "preformatted". Thus, if you format a disk without the /S option and place various files on it, you cannot go back and add the operating system to this data disk to make it bootable. If you try, you will get the error message, "No room for system on destination disk". You get this message regardless of how many bytes are available on the disk. This is because the hidden system files must occupy the first tracks and sectors on the disk. This sounds a little circular. You can't put the system files on a disk unless it's been preformatted with the /S option, but when you format a disk with the /S option, you are putting the system files on it. Why do you then need to know about this apparently useless command? There are two major reasons.

1. If you purchase an applications package that you want to make bootable and the package you purchase is copy protected, (copy protected means that the manufacturer of the applications package has a "lock" on the disk and you cannot use ordinary DOS commands to make a back up copy of the disk), you cannot use the `FORMAT /S` to put the operating system on the applications disk. `FORMAT /S` will place the operating system on the applications disk, but, at the same time, it will erase all the applications programs that are on the disk. You need a special command that puts the operating system on the applications disk, but not erase the program files. This is one use of the `SYS` command. `SYS` is designed to transfer the operating system hidden files, `IBMBIO.COM` and `IBMDOS.COM`, to the proper tracks and sectors of the disk. `SYS` will let you transfer these system files to an applications program disk that is meant to use DOS, but sold without the operating system. In this case, the space required for the DOS files has already been reserved for these files. (NOTE: The application package instructions will tell you if you can use this command. Be sure to read the installation instructions for any package prior to using this or any command.)
2. The second major reason for using the `SYS` command, is when DOS is updated and a new version is released. In this case, all you want to copy is the operating system files. You do not need to reformat the disk. You want to overwrite the current operating system files with the new version. The hidden system files must occupy the proper place on the disk to be bootable.

   `SYS` is designed to copy or transfer the two hidden system files from one disk to another. `SYS` does not transfer or copy the third system file, `COMMAND.COM`. Thus, using the `SYS` command is a two part process. After you finish executing the `SYS` command, you then `COPY command.com.` The syntax of the command is:

   `SYS [d:]`

   `SYS` is an external command. `d:` stands for "designated disk", you do not use the letter `d:`, you substitute the correct letter of the drive to which you wish to copy the files. For example, if you transfer the system files to the disk in Drive B, you substitute `B:` for `d:`

ACTIVITY A3.1 USING THE SYS COMMAND

STEP 1: Boot the system. The DOS System Disk should be in Drive A:.

```
A>_
```

STEP 2: Place the ACTIVITIES disk in Drive B.

STEP 1: Boot the system. You should be logged into the DOS System Disk on Drive C.

```
C>_
```

STEP 2: Place the ACTIVITIES disk in Drive A.

STEP 3: Key in the following:

A>SYS B: <Enter>

```
A>SYS B:
System transferred

A>_
```

STEP 3: Key in the following:

C>SYS A: <Enter>

```
C>SYS A:
System transferred

C>
```

WHAT'S HAPPENING? You are transferring the hidden files to the ACTIVITIES disk. You can do this because this disk was already formatted with the /S option. The ACTIVITIES disk is already bootable. You have overwritten the hidden files. The message, "System transferred" tells you that those hidden files are copied to ACTIVITIES disk. There is one more step to this process.

SYS did copy the hidden files, IBMBIO.COM, and IBMDOS.COM; but it did not copy COMMAND.COM. Remember, that these three files make up the operating system. The COMMAND.COM file must be from the same version of DOS. Thus, you want to be sure to copy COMMAND.COM. Since command.com is not a hidden file, you just use the COPY command.

STEP 4: Key in the following:

A>COPY command.com B: <Enter>

```
A>COPY command.com B:
        1 File(s) copied

A>_
```

STEP 4: Key in the following:

C>COPY command.com A: <Enter>

```
C>COPY command.com A:
        1 File(s) copied

C>_
```

WHAT'S HAPPENING? You have now completed the process for transferring the DOS operating system to the ACTIVITIES disk. One note of caution. Before you do anything with any application package, you must read and understand the "installation" instructions. These instructions come with any applications package you purchase.

Often, more than just upgrading the operating system to a higher version is required. There can be other important files that can be affected, like printer driver files. Thus, if you do not understand the installation instructions and/or the ramifications, DO NOT DO ANYTHING until you understand the installation process or get professional assistance from where you purchased the package.

You now are aware of the SYS command and how to use it. Knowing when to use it is dependent on the specific applications that would be affected.

APPENDIX B: DATA REPRESENTATION: Bits and Bytes

How do you measure the capacity of RAM or a floppy disk (capacity means how much data RAM or a disk can hold). Here begins the world of bits and bytes which represents data. We humans use a decimal counting system, which is comprised of 10 digits that range from 0 to 9 and is called base 10. We can represent any number we wish with a combination of these digits. However, a decimal system is not the only way to represent counting. There is also the binary system. The binary system consists of only two digits (base 2) which represent all numerical values. A computer does not understand actual words, letters or numbers. The CPU recognizes only 0's and 1's; a binary language. Using 0's and 1's turns on or off the integrated circuit switches on the system board to process words, numbers, and graphics.

If you were asked to write the number, 245, you would quickly write down the three digits, 2, 4 and 5 and would know that it represented the number 245. However, this is what you are really doing:

Every number has a position value, in other words, the relative position determines it value. In any numbering system, the rightmost position has a value of the base to the zero power, or one (in a decimal system, $10^0 = 1$). The second position is the base to the first power (in a decimal system, $10^1 = 10$). The third position is the base to the second power, or the base squared (in a decimal system, $10^2 = 100$). The fourth position is the base to the third power, or cubed and so forth. These values are then summed in the Figure 1.0.

Figure 1.0 The Decimal System

DECIMAL SYSTEM

Decimal Position Number:	5	4	3	2	1	
Decimal Values for Positions:	10^4	10^3	10^2	10^1	10^0	
Represented as:	10000	1000	100	10	1	
Values from position only	__	__	2	__	__	2 × 100 = 200
	__	__	__	4	__	4 × 10 = 40
	__	__	__	__	5	5 × 1 = 5
Cumulative total	__	__	2	4	5	245

The binary numbering system works the same way, except that you have only two digits to represent any number. To write 245 binary, would be as shown in Figure 1.1.

Figure 1.1 The Binary System

BINARY SYSTEM

Binary Position Number:	8	7	6	5	4	3	2	1	
Binary Values for Positions:	2^7	2^6	2^5	2^4	2^3	2^2	2^1	2^0	
Decimal as:	128	64	32	16	8	4	2	1	
Values from position only:	1	—	—	—	—	—	—	—	1 × 128 = 128
	—	1	—	—	—	—	—	—	1 × 64 = 64
	—	—	1	—	—	—	—	—	1 × 32 = 32
	—	—	—	1	—	—	—	—	1 × 16 = 16
	—	—	—	—	0	—	—	—	0 × 8 = 0
	—	—	—	—	—	1	—	—	1 × 4 = 4
	—	—	—	—	—	—	0	—	0 × 2 = 0
	—	—	—	—	—	—	—	1	1 × 1 = 1
Cumulative total	1	1	1	1	0	1	0	1	245

Thus, to represent the number 245 in decimal, requires 3 digits. In binary, the number 245 is 11110101. Note that binary takes many more places to represent numbers. However, the binary numbering scheme is perfect for computers because it is easy to translate a 1 for an on state and 0 for an off state. Remember, that is all a computer can do, is indicate on or off. The word bit comes from Binary digIT. A bit is the smallest unit a computer can recognize, an on or off state. However, while a bit may be meaningful to a computer, it is not meaningful to human beings. What we want represented is letters, numbers and symbols, symbols like ? or &. Thus, bits are combined in meaningful groups, much like letters of the alphabet combine to make words. The most common grouping is eight bits. A pattern of eight bits makes one byte. Accordingly, if you have 8 bits, the patterns would be:

0	0	0	0	0	0	0	0	All bits off
0	0	0	0	0	0	0	1	All bits off except 1 on
0	0	0	0	0	0	1	1	All bits off except 2 on

Rather than showing each pattern manually, the total number of patterns can be calculated mathematically by the rules of permutation and combinations: 2^8 calculates to 256 separate patterns into which a 1 and a 0 can be combined. Thus a BYTE can be thought of as a singular letter or number.

However, there is more to a byte than that. There has to be a commonly agreed meaning for these patterns. For instance, jour, meaning day, is a valid combination of letters but only if you speak French. In English, to communicate jour, you combine a different pattern of letters, D A Y. These are arbitrary assignments. The same is true with computers. The most common coding scheme for microcomputers ASCII (pronounced as-key). ASCII stands for American Standard Code for Information Interchange, always referred to as ASCII. Consequently, when you strike the letter M on the keyboard, it is encoded to a bit configuration (pattern of 1's and 0's—M 0100 1101) on input so the computer can interpret. Then in output, it is decoded so we can understand it as the letter M. If the lower case letter m is keyed in, it has a completely different bit configuration (m 0110 1101) because to the computer there is no relationship between upper case M and lower case m.

RAM, ROM and disk capacities are measured in bytes, typically in thousands of bytes or K (Kilobytes) K is the symbol for 2^{10} or 1024. If your computer has 64K of memory, its actual memory size is 64 × 1024 or 65,546 bytes. For simplification, the K is rounded off to a 1000, so that 64K of memory means 64,000 bytes. You should know the capacity of the memory of your computer because it determines how big a program and/or data the computer will hold. For instance, if you had a 64K computer and a program that required 256K, your computer could not hold that program. Disk capacity is also measured in bytes. A single-sided disk holds 180K of data (180,000 bytes), a double-sided disk holds 360K (360,000). Because a hard disk holds so much more than floppy disk, hard disks are measured in millions of bytes. This is known as megabytes or typically referred to as Meg. Typical hard disks are 20 Meg (twenty million bytes) and up.

APPENDIX C: DOS COMMANDS QUICK REFERENCE CHART

(Guide to symbols which indicate the type of command: * Internal command, or # External command. Uppercase letters represent the DOS commands. Lowercase letters are examples of correct syntax.)

COMMAND	SYNTAX/EXAMPLES	DESCRIPTION
*CD	`CD`	Displays the default subdirectory.
	`CD [d:][path]`	Changes the default subdirectory.
	`C>cd`	Would display the default subdirectory.
	`C>cd \dbase`	Would change the default subdirectory to \dbase on the disk in Drive C.
*CHDIR	`CHDIR`	Changes default subdirectory. Same as CD. See CD for full explanation.
	`CHDIR [d:][path]`	
	`CHDIR [d:]`	
#CHKDSK	`CHKDSK [d:][path]`	Examines disks and issues status report.
	`CHKDSK [filname[.ext]]`	Examines disks, issues status report and sees if specified file(s) are contiguous
	`CHKDSK [d:][path][/V]`	Examines disks, issues status report and displays all file names and their path
	`A>chkdsk`	Examines disk in default drive and gives status report.
	`A>chkdsk B:`	Examines disk in Drive B: and gives status report.
	`A>chkdsk myfile.txt`	Examines disk in default drive and sees if file called myfile.txt is contiguous.
	`A>chkdsk B:/V`	Displays all files and paths on disk in drive B and gives status report.
*CLS	`CLS`	Clears the display screen and moves the cursor to the upper left corner of the screen.
	`A>cls`	Clears the screen.
*COMP	`COMP [d:][path]filename.[ext] [d:][path]filename.[ext]`	Compares the contents of the first file(s) to the contents of the second set of file(s).

COMMAND	SYNTAX/EXAMPLES	DESCRIPTION
*COMP *(cont.)*	`A>comp myfile.ext yourfile.txt`	Compares the contents of the file called myfile.ext located on the default drive to the contents of the file called yourfile.txt also located on the default drive.
	`A>comp myfile.ext B:\DOS\yourfile.txt`	Compares the contents of the file called myfile.ext located on the default drive to the contents of the file called yourfile.txt located on the the disk in Drive B in the subdirectory called \DOS.
	`A>comp *.ext *.txt`	Compares the contents of all the files with .ext located on the default drive to all the contents of the files with .txt as an extension also located on the default drive.
*COPY	`COPY [d:][path]filesname.ext [d:][path]filename.ext`	
	`COPY source destination`	Copies files from one location to another.
	`A>COPY myfile.txt B:`	Copies file called myfile.txt (source) on the default Drive A to (destination) disk on Drive B. File on destination Drive B will be given file name of myfile.txt.
	`A>COPY myfile.txt B:newfile.txt`	Copies file called myfile.txt (source) on the default Drive A to (destination) disk on Drive B. File on destination Drive B will be given file name of newfile.txt.
	`A>COPY \DOS\myfile.txt B:\BIN\newfile.txt`	Copies file called myfile.txt in subdirectory called DOS on the default Drive A (Source) to (destination) disk on Drive B in subdirectory called BIN. File on destination Drive B, subdirectory called BIN will be given file name of newfile.txt
	`A>COPY *.txt *.tmp`	Copies all the files on the default Drive A which have the file extension of .text (Source) to the default drive (Destination) but give all the target or destination files the same file name but the file extension of .tmp.
	`A>COPY CON B:myfile.txt`	Copy whatever text is keyed in on the keyboard and displayed on the screen (CON) which is the source and written to a file (Destination) on the disk in Drive B. The new file name on Drive B will be given the file name, myfile.txt.

COMMAND	SYNTAX/EXAMPLES	DESCRIPTION
*COPY *(cont.)*	`A>COPY B:myfile.txt PRN`	Copies the file on the disk in Drive B called myfile.txt (Source) to a device, the printer (Destination).
	`A>COPY myfile.txt + B:\BIN\myfile.txt B:myfile.txt`	Copies the file on the default drive, A, AND the file on the disk in Drive B in the subdirectory BIN called myfile.txt (Source) to a file on the disk in Drive B in the root directory called myfile.txt.
*DATE	`DATE [mm-dd-yy]`	Sets the system date.
	`A>date`	Will display the current month, day and year the computer is set to in the format of: Current date is Wed 11-4-1987 Enter new date (mm-dd-yy)__ If you wish to retain the displayed date, press <Enter>. If you wish to change the date, key in a new date in the format of mm-dd-yy, i.e., 01-02-88.
*DEL	`DEL [d:][path]filename[.ext]`	Deletes a file from a disk.
	`A>del myfile.txt`	Removes the file called myfile.txt from the default drive, A.
	`A>del B:*.txt`	Removes ALL the files on the disk in Drive B that have the file extension of .txt.
	`C>del \dbase\*.*`	Removes ALL the files on the default drive, C, in the subdirectory \dbase.
	`C>del *.*`	DANGEROUS—Removes EVERY SINGLE file in the root directory of the default drive, C.
*DIR	`DIR [d:][path][filename[.ext][/P][W]`	Displays the list of files on a specified disk.
	`A>dir`	Will display a list of all the files on the default drive.
	`A>dir B:`	Will display a list of all the files on the disk in Drive B.
	`A>dir myfile.ext`	Will only look for file called myfile.ext on the default drive—Drive A.
	`A>dir B:myfile.ext`	Will only look for file called myfile.ext on the disk in Drive B.
	`A>dir C:\dbase`	Will display a list of all the files on the disk in Drive C, in the subdirectory \dbase.
	`A>dir C:\dbase\myfile.*`	Will only look for the files with a file name of myfile and any file extension on the disk in Drive C, in the subdirectory \dbase.

COMMAND	SYNTAX/EXAMPLES	DESCRIPTION
*DIR *(cont.)*	`A>dir /w`	Will display a list of all the files on the default drive but the display will spread across the screen (wide mode) and will not display the date, time or size of the file
	`A>dir /p`	Will display a list of all the files on the default drive. The screen display will Pause and stop scrolling as a screen fills with directory information.
#DISKCOMP	`DISKCOMP [d: [d2]]`	Compares two diskettes to see if they are identical disks track for track, sector for sector.
	`A>diskcomp`	Will instruct user to insert source and target disk into Drive A to compare the disks.
	`A>diskcomp A: B:`	Will compare the disk in Drive A to the disk in Drive B.
	`A>diskcomp B:`	Will compare disk in Drive B to disk in Drive A.
#DISKCOPY	`DISKCOPY [d: [d:]]`	Makes an identical copy of an entire disk, track for track, sector for sector
	`A>diskcopy`	Will instruct user to insert source and target disk into Drive A.
	`A>diskcopy A: B:`	Will make an exact copy of disk in Drive A and copy it to disk in Drive B.
	`A>diskcopy B:`	Will make an exact copy of disk in Drive B and copy it to disk in Drive A.
#EDLIN	`EDLIN [d:][path]filename.[ext]`	Edits and creates text files. See EDLIN section for EDLIN specific commands.
	`A>edlin b:myfile.txt`	Would create or edit a text file called myfile.txt on the disk in Drive B.
*ERASE	`ERASE [d:][path]filename[.ext]`	Removes a file from disk. Same as DEL. See DEL for complete examples.
#FORMAT	`FORMAT [d:][/S][/V]`	Prepares a new disk in an acceptable recording format for DOS so that files can be placed on a disk; checks for defective tracks and places a directory and FAT on each prepared disk. Will do the same for a disk with data already on it but will TOTALLY DESTROY all data on the existing disk. BE VERY CAREFUL using this command.

COMMAND	SYNTAX/EXAMPLES	DESCRIPTION
#FORMAT *(cont.)*	`C>format`	DANGEROUS! Will format the disk in the default Drive C.
	`A>format B:`	Will format the disk in Drive B.
	`A>format B:/S`	Will format the disk in Drive B and will place the hidden operating system files and COMMAND.COM on the disk in Drive B making the formatted disk bootable.
	`A>format B:/V`	Will format the disk in Drive B and will allow the user to place an internal volume label on the disk in Drive B.
	`A>format B:/S/V`	Will format the disk in Drive B and will place the hidden operating system files and COMMAND.COM on the disk in Drive B making the formatted disk bootable as well as allowing the user to place an internal label on the disk in Drive B.
#LABEL	`LABEL [d:][volume label]`	Displays the current volume label of any specified disk. Allows user to change label at this time. This command only available in Version 3.0 and above.
	`A>label`	Will display the volume label in the default drive. User can choose to change volume label at this time.
	`A>label B:`	Will display the volume label on the disk in Drive B. User can choose to change volume label at this time.
*MD	`MD [d:][path]`	Creates a subdirectory on a specified disk.
	`C>md \dbase`	Makes a subdirectory on the disk in Drive C called \dbase. It is one level below the root directory.
	`C>md \dbase\reports`	Makes a subdirectory on the disk in Drive C called \reports which is in the subdirectory \dbase. It is two levels below the root directory.
	`C>md A:\letters`	Makes a subdirectory on the disk in Drive A called \letters. It is one level below the root directory on the disk in Drive A.
*MKDIR	`MKDIR [d:][path]`	Same as MD. See MD for complete details.

COMMAND	SYNTAX/EXAMPLES	DESCRIPTION
#MODE LPT#:	`MODE LPT#: [n][,m]`	Changes printer settings for Epson like printer.
	`A>mode lpt1:`	Sets printer characteristics to printer default values (80 CPI, 6 LPI)
	`A>mode LPT1:132,8`	Sets printer characteristics for the first line printer (LPTl) to a compressed mode (132 CPL, 8 LPI)
	`A>mode LPT2:80,8`	Sets printer characteristics for the second line printer (LPT2) to a compressed line mode (80 CPL, 8 LPI)
*PATH	`PATH [[d:]path[[;d:]path...]]`	Where DOS will look for .COM, .EXE or .BAT files if not found in current directory.
	`PATH ;`	Cancels the search path.
	`PATH`	Displays the current search path.
	`C>path`	Displays the current path.
	`C>path C:;\dos;\junk`	Sets the search path to the root directory, then the subdirectory \dos; then the subdirectory \junk.
	`C>path ;`	Cancels the search path.
#PRINT	`PRINT [/C][/T][[d:][path] filename.ext]...]`	Prints contents of a file on the printer. If printing more than one file, each file printed will begin on a new page.
	`PRINT /T`	Terminates all jobs in print queue.
	`PRINT filename.ext /C`	Cancels only filename.ext in print queue.
	`A>print B:myfile.txt`	Prints the file on the disk in Drive B called myfile.txt.
	`A>print B:myfile.txt A:new`	Prints the file on the disk in Drive B called myfile.txt and the file called new on the disk in Drive A.
	`A>print`	Displays the files in queue waiting to be printed.
	`A>print C:\dbase\*.rpt`	Prints all the files with the extension .rpt in the subdirectory \dbase on the disk in Drive C.
	`A>print /T`	Terminates all the files waiting to be printed. Once this command is keyed in, no files are in queue.

COMMAND	SYNTAX/EXAMPLES	DESCRIPTION
#PRINT *(cont.)*	`A>print B:myfile.txt /C`	Cancels only the file called myfile.txt on the disk in Drive B from being printed. It is removed from the queue.
*PROMPT	`PROMPT [text or meta-string]`	Changes the DOS prompt.
	`A>prompt hello`	Changes the prompt from A> to hello.
	`A hello>prompt`	Changes the prompt from hello to A>.
	`A>prompt hello $n$g`	Changes the prompt from A> to hello A>.
	`A>prompt $p$g`	Changes the prompt from A> to A:\>.
	`C>cd \dbase` `C>prompt $p$g`	Changes the subdirectory to \dbase. Then changes the prompt from C> to C:\dbase>. Note, you do not have to change directories first.
*REN	`REN [d:][path]filename[.ext] filename[.ext]`	Changes the name of the file in the first parameter to the given file name in the second parameter. A file can only be renamed in the same physical location. It is just placing a new label on a file folder. The contents and location of the file folder do not change. The file once renamed does not exist any longer under the old name.
	`A>ren myfile.txt yourfile.txt`	Changes the name of the file called myfile.txt located on the default Drive A to a new name of yourfile.txt, also on default drive.
	`C>ren \lotus\myfile.wks yourfile.wks`	Changes the name of the file called myfile.wks located in the subdirectory called \lotus on the default Drive C to yourfile.wks still located on the default Drive C in the subdirectory \lotus.
	`A>ren *.wks *.tmp`	Changes the names of ALL the files on the default Drive A to files with the same file name but with new file extensions of .tmp still located on the default drive.
	`A>ren B:*.wks *.tmp`	Changes the names of ALL of the files on the disk in Drive B to files with the same file name but with new file extensions of .tmp still located on the disk in Drive B.
*RENAME	`REN [d:][path]filename[.ext] filename[.ext]`	Same as REN—See REN for full explanation.

COMMAND	SYNTAX/EXAMPLES	DESCRIPTION
*RD	`RD [d:][path]`	Removes a subdirectory. Subdirectory must be empty of files otherwise you cannot remove it.
	`C>RD \dbase\reports`	Will delete the subdirectory called reports that is under the subdirectory called \dbase that is under the root root directory on the disk in Drive C.
	`C>RD A:\dbase`	Will delete the subdirectory called \dbase on the disk in Drive A.
*RMDIR	`RMDIR [d:][path]`	Removes subdirectories from disk. Same as RD. See RD for complete example.
#SYS	`SYS [d:]`	Transfers the operating system files and boot record on a disk. Note: first tracks and sectors must be available for the system files.
	`A>SYS B:`	Would transfer the system files to the disk in Drive B.
	`A>SYS C:`	Would transfer the system files to the hard disk, Drive C.
*TIME	`TIME [hh:mm:ss:xx]`	Sets the system clock to specified time.
	`A>time`	Will display the current time the computer is set to in the format of: Current time is 13:42:39:61 Enter new time: If you wish to retain the displayed time, press <Enter>. If you wish to change the time, key in a new time in the format of hh:mm:ss:xx, i.e., 14:40. It is a twenty-four hour clock. Setting hours and minutes is usually sufficient. Setting seconds (ss) or hundredths of seconds (xx) is unnecessary.
*TYPE	`TYPE [d:][path]filename[.ext]`	Displays contents of file on the display screen.
	`A>TYPE myfile.txt`	Displays the contents of the file located on the default Drive A called myfile.txt on the screen.
	`A>TYPE B:\DOS\myfile.txt`	Displays the contents of the file called myfile.txt located on the disk in Drive B in the subdirectory DOS on the screen.
*VER	`VER`	Displays the DOS version number on the screen.
	`A>ver`	Displays a number on the screen such as 3.1 to tell the user what version of DOS is being used.

COMMAND	SYNTAX/EXAMPLES	DESCRIPTION
*VOL	`VOL [d:]`	Displays the label of a disk.
	`A>vol B:`	Displays the label of the disk in Drive B.
	`A>vol`	Displays the label of the disk in the default drive.

APPENDIX D: SPECIAL KEYS

Key	Function
<Backspace>	When pressed, will delete any characters to left of cursor.
<Ctrl>	The <Ctrl> key, when pressed in conjuction with another key, gives the other key an additional meaning. The symbol ^ represents pressing the key.
<Ctrl>-<Alt>-<Del>	Pressing these 3 keys will reboot the system.
<Ctrl>-C	Pressing the <Ctrl> key and the letter C will interrupt and stop a command from executing.
<Ctrl>-<Break>	Interrupts function and returns to the default prompt.
<Ctrl>-<NumLock>	When the <Ctrl> key is pressed in conjunction with the <NumLock> key, it freezes and halts whatever is displayed on the screen. Pressing any key releases the freeze.
<Ctrl>-<PrtSc>	The <Ctrl> key, when pressed in conjunction with <PrtSc> key, toggles the printer on or off.
<Ctrl>-Z	Terminates the COPY CON function.
<Enter>	Tells the computer to execute a command.
<Esc>	An abbreviation for Escape. When this key is pressed, it cancels the previously keyed in line. DOS ignores the previously keyed in line.
<Shift>	Pressing the <Shift> key in conjunction with another letter will change the case of the letter to upper case. If the <Caps Lock> key is toggled ON, the <Shift> key when pressed will change the case of the letter to lower. The <Shift> key must always be pressed to display the special characters above the number keys.
<Shift>-<PrtSc>	When these two keys are pressed, whatever is displayed on the screen, is printed.
<F1>	Pressing <F1> will replace a previously entered command one character per tap.
<F3>	Pressing <F3> will replace a previously entered command line.
<F6>	Pressing <F6> will interrupt a command.

APPENDIX E: BATCH FILE COMMANDS

Command Type	Command	Explanation
*PAUSE	`PAUSE`	In a batch file, will halt the processing of a batch file and will wait for the user to strike a key before proceeding with the execution of the rest of the batch file.
*REM	`REM`	Allows the user to put in text. When DOS sees REM, it will not execute that line.
	`rem This is a line.`	When executing the batch file, DOS would display on the screen: `rem This is a line.`

APPENDIX F: EDLIN COMMANDS

(Note: n or m represent any number.)

DISPLAY COMMANDS

Command	Format	Explanation
List	L	Will list the file.
	1L	Will list the file from Line 1.
	nL	Will list the file from n Line
	n,mL	Lists lines n through m

TEXT MODIFICATION COMMANDS

Command	Format	Explanation
Insert line(s)	nI	Inserts line(s) before line n
	I	Inserts a line.
	#I	Begins insertion of line at the bottom of a current file.
Edit a single line	n	Edit/change an existing line
Delete line(s)	nD	Deletes specified line number.
	n,mD	Deletes lines n through m

HOUSEKEEPING COMMANDS

Command	Format	Explanation
End or exit EDLIN	E	Exits, saving your file
Quit	Q	Exits without saving your program

GLOSSARY

Adapter Card A printed circuit board that is installed in a computer to control some type of a device, such as a printer.

Application Software A computer program that is user–oriented, usually for a specific job such as word processing. Application software is also called packages, off–the–shelf or canned software when often sold to consumers.

ASCII An acronym for American Standard Code for Information Interchange, is code used for transmitting text data between computers and peripherals. Each character has its own numerical equivalent in ASCII.

AUTOEXEC.BAT A batch file that automatically executes every time the system is booted.

Back Up The process by which a user makes a copy of an original file or disk for safekeeping. It is an alternate copy of data or programs.

Batch files A text file of DOS commands. When its name is keyed in at the DOS system level prompt, the commands in the batch file are executed.

Batch processing A manner of running programs without interruption.

BIOS An acronym for Basic Input Output System which is a program that controls Input/Output (I/O) devices.

Bit The smallest unit of information that the computer can measure and is expressed in binary numbers, 0 or 1. Eight bits make a byte.

Boot Starting up the computer by loading the operating system into memory.

Byte A unit of measure which represents a character (a letter, number or punctuation symbol). Computer memory and disk storage are measured in bytes. A byte is comprised of eight bits.

Cluster A cluster, comprised of one or more sectors, is the smallest unit of disk space that DOS can write to or read from.

Command An instruction, which is a program, that the user keys in at the DOS prompt. This instruction, then, calls and executes the selected program.

Control key A key marked Ctrl on the keyboard that, when held down with another key, causes that other key to have another meaning.

Concatenate files To combine the contents of two or more text files.

Contiguous files Files that are written to adjacent clusters on a disk.

CPU An acronym for Central Processing Unit. The CPU is the brains of the computer which carries out the instructions or commands given to it by a program. It is the circuitry that does the calculations. In a microcomputer, the CPU is usually on one circuit board.

CRT A cathode ray tube (CRT) is another name for the monitor.

Ctrl key (See Control key)

Data Information in the widest possible sense. Usually it refers to the numbers and text used by the computer to do the work wanted performed by the user.

Default What the computer system "falls back" to if no other specific instructions are given.

Default Drive The disk drive that DOS will look on to locate commands or files.

Delimiter Some character that is used to separate other characters.

Device A piece of computer equipment that does one specific job such as a disk drive or a printer.

Device name A reserved name that DOS assigns to a device such as PRN for printer.

Directory A list of files that DOS maintains on each disk. The DIR command displays this list.

Disk A magnetically coated mylar disc, that permanently stores information.

Disk drive A device that spins the disk so that the computer can read and write information to the disk.

Documentation The written instructions that inform a user how to use hardware (the equipment) or software (programs).

DOS An acronym for Disk Operating System which refers to the most common operating system used on microcomputers.

Drive letter A letter of the alphabet that identifies a specific disk drive.

Dummy data A file of data that in itself has no particular meaning. It is used for test purposes.

Edit To alter the contents of a file.

EDLIN A line editor that comes with PC/MS DOS. It is used to create or modify text files.

Enter key The key that is pressed which sends a signal to DOS that the user has finished keying in a command. It is also called the RETURN key.

Extension (See file extension)

External commands A program that resides on a disk and must be read into RAM before it can be used.

FAT (File allocation table) A map of the disk which keeps track of the spaces on the disk. It maps every track, sector and cluster.

File A program or a collection of related information stored on a disk.

File extension Up to a three character that can be added to a file name to help identify a file. Usually file extensions describe the type of data in the file.

File name The label used to identify a file. Technically, it is the name made up of no more than eight characters. However, when most users refer to the file name, they are actually referring to the file specification which includes the file name and the file extension.

File specification The complete name of the file, including the file name and the file extension.

Fixed disk Another name for a hard disk.

Floppy disk (see Disk)

Format To prepare a disk so that it can be used by the computer.

Function key A programmable key on a keyboard. F1 and F2 are examples of function keys.

Global file specifications (see Wildcards)

Graphics Often referred to as computer graphics which are pictures, representations, graphs and charts produced on the screen or printer.

Hard copy Refers to the printed paper copy of information created using the computer. Also referred to as printouts.

Hard disk A disk that is permanently installed in a computer and that has a larger capacity to store files and programs than a floppy disk. Its capacity is measured in megabytes.

Hardware The physical components or parts of a computer.

Hidden files A file that is not displayed when the DIR command is used. Hidden files cannot be deleted or modified. In PC/MS DOS, the hidden files are the two system files, IBMBIO.COM and IBMDOS.COM.

IBMBIO.COM The hidden system file that is one of the files that make up the operating system. It manages the input/output devices.

IBMDOS.COM The hidden system file that is one of the files that makes up the operating system. It manages the disks.

Input Refers to data or information entered into the computer.

Interactive The abiltiy to update data within the computer system instantaneously.

Interface The hardware and/or software needed to connect computer components. Also used as a synonym when the user interacts with the computer.

Internal commands A part of the third operating system files, COMMAND.COM, that is loaded into memory when the operating system is booted. These commands remain resident in memory until the computer is turned off or rebooted.

I/O Common abbreviation for input/output.

Keyboard The major device used for entering data into a computer. Consists of typewriter-like collection of labeled keys.

Megabyte A unit of measure that is equal to one million bytes.

Memory (See RAM)

Message Information that the computer program supplies to assist the user in completing a task or that informs the user of an error.

Meta-string Symbols used with the PROMPT command that returns a value for the symbol. For example, using the meta-string "d" will return the system date.

Microcomputer A small word, number and graphics processing machine which can be installed on a desk top.

Monitor A device that displays the input and output of the computer. Also called display screen, screen, CRT, or VDT.

Noncontiguous files Files that are written to the disk in nonadjacent sectors.

Operating system A set of programs that manage the operation of all parts of the computer. Also know as system software. Must be loaded prior to any application software.

Overwrite To copy over another file.

Parameter A qualifier or modifier added to a command that will specify the action to be taken.

Path This tells DOS where to look for the programs and files the user needs.

Peripheral Any device connected to a computer such as a keyboard, monitor, printer, etc.

Port A place to connect other devices to a computer. Also allows the computer to send information to and from the device.

Printer A peripheral that produces hard copies of text or graphics.

Program A set of step-by-step instructions that tell the computer what to do.

Prompt A computer program request for the user to either take action or provide more information.

Queue A line up of items waiting for processing. For example, several documents in the print queue that will be printed one after another.

RAM (Random Access Memory) The temporary workspace of the computer where programs and data are stored while they are being processed. RAM is volatile; everything in RAM is lost when the power is turned off.

ROM (Read-Only Memory) Memory that is permanent and contains programs written on ROM chips. The CPU can only read programs from ROM but not change or alter the contents of ROM. ROM is retained when the power is turned off. Usually, holds start-up routines of the computer.

Root directory The main directory that DOS creates on each disk when the disk is formatted. The backslash (\) is the symbol used to represent the root directory.

Sector Data is stored on disks in concentric circles (tracks) that are divided in separate pieces (sectors). Thus, a sector is a portion of the track.

Software The programs that tell the computer what to do as opposed to hardware, the equipment.

Subdirectory A hierarchical filing system that allows the user to divide a disk into manageable portions. Subdirectories have names and are files.

Syntax The proper order or sequence of the computer language or command.

System prompt A symbol on the screen that tells the use that the computer is ready for the next command. The prompt consists of the letter of the current drive followed by a greater than sign (A>, B>, or C>).

Text files A file that contains text as opposed to a program. It consists of data that can be read such as letters and numbers.

Track A concentric circle on the disk where data is stored. Each track is further divided into sectors. All tracks and sectors are numbered so that computer can locate where information is stored.

Utility programs Programs whose purpose is to carry out specific, vital functions that assist in the operation of a computer or software. DOS includes utility programs such as FORMAT with its system disk.

Version The numbering scheme which indicates the progressive enhancements and improvements of software.

Volume label The electronic label for a disk that a user can assign at the time of formatting a disk.

Wildcard The symbols, (*, ?), also called global file specifications, used to represent a character (?) or a group of characters (*) in a file name.

Write-protect notch A cutout on the side of a floppy disk, that, when covered, keeps programs and data from being written to the disk.

Write-protected A floppy disk that cannot be written over, only read from.

INDEX

Chapter 1 Test
Microcomputer Systems: Hardware, Software and the Operating System

MATCHING QUESTIONS

Choose the letter of the answer that best defines the word or phrase in the numbered column.

1.	_____	CPU	A.	Solves problems, handles information and is user-oriented.
2.	_____	RAM	B.	Name of major microcomputer operating system in use today.
3.	_____	ROM	C.	Smallest unit a computer can recognize; an on or off state.
4.	_____	Disk	D.	Temporary work space of the computer.
5.	_____	Disk Drive	E.	Brain of the computer.
6.	_____	Bit	F.	Physical components of a computer system
7.	_____	Byte	G.	Supervises the processing of all application programs and all computer input/output.
8.	_____	K	H.	External storage media.
9.	_____	Monitor	I.	The step-by-step instructions that tell a computer what to do
10.	_____	Hardware	J.	Symbol used for 1024 bytes.
11.	_____	Software	K.	Firmware that often holds start-up routines for the computer.
12.	_____	System Software	L.	A device given a one-letter name.
13.	_____	Application Software	M.	Amount of information required to define a character (letter, number or symbol).
14.	_____	Operating System	N.	A display unit that resembles a television where the CPU writes information.
15.	_____	DOS	O.	Coordinates the operations of all the various hardware components.

TRUE/FALSE QUESTIONS

Write + for True or 0 for False for each question.

16. _____ RAM, ROM and disk capacities are measured in bytes.
17. _____ A dot-matrix printer uses a beam of light to form characters.
18. _____ The system configuration refers to the basic components of a complete microcomputer system.
19. _____ Since RAM is volatile, data and programs are retained on the monitor.
20. _____ The operating system is the program that is always working and always loaded into RAM.

MULTIPLE CHOICE QUESTIONS

Write the letter of the word or phrase that best completes the numbered statement.

21. _____ A printer is:
  A. a device that allows the user to have a hard copy of information.
  B. one of the most commonly used output devices.
  C. both A and B.
  D. neither A nor B.

22. _____ Disks are divided into numbered:
  A. tracks and sectors.
  B. bits and bytes.
  C. RAM and ROM.
  D. none of the above.

23. _____ DOS is an acronymn for:
  A. Data Operations System.
  B. Disk Operating System.
  C. Digital Output System.
  D. none of the above.

24. _____ Internal commands are:
  A. loaded into memory at the time of booting and remain in memory until the power is turned off.
  B. reside on the DOS System Disk and must be called into memory each time you wish to use one of these programs.
  C. not used with a microcomputer operating system.
  D. none of the above.

25. _____ External commands are:
  A. loaded into memory at the time of booting and remain in memory until the power is turned off.
  B. Reside on the DOS System Disk and must be called into memory each time you wish to use one of these programs.
  C. not used with a microcomputer operating system.
  D. none of the above.

Chapter 2 Test

Getting Started With DOS: Booting the System, Using the Keyboard, and Making a System Disk

MATCHING QUESTIONS

Write the letter of the word or phrase that best completes the numbered statement.

1.	_____	Booting	A.	Allows user to delete character to the left of the cursor.
2.	_____	Rebooting	B.	A special key whose purpose is software dependent.
3.	_____	File Specification	C.	Allows the user to cancel a keyed in line if <Enter> has not been pressed.
4.	_____	DIR	D.	Allows the user to make an exact copy of a disk.
5.	_____	Backspace key	E.	Allows the user to display or change the system date.
6.	_____	Function key	F.	When pressed in conjunction with the <Shift> key, it allows the user to print what is on the screen.
7.	_____	Esc key	G.	When pressed together, will freeze the display of the screen.
8.	_____	PrtSc key	H.	Loading the operating system by inserting the system disk and turning on the power switch.
9.	_____	Ctrl-PrtSc	I.	Unique indentifier of a program or data stored on a disk.
10.	_____	Ctrl-NumLock	J.	Loading the operating system by pressing the Ctrl, Alt and Del keys when the power switch is already on.
11.	_____	Ctrl-C	K.	Command that displays the table of contents of a disk.
12.	_____	CLS	L.	Allows the user to display or change the system time.
13.	_____	DATE	M.	When pressed together, toggles the printer on or off.
14.	_____	TIME	N.	When pressed together, will cancel the execution of a command.
15.	_____	DISKCOPY	O.	Will clear the display screen.

TRUE/FALSE QUESTIONS

Write a + for True or 0 for False for each question.

16. _____ The source disk is the disk to be copied. The target disk is where the information will be copied.
17. _____ Keying in January 1, 1988, at the DATE command prompt will change the date.
18. _____ DISKCOMP compares two disks to insure they are identical.
19. _____ When you turn off the power to the computer, you lose everything that is stored on the disk.
20. _____ When you key in the time, you must key it in the format hh:mm:ss.xx.

MULTIPLE CHOICE QUESTIONS

Write the letter of the word or phrase that best completes the numbered statement.

21. _____ When you key in DISKCOPY A: B:
    - A. the system will prompt the user to insert the source disk in Drive A and the target disk in Drive B.
    - B. DISKCOPY is not a command.
    - C. the system will first prompt the user for the current date.
    - D. none of the above.

22. _____ Pressing the Control key and the NumLock key will:
    - A. print what is currently on the screen.
    - B. toggle on the printer.
    - C. cause the display on the screen to freeze.
    - D. all the above.

23. _____ Pressing the PrtSc key and the <Shift> key will:
    - A. print what is currently on the screen.
    - B. toggle on the printer.
    - C. cause the display on the screen to freeze.
    - D. all the above.

24. _____ A program is permanently stored:
    - A. in ROM.
    - B. in the CPU.
    - C. in RAM.
    - D. in a file on a disk.

25. _____ Pressing Ctrl-C will:
    - A. toggle on the printer.
    - B. cancel the execution of a command.
    - C. cancel a keyed in line.
    - D. has no meaning to DOS.

Chapter 3 Test
Command Syntax: Using the DIR Command with Parameters and Wildcards

MATCHING QUESTIONS

Choose the letter of the answer that best defines the word or phrase in the numbered column.

1.	-----	Syntax	A.	Qualifier added to a command to make it more specific.
2.	-----	Command	B.	Will cause the file names to be displayed across the screen. Display will not include the size, date or time the file was created.
3.	-----	Parameter	C.	Is mandatory and must be no longer than eight characters.
4.	-----	Delimiter	D.	A value supplied by the computer system, if the user or program does not provide specific instructions.
5.	-----	DIR /P	E.	A symbol that can represent any character or any group of characters.
6.	-----	DIR /W	F.	The device name of the first floppy disk drive.
7.	-----	DIR myfile.ext	G.	Order of a language.
8.	-----	File name	H.	A place to send or receive information.
9.	-----	File extension	I.	Will look for any file name that has .txt as an extension.
10.	-----	Default	J.	A program that is executed.
11.	-----	Device	K.	Will only look for and display, if found, the file called myfile.ext.
12.	-----	A:	L.	Is optional but, if, included cannot exceed three characters.
13.	-----	Wildcards	M.	A character used to separate other characters.
14.	-----	DIR *.txt	N.	All commands, if given no other instructions, will assume that all the activities will default to the prompt displayed on the screen.
15.	-----	Designated drive	O.	Will cause the directory display to pause when the screen is full.

TRUE/FALSE QUESTIONS

Write + for True or 0 for False for each question.

16. ----- A file specification may not have a <Space> included in its name.
17. ----- The DIR command has the parameters, the /P, /W, or a file specification.
18. ----- A> displayed on the screen indicates the default disk drive is A.
19. ----- DIR exp???.??? will look for any file that has a ? in its file specification.
20. ----- A file specification can be broken into two parts, a file name and a file extension.

MULTIPLE CHOICE QUESTIONS

Write the letter of the word or phrase that best completes the numbered statement.

21. _____ The default drive is A. Which of the following will occur when this command is entered? DIR B:/W

A. A directory of all files on the default drive will be displayed in columns. File sizes, date and times that the files were created will not be shown.

B. A directory of all files on the disk in Drive B will be displayed. File sizes, date and times that the files were created will not be shown.

C. A directory of all files on the default drive that have an extension of W will be displayed.

D. A directory of all files on the disk in Drive B that have an extension of W will be displayed.

22. _____ The default drive is A. Which of the following will occur when this command is entered? DIR /P

A. A directory of all files on default drive will be displayed. When the screen is full, it will pause until the user strikes any key.

B. A directory of all files on the disk in Drive B will be displayed. When the screen is full, it will pause until the user strikes any key.

C. A directory of all files on the default drive that have an extension of P will be displayed.

D. A directory of all files on the disk in Drive B that have an extension of P will be displayed.

23. _____ The default drive is A. Which of the following will occur when this command is keyed in? B:

A. Nothing. B: has no meaning to DOS.

B. All files with a file name of B: will be displayed.

C. The default drive will be changed to B:.

D. None of the above.

24. _____ The default drive is A. Which of the following will occur when this command is keyed in? DIR *.txt

A. A directory of all files on the default drive that have an extension of .txt will be displayed.

B. A directory of all files on the disk in Drive B that have an extension of .txt will be displayed.

C. A directory of all files on the default drive that do not have an extension of .txt will be displayed.

D. A directory of all the files on the disk in Drive B that do not have an extension of .txt will be displayed.

25. _____ The default drive is A. Which of the following will occur when this command is keyed in? DIR myfile.txt

A. A directory of all files on the default drive will be displayed.

B. A directory of all files on the disk in Drive B will be displayed.

C. A directory of all files on the default drive will be displayed in columns. File sizes, date and times that the files were created will not be shown.

D. None of the above.

Chapter 4 Test
Disks and Formatting

MATCHING QUESTIONS

Write the letter of the word or phrase that best completes the numbered statement.

1.	_____	Formatting	A.	Includes bootstrap routine that DOS uses to load itself, if it is a system disk. Always indicates what version of DOS was used to format the disk.
2.	_____	Tracks	B.	Where the actual file or data is stored on a disk.
3.	_____	Sectors	C.	A disk that has the operating system files on it.
4.	_____	Boot record	D.	Are always available in memory, once the system is booted.
5.	_____	FAT	E.	Each track is divided into a block of 512 bytes.
6.	_____	Directory sectors	F.	An external command that prepares a disk for use.
7.	_____	Data sectors	G.	A disk that does not have the operating system on it.
8.	_____	FORMAT	H.	The file allocation table that is a map of the disk and made up of entries that correspond to every cluster on the disk.
9.	_____	Internal commands	I.	Concentric circles on the disk.
10.	_____	External commands	J.	An external command that prepares a disk for use and places the operating system on the disk.
11.	_____	Bootable disk	K.	An external command that prepares a disk for use and places a volume label on the disk.
12.	_____	Nonsystem disk	L.	Defines physical layout of the information on the disk to determine how the information is stored on the disk.
13.	_____	FORMAT /S	M.	An internal command that allows the user to display the label of a disk.
14.	_____	FORMAT /V	N.	Where information about every file on a disk is stored, including the file name, file extension and file attributes.
15.	_____	VOL	O.	Loaded into memory and executed only when the user keys in the command name

TRUE/FALSE QUESTIONS

Write + for True or 0 for False for each question.

16. _____ A new, blank disk does not have to be formatted if it is only going to be used for data.

17. _____ Internal commands are kept in memory, once DOS is booted, and do not need to be read from the disk each time they are invoked.

18. _____ External commands are kept in memory, once DOS is booted, and do not need to be read from the disk each time they are invoked.

19. _____ A bootable disk can also be called a system disk.

20. _____ A data disk does not have a File Allocation Table (FAT).

MULTIPLE CHOICE QUESTIONS

Write the letter of the word or phrase that best completes the numbered statement.

21. _____ When a disk is formatted with the FORMAT command, it will:

A. copy any data stored on it.
B. destroy any data stored on it.
C. leave any data stored on it intact.
d. none of the above.

22. _____ The default drive is A. Which of the following will occur when this command is entered? FORMAT B:

A. The system will look for the FORMAT program on the default disk drive.
B. The system will look for the FORMAT program on the disk Drive B.
C. The disk on the default drive will be formatted.
D. Both A. and C. are true.

23. _____ The default drive is A. Which of the following will occur when this command is entered? FORMAT B:/V

A. The disk on the default drive will be formatted.
B. The disk on Drive B will be formatted.
C. After formatting, the user will be prompted by the system to enter an internal volume label.
D. Both B. and C. are true.

24. _____ The default drive is A. Which of the following will occur when this command is entered? FORMAT B:/S/V

A. The hidden files, IBMBIO.COM and IBMDOS.COM will be placed on the disk being formatted.
B. After formatting, the user will be prompted by the system to enter an internal volume label.
C. Both A. and B. are true.
D. Neither A. nor B. are true.

25. _____ The default drive is A: Which of the following will occur when this command is entered? DIR format.com

A. The disk on the default drive will be formatted.
B. The disk on Drive B will be formatted.
C. The name of the file called format.com on the default directory will be displayed.
D. The name of the file called format.com on the disk in Drive B will be displayed.

Chapter 5 Test
Using Internal Commands: COPY and TYPE

MATCHING QUESTIONS

Choose the letter of the answer that best defines the word or phrase in the numbered column.

1.	_____	COPY	A.	Computer notation for pressing the Control key and the letter z.
2.	_____	COPY source destination	B.	Syntax of the TYPE command.
3.	_____	CON	C.	Files whose contents have no particular meaning.
4.	_____	Ctrl-Z	D.	A system message that is displayed on the screen, after a file is successfully copied.
5.	_____	TYPE	E.	Device name for the printer that means Line Printer 1.
6.	_____	TYPE filename.ext	F.	Device name for the printer that means printer.
7.	_____	F6	G.	Device name for the console.
8.	_____	Dummy files	H.	An internal command that will copy the contents the file called new.one to the printer.
9.	_____	1 File(s) copied	I.	An internal command that will display the contents of the file new.one on the screen.
10.	_____	.EXE	J.	An internal command that will copy any file that has .txt as a file extension, regardless of its file name, to a new set of files that will have the same file name but a different extension, .dat
11.	_____	TYPE new.one	K.	An internal command that takes an original source file and makes an identical copy of it.
12.	_____	COPY *.txt *.dat	L.	An internal command that displays the contents of a file.
13.	_____	PRN	M.	By pressing this function key, a Ctrl-Z is created.
14.	_____	LPT1	N.	Syntax of the COPY command.
15.	_____	COPY new.one PRN	O.	A file extension that means executable code.

TRUE/FALSE QUESTIONS

Below are listed various file names. Indicate which ones follow valid rules for naming files that can be entered into DOS. Write + for True, 0 for False for each question.

16. _____ SALES.1986
17. _____ FALL.DAT
18. _____ CLASS.*
19. _____ PAYROLL.WKS
20. _____ CLASS

MULTIPLE CHOICE QUESTIONS

Write the letter of the word or phrase that best completes the numbered statement.

21. _____ The default drive is A. Which of the following will occur when this command is entered? COPY CON employee.dbf

A. A file named employee with an extension of dbf will be created.

B. The contents of the file employee.dbf can be keyed in from the console.

C. The file named employee.dbf will be written to the default drive.

D. A., B., and C., are true.

22. _____ The default drive is A. Which of the following will occur when this command is entered? TYPE employee.dbf

A. The contents of the file employee.dbf will be displayed on the screen.

B. The contents of the file employee.dbf will be printed on the printer.

C. Both A. and B. are true.

D. Neither A. nor B. are true.

23. _____ The default drive is A. Which of the following will occur when this command is entered? COPY employee.* PRN

A. The contents of all files with a name of employee, regardless of their file extension, will be displayed on the screen.

B. The contents of all files with a name of employee, regardless of their file extension, will be printed on the printer.

C. Both A. and B. are true.

D. Neither A. nor B. are true.

24. _____ The default drive is A. Which of the following will occur when this command is entered? TYPE B:

A. The contents of the file B: will be displayed on the screen.

B. The contents of the file B: will be printed on the printer.

C. You will get an error message saying "Invalid number of parameters."

D. None of the above.

25. _____ COPY is:

A. an internal command that is always available to use and whose syntax is COPY source destination.

B. an external command that is always available to use and whose syntax is COPY source destination.

C. a command that is used to make identical copies of disks.

D. a command that may never use wildcards.

Chapter 6 Test
Expanding the Use of the COPY Command

MATCHING QUESTIONS

Choose the letter of the answer that best defines the word or phrase in the numbered column.

1.	_____	Subdirectory the subdirectory \junk.	A.	An internal command that locates the file called hi.txt on the disk in Drive C and \junk.
2.	_____	COPY new.one B:	B.	An internal command that will copy the file called old.one from the default drive to the default drive giving it a new file name, new.one and verifies it was copied correctly.
3.	_____	Overwrite	C.	An internal command that will make a subdirectory called \junk on the default drive.
4.	_____	COPY *.txt B:*.tmp	D.	An internal command that will copy the file new.one and the file old.one on the default drive and place them in a new file on the disk in Drive B called extra.fil.
5.	_____	DIR C:\junk\hi.txt	E.	An internal command that will display the contents of the file new.one located on the disk in Drive B.
6.	_____	Concatenate	F.	Indicates that this parameter is optional. The letter enclosed in brackets indicates the designated drive. The user would substitute the drive letter he wants.
7.	_____	COPY new.one + old.one B:extra.fil	G.	System message that is displayed when trying to make a copy of a file with same name on the same disk.
8.	_____	MD \junk	H.	An internal command that will copy the file called old.one from the disk in Drive B to the disk in Drive A, giving it a new file name, new.one.
9.	_____	COPY B:old.one A:new.one	I.	Additional directories a user can create and use to help organize files.
10.	_____	File cannot be copied onto itself	J.	Combine the contents of two or more text files.
11.	_____	COPY old.one new.one /V	K.	Writes over what used to be in a file.
12.	_____	TYPE B:new.one	L.	An internal command that changes the default subdirectory to \junk on the default disk drive.
13.	_____	[d:]	M.	An internal command that will copy all the files from the default drive with the extension of *.txt to the disk in Drive B and give the files

			on Drive B the same file name but with the file extension .tmp.
14. _____	CD \junk	N.	An internal command that will copy all the files on the default drive to the disk in Drive B, keeping the file names the same.
15. _____	COPY *.* B:	O.	An internal command that will copy the file called new.one from the default drive to the disk in Drive B, keeping the same file name.

TRUE/FALSE QUESTIONS

Write + for True or 0 for False for each question.

16. _____ COPY A:class.dat B:class.txt will copy the file on the default drive called class.dat to the disk in Drive B with a new file name of class.dat.

17. _____ COPY A:*.txt B: will copy all the files on the disk in Drive A with a file extension of .txt to the disk in Drive B, keeping the same file names.

18. _____ COPY myfile will copy the file called myfile located on the default drive to the disk in Drive B, keeping the same file name.

19. _____ TYPE book.txt PRN will copy the contents of the file book.txt to the printer.

20. _____ COPY [d:][path]filename.ext [d:][path]filename.ext is the correct syntax for the COPY command.

MULTIPLE CHOICE QUESTIONS

Write the letter of the word or phrase that best completes the numbered statement.

21. _____ The default drive is A. Which of the following will occur when this command is entered? DISKCOPY class.txt B:

A. A file named class.txt located on the default drive will be copied to the disk in Drive B.

B. A file named class.txt located on the disk in Drive B will be copied to the disk in Drive A.

C. A file named class.txt located on the default drive will be copied to the disk in Drive B and will have a new name, myfile.txt.

D. None of the above.

22. _____ The default drive is A. Which of the of the following will occur when this command is entered?

COPY book.txt + book.dat B:total.bok

A. The contents of the files, located on the default drive, book.txt and book.dat will be copied into a new file on the disk in Drive B called total.bok.

B. The contents of the files, located on the disk in Drive B, book.txt and book.dat will be copied into a new file on the default drive called total.bok.

C. Nothing. You cannot copy more than one file at a time.

D. None of the above.

Chapter 7 Test
File Maintenance

MATCHING QUESTIONS

Choose the letter of the answer that best defines the word or phrase in the numbered column.

1. _____	DEL	A.	An external command that makes an exact copy of the disk in Drive A and copies it to the disk in Drive B.
2. _____	ERASE [d:][path] filename.ext	B.	An internal command that changes the name of the file from crs.dat located on the disk in Drive B to crs.txt on the disk in Drive B.
3. _____	DEL employee.txt	C.	An internal command that changes the name of the file from crs.dat, located on the default drive, to crs.txt on the default drive.
4. _____	DEL B:employee.txt	D.	An internal command that eliminates a file on a disk.
5. _____	ERASE B:*.txt	E.	A procedure to follow so that, if something happens to the original disk, the user can recover.
6. _____	ERASE *.txt	F.	The correct syntax for the RENAME command.
7. _____	REN	G.	An internal command that allows the user to change the name of a file.
8. _____	RENAME [d:][path] oldfile.ext new.ext	H.	An internal command that would delete the file called employee.txt located on the default drive.
9. _____	REN B:crs.dat crs.txt	I.	An internal command that would delete the file called employee.txt located on the disk in Drive B.
10. _____	REN crs.dat crs.txt	J.	The correct syntax for the ERASE command.
11. _____	Back up	K.	An internal command that copies all the files on the default drive to the disk in Drive B, keeping the same file names.
12. _____	DISKCOPY A: B:	L.	An internal command that will change all the file extensions on the default drive from old to new, keeping the same file names.
13. _____	COPY *.* B:	M.	An internal command that will erase the file called new.one located on the disk in Drive C in the subdirectory \junk.
14. _____	DEL C:\junk\new.one	N.	An internal command that would delete all the the files with an extension of .txt located on the

default drive.

15. _____ REN *.old *.new

O. An internal command that would delete all the files with an extension of .txt located on the disk in Drive B.

TRUE/FALSE QUESTIONS

Write + for True or 0 for False for each question.

16. _____ RENAME cannot be used with wildcards.

17. _____ Backing up a data disk is unimportant; you can always create the data again.

18. _____ The ERASE command can only be used with wildcards.

19. _____ There is no utility program on the DOS System Disk that allows you to recover a file that has been deleted.

20. _____ The RENAME command allows you to change the name of a file.

MULTIPLE CHOICE QUESTIONS

Write the letter of the word or phrase that best completes the numbered statement.

21. _____ The default drive is A. Which of the following is true of this command? REN employee.dat employee.txt

A. The file named employee.dat will be renamed to employee.txt.
B. The file named employee.txt will be renamed to employee.dat.
C. Employee.txt will be the new file name.
D. Both A. and C. are true.

22. _____ The default drive is A. Which of the following will occur when this command is entered? DEL B:class.dbf

A. The file class.dbf will be deleted from the default drive.
B. The file class.dbf will be deleted from the disk in Drive B.
C. Nothing will happen because the entire word DELETE must be spelled out.
D. None of the above.

23. _____ The default drive is A. Which of the following will occur when this command is entered? ERASE class.dbf

A. The file class.dbf will be deleted from the default drive.
B. The file class.dbf will be deleted from the disk in Drive B.
C. Nothing will happen because the word ERASE must be abbreviated to ERA.
D. None of the above.

Chapter 8 Test
Informational Commands: CHKDSK, COMP, VER and LABEL

MATCHING QUESTIONS

Choose the letter of the answer that best defines the word or phrase in the numbered column.

1.	_____	CHKDSK	A.	An external command that gives statistical information about the default disk and computer memory as well as listing all the files on the default disk, including hidden files.
2.	_____	COMP	B.	An external command that gives statistical information about a disk and computer memory.
3.	_____	LABEL	C.	Files whose sectors are all in adjacent clusters.
4.	_____	VER	D.	An external command that allows the volume label on the disk in Drive B to be changed.
5.	_____	Contiguous files	E.	A system message that indicates that, since the files to be compared are different sizes, they are not identical files and the command is done executing.
6.	_____	Fragmented files	F.	A system message that indicates that the contents of two files are not identical.
7.	_____	CHKDSK /V	G.	An internal command that displays the version number of DOS that is in memory.
8.	_____	COMP [d:][path] filename1.ext [d:][path] filename2.ext	H.	Transposes as 655,360 actual bytes.
9.	_____	Compare errors at OFFSET D	I.	An external command that gives statistical information about the default disk and computer memory and will see if the files located on the default disk with the extension of .dat are contiguous.
10.	_____	LABEL B:	J.	An external command that allows the user to compare contents of files.
11.	_____	CHKDSK *.dat	K.	The correct syntax for the COMP command.
12.	_____	Bad command or file name	L.	An external command that gives statistical information about the disk in Drive B and computer memory and will see if the files located on the disk in Drive B with the extension of .dat are contiguous.

13. _____ CHKDSK B:*.dat — M. A system message that can indicate that DOS could not find the program to execute on the default disk.

14. _____ 640K — N. An external command that allows the user to change the volume label of a disk.

15. _____ Files are different sizes — O. Files whose sectors are in non-adjacent clusters.

TRUE/FALSE QUESTIONS

Write + for True or 0 for False for each question.

16. _____ CHKDSK /V will display the volume label of a disk.

17. _____ LABEL is an external command that is available on DOS version 3.0 or above.

18. _____ Software is often revised to add enhancements and fix bugs. These versions are numbered to keep track of the latest release.

19. _____ The COMP command will only compare text files.

20. _____ CHKDSK will let you know how much room is left on a disk.

MULTIPLE CHOICE QUESTIONS

Write the letter of the word or phrase that best completes the numbered statement.

21. _____ The default drive is A: Which of the following is true of this command? CHKDSK B:

A. The command CHKDSK will compare the files on the disk in Drive B.
B. The command CHKDSK is an internal command that is always in memory.
C. A status report will be displayed on the screen which will give the user information about the disk in the default drive.
D. A status report will be displayed on the screen which will give the user information about the disk in Drive B.

22. _____ Which of the following will be displayed in the status report when the following command is entered? CHKDSK B:

A. The amount of total space available on the disk in Drive B.
B. The number of files and the bytes used by those files.
C. The number of hidden files and the bytes used by those files.
D. All the above.

Chapter 9 Test
EDLIN: The Text Editor

MATCHING QUESTIONS

Choose the letter of the answer that best defines the word or phrase in the numbered column.

1. _____	EDLIN	A.	An EDLIN command that allows the user to delete line number 7.
2. _____	EDLIN [d:][path] filename.ext	B.	An EDLIN command that allows the user to list lines of an existing file.
3. _____	EDLIN B:new.fil	C.	Each time this key is pressed, one character from the buffer is written to the screen.
4. _____	i	D.	Each time this key is pressed the rest of a line from the buffer is written to the screen.
5. _____	L	E.	An EDLIN command that allows the user to exit from the current file and write the data to the disk.
6. _____	7	F.	An EDLIN command that allows the user to exit from the current file and not write the data to the disk.
7. _____	E	G.	An external command that will create a file on the disk in Drive B called new.fil.
8. _____	Q	H.	This key allows the user to insert a character or a word in an EDLIN file.
9. _____	7D	I.	An EDLIN command that allows the user to edit line number 7.
10. _____	F1	J.	Will list only lines 7 through 10 in an EDLIN file.
11. _____	F2	K.	This key allows the user to delete a character or work in an EDLIN file.
12. _____	Ins key	L.	A line-oriented text editor.
13. _____	Del key	M.	Will delete lines 7 through 10 in an EDLIN file.
14. _____	7,10L	N.	An EDLIN command that allows the user to enter new lines of data.
15. _____	7,10D	O.	The correct syntax for the EDLIN command.

TRUE/FALSE QUESTIONS

Write + for True or 0 for False for each question.

16. _____ EDLIN creates one file with a .bak file extension each time you edit an existing file.
17. _____ You cannot print a file when you are in EDLIN.
18. _____ DOS internal commands do not work once you are in the EDLIN program.
19. _____ You can edit any text file with EDLIN regardless of whether or not it was created with EDLIN.
20. _____ EDLIN automatically numbers all the lines in an EDLIN file.

MULTIPLE CHOICE QUESTIONS

Write the letter of the word or phrase that best completes the numbered statement.

21. _____ Which of the following is true of EDLIN?
    A. It is a word processor that offers many features such as word wrap, setting margins and tabs.
    B. It is a line editor that allows you to work on one line at a time.
    C. It is an internal command.
    D. You cannot make changes to an EDLIN file, once you have written the data to the disk.

22. _____ The EDLIN command I is used to:
    A. place EDLIN into the insert mode so the user may enter text.
    B. cancel the insert mode.
    C. place EDLIN in the delete mode.
    D. place EDLIN in the interrupt mode.

23. _____ When Ctrl-C is pressed in EDLIN, the following occurs:
    A. stops the insert mode and returns the user to the * prompt.
    B. stops the editing session and returns the user to the system prompt.
    C. places EDLIN into the insert mode so the user may enter data.
    D. none of the above.

24. _____ When #i is keyed in at the * prompt, the following occurs:
    A. insert mode is canceled, and the user is returned to the system prompt.
    B. delete mode is canceled, and the user is returned to the system prompt.
    C. the user is placed in the insert mode at the bottom of the file.
    D. the user is placed in the insert mode at the top of the file.

25. _____ To tell EDLIN that the user is finished using the EDLIN program and wishes to save all text to the file on the disk, he would key in which of the following letters at the * prompt?
    A. Q
    B. E
    C. S
    D. W

Chapter 10 Test
Managing the Printer with the MODE and PRINT Commands

MATCHING QUESTIONS

Choose the letter of the answer that best defines the word or phrase in the numbered column.

1.	_____	Pressing the <Shift> key and the PrtSc key	A.	Will toggle the printer on or off.
2.	_____	Pressing the Ctrl key and the the PrtSc key	B:	Will remove the file new.one from the print queue.
3.	_____	COPY new.one PRN	C.	Will print all the files on the disk in Drive B: that have .txt as a file extension. The contents of each .txt file will begin printing on a new page.
4.	_____	PRINT	D.	Will print all the files on the disk in Drive B that have .txt as a file extension. The contents of each .txt file will be printed as one file.
5.	_____	Background printing	E.	Will allow the user to set the characteristics of the printer so it prints in a condensed mode.
6.	_____	PRINT B:*.txt	F.	Will print what is displayed on the screen.
7.	_____	COPY B:*.txt PRN	G.	An external command that will allow the user to alter the way some parts of the hardware operate.
8.	_____	PRINT /T	H.	Will allow the user to set the characteristics of the printer so it prints in the default mode.
9.	_____	PRINT new.one /C	I.	Copy the contents of the file new.one to the printer.
10.	_____	MODE	J.	Transfers data at the rate of one byte at a time.
11.	_____	MODE LPT1:132,8	K.	Input/output connection.
12.	_____	MODE LPT1:80,6	L.	Describes the process whereby the computer can be doing another task while it is printing.
13.	_____	Serial port	M.	Will cancel the print job.
14.	_____	Parallel port	N.	An external, semi-resident command.
15.	_____	Port	O.	Transfers data at the rate of one bit at a time.

TRUE/FALSE QUESTIONS

Write + for True or 0 for False for each question.

16. _____ Using the PRINT command, you can print files while going on and using other DOS commands.

17. _____ The MODE command can set the print line to any number of characters that the user chooses.

18. _____ The command line, PRINT *.tmp and the command line COPY *.tmp PRN will print each *.tmp file on a new page.

19. _____ A serial port and an asynchronous port mean the same thing.

20. _____ LPT1 is the name for parallel port 1.

MULTIPLE CHOICE QUESTIONS

Write the letter of the word or phrase that best completes the numbered statement.

21. _____ A print queue is a:

A. cable that connects the printer to the system unit.
B. waiting line of files to be printed.
C. list of all the files on a disk.
D. none of the above.

22. _____ The DOS System Disk is in Drive A. The default drive is A. Which of the following will occur when this command is entered? PRINT

A. It will cancel the print queue.
B. It will activate the printer.
C. It will allow you to view the print queue.
D. It will print all the files on the default disk.

23. _____ The default drive is A. Which of the following will occur when this command is entered? COPY DIR PRN

A. A copy of the directory on the default disk will be printed.
B. A copy of the directory on the disk in Drive B will be printed.
C. Both A. and B.
D. Neither A. nor B.

24. _____ The DOS System Disk is in Drive A. The default drive is A. Which of the following will occur the first time this command is entered after booting? PRINT B:*.tmp

A. The following message will appear:
Name of list device [PRN]:_
B. The following message will appear:
Resident part of PRINT installed
C. The following message will appear:
Enter the name of the file you wish printed:_
D. None of the above.

25. _____ The Prtsc key is used in the following ways:

A. The <Shift> key and the PrtSc key print everything currently displayed on the screen.
B. The Ctrl key and the PrtSc key cause each line that is being displayed on the screen to be printed on the printer.
C. Both A. and B.
D. Neither A. nor B.

Chapter 11 and 12 Test
Batch Files and Customized Batch Files

MATCHING QUESTIONS

Choose the letter of the answer that best defines the word or phrase in the numbered column.

1.	_____	Batch file	A.	A message the user will receive if Ctrl-C is pressed while running a batch file.
2.	_____	Autoexec.bat	B.	A process where all instructions to the computer are given in a group. The user cannot interact with the computer.
3.	_____	PROMPT	C.	A tool that can be used to write batch files.
4.	_____	Meta-string	D.	An internal command that allows the user to change the default prompt.
5.	_____	REM	E.	The default system prompt.
6.	_____	PAUSE	F.	A file that contains DOS commands that are executed when the name of the name of the file is keyed in at the prompt. The file must have an extension of .bat.
7.	_____	Dummy parameters	G.	A percent sign followed by a one-digit number that can be included with commands in a batch file that are place holders whose values will be indicated when the batch file is run.
8.	_____	Terminate batch job (Y/N)?	H.	A file that is executed immediately after the system is booted.
9.	_____	PROMPT $d_$n$g	I.	To explain the purpose of a file.
10.	_____	EDLIN	J.	A batch command that allows the user to place explanatory text in a batch file. It does not cause DOS to take any action.
11.	_____	Interactive	K.	A batch command that will cause the batch file to stop executing and allow the user to take some action.
12.	_____	Batch	L.	Characters that represent certain specific values that have pre-defined meaning to DOS.
13.	_____	.COM, .EXE, .BAT	M.	Will change the prompt to the current date with the default drive followed by the > on the next line.
14.	_____	Document	N.	The order in which DOS looks for a program file on the default disk.
15.	_____	A> or C>	O.	A process that allows active communication between the user and the computer and allows an immediate, real-time response.

TRUE/FALSE QUESTIONS

Write + for True or 0 for False for each question.

16. _____ The REM command is used to remove text from a batch file.

17. _____ A batch file can be created using a text editor such as EDLIN.

18. _____ A batch file is executed by entering the file name at the prompt.

19. _____ Dummy parameters allow you to use the same batch files, and just substitute the values you are interested in when you actually execute them.

20. _____ PROMPT is a file that can only be executed at the time of booting.

MULTIPLE CHOICE QUESTIONS

Write the letter of the word or phrase that best completes the numbered statement.

21. _____ A batch file name must include:

A. the file extension .bat.
B. the file extension .exe
C. the file extension .com.
D. no file extension.

22. _____ To cause a batch file to cease operation temporarily and allow the user to take some action, the following command should be placed in the batch file:

A. STOP.
B. CEASE.
C. PAUSE.
D. HALT.

23. _____ A batch file can be stopped from executing by:

A. pressing Ctrl-B.
B. pressing Ctrl-C
C. pressing Ctrl-Z.
D. none of the above.

24. _____ Which of the following are true of an AUTOEXEC.BAT file?

A. It must have the file name autoexec.bat.
B. There can only be one autoexec.bat file per booting disk.
C. Both A. and B.
D. Neither A. nor B.

25. _____ Batch files are primarily used to:

A. cause the system to boot.
B. clear whatever is in memory.
C. clear whatever is on the screen
D. none of the above.

Chapter 13 Test
Subdirectories

MATCHING QUESTIONS

Choose the letter of the answer that best defines the word or phrase in the numbered column.

1.	_____	Root directory	A.	A command that allows the user to erase a subdirectory.
2.	_____	Subdirectory	B.	A command that will allow the user to display the default disk drive and the default subdirectory.
3.	_____	CD	C.	A command that will eliminate the subdirectory \wp that is in a subdirectory \junk on the default drive.
4.	_____	MD	D.	A command that allows the user to to show the current directory or change the directory.
5.	_____	RD	E.	A command that will allow the user to see if a file called new.one is located in the subdirectory called \junk on the default drive.
6.	_____	PATH	F.	A command that will change the default subdirectory to a subdirectory called \text that is in a subdirectory called \wp on the default drive.
7.	_____	PROMPT pg	G.	A command that will cancel the currently set path.
8.	_____	CD ..	H.	A command that allows the user to tell DOS where to look for a program file, if it is not the current directory.
9.	_____	DIR \junk\new.one	I.	A command that will create a new subdirectory called \wp under the subdirectory called \junk on the default drive.
10.	_____	DEL \junk*.*	J.	A command that will allow DOS to look in the subdirectory called \DOS and, then, look in the subdirectory called \TEXT for command programs.
11.	_____	RD \junk\wp	K.	Additional directories that the user can create to help organize files.
12.	_____	CD \wp\text	L.	A command that will delete all the files in the subdirectory \junk on the default drive.
13.	_____	PATH \DOS;\TEXT	M.	A command that allows the user to create a new subdirectory.
14.	_____	PATH ;	N.	A command that will allow the user to move up to the parent directory of the current subdirectory.
15.	_____	MD \junk\wp	O.	The main directory DOS creates on each disk. The \ symbol is used to represent this directory.

TRUE/FALSE QUESTIONS

Write + for True or 0 for False for each question.

16. _____ If <DIR> follows a file name on on directory display, it indicates that it is a subdirectory not just a file.
17. _____ There is no limit to the number of files that the root directory can hold.
18. _____ DEL myfile <DIR> is the proper command to delete the subdirectory called myfile.dir.
19. _____ The PATH command is an external command that must be on the default disk in order to be used.
20. _____ A subdirectory name has no limit as to its length.

MULTIPLE CHOICE QUESTIONS

Write the letter of the word or phrase that best completes the numbered statement.

21. _____ The directory that is always created when a disk is formatted is called the:

A. TWIG directory.
B. BRANCH directory.
C. ROOT directory.
D. LEAF directory.

22. _____ A subdirectory is created using the:

A. MD command.
B. RD command.
C. EDLIN command.
D. DIR command.

23. _____ Which of the following will occur when this command is entered? CD \junk\wp

A. The subdirectory \junk\wp will be displayed.
B. The default subdirectory will be changed to \junk\wp.
C. The subdirectory \junk\wp will be erased.
D. None of the above.

24. _____ A subdirectory can be deleted using the RD command only if:

A. it has files and other subdirectories in it.
B. if it has no files or no subdirectories in it.
C. it has programs in it.
D. none of the above.

25. _____ When using PATH, the search can include:

A. more than one specified drive identifier.
B. more than one subdirectory path.
C. Both A. and B.
D. Neither A. nor B.